E. WAYNE NAFZIGER

The Debt Crisis in Africa

.

THE JOHNS HOPKINS UNIVERSITY PRESS

BALTIMORE AND LONDON

To my colleagues in Africa and North America
who speak out against injustice

Printed in the United States of America
on acid-free paper

The Johns Hopkins University Press
2715 North Charles Street
Baltimore, Maryland 21218-4319

Library of Congress Cataloging-in-Publication Data
Nafziger, E. Wayne.
The debt crisis in Africa / E. Wayne Nafziger.
p.   cm.
Includes bibliographical references and index.
ISBN 0-8018-4476-2
1. Debts, External—Africa, Sub-Saharan.   I. Title.
HJ8826.N34   1993
336.3'435'0967—dc20   92-23735

A catalog record for this book is available
from the British Library.

Contents

■

Contents

Contents

List of Tables

.

List of Tables

List of Figures

■

Abbreviations

■

AL(s)	Adjustment loan(s)—Sectoral adjustment loans (SECALs) of the World Bank or structural adjustment loans (SALs) of the Bank or IMF
APs	Adjustment programs—World Bank/IMF programs involving policy-based ALs
CFAF	Communauté financière africaine franc
CPSP	Caisse de Péréquation et de Stabilisation des Prix, Senegal's monopsony agricultural marketing board
DCs	Developed countries
DRF	Debt Reduction Facility—World Bank section to reduce the debt and debt-service burden of the poorest debt-distressed countries
EC	European Community
ECA	U.N. Economic Commission for Africa
ECAs	Export credit agencies
ESAF	Enhanced Structural Adjustment Facility—IMF section for concessional funds for the poorest members
FAO	Food and Agriculture Organization of the United Nations
G7	Group of Seven Major Industrialized Countries (United States, Canada, Japan, Germany, United Kingdom, France, and Italy)
GATT	General Agreements on Tariffs and Trade—International organization that serves as a multilateral forum for negotiations to reduce tariffs and other trade barriers, and administers rules of conduct in international trade
GSP	Generalized system of tariff preferences
IDA	International Development Association—The World Bank's concessional window, primarily for low-income countries
ILO	U.N. International Labour Office
IMF	International Monetary Fund—International organization established at Bretton Woods, New Hampshire, in

	1944 for the initial purpose of providing credit to ease short-term international payments imbalances
LDCs	Less-developed countries
LIBOR	London Interbank Offered Rate—Virtually riskless interest rate used as a standard for comparing other interest rates
MNCs	Multinational corporations
₦	Naira (Nigeria)
OAU	Organisation for African Unity
ODA	Official Development Assistance—Official aid
ODC	Overseas Development Council
OECD	Organisation for Economic Cooperation and Development—A major bilateral donor group, which includes the United States, Canada, Western Europe, Japan, Australia, and New Zealand
RM	Reichsmark, the German monetary unit from 1924 to 1948
SA	Structural adjustment—The process of undergoing SAPs
SAF	Structural adjustment facility—World Bank or IMF section for policy-based SALs
SALs	Structural adjustment loans—World Bank/IMF loans to affect the supply side, which support sectoral, relative-price, and institutional reform to improve efficiency and long-term growth
SAPs	Structural adjustment programs—World Bank/IMF programs involving policy-based SALs
SDRs	Special drawing rights—Bookkeeping entries in the accounts of member countries of the IMF used as internationalized currency by central banks for official transactions (with the IMF and other central banks)
SECALs	Sectoral adjustment loans—World Bank loans emphasizing trade, agricultural, industrial, public-enterprise, financial, energy, educational, or other sectoral reforms
Sh	Shilling
SOEs	State-owned enterprises
SPA	Special Programs of Assistance—Concessional funds by the World Bank (IDA) and IMF for low-income, debt-distressed countries
UNCTAD	United Nations Conference on Trade and Development, consisting of 127 African, Asian, Latin American, and Central European LDCs
USAID	United States Agency for International Development
Zk	(Zambian) kwacha

Preface

■

In the 1980s, the inability of the Third World to pay its debt was a major international economic concern of American journalists and scholars. Yet in the early 1990s, economists such as Benjamin J. Cohen are asking: Whatever happened to the Third World debt crisis? A partial answer is that, for LDCs, little has changed. In Africa and Latin America, the debt overhang still keeps standards of living down and limits the investment needed to end stagnation. Africa, we will show, has been doubly hurt by a deteriorating global economic environment (including falling export purchasing power) and domestic policy misdirection.

The early 1980s saw health spending, child nutrition, and infant survival fall among Africa's poor. During the late 1980s, real wages, the employment rate, and health and educational expenditure shares declined. For the entire decade, schools, roads, health clinics, and other infrastructure deteriorated. UNICEF blames chronic debt servicing and the substantial net transfer of $30 billion yearly from poor to rich nations for the Third World's failure to reduce malnutrition, disease, and the early death of children.

Meanwhile, however, Third World debt repudiation no longer threatens money-center banks of New York City, such as Citicorp, Manufacturers Hanover, and Chase Manhattan. These banks have reduced their exposure to Third World borrowers, so their defaults endanger neither bank credit ratings and stock prices nor the stability of the U.S. banking system. The policy of the United States in the 1980s, as discussed in this book, focused on saving its banks and averting a debtors' cartel. By 1987 the major creditor banks no longer had to continue lending to LDCs or participate in debt rescheduling to forestall their own collapse. Thus, while the U.S. government and commercial banks have abandoned their preoccupation with the debt crisis, debt continues to drain the Third World generally, while worsening in Africa.

This book discusses the origin and nature of the crisis in Africa and how it has affected wages, employment, economic growth, and income distribution. I argue that substantial African debt relief would cost the United States and other rich countries little and the banking community nothing, while providing a breathing space for Africa to improve its long-term welfare. In our interdependent world, increased African welfare can only benefit the industrialized countries.

This book is for economists, social scientists, students, bankers, business people, government and international agency personnel, and others who wish to understand African debt. A glossary is supplied to help ease the way through economics terminology.

I did the research for this book during five trips to Africa, with funds from Kansas State University (KSU) and the American Philosophical Society. A Hewlett Fellowship at the Carter Center's African Governance Program in Atlanta gave me time to finish my work; however, the Center and the Program bear no responsibility for my views. John Weeks, Howard Stein, and Richard Joseph helped me clarify my thinking on African debt. James Ragan, Daniel J. Socolow, Steve Hochman, Lynora Williams, Sharon Gardner, Lorri E. Rumph, Susan M. Koch, Jeri N. Slagel, and Velda M. Deutsch facilitated my research. I received generous help from librarians at KSU and Northwestern University's Africana Library. Holly Schue found an African map suitable for publication. At the Johns Hopkins University Press, Henry Y. K. Tom, Heather E. Peterson, Barbara B. Lamb, Douglas Armato, James Johnston, Gregg A. Wilhelm, and Jeanne Pinault transformed the manuscript to the book you are now reading. Elfrieda, Brian, and Kevin Nafziger provided the security, support, and intellectual challenge I needed for writing. I am grateful to all these for the strengths they contributed to my work, but I am solely responsible for its weaknesses.

I also thank the following for permission to reproduce copyrighted materials: the World Bank for tables and graphs from *World Debt Tables, Dealing with the Debt Crisis,* and *Global Economic Prospects;* the International Monetary Fund for tables and graphs from the *World Economic Outlook, 1988–1991;* the United Nations for a graph from the *World Economic Survey, 1990;* and Baywood Publishing Company and author M. H. Brenner for a graph from the *International Journal of Health Services.*

Introduction:
Africa's Economic Crisis

.

This study critically examines the approaches of the World Bank, the International Monetary Fund (IMF), the United Nations, the U.S. government, commercial banks, and the Economic Commission for Africa (ECA)/Organisation of African Unity (OAU) toward Africa's debt overhang and negative growth of the 1980s and early 1990s. I argue that the short-run economic adjustment and reform policies prescribed by the World Bank, IMF, and other creditors for Africa exacerbate its decline in material welfare and its international economic crisis. The book, by showing the failure of present debt strategies in Africa, the region with the world's most severe international economic crisis, provides insight into the problem of debt and adjustment in the Third World generally.

A Crisis of Debt and Stagnation

In the 1980s and continuing into the 1990s, sub-Saharan Africa[1] suffered both from an unfavorable international environment (declining terms of trade, reduced aid and credit, and higher real interest rates) and from government policies (exchange-rate, import-substitution, foreign-investment, tariff, pricing, and technology) that worsened stagnation and international deficits.

The crisis that struck Africa after 1973–74 was partly linked to change in the world economy, that is, the abrupt end of a quarter century of rapid post–World War II economic growth. The major factors contributing to fast growth in the earlier postwar years were pent-up demand from preceding years, European and Japanese reconstruction, accelerated technical change (partly from an unused stock of wartime innovations), high profit rates, demand management for full employment, increasing trade and payments liberalization, and a stable international economic system under U.S. hegemony.

African States and Capital Cities

Since 1973, increased raw-materials prices, oil shocks, rise in real interest rates worldwide, cost-push inflationary wage increases, declining profit rates, reduced investment, DC exchange-rate instability, and attempts to control state spending contributed to slower growth and greater economic instability.[2] When the West sneezed (as in 1980–82 and 1991), sub-Saharan Africa, the fringe of the international economic periphery, caught pneumonia.

For the World Bank and IMF, fraternal twins established in Bretton Woods in 1944, Africa's economic crisis during the late 1970s and 1980s resulted from a failure of economic management. Yet what appeared to be policy mistakes and mismanagement were actually strategies pursued in the interest of sub-Saharan elites that were not sustainable in the long run.

The Sub-Sahara's debt overhang, without new money or debt reduction, restrained both investment and adjustment. African countries, with austerity and stagnation since the mid–1970s, could not afford to reduce spending to effect an external transfer. Large future repayments acted as a tax on investment. Paying back debt often meant slowing economic growth to avoid an import surplus.

The debt problem emerged earlier in Africa than in Latin America. Beginning with Zaïre in 1976, ten low-income sub-Saharan countries rescheduled official debt claims nineteen times and commercial bank debt five times before the first Latin rescheduling in 1982. In the 1980s and early 1990s, producers in industrialized countries, seeing that slow Third World growth hindered export expansion, joined bankers in pressing Washington, other DC capitals, and international agencies to resolve LDC debt, but the primary focus was the debt problem of middle-income Latin America, whose crisis hurt Western and Japanese exports much more than the Sub-Sahara's did.

External debt in sub-Saharan Africa was small compared to other Third World regions. In the Sub-Sahara in 1985–87, only Nigeria and Côte d'Ivoire were among those severely indebted (all middle-income) countries termed "the Baker Seventeen." Some 85 percent of the sub-Saharan debt was owed to official creditors. Still, commercial bank claims were a significant problem in some low-income sub-Saharan countries. Indeed, the smallness of the 1990 debt of the Sub-Sahara, $174 billion (14 percent of Third World debt), compared to Latin America's $431 billion (34 percent) or Asia's $350 billion (27 percent), reflected its low income and poor credit rating; the ratio of debt to GNP in the Sub-Sahara was the highest of all world regions. Furthermore, *actual* debt service (interest and principal payments due in a given year on long-term debt) in the Sub-Sahara was 8 percent of GNP and 24 percent of export earnings in 1990, far more than the minimal burden (3 percent of GNP and 15 percent of exports) the depressed region can bear. However, *actual* debt service was less than 40 percent of *scheduled* debt payment; the latter totaled 22 percent of GNP and 65 percent of export earnings![3]

Since 1979–80, virtually all sub-Saharan countries have undertaken Bank/Fund adjustment. Indeed sub-Saharan economic policymaking in the 1980s and early 1990s was primarily shaped by conditions of Bank/Fund loans of last resort in return for requiring adjustment and reform to reduce the external deficit and ameliorate the debt crisis. Some African elites allied with the Bank/Fund, supporting liberalization and becoming (with their accomplices and clients) the emerging economically dominant group, the nouveau riche.[4] Bank/Fund cooperation also enabled elites to protect vested interests from the threat of reform and its new rules. But declining GNP pie slices meant that adjustment came disproportionately at the expense of poverty programs, wages, employment, and public services for working and peasant classes, who received little benefit from the borrowing, rather than the ruling elites and upper classes whose spending had contributed to the external crisis. The popular classes opposed the economic liberalism of the Bretton Woods twins, whose publications emphasized longer-term structural adjustment but whose programs, under constant monitoring, usually carried out demand reduction. To control discussion and opposition, regimes undergoing economic reform in Nigeria, Ghana, Sudan, Kenya, Malawi, and Tanzania (to say nothing of Liberia and Zaïre) arrested, banned, jailed, deported, and in some instances even killed dissenting intellectuals, students, and journalists.

Klein asserts that the Bank and Fund, "ideologues of the new economic orthodoxy . . . may doom democracies" and make "a bad economic situation worse." The Committee for Academic Freedom in Africa (CAFA), which contends that "the most frequent violations of academic rights occur when African governments implement World Bank and IMF policies and meet the protest they generate," even states that the Bank's "policy [emphasizing educational cost reduction] is unequivocally exterminist."[5] UNICEF expresses the view of advocates for the African poor, that the Bank/Fund adjustment of the 1980s exacerbated the economic crisis rather than ameliorating it:

> The common aim of these [economic adjustment] measures is to improve the balance of payments, repay debts and reduce inflation. Important national objectives—such as expanding and protecting employment, ensuring a minimum income for households and providing basic public services—have become secondary. Ironically, the result has often been an aggravation of the economic crisis and a parallel human crisis as unemployment rises, incomes of the most vulnerable groups fall, import-dependent industries cut production, public services are curtailed and public discontent and political instability grow.[6]

Africa's economic distress is worsened by depending on the financial support and program strategies of the Bank/Fund and DC donors, who usually coordinate policies on debt and adjustment. Yet I argue, contrary to Klein and CAFA, that the ruling elites in Africa, who benefit at the expense of the majority of its population, bear much blame for Africa's continuously subordinate relationship to the Bank, the Fund, and the world economic system.

Introduction

The economic crisis deepened in the 1980s, despite far-reaching African reforms. The annual real growth in GNP per person in the Sub-Sahara through 1990 had been virtually zero since 1965 (negative since 1980 and since 1986), compared to substantial positive growth in the rest of the developing world during the same periods. Growth of foodgrain output per person since 1963 was positive in the Third World generally but negative in the Sub-Sahara, the only world region where caloric intake, if equally distributed, was below the Food and Agriculture Organization (FAO) minimal standards. Economies that fail to grow are more likely to encounter or prolong external debt crises.

Sub-Saharan Africa's commodity terms of trade (price index of exports/price index of imports) fell 47 percent from 1970 to 1990. Since export volume remained the same during the same period, export purchasing power also dropped 47 percent, reducing imports, especially during the 1980s. Exports were hurt further in the early 1990s by the reduced demand for Africa's primary products due to the West's recession. The Sub-Sahara's international balance on goods, services, and transfers, negative since 1977, exceeded 20 percent of total exports after 1987. Net financial flows to Africa fell in the late 1970s and the late 1980s. In 1990 and 1991, one-fourth of Africa's export earnings were for servicing debt (interest and principal).[7]

Adjustment and Its Impact

Without debt rescheduling, chronic external deficits and debt over-hang require economic adjustment (structural or sectoral adjustment, macroeconomic stabilization, or economic reform), imposed domestically or (usually) by the World Bank or IMF. Bank sectoral adjustment loans (SECALs) emphasize reforms in trade, agriculture, industry, public enterprise, finance, energy, education, or other sectors. Structural adjustment loans (SALs) by the Bank or Fund, to affect the supply side, support sectoral, relative-price, and institutional reform to improve efficiency and long-term growth. By 1988, 33.8 percent of SALs and SECALs, constituting $19.9 billion (or 24.1 percent) of the Bank's lending, went to the low-income Sub-Sahara. The objectives of IMF stabilization under standby agreements are to decrease demand in order to moderate inflation, and to switch demand from domestic to foreign sources, depreciating domestic currency to reduce an international payments deficit.[8] In Africa, Bank/Fund lending to resolve external crises was usually linked to devaluing, decontrolling prices, reducing social spending programs, privatizing public firms, and integrating the domestic economy into the world economy, but the sequence of these adjustments often exacerbated stagflation and external deficits.

Africa is caught in an export trap, as the growth of primary-product exports faces competition from other economies requiring similar expansion for adjustment. Moreover, DC protectionism limits the growth in Africa of primary-product processing and light manufacturing for export.

UNICEF reported that from 1980 to 1985, when Bank/Fund adjustment programs limited sub-Saharan social spending, child welfare (nutrition, literacy, primary school retention, immunization, and survival) deteriorated. Tanzanian President Julius K. Nyerere asked in 1985: "Must we starve our children to pay our debt?" In 1989, Adebayo Adedeji, ECA's Executive Secretary (1975–91), observed that Africa would not recover without lifting the "unbearable albatross" of debilitating debt burdens, low export prices, and net capital outflow (including capital transfer to the West by the wealthy and politically influential).[9]

The 1985 Baker Plan emphasized expanded lending and the 1989 Brady Plan writedowns and writeoffs to resolve the LDC debt crisis. Indeed, Western bankers advising the Secretary-General of the United Nations recommended a moratorium by commercial creditors on Africa's interest and principal for three years, after which interest rates would be written down to concessional levels. African commercial bank debt instruments sold at a 40–95 percent discount on the secondary market. In Africa, more than in any other region, a Laffer curve exists, where private creditors as a whole could increase expected debt paybacks by writing down debt. Commercial lenders widely recognized that Nigeria, Côte d'Ivoire, Sudan, and several other sub-Saharan debtors could not fully service their debts at market terms. Frequently no Bank/Fund program for full debt servicing made an African country better off than partially suspending payments.

In the early 1990s, creditors had little success in debt reduction, especially for Africa, where settlements would have set damaging precedents for larger debtors. The inherent barrier to voluntary, piecemeal arrangements is that nonparticipating creditors holding claims that will subsequently rise in value are better off than the participants. Brady debt writedowns work only with concerted debt reduction, where all commercial creditors and debtors participate on a prorated basis (as in U.S. Chapter 11 bankruptcies) under international agency auspices to exclude nonparticipants' free riding.

Introduction

Multilateral institutions, primarily the World Bank and IMF, which receive about one-third of the sub-Saharan debt service, do not write down debt. Indeed the IMF, unlike the Bank, received at least an annual $4.5 billion net resource transfer from sub-Saharan countries from 1984 through 1990. The major shareholders of the IMF need to provide it more concessional funds to avoid a sub-Saharan negative transfer when the debt-servicing burden already is so high.

The World Bank, donor governments, and commercial banks rely on a Fund "seal of approval" (usually contingent on the borrower's reducing demand) before arranging adjustment loans and debt write-offs for sub-Saharan countries. These countries would benefit from the breaking up of this loan and policy cartel through increasing the resources of U.N. and other international agencies and strengthening independent financial centers, such as the EC, the Middle East, or East Asia. Moreover, sub-Saharan states should put together their own programs of adjustment, and donors should base loans on the financial capability of the borrowers rather than on meeting conditions on national economic policy.

For low-income Africa, debt writedowns, trade liberalization by industrialized countries, increased foreign aid and investment, and indigenous government formulation of adjustment programs can achieve the economic turnaround that the ECA admits has not yet occurred. If the cartel refuses to provide funds without Bank/Fund policy conditions, Africa may have no choice but to default and manage its own adjustment, while cooperating with other LDCs to undermine the cartel's stranglehold.

However, DCs have an interest in assisting low-income Africa while supporting African management of economic planning. Although the immediate cost to multilateral agencies and Western and Japanese governments and banks is negligible, this breathing space might enable some African political leaders to form wider coalitions emphasizing long-range planning. While political conflict or blatant corruption might preclude effective capital use in some African countries, a major international effort can stabilize political institutions and improve mass economic welfare in Nigeria, Ghana, Côte d'Ivoire, Senegal, Benin, Zimbabwe, Zambia, and Tanzania, to name just a few.

The Organization of This Study

Chapter 1 identifies the leading Third World debtors and the measures of their debt burden. Chapter 2 sketches the Sub-Sahara's contemporary economic plight. Chapter 3 examines elite policies contributing to poverty and external imbalance. Chapter 4 investigates the effect of foreign trade, aid, investment, and capital flight on debt and poverty. Chapters 5 through 7 analyze World Bank and IMF policies toward indebted African countries and critiques by ECA/OAU, UNICEF, structuralists, and scholars and policymakers from a wide range of perspectives. Chapters 8 and 9 suggest approaches to resolving the African debt crisis.

The starkness of Africa's economic experience enables us to see plainly how debt and stagnation interact and how some of our findings can be applied to other debt-ridden developing regions, such as Latin America, Central Europe,[10] and the former Soviet Union.

1

The Third World External Debt Crisis

■

If you owe a bank $1, the bank owns you, but if you owe a bank
$1 million, you own the bank.
—**Edward John Ray**

The U.S. Bankers' Perspective

The Third World debt crisis has been a dominant factor in relations
between rich and poor countries since 1982. During the 1980s and
early 1990s, U.S. (and British and some European) commercial banks
were vulnerable to default by LDCs. LDC debts to U.S. banks as a
percentage of their capital grew from 110 percent in 1978 to 154
percent in 1982, before falling to 114 percent in 1986 to 63 percent
in 1988. For the nine major U.S. banks, this percentage was even
higher: 163 percent in 1978, 227 percent in 1982, 154 percent in 1986,
and 198 percent in 1988.

Assume a bank's LDC debt-capital ratio is 100 percent, and the bank
writes off 60 percent of LDC debt but none of the other debt. If the
loan-capital ratio is 1200 percent (this ratio typically varies between
1000 and 1700 percent for U.S. banks), then bad loans as a percentage
of capital are at the precarious level of 5 (60/1200) percent.

A complete writeoff of Third World debts in the early 1980s would
have wiped out many major U.S. commercial banks, which had more
exposure to LDC debt than banks in any other country. In response
to nonperforming LDC loans and petrodollar shrinkage from low
world oil prices, U.S. banks reduced their loans to non-OPEC developing countries from $120.6 billion in 1982 to $117.6 billion in 1984
to $100.2 billion in 1986, and after 1988 did not plan to resume 1982

1

lending levels without major loan restructuring. From 1984 to 1988, net commercial bank lending by Japan was double that of the United States, the world's second-ranking lender.[1]

U.S. bank exposure to LDC foreign debt declined in the mid-1980s from loan writeoffs, writedowns, asset sales, and reduced LDC lending. On 19 May 1987, John S. Reed, chairman of the largest U.S. commercial bank, New York's Citicorp, added $3 billion to bank reserves for future LDC loan losses, acknowledging uncertain debt repayment and starting a chain reaction that resulted in losses and increased reserve allocations for several other major banks in 1987. It also struck a death blow to the U.S. official strategy (the Baker Plan, discussed in chapter 8), which emphasized new loans. In 1988–90, Citicorp's reserves were only 56 percent of nonperforming loans, compared to 70 percent for competitors of the same size, so Moody's Investor Service and Standard and Poor's downgraded the credit ratings of Citicorp, as well as four other New York money-center banks with similar problems. In early 1991, as a result of rising concern about commercial loans, especially to LDCs, Moody downgraded Citicorp's ratings further. Table 1.1 indicates the LDC exposure of ten leading U.S. commercial banks.

In 1988, Latin American, Philippine, and Polish loans held by U.S.

Table 1.1. U.S. Commercial Bank Reserve Positions, 1990 ($ millions)

| | (1) | (2) | (3) | (4) |
| | Long-term Exposure to | | col. (2) / col. (1) | Charge-off of LDC |
Commercial Bank	LDC Loans	Reserves	%	Loans
Citicorp	7,800	2,415	31.0	891
Manufacturers Hanover	4,500	1,481	32.9	730
BankAmerica	4,050	1,739	42.0	556
Chase Manhattan	4,000	1,730	43.3	815
Chemical Bank	2,370	1,187	50.1	550
Bankers Trust	2,271	1,930	85.0	388
J. P. Morgan	1,500	1,736	115.7	519
Bank of New York	544	313	57.5	214
First Chicago	450	183	40.7	464
Security Pacific	250	130	52.0	33

Sources: World Bank, vol. 1, *Analysis and Summary Tables* (1990b: 87), citing Salomon Brothers and Standard and Poor's.

Table 1.2. Secondary Market Prices of Bank Debt for Severely Indebted Middle-Income Countries (The "Baker Seventeen") (7/20/89) (Face Value = 1)

Argentina	.18	Côte d'Ivoire	.06	Peru	.04
Bolivia	.11	Ecuador	.14	Philippines	.54
Brazil	.32	Jamaica	.42	Uruguay	.55
Chile	.64	Mexico	.44	Venezuela	.40
Colombia	.60	Morocco	.44	Yugoslavia	.54
Costa Rica	.14	Nigeria	.24		

Sources: Rogoff (1990: 4); Kenen (1990: 9); and Salomon Brothers, *Indicative Prices for Developing Country Debt* (July 1989).

Note: By 1991, Congo, Egypt, Honduras, Hungary, Nicaragua, Poland, and Senegal were added to and Nigeria (demoted to low-income country), Colombia, and Jamaica were deleted from the middle-income severely indebted countries. World Bank, vol. 1, *Analysis and Summary Tables* (1990b: 121).

banks sold at a 40–70 percent discount on the secondhand market, indicating market expectation of partial default. Table 1.2 shows the secondary market prices of bank debts of severely indebted countries, ranging from 4 percent for Peru and 6 percent for Côte d'Ivoire to 24 percent for Nigeria to 64 percent for Chile. (Additionally, Sudan's secondary price was 2 percent and Zaïre's 19 percent.) Steadily increasing discounts for LDC bank debt (fig. 1.1), together with the rising risk premium (interest rates 1–2 percentage points in excess of LIBOR for Brazil, Argentina, and Mexico and once as much as 9 percentage points for other LDCs), the reduction of commercial lending to LDCs during the 1980s, and the increasing interest and principal arrears (to $52 billion in December 1988), indicate how much debtor countries' creditworthiness deteriorated. Banks exacerbated instability, overexpanding during the upswing of LDCs and contracting during their downswing.[2]

While many scholars, such as McKinnon, Guttentag, and Herring, blame managers' herd behavior for the big banks' precarious positions, few scholars think we should allow these banks to fail. The failure of large banks may engender general financial collapse and economic chaos, especially in the United States. Contrary to the prevailing view before 1980, the Federal Deposit Insurance Corporation (FDIC) does not have resources sufficient to protect all insured depositors from a proliferating bank panic. FDIC fund shortages expose U.S. taxpayers to substantial payments, while big bank collapses would probably depress the U.S. and the international economies.[3]

Figure 1.1. Secondary Market Bids on Bank Debt of
Developing Countries, 1986–1990

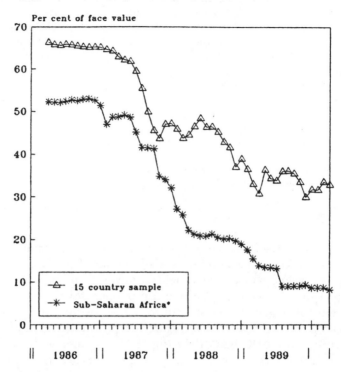

Source: U.N. (1990: 89).
* Excluding Nigeria.

The LDC Perspective and DC Interdependence

From 1970 to 1980, LDC total external debt increased from \$67.0 billion to \$572.2 billion, an eightfold increase and a harbinger of the debt-servicing problems of the 1980s; in 1990, total debt was \$1280.6 billion (table 1.3). Debt-payment problems are portended by such maladies as arrears on interest and then principal, IMF borrowing beyond the reserve tranche, and rescheduling loans. The world press focused on the LDC debt crisis in 1981, when Poland could not meet its obligations to European banks, and in August 1982, when Mexico, facing rapidly falling oil export prices, announced its inability to pay its external debt obligations to (primarily U.S.) banks. From September to December 1982, the Bank for International Settlements (an agency promoting cooperation between DC central banks and supplying additional facilities for international financial transactions) and U.S. and other bilateral official sources provided bridge financing to enable Mexico to service its debts. In February 1983, bank creditors agreed to provide new funds to Brazil and to reschedule debt obligations. The next month banks disbursed new money to Mexico so that it could pay new debt obligations. Yet in early 1983, the World Bank was optimistic, arguing: "There is no generalized debt crisis; rather the mutual difficulties of developing countries in servicing foreign borrowing and of commercial banks in obtaining service payments on foreign lending are an outgrowth" of transitory problems of the 1979–82 global disinflation.

By June 1984, the Group of Seven (G7), the major industrialized capitalist countries (the United States, Japan, West Germany, the United Kingdom, France, Italy, and Canada), agreed to resolve debt case-by-case. Beginning in 1985, several LDCs renegotiated foreign debts through multilateral agreements with the Paris Club, with official creditor groups, or with commercial banks (multiyear restructuring agreements, or MYRAs), lengthening or modifying repayment terms. In October 1985, U.S. Secretary of the Treasury James Baker announced a plan emphasizing adjustment with growth, while encouraging new public and commercial lending.[4]

DC banks improved their financial position in the late 1980s, reducing governmental concern that debt repudiation would bankrupt commercial banks and threaten banking stability. The main focus then became the fall in living standards of LDCs, where external debt was $937 billion in 1985, increasing to $1135–1280 billion for each of the years 1987–90 (table 1.3). Living standards declined in several indebted countries, especially Latin America, where external debt exceeded $400 million in 1985 and peaked at $466 million in 1987, and sub-Saharan Africa, where debt increased steadily from $56 million in 1980 to $97 million in 1985 to $174 million in 1990 (table 1.4).[5] Among the World Bank's severely indebted middle-income countries in 1989, the Baker Seventeen listed in table 1.2, only Yugoslavia, the Philippines, and Morocco were outside Latin America and the Sub-Sahara.

In 1987, the low-income African countries owed a debt of 504 percent of their annual exports, compared to 357 percent for severely indebted middle-income countries and 158 percent for low-income Asia (Bangladesh, Bhutan, Burma, China, India, Laos, Maldives, Nepal, Pakistan, Sri Lanka, and Vanuatu). Almost half of low-income Africa's debt was concessional (where the grant component is 25 percent or more), compared to 5 percent in the highly indebted middle-

Table 1.3. External Debt, GNP, and Exports of 109 Reporting Less-Developed Countries, 1970–1990 ($ billions and percent)

	1970	1975	1980	1981	1982	1983	1984	1985	1986	1987	1988	1989	1990	1991 (projected)
Total external debt (EDT)	67.0	166.7	572.2	673.7	752.9	806.7	843.1	936.9	1027.6	1151.7	1136.5	1146.7	1280.6	1280.8
Long-term public guaranteed debt (DOD)[1]	47.2	126.8	365.1	407.5	462.8	633.2	674.8	767.8	867.3	980.5	959.8	958.8	1047.0	1050.2
Gross national product (GNP)	461.4	1024.1	2059.5	2205.5	2107.1	1997.8	2024.8	2054.5	2112.4	2244.0	2500.0	2748.4	3060.6	3339.2
Exports of goods and services (XGS)	55.0	171.8	432.7	497.4	430.6	400.7	447.1	438.4	425.9	497.1	566.1	614.6	724.3	726.9
DOD/GNP (%)	10.2	12.4	17.7	18.5	22.0	31.7	33.3	37.3	41.1	51.3	38.4	34.9	34.2	31.5
DOD/XGS (%)	85.8	73.8	84.4	81.9	107.5	158.0	150.9	175.1	203.6	197.2	169.5	156.0	144.6	144.5
EDT/GNP (%)	14.5	16.3	27.8	30.5	35.7	40.4	41.6	40.4	48.6	51.3	45.5	41.7	34.2	38.4
EDT/XGS (%)	121.8	97.0	132.2	135.4	174.8	201.4	188.6	201.4	241.3	231.7	200.8	186.6	176.8	176.2
EDT annual growth rate (%)		20.0	21.9	17.7	11.8	7.1	4.5	11.1	9.7	12.1	-1.3	0.9	11.7	0.0
DOD annual growth rate (%)		21.9	23.6	11.6	13.6	36.8	6.6	13.8	13.0	13.1	-2.1	-0.1	9.2	0.3
GNP annual growth rate (%)		17.3	15.0	7.1	-4.5	-5.2	1.4	1.5	2.8	6.3	11.4	9.9	11.4	9.1
XGS annual growth rate (%)		25.6	20.3	15.0	-13.4	-6.9	11.5	-1.9	-2.9	16.7	13.9	8.6	17.8	0.4

Sources: World Bank, World Debt Tables, First Supplement (Washington, D.C., 1971–88); World Bank (1990b: 4); World Bank, vol. 1, Analysis and Summary Tables (1990c: 112, 126); and World Bank, vol. 1, Analysis and Summary Tables (1991b: 120).
[1]Long-term debt is debt with an original maturity of more than one year; short-term debt is debt with an original maturity of one year or less.

Table 1.4. External Debt, GNP, and Exports of Sub-Saharan Africa, 1970–1990 ($ billions and percent)

	1970	1980	1983	1984	1985	1986	1987	1988	1989	1990	1991 (projected)
Total external debt (EDT)	—	56.2	79.8	83.4	96.5	113.8	138.8	141.5	147.0	173.7	175.8
Long-term public guaranteed debt (DOD)[1]	5.7	43.5	62.5	64.4	76.1	93.4	117.6	119.6	125.0	146.2	149.2
Gross national product (GNP)	n.a.	204.7	183.8	182.3	178.7	152.5	132.9	143.8	149.6	156.3	165.7
Exports of goods and services (XGS)	8.6	57.8	35.6	38.9	39.6	33.8	37.9	37.1	39.7	52.7	51.6
DOD/GNP (%)	—	21.3	34.0	35.3	42.6	61.2	88.5	83.2	83.6	93.5	90.0
DOD/XGS (%)	66.2	75.3	175.6	165.6	192.2	276.3	310.3	322.4	314.9	277.4	289.1
EDT/GNP (%)	—	27.5	43.4	45.7	54.0	74.6	104.4	98.4	98.3	111.1	106.1
EDT/XGS (%)	—	97.2	224.2	214.4	243.7	336.7	366.2	381.4	370.3	329.5	340.8
EDT annual growth rate (%)			12.4	4.5	15.7	17.9	21.9	1.9	3.9	18.2	1.2
DOD annual growth rate (%)		22.5	28.4	3.0	18.2	22.7	25.9	1.7	4.5	17.0	2.1
GNP annual growth rate (%)			−3.5	−0.9	−2.0	−14.7	−12.9	8.2	4.0	4.5	6.0
XGS annual growth rate (%)		20.9	−14.9	9.3	1.8	−14.6	12.1	−2.1	7.0	32.7	−3.7

Source: World Bank, vol. 1, *Analysis and Summary Tables* (1990c: 112, 130); and World Bank, vol. 1, *Analysis and Summary Tables* (1991b: 124).

Note: N.a. = data not available.

[1] Long-term debt is debt with an original maturity of more than one year; short-term debt is debt with an original maturity of one year or less.

income countries. Yet if we adjust Africa's debt by its grant equivalent, Africa's ratios of debt to GNP and to exports are still higher than for the highly indebted middle-income countries. And Africa's capacity to bear this burden is more limited, since its economies are weaker and more rigid.[6]

Sub-Saharan Africa's high ratio of payment on debt to exports, without new foreign inflows or debt rescheduling, dampened new capital formation and external adjustment. Africa, after years of negative growth, could not reduce consumption to facilitate the international transfer; thus these countries shifted the adjustment to reduced investment or capital flight. Large payments to creditors reduce investment. Servicing the debt often meant decelerating growth to avoid an international balance on goods and services deficit.[7] Moreover, the Sub-Sahara's oligopolistic money markets, the repression of financial market prices, and the sluggish expansion in response to improved prices in export and import substitution industries prevented timely adjustments to changes in the exchange rate and capital market (see chapters 5 and 7). Real GNP per capita fell 3.5 percent yearly in severely indebted low-income (primarily sub-Saharan) countries and 0.9 percent in severely indebted middle-income countries, 1980–88 (table 1.5), compared to substantial positive growth rates in other LDCs during the same period.

In mid-1985, Peru's President Alan Garcia limited debt payment to 10 percent of exports. Fear that other Latin American countries would

Table 1.5. Average Annual Growth of Severely Indebted Countries in Real GNP per Capita by Income Category (percent per year)

	1965–80	1980–85	1985–88
Severely indebted countries			
Low-income	2.5	−4.6	−1.6
Middle-income	3.8	−2.2	0.9
Total	3.5	−2.8	0.2
High-income OECD countries	2.7	1.7	2.7

Source: U.S. President (1990: 236), from World Bank data.

Note: Low-income countries consist of Ethiopia, Ghana, Kenya, Liberia, Malawi, Niger, Sierra Leone, Sudan, Tanzania, Zaïre, Zambia, Indonesia, India, Pakistan, and Sri Lanka. Middle-income countries are those listed in Table 1.2, including Nigeria, a low-income country in 1989. World Bank (1989b: xi, 154).

join Peru in a debtors' cartel set into motion the Baker Plan later that year. In February 1987, Brazil's President José Sarney put a moratorium on interest payments for twelve months, explaining his country's impatience by indicating "A debt paid with poverty is an account paid with democracy."[8] Creditors cut Brazil's short-term credits, although the U.S. Federal Reserve and Treasury arranged a short-term debt settlement a year later (1988). In early 1987, Nigeria and Zambia imposed a ceiling on the percentage of exports they would pay for debt servicing, while in May 1987 Côte d'Ivoire introduced a debt moratorium to draw attention to its plight. At a meeting of leaders of debtor nations in late 1987, Argentine President Raúl Alfonsín indicated that the West must recognize how "current economic conditions impede our development and condemn us to backwardness. We cannot accept that the south pay for the disequilibrium of the north." In September 1989, Brazil, the Third World's largest debtor, suspended interest payments on half its debt, medium- and long-term commercial bank debt, while continuing to pay most interest owed to Western governments and international agencies,[9] but missing out on debt rescheduling, exchanges, buybacks, and swaps that banks arranged with Mexico and Argentina, the LCDs' other two largest debtors, in 1990–91.

The debt overhang limited LDC import expansion. LDC import volume, which grew 8.2 percent annually, 1971–81, fell 1.8 percent yearly, 1981–86, the period of fastest debt increase, before recovering to a 3.2 percent annual growth, 1986–90.[10] The Overseas Development Council (ODC) indicates that real imports fell from 1981 to 1985 for nine of the ten largest Third World debtors—Brazil, Mexico, Argentina, Indonesia, Venezuela, the Philippines, Chile, Yugoslavia, and Nigeria (63 percent, from 20.4 billion to 7.5 billion). Meanwhile real imports were increasing for South Korea, which rolled over its debt, as its adjustment programs (such as a 1980–81 program in response to oil shocks and price rigidities) were timely and effective and its export and output capacity grew rapidly. ODC estimates that the direct loss to the United States from LDC declining imports from rising debt (1980–86) was $12.7 billion exports and 1.7 million jobs.[11] In the mid- to late 1980s and early 1990s, DC producers, seeing how slow LDC growth dampened export expansion, joined bankers in pressing Washington, other DC capitals, and international agencies to resolve LDC debt.

The rich countries' interest is broader than bankers' and exporters' profits. DCs have motives of humanitarianism and maintaining a sta-

9

ble, global political system. The United States, Canada, Western Europe, Japan, and other OECD countries want an international order that avoids war, widespread hunger, resource depletion, and financial collapse. Aid helps to build a stable world order.

The Sub-Sahara's debt rescheduling began in the late 1970s, several years before that of the severely indebted Latin American countries. Yet during most of the 1980s, Americans and Europeans concentrated on addressing debt in Latin America and the Pacific Rim, whose income and trade made them important economic actors. However, by the late 1980s the world community became increasingly aware of Africa's threat to global stability. Latin American import volume, which expanded 6.4 percent yearly, 1971–81, declined 7.0 percent annually, 1981–86, but grew 3.5 percent, 1986–90. On the other hand, sub-Saharan Africa's volume of imports, which grew 2.4 percent per annum, 1971–81, and dropped 2.7 percent yearly, 1981–86, increased only 0.6 percent annually, 1986–90. The purchasing power of the Sub-Sahara's exports (the value index of exports divided by the price index of imports) fell by 17 percent, 1984 to 1990 (see chapter 4).[12]

External debt in sub-Saharan Africa, two-fifths that of Latin America in 1990 (table 1.6), was not large in comparison to other LDC world regions; 51 percent of the sub-Saharan debt was owed to governments and 34 percent to multilateral institutions such as the IMF and the World Bank. Additionally, only Côte d'Ivoire and Nigeria were classified as middle-income severely indebted countries. Only a few sub-Saharan countries owed 70 percent or less to official creditors; these included Côte d'Ivoire with 38 percent, Nigeria with 52 percent, Congo with 53 percent, Gabon with 55 percent, Sudan with 63 percent, and Cameroon with 70 percent.

The exposure of international commercial banks to the low-income Sub-Sahara (excluding Nigeria and Côte d'Ivoire) was less than $10 billion in 1988, a small sum compared to their exposure in either Brazil or Mexico. Nevertheless, commercial bank claims were a significant problem in some low-income sub-Saharan countries.[13] The low rank of the Sub-Sahara among LDC debtors reflected its low creditworthiness, as its debt-GNP ratio has been the highest in the world, more burdensome than that in either Latin America or Asia (see below). Sutcliffe notes ironically that "for other countries the 'debt crisis' tends to mean that they are too much in debt to the banks. Africa's debt crisis is in a sense the opposite—it has been unable to get into debt."[14]

What IMF economist Khan states about severely indebted countries is also true for sub-Saharan Africa in the 1990s: "External flows to

Table 1.6. Total External Public Debt (EDT) of Developing Countries by Region and Debt Category, 1990

Region/Debt Category	$ billions
All developing countries	1280.5
Region	
Sub-Saharan Africa	173.7
East Asia	234.7
Europe and the Mediterranean	184.1
Latin America	431.1
Middle East	141.5
South and Southeast Asia	115.4
Indebtedness classification	
Severely indebted low-income	165.0
Severely indebted middle-income	505.6
Moderately indebted low-income	183.8
Moderately indebted middle-income	193.7
Other countries	232.4

Source: World Bank, vol. 1, *Analysis and Summary Tables* (1991b).

indebted countries . . . are sharply down; these countries need a lot of external financing to revive their growth rates; and they are unlikely to get it unless something radical . . . is done."[15]

For Western commercial bankers, a country's creditworthiness may reflect not overall economic development or population of the country but the following factors: (1) dependence on foreign capital for development, (2) growth of external debt compared to domestic growth and current-account gap, (3) import dependence, (4) the vulnerability of export earnings, including reliance on a few commodities, (5) debt-servicing burden, (6) extent to which the government's monetary and fiscal policies control expenditures and inflation, (7) hospitality to private and foreign capital, indicative of willingness to respect international financial obligations and welcome private-sector activities, (8) comparative international importance of the country, and (9) political risks, including determining whether the country will repay debts, whether reschedulings have been smooth, and the potential for solving financial problems.[16]

The debt crisis forced many sub-Saharan and Latin American states to curtail poverty programs, wages, employment, and public services throughout the 1980s, even though few of these programs were funded from foreign borrowing. Cuddington sees debt-distressed "developing countries in Latin America and Africa remain[ing] in a state of siege, threatened by impatient creditors, on one hand, and restless domestic constituents, on the other," despite a 1987 debt restructuring of $136 billion that represented 13 percent of the total outstanding external debt of LDCs. While maintaining the status quo is untenable, adjustment can impose a heavy political and economic cost, leading to repudiation of IMF or World Bank programs as it did in Zambia and Argentina in the late 1980s. Fischer credits academics for first pointing out that the stabilization focus of adjustment programs imposed on debtors in the early 1980s was necessary but not sufficient for growth. For growth, Fischer indicates, debtor countries need to restore investment, possible only if resource outflows can be slowed or even reversed.[17]

Major LDC Debtors

Brazil, Mexico, and Argentina were the three leading LDC debtors in the 1980s, with 1989 debts of $111 billion, $96 billion, and $65 billion, respectively (table 1.7), accounting for 65 percent of 1989 LDC debt to commercial banks. Moreover, 66 percent of the three countries' external debt was held by commercial banks.

According to the Organisation for Economic Cooperation and Development (OECD), the thirty-two countries listed in table 1.7 and its notes (except Poland, Hungary, and Romania) accounted for 81 percent of the total 1987 LDC debt of $1,276 billion (a total debt in excess of World Bank estimates in table 1.3). (The last paragraph in table 1.7 indicates some countries listed by the OECD but not by the World Bank.) The 1988 GNP per capita was: $1,530 for the Baker Seventeen, $750 for LDCs, $1,840 for Latin America, $330 for sub-Saharan Africa, and $320 for South Asia. According to the OECD, the seventeen were all middle-income countries and paid 77 percent of the $177.9 billion debt service and owed 64 percent of the $1,240 billion LDC external debt in 1988. (The World Bank reclassified Nigeria as a low-income country in 1989).)[18]

In 1982 the seventeen severely indebted middle-income countries incurred external debt that was 1 percent of GDP. By 1988, these seventeen paid 4.7 percent of GDP in debt service, still too small to cover the interest due! By the end of 1989, their debt outstanding was $506 billion, 30 percent higher than in 1982. And in 1989 net transfers

Table 1.7. Total External Public Debt (EDT)
by Country—Less-Developed Countries, 1980–1990 ($ billions)
($10 billion or more in 1989, ranked by 1989 debt)

Country	1980	1982	1985	1987	1989	1990
Brazil	70	93	106	124	111	116
Mexico	57	86	97	109	96	97
Argentina	27	44	51	58	65	61
India	21	27	41	55	63	70
Indonesia	21	26	37	52	53	68
Egypt	20	29	40	49	49	40
China	5	9	17	35	45	52
Poland	0	0	33	43	43	49
Turkey	19	20	26	41	42	49
South Korea	29	37	47	40	33	34
Nigeria	9	13	20	31	33	36
Venezuela	29	32	35	35	33	33
Philippines	17	25	27	30	29	30
Algeria	19	18	18	25	26	27
Thailand	8	12	18	21	23	26
Morocco	10	12	16	21	21	24
Hungary	10	10	14	20	21	n.a.
Peru	10	12	14	19	20	21
Yugoslavia	18	20	22	22	20	n.a.
Malaysia	7	13	20	23	19	20
Pakistan	19	12	13	17	19	21
Portugal	10	14	17	18	18	20
Chile	12	17	20	22	18	19
Colombia	7	10	14	17	17	17
Côte d'Ivoire	6	8	10	14	15	18
Sudan	5	7	9	12	13	15
Ecuador	6	8	9	10	11	12
Bangladesh	4	5	7	10	10	12

Source: World Bank, vol. 2, *Country Tables* (1990c); and World Bank, vol. 1, *Analysis and Summary Tables* (1990b: 25).

The following countries, not listed in the World Bank source, had $10 billion or more EDT in 1987: Israel ($34 billion), Greece ($32 billion), Taiwan ($20 billion), Saudi Arabia ($17 billion), Iraq ($16 billion), and Cuba ($10 billion). Romania had $10 billion EDT in 1980 and 1982 but fell to less than $10 billion in subsequent years ($0.5 billion in 1989). OECD (1989: 79–213).

Notes: External public debt also includes government-guaranteed private debt. N.a.=data not available.

Table 1.8. Total External Public Debt (EDT) by Country—Sub-Saharan Africa, 1980–1990 ($ billions) ($1 billion or more in 1989, ranked by 1989 debt)

Country	1980	1982	1985	1987	1989
Nigeria	9	13	20	31	33
Côte d'Ivoire	6	8	10	14	15
Sudan	5	7	9	12	13
Zaïre	5	5	6	8	9
Zambia	3	4	5	7	7
Kenya	4	4	4	6	6
Tanzania	3	3	4	5	5
Cameroon	3	3	3	4	5
Mozambique	0	0	3	4	5
Congo	1	2	3	4	4
Senegal	1	2	3	4	4
Madagascar	1	2	2	4	4
Gabon	2	1	1	3	3
Ghana	1	1	2	3	3
Ethiopia	1	1	2	3	3
Zimbabwe	1	2	2	3	3
Guinea	1	1	1	2	2
Mali	1	1	1	2	2
Somalia	1	1	2	2	2
Mauritania	1	1	2	2	2
Uganda	1	1	1	2	2
Liberia	1	1	1	2	2
Niger	1	1	1	2	2
Malawi	1	1	1	1	1
Togo	1	1	1	1	1
Benin	0	1	1	1	1
Sierra Leone	0	1	1	1	1

Source: World Bank, vol. 2, *Country Tables* (1990b). Angola, not listed in the World Bank source, had $2 billion EDT in 1987. OECD (1989: 79–213).

Note: External public debt also includes government-guaranteed private debt.

abroad from these seventeen countries was 24 percent of export earnings.[19]

The three major sub-Saharan African countries with 1989 external debt of $10 billion or more were Nigeria ($33 billion), Côte d'Ivoire ($15 billion), and Sudan ($13 billion). Twenty-four other sub-Saharan countries with $1 billion or more are also listed in table 1.8. Nigeria,

Côte d'Ivoire, and Zaïre accounted for roughly half of the Sub-Sahara's 1991 total scheduled debt service.[20]

In 1991, three middle-income (Congo, Côte d'Ivoire, and Senegal) and twenty-four (of twenty-six) low-income countries were classified as severely indebted: They were countries in which three of four key ratios were above critical levels. These levels and ratios were debt to GNP (30–50 percent), debt to exports of all goods and services (165–275 percent), accrued debt service to exports (18–30 percent), and accrued interest to exports (12–20 percent). Low-income countries had a 1989 GNP per capita no more than $580, while middle-income countries had a GNP per capita more than $580 and less than $6,000.[21]

Twenty of twenty-seven sub-Saharan African countries listed in table 1.8 were low-income countries in 1989, compared to only five (highly populated India, Indonesia, China, Pakistan, and Bangladesh, with low external debt per person) of the thirty major Asian and Latin American debtors listed in table 1.7. While twenty-one of the sub-Saharan twenty-seven were poor enough to be eligible for International Development Association (IDA) concessional loans, only Bangladesh of the Asian-Latin debtors was, as most were middle-income countries with higher credit ratings among commercial banks than African countries.

Poor countries also need heavy borrowing for infrastructure to increase spillovers from which directly productive investors can benefit. Multilateral agencies, especially the IDA, have a major role in funding poor countries. Fifty-four percent of the Sub-Sahara's 1987 debt was owed by IDA-eligible countries, 32 percent by the region's middle-income oil exporters (including Nigeria), 14 percent by middle-income oil importers, and the remainder by low-income countries not IDA-eligible.

Commercial bankers do not lend unless they anticipate enough bargaining power over the sovereign borrower or its guarantor to recover the cost of the funds. This suggests that the lack of private creditors for the Sub-Sahara results from insufficient projects with expected above-market rates of returns or governments unable to appropriate the returns to pay back the creditors. No LDC rescheduling debt has regained access to commercial credit except as part of a cofinancing agreement with the World Bank.[22] Yet while the Sub-Sahara owed only 37 percent of its debt to private creditors compared to 54 percent for other LDCs in 1987, the Sub-Sahara's debt grew faster than that of other LDC regions, 1975 to 1990.[23]

Indicators of Debt

Low-income Sub-Sahara (excluding Nigeria) had a 1989 debt less than either Brazil's or Mexico's. Total external debt as a percentage of LDC GNP increased from 15 percent in 1970 to 28 percent in 1980 to 42 percent in 1984 to 51 percent in 1987 (and the Sub-Sahara's percentage grew even more rapidly) (tables 1.3 and 1.4), reflecting both the collapse in GNP growth and the surge in debt level.

In 1987, the debt-GNP ratio was 63 percent in Latin America and 104 percent in sub-Saharan Africa. Debt in fact exceeded GNP in 1987 for Chile, Costa Rica, Bolivia, Panama, Nicaragua, Chad, Côte d'Ivoire, Congo, Liberia, Madagascar, Malawi, Mali, Mauritania, Mozambique, Niger, Senegal, Somalia, Sudan, Tanzania, Togo, Zaïre, and Zambia (debt-GNP ratio 3.43) but not in major debtors Brazil, Mexico, Argentina, Venezuela, Peru, Colombia, and Ecuador.[24]

The debt-service ratio is figured by dividing interest and principal payments by the exports of goods and services in a given year. The LDC debt-service ratio increased from 9 percent in 1970 to 21 percent in 1980 to 34 percent in 1987, before falling to 27 percent in 1989 and 21 percent in 1990, while the Latin American ratio remained in excess of 30 percent and the sub-Saharan ratio in excess of 20 percent in the 1980s. The 1990 ratio was 27 percent in Latin America and 24

Table 1.9. Debt-Service Payments as a Percentage of Export Earnings and GNP by World Region and Indebtedness Class, 1990

World Region/Indebtedness Class	Debt Service Payments/GNP	Debt Service Payments/ Export Earnings
Sub-Saharan Africa	7.8	24.4
Middle East	10.6	29.4
Latin America	5.0	27.0
South and Southeast Asia	2.8	25.9
East Asia	4.0	14.4
Severely indebted low-income	7.7	28.4
Severely indebted middle-income	5.4	26.1
Moderately indebted low-income	7.4	32.4
Moderately indebted middle-income	9.0	31.3
All LDCs	5.0	21.1

Source: World Bank, vol. 1, *Analysis and Summary Tables* (1990b).

percent in sub-Saharan Africa (table 1.9), a percentage twice what it would have been if exports had grown at the rate of LDCs generally, rather than rising only 1.5 percent annually between 1980 and 1990. Ratios in 1989 varied from Chad's 5.2 percent to Uganda's 81.2 percent; both were IDA-eligible countries with poor credit ratings. The ratios of Madagascar, Ghana, Côte d'Ivoire, and Colombia exceeded 40 percent; those of Mexico, Ethiopia, Somalia, Kenya, Niger, and Brazil were more than 30 percent; Senegal's, Malawi's, Chile's, Congo's, Mozambique's, Zaïre's, and Nigeria's were in excess of 20 percent; Cameroon's, Tanzania's, Zambia's, and Korea's exceeded 10 percent; and Burkina's, Sudan's, and Benin's were less than 10 percent (patterns suggesting little correlation between ratios and creditworthiness).

Sometimes lower ratios reflect substantial default or debt rescheduling. For example, while the Sub-Sahara's and Latin America's actual ratios varied little, the Sub-Sahara's 1990 *scheduled* debt payments percentage was more than twice Latin America's, as *actual* percentages as a proportion of *scheduled* percentages were 37 percent in the Sub-Sahara and 91 percent in Latin America. Finally, the Sub-Sahara's *debt service to GNP* rose from 1 percent in 1980 to 6 percent in 1985 to 8 percent in 1990, while Latin America's increased from 6 percent in 1980 to 7 percent in 1985 before falling to 5 percent in 1990.[25]

Almost 90 percent of total debt carried by IDA-eligible sub-Saharan countries represents claims directly from or guaranteed by bilateral or multilateral official agencies (table 1.10). Most creditor effort to reduce Africa's debt burden must be by official rather than private agencies.

In 1980 and 1990, 60–61 percent of official claims was bilateral, including private loans guaranteed by official export credit agencies (ECAs), which comprise one-quarter of the low-income sub-Saharan countries' nonconcessional, bilateral debt (and 8 percent of total debt).[26] Fifty-two percent of bilateral official and creditor-guaranteed debt was nonconcessional. Multilateral creditors, including the IMF, held 39 percent ($25 billion) of the claims on low-income countries, with more than 60 percent of the claims at concessional interest rates. IDA was the largest creditor of the thirty-four low-income countries, holding 15 percent of multilateral long-term debt although receiving only 3 percent of multilateral debt-service payments.[27]

Only 13 percent of low-income African debt is held by private commercial lenders (not guaranteed by creditor governments or agencies), and most of this is short-term. African debt structure contrasts sharply with that of the highly indebted middle-income countries, two-thirds of whose debt is held by private creditors (table 1.11).

17

Table 1.10. IDA-Eligible Sub-Saharan African Countries: External Debt at
Year-End, 1987

	$ billions	Percentage share
1 Total debt	71.6	100.0
2 Long-term debt	59.4	83.0
3 Public and publicly guaranteed	58.2	81.3
4 Official creditors	50.8	71.0
5 Multilateral	19.9	27.8
6 Concessional	15.4	21.5
7 Nonconcessional	4.5	6.3
8 Bilateral	30.9	43.1
9 Concessional	17.9	25.1
10 Nonconcessional	12.9	18.1
11 Private creditors	7.4	10.3
12 Paris Club eligible	6.0	8.4
13 Other	1.4	2.0
14 Private nonguaranteed	1.2	1.7
15 IMF	5.6	7.8
16 Short-term[a]	6.6	9.2
Memorandum items		
17 Concessional debt	33.3	46.6
18 Nonconcessional debt	38.2	53.4
19 Exposure of private creditors (13+14+16)[b]	9.2	12.8
20 Exposure of official creditors (4+12+15)[b]	62.4	87.2

Source: Charles Humphreys and John Underwood, "The External Debt Difficulties of Low-Income Africa," in Husain and Diwan (1989: 60).

Note: Guaranteed debt in this table is that guaranteed by debtor governments. Debt presumed to be guaranteed by creditor governments is shown as Paris Club–eligible.

[a]Including interest arrears on long-term public debt.

[b]A small share of the short-term debt is likely to be from an official source or to carry an official guarantee.

The Burden of the Debt

The low-income sub-Saharan countries are much less creditworthy than anticipated when the original hard loans were made. The sub-Sahara's debt problem cannot be solved by marginal adjustments. Additional borrowings, if creditors were prepared to lend, would push future debt-service payments to levels in excess of what the Sub-Sahara has been able to meet in the past.

Given World Bank assumptions of constant annual OECD real net transfers and 1 percent annual growth in real imports per capita, or 8 percent nominal annual import growth, 1988–95, donors have to increase grants from $5.5 billion in 1987 to $9.5 billion in 1995 for low-income Africa's nonconcessional debt-export ratio (330 percent) to remain constant. To reduce this ratio to 200 percent, which roughly divides countries that have maintained creditworthiness from those that experienced debt-servicing difficulties, donors would have to increase grants to $11.9 billion by 1995, ensuring that the grant element of resource flow, 1988–95, would be 91 percent.[28]

Ironically, the high ranking of middle-income countries (all those with $20 billion or more debt in 1989 in table 1.7 except Nigeria, Indonesia, India, and China) among LDC debtors compared to low-income Africa (all those with $14 billion or less debt except Congo, Cameroon, Senegal, Gabon, and Zimbabwe in table 1.8) usually indi-

Table 1.11. Debt Structure at Year-End, 1987 (by Debt Category)

Debt Category	Severely Indebted Low-Income Africa	Severely Indebted Middle-Income Countries
Official direct bilateral		
$ billions	30	44
Percent	42	10
Creditor-guaranteed[a]		
$ billions	6	34
Percent	9	6
Multilateral		
$ billions	26	83
Percent	36	16
Private (including short-term debt[b])		
$ billions	9	357
Percent	13	68

Source: Charles Humphreys and John Underwood, "The External Debt Difficulties of Low-Income Africa," in Husain and Diwan (1989: 50).

[a]Defined as suppliers' credits and fixed-rate commercial bank loans.

[b]Defined as private loans not guaranteed by debtor governments, variable-rate commercial bank loans, short-term debt (which may include interest in arrears on public loans), and nationalization obligations.

19

cated a high credit rating among commercial banks. South Korea has shown that a large debt need not be a problem as long as the country can borrow enough to cover debt services and imports and foreign creditors believe the economy can service its debt. Although South Korea's debt increased—from $2 billion (1970), to $15 billion (1979), to $37 billion (1982), to $47 billion (1985)—its exports grew so rapidly that its debt-servicing capacity improved considerably.[29]

While only three major debtors were from sub-Saharan Africa, its 1989 external debt of $155 billion, only three-fourths of Brazil's and Mexico's total, was probably more burdensome than for any other world region. By the end of 1986, two-thirds of the forty-five countries under the IMF's African Department had credit outstanding averaging 134 percent of their quotas,[30] compared to only 25 percent unconditional borrowing rights, the reserve tranche. In the 1970s and early to mid 1980s, the rulers of Nigeria, Zaïre (most principal and interest from 1971–74 borrowing), and Ghana squandered their loan funds, sometimes expanding patronage for intermediaries and contractors so fast that they lost track of millions of dollars borrowed from abroad. The inefficiency and poor national economic management by the ruling elites in Nigeria, Zaïre, and Ghana, much like Latin American military governments such as Argentina's in the 1970s, meant no increased capacity to facilitate the export surplus to service the foreign debt. The three African countries had to reschedule their debts— Ghana in 1974, after an abrupt decline in the prices of cocoa exports; Zaïre, in 1980–89 after several years of depressed copper export prices; and Nigeria, in 1983 and 1986, during a prolonged oil-price slump. Compared to Asian and Latin countries, these three African countries have had poorer credit ratings among commercial banks because of poor national economic management, as reflected in previous balance-of-payments crises, and a slow growth in output and exports.

The 1930s as a Historical Comparison

A comparison with the 1930s is useful because Africa's and Latin America's economic collapse in the 1980s and 1990s parallels that of LDCs (primarily Latin American) in the 1930s. Lenders in the 1920s were as sophisticated as in the contemporary period, but issue houses, like governments in the 1970s, encouraged hesitant lenders to expand debt instruments. Starting in 1928, the sudden decline in lending by the United States, global commodity price and other external shocks, and the increased government budget deficits reduced the debt-servicing capacity of debtors. Debtors in the 1930s reduced imports, expanded import-substitution production, and undertook contractionary monetary and fiscal policies. Countries facing external crises then were more likely to default on bonds rather than press for bank rescheduling or renegotiation as they would today. Those countries that stopped paying their debt service recovered from the Great Depression more quickly than countries that resisted default and had virtually identical access to post–World War II capital markets. Yet the widespread default resulted in a depression of portfolio lending that lasted for twenty to thirty years, until the 1950s.

The resolution of the crisis of the 1930s was slow, with sporadic suspension and renegotiation and long periods of uncertainty. Governments in the 1930s and 1940s intervened to maintain debt service but were more likely than today to pressure creditors as well as debtors to reach an early agreement. Despite defaults, both British and American creditors overall recovered their principal while receiving interest payments almost as high as those on domestic treasury bonds.

Global solutions proposed today—a special international lending facility, injections of new funds, debt buybacks, and conversions of existing assets into new assets with different contingencies—were first proposed in the 1930s. Global schemes failed then because of disagreements about who should fund and control the administration, an experience that leaves economic historians pessimistic about resolution in the 1990s.[31]

Yet country default in the 1990s is likely to be more costly than it was in the 1930s, when debt was held among scattered bondholders ranging from retired individuals to large corporations, so that creditor collusion was virtually impossible. Currently debt is, in contrast, largely held by an oligopoly of international commercial banks, which hold the lion's share of LDC international reserves, dispense LDC credit, maintain close communication with each other, and coordinate action with the IMF and DC central banks. Moreover, contemporary LDCs face a relatively prosperous, not a depressed and divided, North. Furthermore, today's bank cartel insists on a case-by-case approach, thus increasing their bargaining power vis-à-vis debtors.[32]

Conclusion

Total Third World external debt rose from $70 billion in 1970 to $570 in 1980 to $1280 billion in 1990. Indeed, in the 1980s this debt crisis was a dominant factor in relations between DCs and LDCs. The U.S. press and political establishment paid attention to the crisis because of the possible effect of LDC default on DC commercial-bank insolvency.

Nigeria, Côte d'Ivoire, and Latin America owed substantial commercial debt and low-income Africa much official debt. In the face of rising debt, the U.S. proposed the 1985 Baker Plan to encourage expanded lending, especially for highly indebted countries like those in Latin America. But the debt overhang in Latin America and sub-Saharan Africa continued to increase during the 1980s and early 1990s, reducing output, imports, and social spending per person. The debt crisis forced many sub-Saharan and Latin states to borrow from the World Bank and IMF, whose adjustment programs often forced the reduction of poverty programs, wages, employment, and public services.

While no sub-Saharan debtor ranked among the top ten LDC debtors and the Sub-Sahara's 1990 debt, $174 billion, was small compared to Latin America's $431 billion, Africa's debt may have been more burdensome than Latin America's if we examine debt/GNP and debt/export ratios. Despite the low creditworthiness of Africa and the low percentage of its debt held by commercial lenders, Africa faced widespread debt rescheduling in the 1980s and the early 1990s, and it depended on the IMF as the lender of last resort. From 1980 through 1991, thirty of the forty-four sub-Saharan countries resorted to rescheduling, mainly official bilateral debt reschedulings at the Paris Club. When Nigeria and Senegal became IDA-eligible in the early 1990s, all but five (Cameroon, Côte d'Ivoire, Congo, Gabon, and Zimbabwe) of the forty-four were IDA-eligible.

2

The Great Descent:
Stagnation and External Deficits

．

We are . . . in a world turned upside down, a world in which those
who stress the urgency of material problems such as poverty and
unemployment are considered hopeless romantics, and those who
restrict themselves to the rarefied world of high finance are hard-
headed realists.
                                          —**John F. Weeks**

Sub-Saharan Africa's external deficit and debt affected and were affected by stagnation, poverty, and inequality. Exchange-rate, import-
substitution, foreign-investment, tariff, and pricing policies, combined
with global economic trends (declining terms of trade, reduced concessional lending, and higher interest rates), increased the interrelated
evils of poverty, inequality, external imbalance, and debt burden in
the Sub-Sahara that began in the 1970s, worsened in the 1980s, and
continue into the 1990s.

IMF Rules of Adjustment

John Maynard Keynes, head of the British delegation negotiating the
creation of the IMF at Bretton Woods, New Hampshire, in July 1944,
argued for an international system in which the burden for balance-of-
payments and financial policy adjustments would be borne by surplus
nations. He supported expansionary policies for external surplus
countries to reduce the need for painful adjustments (devaluation and
contractional monetary and fiscal policies) by deficit countries. Harry
Dexter White, Deputy Secretary of the Treasury, reflecting the interests of the United States, soon to be the major postwar creditor nation,
proposed a plan that placed the initiative for removing international

disequilibrium on deficit countries. This approach was largely adopted and continues to the present.[1]

Applying Keynes's concern for reducing deficit-country adjustment to the post-1973 world of managed floating exchange rates would indicate that the IMF should require surplus countries, mostly DCs, to appreciate their currencies relative to foreign currencies. On the contrary, the contemporary IMF, together with the World Bank, provides loans to Africa and other LDCs with international deficits that require disinflation, spending reductions, and (often) currency depreciation, indicating, in Tanzania's former President Julius K. Nyerere's words, that the Bank and Fund have "usurped the role of 'finance minister of the Third World.' "[2]

Africa and other LDCs are required to adjust to conditions created by external change beyond their control, that is, recession, high interest rates, and fluctuating commodity prices. The FAO notes the irony of this;

> Given that the economies of the developed countries are generally much stronger and more flexible, the pressure on developing countries to adjust is striking for its asymmetry. Relevant adjustments by the developed countries could have been a reduction in the excessive levels of farm support, freer trade in primary products, and measures to achieve private and public debt relief.[3]

The global economic system lacks a mechanism for encouraging DC adjustment. Requiring poor deficit countries to adjust redistributes income from poor to rich countries.

One 1988 World Bank seminar participant from an African finance and planning ministry observes that the Bank and Fund view LDCs in isolation from the international economy. According to this participant, the approach of the Bretton Woods institutions is derived from

> a vision of a world composed of deficit countries (not counting the more powerful deficit countries such as the United States) that need adjustment, and surplus countries whose policies are deemed appropriate. It is based on an image of the world in which commodity markets, capital markets, and so on are free and uncontrolled. Thus, a quasi-religious belief in liberalization as a panacea is made that much more credible. In the final analysis, however, the approach leads to a shift of the burden of adjustment of the world system to the least developed countries.[4]

When growth or foreign flows fell, Africa's disadvantaged classes usually were hurt the most. While African rulers incurred debt partly to expand patronage, they responded to external pressures by reducing social programs, especially for small farmers, workers, the unemployed, the sick, and the elderly. Even attaining external balance at the expense of domestic goals of employment, state spending, or price stability means external disequilibrium, according to Nurkse's classic definition.[5]

Social Costs of Adjustment

Bank/Fund conditions for adjustment loans to pare the external deficit usually involved reduced social spending to dampen inflation and imports. UNICEF contends that

> the common aim of these [Bank/Fund economic adjustment] measures is to improve the balance of payments, repay debts and reduce inflation. Important national objectives—such as expanding and protecting employment, ensuring a minimum income for households and providing basic public services—have become secondary. Ironically, the result has often been an aggravation of the economic crisis and a parallel human crisis as unemployment rises, incomes of the most vulnerable groups fall, import-dependent industries cut production, public services are curtailed and public discontent and political instability grow.[6]

Another UNICEF study shows that from 1980 to 1985, during a period of negative growth resulting from external debt limiting social spending, child welfare deteriorated in most of sub-Saharan Africa; that is, rates of infant mortality, child death, child malnutrition, primary school dropout, illiteracy, and non-immunization all increased. The fall in birth weight occurring throughout the Sub-Sahara also indicated declining welfare. Moreover, an ECA paper indicates that killer diseases like yaws and yellow fever, virtually eliminated by the end of the 1950s, re-emerged in the 1980s.[7]

Ghana's prolonged economic decline from the 1960s through the early 1980s contributed to the decline of health expenditure per capita by 20 percent (with infant mortality rates rising from 80 per 1,000 in the 1970s to 100 in 1980 and 115 in 1983–84). A 1983 project to immunize against yellow fever met only 50 percent of its target; project vehicles were withdrawn because of a fuel shortage. In the middle of the same year in the Accra region, twenty of fifty-seven project refrigerators were not functioning. Mozambique could not acquire the drugs and equipment needed for primary health care because of shortages of foreign exchange. Zaïre's budget cuts reduced teachers by 7,000. In Addis Ababa, Ethiopia, four primary school students shared one textbook.[8] Chapter 7 provides more detail on the social costs of adjustment to African peoples.

The Transfer Problem

While the savings of private business firms (including land clearing and drainage by peasant households) retained from earnings constitute a leading source of investment in Africa, most household savings plans do not coincide with business investment plans. The following equation shows private investment minus private savings, the budget deficit (the deficit of public-sector enterprises plus government purchases of goods and services minus taxes paid to government), and the international balance on goods and services deficit (imports minus exports of goods and services), and how a country finances its external deficit and savings gap (government and private investment minus savings) by net capital inflows, that is, borrowing, attracting investment, or receiving grants from abroad.

$$\text{Net Capital Inflows} = \text{Imports} - \text{Exports} =$$
$$\text{Private Investment} - \text{Private Saving} + \text{Budget Deficit}[9]$$

Economic policy that reduces the demand for imported goods and services, cuts investment demand, or avoids inflationary financing of the government budget makes it easier to effect the transfer of real purchasing power to the creditor country. If the transfer causes the debtor country's income terms of trade or export purchasing power (the *value* index of exports divided by the price index of imports) to fall, the creditor country enjoys a further gain of purchasing power. However, if the creditor country's monetary and fiscal policies fail to translate the extra purchasing power into effective overall demand, especially the demand for foreign goods, the debtor country's transfer problem worsens. As an example, if the creditor country protects its less competitive industries, transfer by the debtor country is difficult. The larger the debtor's net financial transfer relative to GNP, the greater the required cut in domestic claims on GNP and the less likely the transfer can be financed exclusively by reduced government spending.[10] Government dissavings through a budget deficit (without foreign or domestic non-bank financing) will involve money creation, exacerbating excess aggregate demand or spending and igniting inflation, making the transfer more difficult. Sub-Saharan Africa's central government fiscal deficits as a percentage of GDP were more than 5 percent every year, 1980–90, while highly inflationary Latin America's excess deficits over sub-Saharan Africa's rose from 1983 through 1989.

Devlin compares Latin America's contemporary debt payments to war reparations by France in the 1880s after the Franco-Prussian War and Germany's payment to the victorious allies after World War I.

According to Keynes in 1929, given the allies' restrictions on mark devaluation, Germany could pay the reparations only by depressing the economy. Latin America's negative resource balance with foreign creditors and investors, roughly 5 percent of GDP and 30 percent of export earnings, 1982–85, was comparable to France's and double the 2.5 percent for Germany, 1924–32, that contributed to the discontent giving rise to Hitler's Nazi Germany. The percentages for Brazil, Mexico, and Venezuela in the late 1980s (table 2.1), lower than those for the early 1980s, were still comparable to Germany's ratios for war reparations.

Africa's percentages in table 2.1, chosen to illustrate the right (high-valued) tail of the distribution, were comparable to war reparations for the years selected but were not as sustained as Latin America's, France's, or Germany's over a multi-year period, because of Africa's lesser per capita borrowing (with inferior creditworthiness), greater concessional borrowing, and positive official transfer (table 2.2). The closest African approximation of a war-reparations burden was borne by Nigeria, 1984–86, which experienced a negative net transfer of 1.8 percent of GNP and 12.5 percent of exports over a three-year period, 1984–86. But Nigeria's resource balance was positive in 1987, two years before chronic negative growth made her eligible for IDA funds.[11]

Stages in the Balance of Payments

While foreign loans enable a country to import in excess of its exports, eventually the borrowing country must service (with interest plus re-payment of principal) the foreign debt. Sometimes a country can arrange debt relief, convert debt into equity, or postpone payment by rescheduling the debt or borrowing in excess of the debt due for the year. In rare instances, a country may repudiate its debts despite potential economic sanctions and credit restraints.

Paying back the loan requires a country to produce more than it spends, save more than it invests, and export more than it imports. Doing this need not be onerous, however. In fact a country in early stages of development typically encounters a growing debt. The United States, from the Revolutionary War until after the Civil War, was a young and growing debtor nation, borrowing from England and France to finance an import surplus for domestic investments, such as railroads and canals. However, the United States proceeded to a subsequent stage, mature debtor nation, 1874 to 1914, when the

Table 2.1. Comparison of Developing Countries' Negative Resource Balance with the War Reparations of Germany and France

	Negative Transfer as Percentage of GNP[a]	Negative Transfer as Percentage of Exports[b]
Germany, 1925–1932[c]	2.5	13.4
France, 1872–1987[d]	5.6	30.0
Congo, 1989	9.6	16.2
Brazil, 1989	2.6	23.9
Mexico, 1989	3.8	19.6
Venezuela, 1989	4.9	13.0
Cameroon, 1985	3.6	9.8
Nigeria, 1985	2.7	17.4
Zaïre, 1985	3.3	11.2

Sources: Germany and France: Devlin (1987: 81); and LDCs: World Bank, vol. 2, *Country Tables* (1990c).

Note: Comparisons should be viewed with caution and taken as rough estimates.

[a]The denominator is GNP for developing countries in the 1980s and national income in the cases of Germany and France. GNP is larger than national income.

[b]Goods and services for developing countries in the 1980s and goods for France and Germany.

[c]War reparations to victorious nations of RM10,720 million in currency and payments in kind as indicated in the 1919 Treaty of Versailles.

[d]War reparations of Fr. 5,000 million as part of the 1871 peace treaty of Frankfurt, which ended the Franco-Prussian War.

economy's increased capacity facilitated the export surplus to service the foreign debt. Similarly, contemporary developing countries effectively using capital inflows from abroad should usually be able to pay back loans with increased output and productivity.[12]

A Rising Balance on Goods and Services Deficit

Double-entry bookkeeping ensures that current (income) and capital accounts equal zero in the balance-of-payments statement, an annual summary of a country's international economic and financial transactions. A major measure of the deficit is the international balance on goods and services account, or exports minus imports of goods and

Table 2.2. Net Resource Transfers to LDC Debtor Countries, 1981–1988[a] ($ billions)

	Year							
	1981	1982	1983	1984	1985	1986	1987	1988
Total LDC debtor countries	25.2	22.9	12.2	0.7	−12.7	−19.4	−28.8	−39.0
Official creditors	16.6	14.5	12.6	11.9	5.4	4.6	0.9	1.4
Private creditors	9.0	8.4	−0.4	−11.1	−18.1	−24.0	−29.6	−41.3
Latin America	7.2	6.2	−1.3	−6.5	−14.0	−15.6	−12.5	−20.8
Official creditors	3.0	3.0	1.9	2.8	2.1	1.8	−0.2	−1.1
Private creditors	4.2	3.2	−3.2	−9.3	−16.1	−17.4	−12.3	−19.7
Sub-Saharan Africa	5.6	6.2	3.5	0	−1.4	1.5	2.6	0.5
Official creditors	3.2	3.5	3.6	2.3	1.3	2.6	2.9	2.1
Private creditors	2.1	2.7	−0.1	−2.3	−2.7	−1.1	−0.3	−1.6

Source: John T. Cuddington, "The Extent and Causes of the Debt Crisis of the 1980s," in Husain and Diwan (1989: 18–19).

[a]Long-term public and public-guaranteed debt only. Note that a large proportion of debt by private entities in LDCs is guaranteed by government.

services. Table 2.3, which illustrates international balance-of-payments concepts, shows that in 1991 Ghana pays for its $728 million balance on goods and services deficit and $90 million reduced official liabilities through net capital inflows ($367 million) and net grants and transfers from abroad ($451 million). Aid, remittances, loans, and investment from abroad enable Ghana to finance the deficit so that it spends more than it produces, imports more than it exports, and invests more than it saves. These funds provide time and resources for Ghana to adjust, as long as the investments, imports, and reforms that Ghana undertakes increase its capacity to produce and export (thus being able to repay the funds).

Oil-importing developing countries had a deficit, 1974–79, with a series of global price shocks, including the quadrupling of oil prices over four months in 1973–74 and oil-price rises reducing non-oil LDCs' terms of trade, 1979–80. This deficit continually increased, 1974–79, except for 1976 and 1977. Non-oil developing countries had a deficit every year in the 1980s, increasing during the 1980–83 OECD recession (with sharply falling commodity prices, slowed export expansion, and greater OECD protectionism) but falling from 1983 to 1988, before rising in 1989. Overall the non-oil LDC deficit as a percentage of GNP increased almost twofold from before the 1973–74 oil shock

Table 2.3. Ghana's International Balance of Payments, 1991 ($ millions)

	Goods and Services Account	Current Account	Capital Account (+ Increases in Foreign Liabilities)
	(− Debits or Payments)		
Merchandise exports	+948		
Merchandise imports	−1313		
Service exports minus service imports (net travel, transport, investment income, and other services)	−363		
Balance on goods and services		−728	
Net grants, remittances, and unilateral transfers		+451	
Balance on current account		−277	
Net capital inflows			+367
Net official reserve asset change			−90
		−277	+277

Source: Africa Research Bulletin (Economic Series) 28 (15 September 1991): 10501.

to the late 1970s, with little adjustment to the shock. Oil-exporting developing countries (including high-income Middle Eastern oil exporters) had surpluses from 1974 to 1985, declining to deficits during the real oil price slump of the late 1980s. (Table 2.4 combines oil-importing and oil-exporting countries.)

Africa, largely an importer of oil, followed a pattern similar to oil-importing LDCs, with the deficit gradually increasing from 1974 to 1979, falling in 1980, rising during the DC recession in the early 1980s, declining in the mid-1980s, and increasing slowly in the late 1980s. Even Nigeria, sub-Saharan Africa's major oil exporter, had a surplus only in 1973–75 and 1979–80, during two price peaks, and in the late 1980s, when debt-servicing burdens forced import reductions, especially of services.[13] (Chapter 4 provides more detail about how declining and fluctuating export prices contribute to debt crises.)

Aid includes concessional loans and grants. In the late 1970s, aid (official development assistance) to sub-Saharan Africa fell in real terms, while commercial loans remained sparse; African countries

Table 2.4. Developing Countries' Balance on Goods and Services Deficit and Finance Sources, 1980–1991 ($ billions)

Item	Year											
	1980	1981	1982	1983	1984	1985	1986	1987	1988	1989	1990	1991
Balance on goods and services deficit	(12.9)[a]	57.9	89.3	73.8	46.2	43.0	67.1	24.0	40.0	40.5	48.5	53.0
Financed by:												
Private transfers	12.3	7.7	4.2	6.6	8.1	7.7	11.1	12.7	11.8	11.1	12.3	13.6
Official development assistance (grant component)	5.4	7.0	8.0	9.4	10.5	13.4	14.6	13.8	14.9	15.6	16.3	16.1
Private direct investment	4.3	17.6	19.7	13.3	13.4	11.1	9.9	13.1	14.0	10.0	14.1	17.7
Loans (commercial and official) at bankers' standards	99.2	114.1	88.6	63.3	44.3	33.0	49.0	50.5	36.4	42.8	52.5	46.6
Short-term borrowing	−89.2[b]	−98.9	−74.8	−20.8	−22.1	−14.0	−13.4	−14.7	−34.9	−13.2	−20.3	−12.6
Changes in reserves	−44.9	10.4	43.6	2.0	−8.0	−8.2	−4.1	−51.4	−2.2	−25.8	−26.4	−28.4

Sources: IMF (1988: 97, 108); IMF (1989b: 110, 120); and IMF (1990: 160, 170).
[a]Parentheses indicate a balance on goods and services surplus.
[b]Minus sign indicates an increase in reserves.

Table 2.5. Africa's Balance on Goods and Services Deficit and Finance Sources, 1980–1991 ($ billions)

Item	Year											
	1980	1981	1982	1983	1984	1985	1986	1987	1988	1989	1990	1991
Balance on goods and services deficit	6.2	27.2	26.2	17.3	12.8	7.4	17.9	13.4	19.6	18.2	17.6	18.6
Financed by:												
Private transfers	0.4	1.1	1.3	1.3	1.5	1.9	2.5	3.2	3.1	3.1	3.5	3.6
Official development assistance (grant component)	3.1	2.8	4.4	4.0	5.3	6.4	6.9	6.5	6.9	7.3	7.4	7.7
Private direct investment	0.4	0.5	1.0	0.1	−0.1	−0.1	0.2	0.3	0.3	0.3	0.4	0.5
Loans (commercial and official) at bankers' standards	10.8	14.4	15.9	11.0	7.1	2.2	9.7	7.0	7.9	9.4	8.7	7.0
Short-term borrowing	−2.3[a]	−1.5	−1.6	−2.3	−1.4	−1.5	−0.8	−0.8	−0.1	−0.2	−0.3	−0.2
Changes in reserves	−6.2	9.9	5.2	3.2	0.4	−1.5	−0.6	−2.8	1.5	−1.7	−2.1	0.0

Sources: IMF (1988: 97, 110); IMF (1989b: 110, 122); IMF (1990: 158, 160, 172); and OECD (1989).
[a] Minus sign indicates an increase in reserves.

lacked the credit standing to receive many loans at bankers' standards. In the 1980s, donor countries increased the share of aid to the forty-one least-developed countries, designated by the United Nations on the basis of low per capita income, low share of manufacturing in gross product, and low literacy rates. Since twenty-one of the thirty-six sub-Saharan African states (with a population of one million or more) are considered least developed, aid rose gradually during the early to mid-1980s. The trickle of commercial loans fell sharply in the late 1980s.

Africa received $667 million in U.S. aid in fiscal year 1984 (14 percent of the total $471,429 million), dropping to $575 million in fiscal year 1990 (11 percent of $522,727 million). In that year, Zaïre, with 6 percent of Africa's population, received $61 million (11 percent) of the $575 million official American aid to Africa, even though a substantial share of aid left Zaïre through capital flight.[14]

A Rising External Debt, 1970–1990

Sub-Saharan Africa's debt rose from $5 billion in 1970, $14 billion in 1976, $56 billion in 1980, $83 billion in 1984, $114 billion in 1986, $142 billion in 1988, to $174 billion in 1990 (tables 1.3 and 1.4). The chronic and rising African external deficit required greater foreign borrowing, thus increasing future external debt. Indeed, an African ministry official commented in 1988 that most external funds Africans obtain are earmarked for paying debt, leaving little scope for adjustment with growth. A Comoro official contended that

> the current program with the [World] Bank stresses stabilization and reduction of internal and external indebtedness. Little is allocated to investment. According to the Bank, meeting external obligations will lead to new inflows of resources. These resources, however, have yet to materialize. As a result, there is an important segment of the population for whom the adjustment program is simply aimed at enabling Comoro to pay its external debts.[15]

Net Resource Transfers

While hard-loan disbursements to LDCs by the Bank/Fund exceeded its debt service and fees from 1982 to 1985, disbursements were less than debt service and fees, 1985–89. Inter-American Development Bank and Asian Development Bank disbursements minus debt service were negative for the same period, indicating a net transfer from poor to rich countries. Even the net transfer from the Bank's soft-loan agency, the IDA, was negative in 1988 for the first time in history. Moreover, annual loans at banking standards fell substantially between 1980–83 and 1984–90 for LDCs and Africa (tables 2.4–2.5). (In 1989, the Sub-Sahara held 56 percent of the total external debt of Africa and 47 percent of its debt service.)[16]

Net resource transfers to sub-Saharan Africa peaked in 1982 at $6.2 billion (or 15.5 percent of exports of goods and services).[17] Private debt-service obligations exceeded net transfers of capital by private creditors beginning in 1983, a reversal of the direction of private flows during the twenty years before. However, net private transfers rose from 1985 to 1987 (all negative), not from resumed lending but from falling debt-service payments.

Net private *and* official transfers to reporting LDC debtors, on the other hand, were first negative in 1985 and fell steadily throughout the late 1980s, as debt-service repayments exceeded new loan disbursements (table 2.2). The World Bank indicates net transfers declining from −$39.0 billion in 1988 to −$44.2 billion in 1989, rising to −$28.6 billion in 1990 before falling to −$36.4 billion in 1991.

Total new net *lending* to LDCs in 1989 declined 25 percent to $19 billion. Net transfers in 1989 were much less than previous projections because disbursements were lower than expected.

The IMF received net transfers from sub-Saharan Africa, 1983 to 1990, as repayment obligation exceeded new loans, even though the Fund introduced concessional adjustment facilities in the late 1980s. During the same period, net transfers from the World Bank (including its IDA concessional window) to the Sub-Sahara have been large and positive every year as a result of a tripling of dollar resources during this period. This aversion of negative net transfers to the most debt-distressed world region may be deliberate, even though the Bank refuses to confirm the policy, perhaps for fear of establishing a precedent. Ironically, the African Development Bank, short of replenishments of concessional funds from DC contributors, received net transfers from the Sub-Sahara for several years during the 1980s.[18]

On the other hand, South Korea, Taiwan, Singapore, Hong Kong, Thailand, and Malaysia made efficacious use of funds borrowed in earlier periods through investing in education and training, infrastructure, and plant, equipment, and buildings that substantially increased capacity output (especially in the tradable goods sector), enabling these Asian countries to service debts and avoid a debt crisis. Indeed, in 1988 Korea and Taiwan emerged as capital exporters.[19]

African States

Sub-Saharan African states are soft states, in which the authorities who decide policies rarely enforce them (if enacted into law) and only reluctantly place obligations on people.[20] These states are dependent on buying political support through concessions to powerful interest groups. Regime survival in Africa's politically fragile states required the support of urban elites (business people, professionals, executives, and high-ranking military officers, civil servants, and parastatal employees) and large landowners and commercial farmers through economic policies that sacrificed growth, income distribution, and external balance. Expanding the state to disperse benefits to allies and clients necessitated increased borrowing from abroad and joint ventures with multinational corporations (MNCs). Thus, political elites, even under African socialism, pursued policies that exacerbated stagnation, increased income inequality, and external disequilibrium. In order to prescribe policies to deal with these problems, we need to identify policies that not only promote growth, income distribution, and external balance but also create immediate and sustained constituencies— while not threatening the political security of governing elites.

African socialism has differed from the Western socialist concept of the ownership of most capital and land by the state. The African variety included the following: substantial state ownership in modern sector industry, agriculture, transport, and commerce; public control of resource allocation in key sectors; a deemphasis on international trade and investment; inward-looking production; and rapid Africanization of professional, managerial, and technical jobs.[21]

African states overvalued domestic relative to foreign currency, set farm prices far below world prices, protected manufacturing at the expense of agriculture, used the surplus from these policies to expand inefficient import-substitution industry, and emphasized high-technology, capital-intensive, Western-type, consumer-goods production in the MNC-parastatal sector.

Poverty and Immiserization

Africans entered the last half of this century with high expectations. Kwame Nkrumah, Ghana's president, 1957–66, prophesied in 1950, "If we get self-government, we'll transform the Gold Coast into a paradise in ten years."[22] In the 1960s, Patel and Hance were more optimistic about Africa's economic potential than that of other LDCs.[23]

But the great ascent expected in the 1960s has, in Africa, become the great descent.[24] The IMF indicates Africa's annual real (inflation-adjusted) GDP per capita growth as 2.1 percent 1965–71 (less than a percentage point slower than LDCs generally), −0.1 percent 1972–81 (2.5 percentage points slower than LDCs), and −0.85 percent 1981–91 (3.5 to 4 percentage points slower than LDCs). Real GDP per capita, with a base of 100 in 1970, reached 108 in 1972, then fell to 107 in 1981 and to 100 in 1991; average GDP shows no growth since 1970 and a 7.4 percent drop since 1972 (fig. 2.1). Sub-Saharan Africa's annual real growth in GNP per capita, 1965–89, 0.3 percent, was below LDCs', 2.5 percent (table 2.6). The declining terms of trade and increased proportion of GNP produced for the market indicate that official figures *overstate* the Sub-Sahara's purchasing-power adjusted growth.[25] (GNP encompasses income earned by a country's residents; GDP, income earned within a country's boundaries.) Twenty-four of the thirty-six least-developed countries—so designated by the United Nations because of their low per capita income, low share of manufacturing in gross product, and low literacy rates—are in the Sub-Sahara.

For the ECA, Africa, the "sick child of the international economy," was suffering its worst economic crisis since the 1930s' Great Depression. Indeed, ECA Executive Secretary Adebayo Adedeji indicated a "growing recognition by the African people, their leaders and governments, that the independence and credibility of the African polity is seriously endangered because the economy is on the verge of collapse."[26] Recognizing this, the United Nations devoted its thirteenth special session in 1986, at the peak of Africa's decline and debt crisis, to develop a Programme of Action for African Economic Recovery and Development, 1986–1990, to safeguard Africa's economic survival.[27]

The *Khartoum Declaration*, expressing the views of the U.N. Inter-Agency Task Force and numerous African ministers, high-ranking officials, and senior experts from government, stated in 1988:

> Regrettably, over the past decade the human condition of most Africans has deteriorated calamitously. Real incomes of almost all households and families declined sharply. Malnutrition has risen massively, food production has fallen relative to population, the quality and quantity of health and education services have made tens of millions of human beings refugees and displaced persons. In many cases, the slow decline of infant mortality and of death from preventable, epidemic diseases has been reversed. Meanwhile, the unemployment and underemployment situation has worsened markedly.[28]

The U.N. Development Programme (UNDP), in a report coauthored with the World Bank, differs from other U.N. agencies (ECA

Table 2.6. Indicators of Development (by LDC Region and Income Group)

LDC Region/ Income Group	Population (millions) mid–1991	GNP per Capita, 1989 ($)	Average Annual Growth Rate of GNP per Capita, 1965–89 (percent)	Percentage of Population in Poverty, 1985[a]	Life Expectancy at Birth, 1990 (years)
LDC Region					
Sub-Saharan Africa	531	340	0.3	47	52
South Asia	1,147	325	1.8	51	57
Southeast Asia	445	760	3.8	59	61
East Asia	94	4,210	3.9	20	68
China	1,151	350	5.7	20	68
Middle East	349	2,180	2.1	31	61
Latin America	451	1,950	1.9	19	67
Country Income Group					
LDCs	4,168	800	2.5	33	61
High-income oil exporters	21	8,250	3.8	n.a.	63
DCs	868	19,090	2.5	n.a.	76
U.S.S.R. & Central Europe	327	n.a.	n.a.	n.a.	n.a.
World	5,384	3,980	2.5	25	64

Sources: World Bank (1991c: 204–5); World Bank (1990d: 29); World Bank (1980b); and Population Reference Bureau (1991).

Notes: Southeast Asia contains the Philippines. LDCs comprise the low- and middle-income countries in World Bank (1991). DCs do not include Central Europe and the old Soviet Union. High-income oil exporters consist of the United Arab Emirates, Kuwait, Saudi Arabia, Libya, and Oman. N.a.=data not available.

[a]People in poverty include those in households with less than $370 per capita income, with purchasing power adjustment, which is based on converting income in local currency into international dollars by measuring the country's purchasing power relative to all other countries rather than using the exchange rate. See Nafziger (1990: 24–25, 110–13).

Figure 2.1. Developing Countries: Real GDP per Capita by Region,* 1970–1992
(1970 = 100)

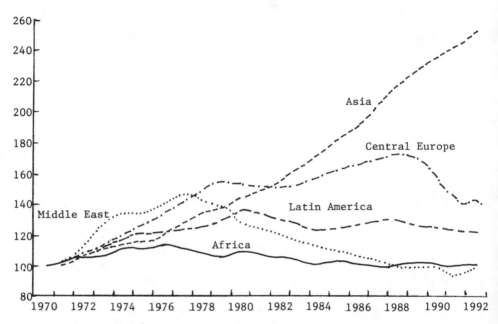

Source: IMF, *World Economic Outlook,* October 1991, p. 16.
* Composites are averages for individual countries weighed by the average U.S. dollar value of their respective GDPs over the preceding three years.

and the General Assembly) in assessing African development in the late 1980s. The Bank-UNDP analysis perceives "signs of a turnaround" in sub-Saharan Africa, 1985–87, with countries adopting strong Bank/ Fund structural adjustment programs improving markedly. When writing about Bank/Fund adjustment programs, IMF Managing Director Michel Camdessus entitles his article, "Good News Out of Africa." In response to such contentions, ECA's Adedeji argues that "it is only by appreciating the reality—sometimes the bitter reality—that the rest of the international community can continue to rally round with support." It is wrong, he maintains, "to portray the economic situation currently prevailing in Africa in rosy terms, to minimize the impact of an adverse external environment, and to depict the effects of structural adjustment programs as having been always positive." Even World Bank economist Ramgopal Agarwala admits it is "time to recognize that we've all failed" in Africa and that new strategies beyond Bank/ Fund structural adjustment lending are desperately needed. Moreover, even the World Bank/UNDP report indicates that growth in GDP per capita was negative, 1985–87, so that per capita income was around 15 percent below its level the decade before.[29] In 1991, the U.N. General Assembly pointed out that African economic and social conditions had worsened over the five years of the United Nations' action program, 1986–90, despite African countries' far-reaching reforms.[30] For most of sub-Saharan Africa, the issue was not restoring but launching growth, as many countries had experienced no growth at all since achieving independence.

Furthermore, the few data over time indicate stagnation and external deterioration were accompanied by rising inequality in Zambia, Ghana, Malawi, Tanzania, and Kenya from the 1960s to the 1980s. President Nyerere admitted at the Arusha Declaration's tenth anniversary (1977) that Tanzania had fallen short of its goals. Tanzania, he indicated, was neither socialist nor self-reliant, and had substantial poverty and inequality. Sub-Saharan Africa's growing inequality, together with economic stagnation, indicated increasing poverty rates, 1965–90, while LDC poverty rates generally fell in the midst of 2.7 percent annual real growth in GNP per capita. Sub-Saharan poverty and immiserization accelerated in the 1980s; income per capita declined as spending fell in response to mounting external debt, primary product prices collapsed, and the net flow of public and private resources from abroad contracted.[31]

Table 2.7 indicates several differences between severely indebted middle-income countries and low-income sub-Saharan Africa, including sub-Saharan savings and investment rates lower than any other world region. Additionally, the Sub-Sahara's high export commodity concentration ratio, poorly educated population, and poorly developed health-care system inhibit the success of adjustment and growth programs.

In the proceedings of the African Leadership Forum, it is observed, "Everywhere, the evidence is of a continent in dereliction and decay, rapidly becoming 'the third world of the Third World.' " In many African countries people do without public services, as governments concentrate on sheer economic and political survival. Frequently trucks no longer run because no spare parts are available; roads are impassable, and airplanes no longer land at night because there is no electricity for runway lights. As Mkandawire points out, "The dilapidated buildings, abandoned factories, pot-holed roads are all the visible outcomes of the working out of negative exponential on Africa's physical stock."

ECA's projection to 2008, with continuing external constraints, envi-

Table 2.7. Indications of Structural Economic Differences between Low-Income
Sub-Saharan Africa and Severely Indebted Middle-Income Countries

Indicator	Severely Indebted Low-Income Africa	Severely Indebted Middle-Income Countries
Average population per country (millions, 1987)	9	36
Population growth (annual percentage, 1988)	3.2	2.0
GNP per capita ($, 1988)	288	1,632
Gross domestic savings (percentage of GDP in current prices, 1986–87)	6	14
Gross domestic investment (percentage of GDP in current prices, 1987–88)	14	22
Exports[a] as share of GDP (percent, 1987–88)	18	16
Imports[a] as share of GDP (percent, 1980–86)	28	15
Share of manufacturing in exports (percent, 1987–88)	8	43
Infant mortality (deaths per 1,000 live births, 1987)	110	55
Primary school enrollment (percentage of age group, 1986)	67	100
Official development assistance (share of GDP, 1987)	8.2	0.6
Long-term official debt (as percentage of debt, 1989)	67	35

Source: Charles Humphreys and John Underwood, "The External Debt Difficulties
of Low-Income Africa," in Husain and Diwan (1989: 48); and Husain and Underwood
(1992: 32).

Note: Averages are weighted.

[a]Goods and nonfactor services. For exports, factor services are a country's residents'
and companies' profits, wages, interest, and rents abroad.

sions a nightmare of explosive population growth pressing on physical
resources and social services. Maintaining past trends means degrad-
ing human dignity for the majority, with a rural population surviving
on intolerable toil, amid disastrous land scarcity. It means a worsening
urban crisis, with more shanty towns, congested roads, unemployed,

beggars, crime, and misery festering alongside the few conspicuous consumers unashamedly shopping at national department stores filled with luxury imports. ECA expects these discrepancies to create social tensions and financial crises that will threaten national sovereignty.[32]

Hunger and Food Production

Annual food output growth per capita, 1960–89, was 0.4 percent in DCs, 0.5 percent in LDCs generally, 0.8 percent in Latin America, 1.3 percent in East Asia (excluding Japan and China), 0.5 percent in South and Southeast Asia (0.5 percent in India), and −0.9 percent in sub-Saharan Africa, the only world region where caloric intake, even if equally distributed, is below minimal nutritional standards (fig. 2.2).

African food insecurity is high (and increasing since the 1960s) not only because of large food deficits but also because of domestic output and foreign-exchange reserve fluctuations, as well as foreign food-aid reductions. Cereals consumption per capita has had a high coefficient of variation since 1965. Adedeji speaks of "the humiliation it has brought to Africa in having to go round with the begging bowl for food aid."[33] Some relief agencies projected 20 million deaths from severe malnutrition in 1991 in six African countries where food trade was disrupted by domestic political conflict—Ethiopia, Liberia, Sudan, Somalia, Angola, and Mozambique. Indeed, in early 1991 the United Nations identified seventeen sub-Saharan countries that had food emergencies. The 5 million or so refugees fleeing civil wars, natural disasters, and political repression (including, before 1990, South Africa's destabilization) have added to Africa's food shortages.[34]

Illustrative of the enormity of the Sub-Sahara's difference from other LDCs is that while the Sub-Sahara and India both produced 50 million tons of foodgrains in 1960, in 1988 India produced 150 million tons (after the Green Revolution and other farm technological improvements) and sub-Saharan Africa (with faster population growth) was still stuck at little more than 50 million tons. India's yield per hectare increased by 2.4 percent yearly, while the Sub-Sahara's grew at a negligible annual rate of 0.1 percent. Thus, the Sub-Sahara, which was at parity with India in 1960, produced only about one-third of Indian output in 1988.[35] According to the FAO, the average North American agricultural worker produces more than 100 times as much farm output as the average African.[36]

An International Food Policy Research Institute projection shows sub-Saharan Africa's food deficit as a percentage of food consumption

Figure 2.2. Index of Per Capita Food Production, 1960–1989 (1960 = 100)

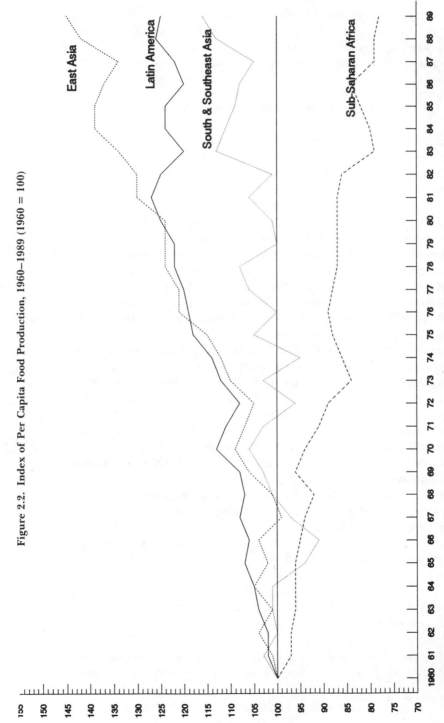

Sources: U.S. Department of Agriculture, International Economics Division, *World Indices of Agricultural and Food Production, 1950–85* (Washington, D.C., 1986); U.S. Department of Agriculture, Economic Research Service, *World Indices of Agricultural and Food Production, 1976–85* (Washington, D.C., 1986); U.S. Department of Agriculture, Economic Research Service, *World Indices of Agricultural and Food Production, 1977–86* (Washington, D.C., 1988); and FAO (1991: 167–69).

Note: East Asia excludes Japan and China.

rising from 7 percent in 1980 to 29 percent in 2000, a figure much higher than for any other LDC region (except the oil-rich Middle East).[37] Yet this projection, while consistent with the bleakness of other African food data, should not obscure the fact that the crises in urban food supply, overall food production, and external imbalances are somewhat distinct. With rapid urbanization and changes in urban diets and the importation of much of urban food supply, we would expect food imports to rise from 1980 to 2000, regardless of food output trends. African farmers are largely self-sufficient in basic calories; price changes have little impact on the output of subsistence crops, since most production is for self-consumption. Export crops drive cash income and capacity to import. Falling primary export prices are a major contributor to Africa's economic crisis. The fact that cereal imports are 25–30 percent of cereals consumed there does not mean that imported grains sustained one-quarter of the sub-Saharan population. Madagascar, Southern Nigeria, Uganda, and Ghana depend much on roots and tubers, while Somalia and Northern Nigeria rely heavily on cereals. Rising cereal imports mean increased quality of cereals consumed in urban areas (rice and wheat), and a shift from coarse grains (sorghum and millet), roots, and tubers. While food management in Africa has not deteriorated from the (low) level of the 1960s, real food prices have fallen substantially.[38]

Climatologist Shukla argues that while China, India, and the African Sahel experienced declining and below-normal rainfall in the 1960s from unfavorable natural change, the Sahel, unlike India and China, failed to recover normal and above-normal rainfall after the late 1960s, because of African deforestation, overgrazing, and increased long-run population pressures. Thus, while random natural factors started the Sahelian drought of the 1960s, human intervention (i.e., ecological mismanagement) made the drought worse by preventing the cyclical recovery of substantial rainfall. Additionally, the greater amplitude of rainfall and weather volatility in Sahel than in other regions contributed to a much more adverse consequence of deforestation and over-population in the Sahel than in India. For Shukla, there is no precedent in the last century for the severity of the Sahel drought; never had human activity so exacerbated natural factors that they impeded the reversal of rainfall deficiencies. The interference by the Sahel and surrounding regions in natural climatic changes means that the Sahel drought will not, as it has in previous epochs, be terminated naturally. To reverse this vicious cycle, Shukla indicates that countries *near* the Sahel will need massive investments in tree planting, while the Sahel will need to reduce human and animal pressures. Because the ecology of the desert and the tropical rain forest are interconnected, Nigeria, for example, needs substantial tree plantings in the southern rain forest to reduce the drought of the north.[39]

Conclusion

The growth of sub-Saharan Africa since the early 1970s has been too slow to enable it to increase its capacity to export enough to avoid an external deficit and debt crisis. The asymmetry of IMF pressure on deficit nations to contract, without an obligation for surplus countries to expand, exacerbates the deficit problem. While the U.N. Development Programme, World Bank, and IMF contend that Bank/Fund adjustment programs have spurred a turnaround in African development, ECA argues that these programs have been based on flawed premises and have, thus, failed to bring about positive economic growth.

3

Ruling Elites and External Disequilibria

·

It is not Fund conditionality that is unduly harsh. It is the difficult
underlying economic problems that demand rigorous economic discipline in the countries seeking Fund help. Quite simply, countries
cannot live beyond their means.
—Michel Camdessus, Managing Director, IMF (1988)

After some three decades of independence, nowhere in Africa have we
either Independence or Socialism, whether defined in terms of social-
democracy or Marxism-Leninism. What we do have though are "national
liberation movements," ruling through the barrel of a gun; "mass parties"
riding on the backs of the masses and presiding over authoritarian legal
and political systems; marxist-leninist vanguard parties napalming oppressed nationalities and eliminating youthful opposition, all in the name
of "Great Red Terror." And we do have the state commanding the
commanding heights of the economy, with the socialist cadres strategi-
cally in command bankrupting the state kitty pitilessly.[1]

The major focus of this chapter is to show how the economic policies
of sub-Saharan African ruling elites contribute to external debts, deficits, and disequilibrium. I examine elite policies on taxes, the public
sector, indigenization of enterprises, agriculture, and exchange rates.

Class Conflict under Socialism

As noted earlier, African socialism lacked the Western concept of state
ownership of the means of production. It also differed in that socialism
in Africa was not introduced by revolutionary struggle but by a ruling
elite coping with the instability of modernizing under capitalism. In-

deed, Ghana's first president, Kwame Nkrumah, branded African socialism a myth, arguing that its supporters neglected the fierce class struggle "between the oppressors and the oppressed in Africa." While class divisions were temporarily submerged during the struggle to eject the colonial power, they returned with increased intensity, Nkrumah contended, "particularly in those states where the newly independent government embarked on socialist policies."[2]

Self-proclaimed "socialist" governments, such as Nkrumah's Ghana (1957–66), Sekou Toure's Guinea (1958–84), Nyerere's Tanzania (1961–85), and Kenneth Kaunda's Zambia (1964–91), tried to eliminate class privilege and prevent bourgeois rule. Nearly all, like the former Soviet Union, produced domination by a ruling elite, a managerial bourgeoisie, antagonistic to worker interests.[3]

The Ruling Class

The African ruling class includes, in addition to private capitalists, groups of high-ranking politicians, military officers, senior civil servants, government administrators, managers of parastatal corporations, top professionals, chiefs, and emirs.[4] This broad class rules primarily through controlling state power over the means of production.[5] Although income and occupation do not correspond one-to-one, in nearly all African countries such a top class is followed by clerical and sales staffs and skilled workers and then by unskilled workers, farmers, and seasonal workers.

Classes are based on ownership or control of land and physical and human capital. The African ruling classes use the accumulated advantages of wealth and power to reproduce their class standing in subsequent generations through education, training, experience, and other human investment, as well as investment in physical property.

Changing modes of production create new class alignments. Although colonialism's demand for educated clerks and business collaborators produced new classes, the most crucial years for Africa's new class formation and re-formation were the 1950s (generally late colonialism) through the early 1990s. Yet class formation varied widely between and within African countries. Within Nigeria, for example, formation in the north occurred within the traditional emirate order structured by feudal principles of aristocratic rank, while in the south, which lacked rigid class stratification, the rise of the dominant class was a product of modern social change—Western education, urbanization, and capitalist development.

Ruling Elites and External Disequilibria

Class is determined by the interaction of power and productive relations. Controlling political power is essential for, yet dependent on, controlling relations of production. Fusing elites is critical in forming a dominant class. While the sources of power of business, government, political, military, professional, and traditional elites varied, they united in the terminal colonial and independence period to form a class to control the state. Political parties and government agencies were agents of class formation, creating elaborate systems of patronage, not only with the bureaucracy and parastatals, but also by liberally using public funds to promote African private enterprise.[6] Nor does the struggle for power by coalitions of classes and communities ever end, as regimes are forced to modify policies, include new interests, or are even overthrown. Ruling classes contract in size when growth becomes negative, as in parts of Africa, 1965–91, where disunity grew within a previously dominant class.

Control of the means of production is highly correlated with income and class. Many African professionals, and technical and other white-collar workers do not initially own or control substantial property. However, they not only are leading investors in human capital but also make enough income to accumulate wealth, including housing. Moreover, they identify with the ruling class that created and protected their privileges.

In Africa, managerial, executive, and technical relative to unskilled wages and salaries increased during one or two decades to become among the highest in the world in the 1970s and continued to expand, especially as adjustment programs reduced real unskilled wages in the 1980s. Moreover, the substantial urban-rural differentials of the 1960s that were legacies of the colonial period narrowed considerably in the 1980s, with wage reductions and increased average farm family income. Nevertheless, income inequality continued to worsen from the 1960s through the 1980s, and probably even during the period of negative growth, and Bank/Fund adjustment programs of the 1980s, increasing immiserization. The poor include not only the families of peasant smallholders, farm workers, single female farmers pushed by land shortages to marginal land, farmers in isolated and peripheral areas, victims of prolonged drought or ecological degradation, war victims losing access to social services and tools, and refugees, but also households of (especially unskilled) wage earners whose real wages frequently plunged sharply with adjustment and various informal-sector operators and operatives. The rich consist of large farm owners, as well as urban formal-sector entrepreneurs (paying lower real wages), professionals, managers, executives, and white-collar workers.[7]

47

While class implies antagonism, African class conflict does not involve a Marxist scenario of a united proletariat overthrowing a capitalist state. Nigeria, which has the largest private capitalist class in tropical Africa, would thus seem ripest for revolution for the Marxist. Yet, the Nigerianists at the Soviet Academy of Science in the late 1970s indicated that even Nigeria's industrial working class was too weak to lead revolution.[8]

Classes exist even where people are not conscious of them. Officials in the capital may live in isolation from the country's problems. And many of Africa's poor are beyond the gaze of the casual visitor to a village—away from roads, away from markets, or living on the outskirts. Even workers may not be conscious of class, as ethnic or regional identity, or a common interest in fighting the colonial power or some other enemy can override class divisions and divert class conflict.

The World Bank criticizes African states for overextending parastatal operations, suggesting that the state should be directed by market forces.[9] But it is unrealistic to expect the dominant political leadership and bureaucracy to implement a decentralized market approach. Dispersing decision-making power to the numerous petty traders, artisans, and small industrialists without a quid pro quo would threaten the ruling class, whose patronage base is enhanced by the viability and monopoly returns of large private-business allies and public corporations. Wasteful industrial policy and parastatal management, which contribute to interest payments on debt as a large proportion of the domestic budget and external deficits, serve specific class interests. The question is not just what policies but also which class alliances would increase efficiency.

Since independence, African politicians have tried to replace the market with a political marketplace. Most African countries practiced price discrimination against farmers. Government intervention in pricing inputs and outputs and replacing private with state trading was negatively correlated to output and export growth in agriculture during the 1970s and early 1980s.[10]

African governments preferred project-based to price-based policies to increase agricultural supplies, because projects reinforce a patron-client system. Government leaders profited more by subsidizing farm implements, fertilizer, and seed costs than by freeing farm prices. Those controlling the state bourgeoisie could manipulate farmers better through market intervention than with a free market.[11]

Most government marketing boards bought crops from farmers to sell on the world market. While these monopsony boards transferred funds from agriculture to industry, they also often diverted resources to members and clients of the state bourgeoisie, who frequently allied with processors, urban consumers, and industrial employers to keep farm prices low. Cash-crop disincentives reduced export receipts, while price ceilings on food increased dependence on imported food-stuffs.

The Public Sector

A series of World Bank-IMF studies points out some determinants of public-enterprise success. State enterprises perform better with competition; without investment licensing; without price, entry, or exit controls; and with liberal trade policies—low tariffs, no import quotas, and exchange rates close to market prices (although as chapter 7 indicates, there are major problems, at least during a substantial transition, with external deficits and inflation during trade liberaliza-tion). Successful public firms have greater managerial autonomy and accountability than others do, moreover, their governments keep the size of the public sector commensurate with technical and managerial skills.[12] Few of these determinants are present in sub-Saharan Africa.

A 1984 World Bank study indicates that seven Eastern African countries—Mozambique, Sudan, Uganda, Zaïre, Madagascar, Tanza-nia, and Zambia—had negative industrial growth after nationalization. Few foreign private investors were interested in investing in these countries. On the other hand, those Eastern African countries that avoided forcible takeovers of private assets, namely, Kenya, Malawi, and Zimbabwe, had the fastest industrial growth.[13]

Yet the impressions of the superior performance of private enter-prise in LDCs, which often originate in anecdotes of Western business people and aid officials, are not necessarily supported by comparative studies. The Millward survey indicates that the efficiency of public and private enterprises in LDCs is comparable, given a certain size of firm. However, public firms are more likely than private firms to choose an excessive scale of operations. Moreover, African public firms have easier access to state finance to mute bankruptcy and more pressure to provide jobs and contracts to clients and relatives than do private enterprises.[14] Many of Africa's parastatal enterprises are effective con-duits for patronage but wasteful, with low capacity utilization and substantial losses, indicating inefficient resource allocation and an ero-sion of available capital resources.

In the early 1980s, government employment as a percentage of total nonagricultural employment was 54 percent in Africa, compared with

36 percent for Asia, 27 percent in Latin America, and 24 percent in the OECD. In Benin, Ghana, and Zambia, the ratio was more than 70 percent. Furthermore, the size of the government sector in Africa rose rapidly after independence. Indeed, although the mean number of administrators per 100 population was rather similar for DCs and LDCs, African countries had the highest administrator ratio and Asian countries the lowest for world regions.[15]

In Nigeria, government expenditures as a percentage of GDP rose from 9 percent in 1962 to 44 percent in 1979 but fell to 17 percent from World Bank structural adjustment programs (SAPs), such as the one in effect from 1986 to 1990, which emphasized privatization, market prices, and reduced government expenditures. Nigeria centralized power during its 1967–70 civil war with the breakup of regions, and in the 1970s, as the oil boom enhanced the center's fiscal strength. Expansion of the government's share of the economy did little to increase political and administrative capacity, but it did increase incomes and jobs that governing elites could distribute to their clients.[16]

Tanzania's state bureaucracy grew rapidly after the 1967 Arusha Declaration and 1972 "decentralization" (which increased central government personnel in the regions). From 1966 to 1976, total annual economic growth increased 4 percent, wage employment 3 percent, and civil service employment 13 percent.[17] As in Nigeria, the government sector's share in Tanzania fell in the 1980s with slower growth and Fund/Bank adjustment programs.

Parastatals' share of employment and output increased rapidly from independence through the mid-1970s, especially in Zambia and Tanzania. In Tanzania, parastatal share of employment increased from 23.1 percent in 1968 to 49.7 percent in 1974 and gross capital shares from 30.4 percent to 44.9 percent, while in Zambia employment shares increased from 14 percent to 37 percent and output shares from 10 percent to 45 percent, 1968–74. The IMF points out that in Africa "over the years, inefficiency has flourished in many state enterprises, its overt consequences masked by the ready availability of budgetary support."[18]

In 1984, Tanzanian Commissioner for Public Investment M.A.M. Mkulo stated that the "public enterprise sector in Tanzania has been in existence for almost 19 years, but the performance has been disappointing." The empirical data for Africa generally show that state-owned enterprises (SOEs) yielded a very low rate of return to investment. An IMF study indicated that public enterprises in seven of eight African countries had deficits during the late 1970s. Nellis's World

Bank sample from twelve West African countries in the early 1980s showed 62 percent of the SOEs with net losses, while 36 percent had a negative net worth!

With monopoly power, price controls, subsidies, and hidden transfers make precise evaluation difficult, they indicate that public-sector performance is probably overstated. African state enterprises are plagued by price distortions, overstaffing, illiquidity, fragmented or overlapping administrative control, unclear and contradictory objectives, and excess political interference. Sierra Leone, which restricted the prices of its state petroleum refining company, still expected that company to contribute profits to government revenues.[19]

In Africa, ruling elites, who use public firms to dispense benefits to clients, build these enterprises beyond management capacity. Business intermediaries and government officials in Kenya, Malawi, and many other African countries depend critically on external investment and assistance for state-enterprise expansion, with its income, patronage, and power. Yet even Nkrumah did not condone the low capacity utilization and substantial losses of the parastatals.

> I must make it clear that these State Enterprises were not set up to lose money at the expense of the tax payers. Like all business undertakings, they are expected to maintain themselves efficiently, and to show profits. Such profits should be sufficient to build up capital for further investment as well as to finance a large proportion of the public services which it is the responsibility of the state to provide.[20]

Yet the transition from state enterprises, centrally managed, to a liberal privatized economy is politically and technically difficult. Prices formerly masked by controls inevitably rise. Forcing inefficient firms to close is likely to be unacceptable where labor is not mobile. Pent-up demand for imports may hurt the balance of payments. Indigenous skilled managers are usually scarce. Improving parastatals requires macroeconomic liberalization, micro-level reforms, and sectoral assistance.[21]

However, the shrinking of salaries and amenities of government and parastatal employees under Bank/Fund adjustment during most of the 1980s had a devastating impact on morale, efficiency, and honesty. Without resources that enable them to perform effectively, many civil servants become time-servers or turn to bribes, embezzling public funds, or moonlighting to supplement their meager pay. Mamdani indicates that in Uganda, "the system of official remuneration has the consequence of putting on sale public employees to the highest

51

bidder." Sandbrook contends that lower remuneration resulting from adjustment had similar effects in Zaïre, Nigeria, Guinea, Somalia, Sierra Leone, and Tanzania.[22]

Ruling-Class Misdirection

Numerous countries misused borrowed resources, buttressing consumption, delaying adjustment, or investing in projects with low rates of return.[23] Many African countries borrowed (or, as in 1973–75 Nigeria, spent) in excess of absorptive capacity, deficient because skilled personnel were scarce. Schatz describes Nigerian planning right after the quadrupling of world oil prices in 1973–74 as euphoric planning:

> Projects involving huge sums were added hastily, with little investigation or appraisal. Issues of project interrelation and coordination were ignored in the belief that rapid economic growth would ensure the utility of whatever was undertaken. Economic reasoning gave way before economic enthusiasm. Problems of executive capacity (the ability to carry out the Plan) were ignored.[24]

The use of state levers by Nigeria's insecure military or civilian political elites (turning over frequently from coups), civil servants, and intermediaries for foreign capital not to support capitalist production but to further their own private interests (substantially purchasing goods from, and transferring money to, foreign countries) was labeled "pirate capitalism" by Schatz.[25] Nigeria was a net foreign borrower for most of the period 1976 to 1989.

Oil exporters Indonesia and Nigeria, which had more than 40 percent of pre-1973 GNP originating in agriculture, provide a revealing contrast in national management. While Indonesia's agricultural output increased 3.7 percent annually, output in Nigeria declined 1.9 percent and exports 7.9 percent yearly, 1973–83. Agricultural imports as a share of total imports rose from 3 percent in the late 1960s to 7 percent in the early 1980s in Nigeria, while in Indonesia, the share remained unchanged at about 1 percent.

Several differences in pricing and investment explain Indonesia's more favorable agricultural development. The real value of the Nigerian naira appreciated substantially, 1970–72 and 1982–83, depreciating relative to the dollar only under pressure in 1986, while the real value of Indonesia's rupiah increased much more slowly and depreciated vis-á-vis the dollar, 1978–83. Additionally, Indonesia invested many government funds in agriculture, especially rice, while less than 10 percent of the Nigerian plan's capital expenditures were in agriculture. A belated attempt by Nigeria, beginning in the mid-1980s, to increase incentives and investment in agriculture had little impact.[26] Nigeria will require sustained policy changes to reverse the effects of years of neglect.

Furthermore, in Africa, accounts are sometimes so inadequate that a cost breakdown is not possible. During the first decade of independence, a Nigerian shoe manufacturer established as a joint public-private firm by influential politicians and traders operated for a year before it undertook an audit. The audit revealed variable cost had exceeded revenue by more than ₦2 (£1) per pair of shoes![27]

Tax Policies

LDC debtors are more likely to reduce investment than to tax or reduce the consumption of high-income groups. Raising taxes to maintain investment is more likely to be a problem when tax-income ratios and tax elasticity (percentage change in taxation divided by percentage change in GNP) are low, as in Africa and other developing countries. Despite the widespread LDC ideology of systematic state intervention to stimulate economic development, tax ratios increase with GNP per capita. Taxes as a percentage of GNP in the early 1980s were 15.0 for the Sub-Sahara, 12.9 percent for low-income countries, 23.1 for middle-income countries, and 37.7 percent for high-income countries.[28] Percentages range from a high of 53.1 for high-income Sweden to 36.5 and 29.8 for Israel and Egypt (middle-income countries), respectively, and 2.6 and 5.5 for Uganda (where government ceased to operate in many areas during a civil war in the early 1980s) and Ghana (low-income countries), respectively.

The increase in tax ratio with GNP per capita is a reflection of both demand and supply factors—demand for social and collective goods like education, highways, sewerage, flood control, and national defense, and the capacity to levy and pay taxes.

Wagner's law states that, as real GNP per capita rises, people demand relatively more social goods and relatively fewer private goods. A poor country spends a high percentage of its income on food, clothing, shelter, and other essential consumer goods. After these needs have been largely fulfilled, an increased proportion of additional spending is for social goods,[29] which are highly foreign-exchange intensive.

Sub-Saharan Africa and other LDCs find it difficult to mobilize resources for public expenditure. A major reason tax ratios increase with GNP per capita is that DCs rely more heavily on taxes with greater elasticity. An elastic tax, whose coefficient exceeds one, rises more rapidly than GNP. Direct taxes—primarily property, wealth, inheritance, and income taxes (such as personal and corporate taxes)—are generally more elastic than indirect taxes such as import, export, turnover, sales, and excise taxes (except for sales or excise taxes on goods purchased mostly by high-income groups).

Direct taxes account for 31.8 percent of the revenue sources in LDCs. The two leading direct taxes, the corporate income and personal taxes, comprise only 19.0 percent and 10.3 percent of total LDC revenue sources, respectively.

The major source of tax for LDCs is international trade, an indirect tax consisting of 30.6 percent of the total—with import duties 25.0 percent and export duties 5.6 percent. Other important indirect taxes—the excise, sales, and other taxes on production and international transactions—account for 27.9 percent. Social security and other payroll taxes comprise the remaining 9.7 percent of the total.

The proportion of taxes raised from direct taxes is 22 percent in low-income countries, 42 percent in middle-income countries, and 65 percent in high-income countries.[30] Accordingly, the average ratio of direct taxes to GNP is 2.9 percent in low-income countries (mostly sub-Saharan African and South and Southeast Asian), 9.4 percent in middle-income countries, and 24.5 percent in high-income countries.

Although personal income taxes rarely comprise more than 5 percent of GNP in LDCs, they often account for 10 to 20 percent of GNP in the DCs. In most DCs, the income tax structure is progressive, meaning people with higher incomes pay a higher percentage of income in taxes. Many people feel that the progressive tax is just—that those with higher incomes should bear a larger tax burden, since they have a much greater ability to pay. Moreover, a progressive income tax has an elasticity greater than one, so that a rising GNP pushes taxpayers into higher tax brackets.

Tanzania, under President Nyerere, 1974–85, was the only African country that used its tax system to redistribute income to low-income classes. Few African countries rely much on income taxes, because they have trouble administering them. The following conditions must be met if income tax is to become a major revenue source for a country: (1) existence of a predominately money economy, (2) a high standard of literacy among taxpayers, (3) widespread use of accounting records honestly and reliably maintained, (4) a large degree of voluntary taxpayer compliance, and (5) honest and efficient administration. Even the United States and Europe, to say nothing of Africa, have trouble fulfilling these conditions.[31]

Taxes on international trade are the major source of tax revenue in LDCs, especially for low-income countries with poor administrative capacity. Exports and imports usually pass through a limited number of ports and border crossings. A relatively small administrative staff can measure volume and value and collect revenue. To be sure, traders may underinvoice goods or seek favors or concessions from customs officials. However, these problems are not so great as those encountered with an income tax.

Yet during the world recession, 1979–82, real international trade and trade taxes fell in many African countries. Taxes on international trade as a percentage of total government revenue dropped, 1979–82, from 58 percent to 25 percent in Zaïre, from 51 to 22 percent in Tanzania, from 48 to 14 percent in Zambia, from 42 to 35 percent in Madagascar, and from 38 to 24 percent in Kenya. At the same time, the recession spurred government to increase claims through price subsidies, state employment, and welfare programs.[32]

Furthermore, politics may be as obstructive as administration in using direct taxes in sub-Saharan Africa and other LDCs. Property owners and the upper classes often successfully oppose a progressive income tax or sizable property tax, introduce tax loopholes beneficial to them, or evade tax payments without penalty.

The United States has a reputation for less legal tax avoidance and illegal evasion than a typical Third World country. However, Pechman and Okner indicate that, even in the United States, taxes as a percentage of income remain nearly constant for virtually all income levels because of tax loopholes and the effect of indirect taxes. Furthermore, the U.S. Internal Revenue Service assumes that the average U.S. citizen is rather resistant to taxation. Tax evasion is low because of the high probability and serious consequences of being caught.[33]

Tax collection in sub-Saharan Africa depends not only on the appropriate tax legislation, but also, more importantly, on administrative capability and political will. Kaldor writes:

> In many underdeveloped countries the low revenue yield of taxation can only be attributed to the fact that the tax provisions are not properly enforced, either on account of the inability of the administration to cope with them, or on account of straightforward corruption. No system of tax laws, however carefully conceived, is proof against collusion between the tax administrators and the taxpayers; an efficient administration

consisting of persons of high integrity is usually the most important requirement for obtaining maximum revenue, and exploiting fully the taxation potential of a country.[34]

Given difficulties in raising revenue, it is not surprising that sub-Saharan Africa's central-government fiscal deficits were substantial throughout the 1980s.

Indigenization

Immediately after independence, African governments relentlessly pursued Africanization of their civil services, catapulting Africans overnight to positions of high responsibilities and salaries, with increasing propensities to consume imports, such as automobiles, appliances, and expensive education—goods and services that were capital- and foreign-exchange intensive, even when produced locally. After civil services were Africanized, governments turned to Africanize their national economies in the 1960s and 1970s. With few exceptions, each African country nationalized at least one foreign enterprise, concentrating on banking, insurance, and petroleum distribution.

Indigenization often meant a partnership between the African ruling class and international capitalism, where the state captured social resources in the name of the people but for the primary benefit of the state bourgeoisie. Africanization often increased indigenous inequalities. In Nigeria, indigenization in the early 1970s became an instrument for a few civil servants, military rulers, business people, and professionals to amass considerable wealth through manipulating state power.[35] Ironically, an indigenization policy designed partly to reduce foreign concentration created Nigerian oligopolies, especially among those with the wealth and influence to obtain capital and government loans to purchase foreign shares.

Corruption was so rife in Nigeria that in 1983, at the fall of the Second Republic, people burned the NET building (the tallest building in Africa), the Ministry of External Affairs, and the accounts section of the Federal Capital Development Authority, Abuja, apparently to conceal widespread fraud.[36]

Agricultural Policies

In Africa, the earlier scholarly assumptions of land abundance and the prevalence of subsistence family production are no longer valid and overstate rural equality. After independence, government spending was biased in favor of large-scale, prosperous farmers.

Among Kenya's African population, rural inequality and land concentration increased from the late 1960s through the 1980s. The Kenyan bourgeoisie, bureaucracy, and their clients used state support to appropriate land (mostly white settlers') to create large-scale capitalist farms and to obtain import licenses, credit, and inputs. Land in Kenya is almost as unequally distributed as in Latin America. The World Bank's second structural adjustment program, 1982–83, offered President Daniel arap Moi and other Kenya African National Union (KANU) leaders with a personal stake in agribusiness the opportunity to remove farm "distortions" while distributing perquisites to ruling party members and their allies.[37]

African peasants have traded their dependence on nature for a dependence on the state bourgeoisie. Even peasants that spend most of their time producing for their own families are not free of government policies regarding land transfer, cooperative and state agriculture, commodity prices, off-farm employment, and benefits of education, water, electricity, and roads. Hyden's "uncaptured" peasant, free from state machination, has almost vanished in Africa.[38] The peasant wishing to escape the state's influence on his livelihood has few places to go.

"Nigerian Disease"

Roemer analyzes "Dutch disease," named when the booming North Seas' gas export revenues in the 1970s appreciated the guilder, exposing industries of the Netherlands to more intense foreign competition and higher unemployment.[39] Analogously, the United States suffered from a similar disease, 1980–84, experiencing a farm export crisis and deindustrialization from the decline of traditional export industries (automobiles, capital goods, high technology, railroad and farm equipment, paint, leather products, cotton fabrics, carpeting, electrical equipment and parts, and basic chemicals) as substantial capital inflows strengthened the U.S. dollar. The pathology that became the "Nigerian disease," was an economic distortion of the 1970s resulting from dependence on a single booming export commodity, petroleum. While 90 percent of export value in 1962 and 65 percent in 1966 was from non-oil primary products (mainly groundnuts, cocoa, palm products, and rubber), after 1973 all of these products except cocoa virtually disappeared from Nigeria's export list.

Nigeria illustrates sub-Saharan Africa's overvaluation in the late 1970s and early 1980s. Like most of Africa, Nigeria's 1970s foreign-exchange rate discouraged the growth of agriculture, especially in goods for export. Nigeria's petroleum exports, rising from ₦74 million in 1968 (18 percent of export value) to ₦1,186 million in 1972 (82 percent of value) to ₦9,439 million in 1979 (93 percent of value), resulted in an enormous influx of foreign exchange, causing the real U.S. dollar price of the naira to rise substantially. In 1968 (the base year) $1.40=₦1, while the consumer price indices in both the United States and Nigeria were 100. By 1979, $1.78=₦1, while the United States' consumer price index was 208.5 and Nigeria's was 498.0. The real exchange rate, calculated as

$$\frac{\text{Nigerian consumer price index}}{\text{U.S. price index}} \times \text{dollar price of naira}$$

was $1.40 = ₦1 in 1968 and $4.25 = ₦1 in 1979, roughly a tripling of the naira relative to the dollar over the eleven-year period. Naira appreciation made imported goods cheaper relative to nontradable goods and caused naira proceeds of exported agricultural goods (denominated in dollars) to decrease from 1968 to 1979. Cocoa fell from 24.5 percent of total exports to 4.1 percent; palm kernels, from 18.0 percent to 0.1 percent; rubber, from 3.0 to 0.1 percent. Peanuts (18.0 percent), peanut oil and cake (6.8 percent), and raw cotton (1.6 percent), all fell to 0.0 percent. These farm exports comprised 90 percent of Nigeria's annual export proceeds in 1962 and 65 percent in 1966, but only 8 percent in 1974–78, when 92 percent was petroleum. Even the aggregate index of the volume of output of Nigerian agricultural export commodities declined from 100 in 1968 to 50.1 in 1978.[40]

The naira's appreciation, 1968–79, reduced greatly the domestic currency price of food and consumer goods purchased from abroad. Thus, food imports increased from ₦7.1 million in 1968 to ₦126.5 million in 1973 to ₦2,115.1 in 1981, and overall consumer goods imports from ₦35.6 million to ₦417.5 million to ₦5,736.3 million, even though the consumer price index increased only five- to sixfold. Overall, Nigeria's balance on current and non-reserve capital account, ₦3,102.4 million in 1974 (with the oil boom), fell to ₦339.0 million in 1976 and −₦1,382.0 million in 1978, before rising with the next increase in oil prices to ₦1,822.7 million in 1979, then falling to −₦3,068.9 million in 1981, and rising to ₦906.6 million in 1985 (when ₦4.60 = $1). This external surplus resulted from the austerity measures of Major General Muhammed Buhari, who led a 31 December 1983 military coup that overthrew the newly re-elected government of President Shehu Shagari, who had held his National Party of Nigeria together by expanding the benefits of office to business and civil servant allies and clients. Major General Ibrahim Babangida, who overthrew Buhari on 27 August 1985 after mounting discontent, faced consistent external deficits in 1986–89, as real world petroleum prices failed to recover to 1980 levels.[41]

The strengthening naira reduced the price of export crops and imported industrial goods relative to that of domestically produced food, increasing income inequality among food producers but diminishing export farm income. And the multiplier and revenue effects of the oil boom had little effect on rural disposable income.[42]

Nevertheless, the strong naira was optimal for the oil export industry, which overwhelmed Nigeria's exchange-rate determination. Since oil prices are determined on the world market in dollars, a weaker naira would not have increased the dollar value of exports but would have increased import costs for the national oil company. At the same time the dollar proceeds from selling local inputs to foreign oil companies would have decreased. One way of retaining the advantages of the strong naira for oil transactions, while promoting exports and import substitution with a weak naira, would have been a dual exchange rate. This would have achieved greater protection of domestic production without the cost of repressing price signals in a regime of high tariffs and quotas, and it would have eliminated the bias against exports without costly subsidies and tax allowances. While a dual rate spurs some people to acquire foreign currency cheaply in one market and sell it expensively in the other, this cost would have been less than the benefits of rationalizing exports and import substitution and reducing the current-account deficit, 1976–78 and most years of the oil glut, 1981–88.

In Nigeria, the critical factor producing income inequality was the sharp increase in labor productivity and the per capita differentials between rural and urban populations during the 1970s. In 1975, the ratio of nonagricultural to agricultural labor productivity was 7.2. That figure would have been only 3.0 without oil—little more than the 1966 ratio of 2.5. The public expenditure pattern of the Nigerian government, fueled by oil revenue, increased maldistribution of income markedly in the 1970s. Without oil's impact, Nigeria's income inequality would have been low among LDCs.[43] Of course, Nigeria's GNP per capita increased and its poverty fell during the 1970s. But with more long-term planning, Nigeria could have reduced its inequality in the 1970s and prevented some of the retrogression of the 1980s.

A minor oil boom in 1990 increased oil prices from 1989. The *Economist* estimated that a rise in the current price of North Sea Brent oil from $18 per barrel in 1989 to $30 in 1990 would have increased Nigeria's oil revenue by 13 percent of its GNP, but that of Mexico, one-fourth of whose 1989 export receipts were petroleum, by only 3 percent. On the other hand, paying for oil would reduce Poland's dollar export purchasing power by 35 percent and Czechoslovakia's by 75 percent![44]

Chapters 7 and 8 mention further issues related to devaluing domestic currencies.

Cameroon and Nigeria Compared

Cameroon, which began oil production off its west coast in 1978, avoided much of the Nigerian syndrome. While Cameroon's crude petroleum output was only one-tenth of Nigeria's, its potential for economic distortion was as great, since most of its export earnings were also from oil and its population was also about one-tenth of Nigeria's. But in the 1970s, the Cameroon CFAF's real domestic currency depreciation compared to the naira's real appreciation made Cameroon's agricultural exports price competitive while Nigeria's traditional exports, as indicated above, fell precipitously. Indeed, Nigeria's agricultural exports as a percentage of total LDC agricultural exports declined during the oil boom, falling 5.7 percent annually from 1965 to 1983.[45]

The Cameroon government planned better than the Nigerian government, accumulating substantial foreign exchange reserves abroad, repaying external debt during the 1979–81 oil price increase, and avoiding some of the painful adjustments of the 1980s' oil price fall. Moreover, Cameroon used much of its oil revenues for manufacturing and agriculture, including the maintenance of producers' coffee and cocoa prices despite softening world prices.[46]

Other African countries experiencing the Nigerian disease in the 1970s or 1980s include Zambia, Zaïre (copper), Ghana (cocoa), Côte d'Ivoire (cocoa, coffee), Kenya (coffee, tourism), and Egypt (tourism, remittances, foreign-aid inflows). As in Nigeria, growth in the booming export sector strengthened domestic currency relative to foreign currency. Strong domestic currency reduced incentives to export other goods and to substitute imports with domestic production. Moreover, labor moved from the lagging export and import-substitution sectors to the booming sectors not competing with international trade. Other ill effects of the export boom have been a neglect of agricultural development, relaxed fiscal discipline, an increase in capital-intensive projects, wage dualism, inability to absorb capital, a crowding out of the private sector's access to scarce managers and technicians, an increased dependence on foreign management of investment projects, unstable export earnings and government revenue, and a diversion to quick, high returns from trade and urban real estate.

Political elites kept the domestic currency overvalued for the non-mineral sector for a number of reasons. In Nigeria, urban middle classes and commercial interests, who had gained from naira appreciation in the 1970s, feared erosion of purchasing power (for food and other consumer goods), the loss of subsidies, and less profitable commercial opportunities.[47] Furthermore, those fortunate enough to get foreign-exchange licenses not only acquired an input in short supply, but also paid below market price. But making scarce foreign currency available at a low price, together with poorly stated criteria for awarding it, resulted in charges of bribery, influence peddling, and communal or political prejudice in Nigeria.

"Reverse Nigerian Disease"

Nigerian disease from the oil boom in the 1970s may seem a mild case of influenza compared to reverse Nigerian disease from the oil bust of the 1980s. For a top Nigerian economic official in 1988, striking it rich on oil in the 1970s was "like a man who wins a lottery and builds a castle. He can't maintain it, and then has to borrow to move out."[48] Nigeria's experience during the oil bust demonstrates the necessity of long-range planning to ameliorate substantial export price fluctuations.

Conclusion

African socialism and capitalism are both beset by class conflict and economic disparities. In both systems, the ruling class uses the economic levers of the state to enlarge the class's influence and prosperity.

Much of what appears to be mismanagement is deliberate policy, pursued in the interest of the African elites at the expense of the masses. Stagnation and a balance-of-payments crisis are interconnected, linked to a ruling class whose affluence and political survival are threatened by policies promoting decentralized economic decision making, increased competition, and redistribution to the underprivileged. The ruling-class use of the state to transfer resources from peasants, small farmers, unskilled workers, and the poor to parastatal managers, civil servants, middlemen, large commercial farmers, and other members of the elite reduces growth, equality, and external balance.

Overvaluation of a low-priced foreign currency is just one example of strategies that benefit elites at the expense of overall economic growth and the balance of payments. Nigeria's policies during the 1970s' oil boom, for example, altered incentives, raised expectations, and distorted and destabilized non-oil (especially agricultural) output. Elites in other African countries experiencing a boom also overvalued domestic currency, making scarce foreign-exchange licenses available to allies at concessional prices.

The control of the public sector by elites is a major source for distributing patronage. Political leaders pressure state-owned enterprises to meet clients' pressures for jobs and contracts. Easy access to official credit and the political opposition to closing down inefficient firms contribute to enterprise expansion beyond optimal output and market size. State intervention in the market exacerbates poverty, inequality, and (through increased high-technology, capital-intensive, and foreign-exchange-intensive production) external imbalance.

Moreover, elites lack the administrative ability and political will to raise taxes to mobilize spending on health, education, and infrastructure. Upper classes, who frequently avoid or evade taxes, oppose using the tax system to redistribute income.

Economic development usually requires access to foreign technology as well as development of indigenous business people and technicans who accumulate capital and create and adapt technology. Can the indigenization of foreign or joint enterprises help African capitalists and business leaders learn by doing? In theory, yes. In practice, indigenization decrees in Africa have been more likely to be used to help officials acquire access to patronage networks with intermediaries and to increase local concentration of power.

Bureaucratic contacts thus become as important to African capitalists as production and marketing knowledge. Public office often becomes the main road to private-sector wealth. Officials and intermediaries in much of Africa depend critically on external aid, investment, and trade for increasing income, dispensing patronage, and controlling state power (see chapter 4).

When an African LDC undertakes reform instigated by the World Bank or IMF, workers, peasants, and other disadvantaged classes, who have little effect on policy revision, usually suffer the most. Africa's ruling elites, on the other hand, use Bank/Fund lending and programs to expand their patron-client network but react to pressures to reduce spending by cutting back disproportionately on programs to benefit the sick, the elderly, workers, small farmers, and the poor.

4

External Trade, Aid, Investment, and Debt

.

While the approaches of adjustment packages have not differed greatly between [developing] countries despite their widely varying situations, after ten years of experience, the results have been mixed. Individual country performances have varied according to a number of . . . factors. . . . External factors have included, at different times: deteriorating terms of trade; rising protectionism; historically high interest rates; declining markets because of recession in the developed countries; as well as other events beyond a government's control such as prolonged droughts. In fact, the 1980s clearly demonstrated that external factors alone are enough to push the adjustment process completely off course.
—Food and Agriculture Organization of the United Nations

As they were being dispatched to the periphery, the bailiffs of global capital, the IMF and World Bank, knew—as indeed we all do—that the mega fortunes of the Samozas, the Duvaliers', the Dikkos', the Marcos', the Mobutu's and their cliques were the diverted booty of the lending days of the mid-1970s when the international banking system was flush with recycled petro-dollars and had proceeded to pour them down the bottomless pits of third world sovereign borrowers, state-owned enterprises and private contractors.
—Ankie Hoogvelt

Brazil's Finance Minister Mario Simonsen explains the rising debt in LDCs by the growth of interest rates exceeding the growth in exports. Cline focuses on global macroeconomics, including the first oil-price shock, 1973–74, and world disinflation and recession, 1980–82, triggered partly by the United States' policy shift toward increased monetary restraint. Sachs stresses country-specific factors more than global shocks. Other economists blame overlending by commercial banks, which operated under inadequate supervisory regulations, underesti-

64

mated risks because of inadequate information, and took calculated gambles, expecting official support in the event of adverse outcomes.[1] This chapter elaborates on some major international factors contributing to the debt crisis and its relationship to economic growth and income distribution.

Trade Dependence

Neocolonialism, which is economic domination without direct colonialism, requires ruling-class interests that are allied to foreign capitalists and governments that uphold their joint interests in economic policy. But neocolonialism can be unstable, leading to growing class polarization as inequality becomes more apparent. Income redistribution to avert class conflict is usually at the expense of indigenous ruling classes or foreign capitalists, threatening the benefits of the alliance. However, fast growth, as in South Korea and Taiwan, makes benefits possible for foreign capital, domestic capital, workers, and farmers.

G.E.A. Lardner, the ECA's former Policy and Program Coordination Office director, argues that independent Africa retained neocolonial policies, including: maintaining monoproduct and other export dependence, relying on external initiative for changing this pattern, and intensifying monoproduct export output to secure foreign exchange for needed inputs.[2]

The overwhelming majority of Africa's international trade has been with DCs. In 1983, 83.3 percent of exports was to DCs, 4.8 percent to developed socialist countries, 11.3 percent to LDCs (3.4 percent to other African countries) and 0.6 percent not specified. The same year, 74.2 percent of imports was from DCs, 7.8 percent from socialist, and 18.0 percent from LDCs (3.0 percent from other African countries).[3]

Francophone countries, with European Community associate status, have maintained especially strong trade ties with the colonial power. In 1987, imports from France as a share of the total were: Senegal, 36 percent; Cameroon, 43 percent; Côte d'Ivoire, 32 percent; Benin, 19 percent; Togo, 30 percent; Niger, 34 percent; Burkina, 31 percent; Chad, 26 percent; Congo, 53 percent; and the Central African Republic, 52 percent. Export shares to France were: Senegal, 28 percent; Cameroon, 21 percent; Côte d'Ivoire, 15 percent; Benin, 9 percent; Togo, 11 percent; Niger, 82 percent; Burkina, 34 percent; Chad, 9 percent; Congo, 15 percent; and the Central African Republic, 42 percent.[4]

LDCs' balance on current account was negative every year from

1977 through 1991 (except 1979 and 1987); sub-Saharan Africa's balance was negative every year during the same period. The Sub-Sahara's annual balance was −$6.5 to −$9 billion, 1987 through 1991, all less than minus 20 percent of exports of goods and services. Sub-Saharan Africa's debt-service ratio varied from 20 to 25 percent, 1985 through 1991.[5]

External financial flows to Africa declined from the late 1970s to the 1980s. The decline in resource flows and export earnings forced a sharp drop in Africa's import volume—by nearly 20 percent between 1980 and 1985, reducing imports of consumer goods, spare parts, investment goods, and inputs needed for domestic and export production and curtailing economic growth.[6] While much external borrowing was for projects to benefit or build patronage for a small elite, the debt crisis limited overall growth and the state's ability to continue meager antipoverty programs.

Africa's vulnerability is worsened because of high export commodity concentration, which is associated with volatile export prices and earnings. The summation of all sub-Saharan African countries' three principal exports as a share of total export earnings was 79.1 percent in 1976–78, an increase from 60.6 percent in 1961. In eight countries, the 1976–78 share was more than 90 percent. Indeed in 1985, tropical beverages (coffee, cocoa, and tea) accounted for 24 percent and six primary commodities for more than 70 percent of sub-Saharan Africa's export earnings. In 1990, five commodities—tobacco, tea, sugar, cotton, and coffee—comprised more than 70 percent of total agricultural export earnings in Malawi, Tanzania, Zambia, and Zimbabwe. Additionally, the fall in the price of copper in the 1970s hurt Zambia and Zaïre, and the 1980s' drought reduced the volume of some of Africa's major exports. Principal export product revenues as a percentage of overall export earnings, 1980–82, were: Nigeria, 97 (crude petroleum); Uganda, 96 (coffee); Somalia, 94 (livestock); Burundi, 90 (coffee); Zambia, 89 (copper); Rwanda, 68 (coffee); Ethiopia, 65 (coffee); Ghana, 59 (cocoa); Madagascar, 47 (coffee); Zaïre, 43 (copper); Burkina, 40 (cotton); and Sudan, 39 (cotton). Many other sub-Saharan African countries have export commodity concentration ratios (that is, the value of the four leading export commodities as a percentage of total merchandise exports) of more than 60 percent, including Liberia, Malawi, Côte d'Ivoire, and Kenya.[7]

Africa is vulnerable to relative international price instability not only because of its dependence on volatile primary product exports but also because of a high concentration of exports in a few commodities and to a few countries. The resulting wide swings in export prices have had a disastrous effect on government budgets and external balances.[8]

The predominantly non-oil primary products that Africa exports and the manufactured products exported by DCs and a few newly industrializing countries are not priced the same way. Although global marketing for most primary products is oligopolistic, the African farmer is a price taker, having no influence on market price; however, widespread commodity productivity gains can result in lower prices. On the other hand, most industrial production and marketing are monopolistic, with productivity gains leading to higher prices.

In his 6 December 1988 Independence Day address, Côte d'Ivoire's President Felix Houphouët-Boigney blamed Africa's difficulties on "insufficient remuneration received from the sale of our raw materials."[9] Sub-Saharan Africa, disproportionately producing and exporting primary products, suffered from both fluctuating and declining prices of exports relative to imports, which were predominantly industrial goods. The Sub-Sahara's commodity terms of trade (the price index of exports divided by the price index of imports) plummeted from 100 in 1970 to 77 in 1980 to 53 in 1990, a 47 percent reduction in 20 years! Indeed, from 1985 through 1991, the sub-Saharan terms of trade declined every year, falling 34 percent (fig. 4.1). Export volume fell from 100 in 1970 to 86 in 1980, only recovering to 100 for the first time in 1990. Export purchasing power (or income terms of trade), the commodity terms of trade times export volume, dropped from 100 in 1970 to 66 in 1980 to 53 in 1990, indicating, again, a reduction of 47 percent during the 20-year period. These declines contributed to a falling goods and services balance and a continually worsening external crisis during the 1980s.[10]

The trend line for commodity terms of trade of Nigeria (see table 4.1), highly dependent on oil exports since the early 1970s, follows closely the pattern of world crude oil prices in figure 4.3 (below). In the 1970s, the terms of trade rose for oil-exporting countries vis-à-vis both DCs and non-oil LDCs. Thus, Nigeria's terms of trade rose dramatically, threefold from 1970, the end of its civil war to 1975, following the fourfold increase in world oil prices in 1973–74, and almost double between 1975 and 1980–81, two years of peak real oil prices.

From 1980 to 1987, industrialized countries' terms of trade increased at the expense of LDC primary exporters (whose terms fell 22.1 percent) and LDC oil exporters, whose terms fell 42.2 percent before falling a further one-fifth in 1988, then making substantial gains in 1989–90. Oil-exporter Nigeria's terms of trade in the late

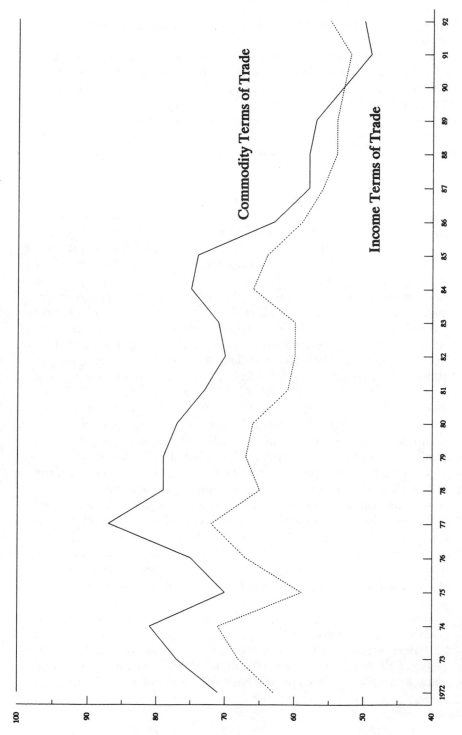

Figure 4.1. Sub-Saharan African Commodity and Income Terms of Trade, 1972–1992 (1970 = 100)

Source: IMF, *World Economic Outlook*, various issues.

**Table 4.1. Nigeria's Commodity and Income Terms of Trade,
1970–1990 (1980 = 100)**

Year	Net Commodity Terms of Trade	Income Terms of Trade
1970	18	14
1975	59	47
1980	100	100
1981	112	53
1982	76	28
1983	81	40
1984	84	48
1985	78	43
1986	36	23
1987	43	23
1988	35	20
1989	38	22
1990	36	21

Source: Central Bank of Nigeria.

1980s, as well as 1970, were one-third to one-sixth the 1981 oil-driven peak.

The extraordinary fall in the Sub-Sahara's commodity terms of trade over a period of two decades is consistent with the Prebisch-Singer thesis that the terms of trade of countries (mainly LDCs) producing primary goods (food, raw materials, minerals, and organic oils and fats) decrease in the long run. This thesis, based on declining primary-product prices from the 1870s to 1938, states that the terms of trade deteriorate because of differences in the growth of demand for, and the market structure in, primary and manufacturing production. Engel's law indicates that as income increases, the proportion of income spent on manufactured goods rises and the proportion spent on primary products falls. If resources do not shift from primary to manufacturing output, there will be an excess supply of, and declining relative price in, primary products and an excess demand for, and increasing relative price in, manufactured goods. Moreover, primary production is relatively competitive, so that the productivity gains result in lower prices, but manufacturing is relatively monopolistic, with productivity gains leading to higher prices.[11]

Is the Prebisch-Singer thesis adequate? The bulk of the extensive evaluation of this thesis during the 1950s through 1970s, which I summarize elsewhere,[12] indicated the inadequacy of data sources used by Prebisch and Singer. However, Spraos's careful statistical study for the United Nations in 1983 showed that, when we adjust for biases, these data sources would still indicate a deterioration of primary producers' terms of trade, although by a smaller magnitude than Prebisch and Singer thought.[13] Figure 4.2 shows a declining trend for the price of *non-oil* commodities relative to exports of manufactures since 1948.

In 1956, Kindleberger, while not supporting deteriorating long-run terms of trade for *primary product exporters,* observed that *LDCs* are especially vulnerable to declining terms of trade because they cannot easily shift resources as patterns of comparative advantage change.[14] The primary-product export concentration mentioned above, the dependence of African primary exports on foreign multinational corporations for processing, marketing, and financing (see "Primary-Product Export Glut," below), and limitations on the expansion of processing indicate Africa's inability to shift resources with changing demand and technologies.

But while falling commodity terms of trade and slow growth in export volume—with substantial competition against other primary

Figure 4.2. Non-Oil Commodity Prices Relative to Unit Value of Exports of Manufactures, 1948–1990

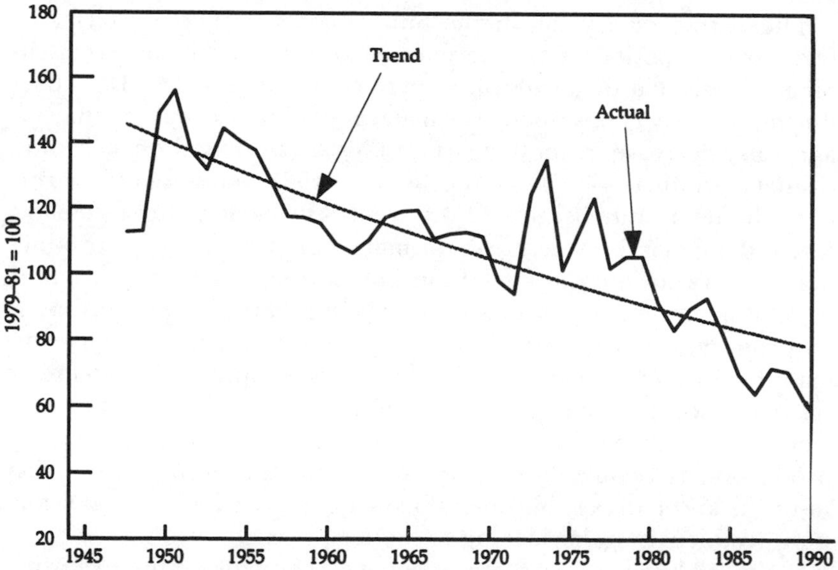

Sources: World Bank (1991a: 46).

producers expanding output to reduce external imbalances—indicate African dependence on factors beyond its control, price policies instituted by much of Africa in the 1970s and early 1980s suggest, at first glance, variables that it could control. Policy set low prices for foreign currency, which discourage primary product exports; fixed price ceilings on food; and set minimum prices for industrial goods. Yet to admonish African governments, as the World Bank does, to "get prices right" in order to expand exports exhibits a fallacy of composition: What is true of the individual case is not necessarily true of all cases combined. Thus, while policies promoting domestic-currency prices favorable to primary-product exporters might help a given country (whose global market share is probably too small to affect world price adversely), the adoption of these policies by numerous African and other developing countries under pressure to improve external balances results in market glut from increased export volume, which reduces total export receipts when the price elasticity of demand (the absolute value of the percentage change in quantity demanded divided by the percentage change in price) is less than one (inelastic). Inelastic demand can be illustrated by the doubling of cocoa exports (in tons), thereby reducing their prices per ton 75 percent so that total export receipts fall by 50 percent.

Most African policymakers perceive the World Bank's Berg report strategy (1981) as focusing on a narrow range of agricultural exports. African countries adopting Bank/Fund structural adjustments, including agricultural export expansion through currency devaluation and price decontrol, face severe competition from other LDCs whose adjustment programs required similar policies.[15] Although expanding primary-product and light-manufacturing exports and achieving market-clearing exchange rates were strategies successful in Meiji Japan, 1868–1912, which had little competition from other LDCs, today's African countries face export expansion limitations from numerous LDC competitors producing commodities in markets with low income and price elasticities.[16]

Manufacturing now comprises a small share of Africa's exports. Industrial exports as a percentage of total exports were 44 percent in Zimbabwe and 7 percent in Côte d'Ivoire in 1989, compared to 69 percent in Asian LDCs. Also in 1989, only 11 percent of African merchandise exports were manufactures, compared to 53 percent for LDCs generally. Between 1967 and 1978, however, Côte d'Ivoire and Zimbabwe were the most diversified manufacturing exporters in Africa. Côte d'Ivoire was among the top three sub-Saharan exporters of equipment, textiles, chemicals, and food products, and Zimbabwe, an exporter of steel, textiles, chemicals, and vehicles, expanded its industrial foundation during the U.N. sanctions against the white-minority government of Rhodesia.[17]

Africa's industrial comparative advantage may lie in the processing of natural resource-based goods; for example, Zambia might export refined copper, and Kenya and Tanzania might export coffee essences or extracts. DC nominal tariff rates appear low (5–6 percent of value after GATT's 1974–79 Tokyo Round trade negotiations); however, on processing and manufacturing, DC effective rates of protection, which are a measure of protection as a percentage of value added by production factors at each processing stage, have been high. Tokyo Round effective protection on LDC commodities according to processing stage, not lowered during GATT's Uruguay Round, 1986–92, was 3 percent on stage 1 (the raw material, for example, raw cotton), 23 percent on stage 2 (low-level processing, as of cotton yarn), 20 percent on stage 3 (high-level processing, as of cotton fabrics), and 15 percent on stage 4 (the finished product, for example, clothing). DC effective rates of protection, which are highest at low levels of processing where poor countries concentrate their industrial activities, have encouraged importing raw materials at the expense of processing, especially at lower levels. Fifty-four percent of DC imports from LDCs are at stage 1, 29 percent at stage 2, 9 percent at stage 3, and 8 percent at stage 4. Zambia, which has the largest nonagricultural share of GDP in the sub-Sahara and a high elasticity of employment growth with respect to nonagricultural output growth, has expanded from consumer goods to intermediate and capital goods. But high effective protection rates on processing have diverted Zambia's industrial growth from exports to import substitution. Indeed, until the late 1980s, MNCs with subsidiaries in Zambia, Zaïre, Botswana, and Namibia built most of the fabricating and processing plants in South Africa and in the West. Moreover, since the Tokyo Round, DCs have promulgated new trade restrictions—Multifiber Arrangements (MFA), "voluntary" export restraints (often imposed in anticipation of more severe restrictions levied by DC parliaments), trigger price mechanisms, antidumping duties, industrial subsidies, and other non-tariff barriers, especially on labor-intensive goods in which LDCs are more likely to have a comparative advantage.[18]

Sub-Saharan Africa is caught in an export trap. In the 1970s and 1980s the purchasing power of exports, which comprise 20–25 percent of GNP in the Sub-Sahara, fell more than one-half, spreading negative multiplier and linkage effects to other sectors of the economy. Primary-product export expansion encountered competition from other economies requiring export expansion for adjustment. Furthermore, DC tariff structure limits growth in processing and agro-industry exports in Africa. Indeed, international economic factors, such as low and falling export relative to import prices, increased economic pressures on Nigeria's Second Republic, 1979–83, and the Mohammed Buhari military government, 1983–85, both of which were overthrown, and on the subsequent Ibrahim Babangida regime, which faced discontent evidenced by several aborted coups. Additionally, declining relative export prices added to the pressures on political leaders Felix Houphouët-Boigney (Côte d'Ivoire), Mobutu Sese Seko (Zaïre), Kenneth Kaunda (Zambia), Jerry Rawlings (Ghana), Hastings Kamuzu Banda (Malawi), Daniel arap Moi (Kenya), and the late Samuel K. Doe (Liberia).

Oil Shocks and Their Aftermath

During the quadrupling of world oil prices in 1973–74, a few oil-exporting countries such as Saudi Arabia, Libya, Kuwait, and the United Arab Emirates, with large deposits of oil per capita, accumulated enormous external surpluses, pouring tens of billions of petrodollars into the global banking system, especially in New York City. Commercial banks, encouraged by the United States and other DC governments, recycled petrodollars into loans to LDCs, which would help maintain DC exports to LDCs. Many bankers believed the government would bail them out of difficulty, given the importance of bank intermediation in international trade.

From 1974 to 1981, lending to major oil-exporting countries, like Mexico, Indonesia, and Nigeria, was considered as "good as gold." Mexico's President José López Portillo encouraged this illusion by declaring: "There are two classes of countries, those that have oil and those that don't; we have it." The banks loaned Mexico more than $20 billion in 1981, the year before Mexico announced its inability to service external debt obligations and the beginning of a five-year slide in oil prices. Figure 4.3 shows world oil market volatility.

LDCs, like U.S. business people and farmers, reacted to the input price hikes of 1973–75 by increasing borrowing, lured by abundant funds and negative world real interest rates (the nominal rates of interest minus the inflation rate), which were −7 percent in 1973, −16 percent in 1974, and −5 percent in 1975. Perhaps because of inexperience with rising inflation, savers were slow to demand interest rates that compensated for inflation. Real interest rates, 1976–82, for

73

Figure 4.3. World Crude Oil Price, 1970–1990
(in U.S. dollars per barrel)

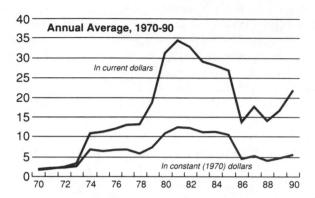

Source: IMF (1991: 77).

Notes: Data from 1984 are the unweighted average spot market price of Brent, Dubai, and Alaska North Slope crude oils representing light, medium, and heavier crude oils, respectively, in three different regions.

In data on constant (1970) dollars, the deflator used is the index of the export prices of manufactures of the industrial countries.

leading debtors varied from −20.5 percent for Turkey to 3.1 percent for Thailand, the only country listed in table 4.2 (below) that paid more than the United States' real interest rate, 1.9 percent. Among sub-Saharan borrowers, Nigeria paid −10.3 percent, Kenya −3.3 percent, Zambia −4.7 percent, Cameroon −5.3 percent, and Zimbabwe −5.2 percent. Many of these debts came due in 1981–86, when high nominal interest rates and low inflation rates meant real interest rates of 9 to 17 percent. Middle-income countries were especially hurt, as more of their bilateral and private debt carried variable rates. The borrowers, with large arrears, have had a demand for credit in excess of the lending countries' limit.[19]

The Credit Cycle

Private capital flows are highly cyclical between periods of boom and collapse. LDCs, typically peripheral to bank lending cycles, and the Sub-Sahara, the periphery of the periphery, experienced even greater credit volatility.

Table 4.2. Real Interest Rates (Nominal Rates of Interest Minus Inflation Rate), Less-Developed Countries, 1976–1982 (in percent)

Brazil	−14.7	Nigeria	−10.3
Mexico	−0.8	Thailand	3.1
Argentina	−6.6	Morocco	−3.5
Indonesia	−0.5	Peru	−17.8
India	1.1	Colombia	1.0
South Korea	−4.3	Ecuador	−6.1
Egypt	−6.4	Kenya	−3.3
Turkey	−20.5	Zambia	−4.7
Philippines	−3.5	Cameroon	−5.3
Venezuela	−14.4	Zimbabwe	−5.2

Source: Erbe (1985: 274).

U.S. regulations restricting interstate commercial bank activity and the rates that banks could pay for deposits enhanced incentives for American and European banks in the 1960s and 1970s to expand into the market for dollar deposits (eurodollars) located in the regulatory no-man's-land of London, Zurich, Paris, Amsterdam, Hong Kong, Singapore, Panama, Nassau, Grand Cayman, Luxembourg, and Bahrain. The successive waves of new U.S., European, and Japanese banks entering the eurocurrency market, with no reserve requirements, fueled credit expansion, especially in the 1970s. Although LDC borrowers faced a concentrated world financial market, with the 25 largest banks holding 32 percent and the 100 largest banks holding 74 percent of total assets in 1975 (and about the same in 1980), European, Japanese, and American regional banks challenging leading American bank domination sought new markets in the 1970s. After 1974, as capital-surplus oil-exporting countries recycled petrodollars to expand credit supply while Western demand for credit contracted, bankers viewed LDCs as a new frontier for lending. LDC borrowers were attractive, as they paid a premium of two percentage points or more over LIBOR and were thought to pose little risk since borrower or guarantor governments, deemed incapable of bankruptcy, would service their debt. In the 1970s, bank loans to LDCs expanded faster than official loans, and aid fell. The *Wall Street Journal* characterized creditor practices as a "glad-handed name your price approach," while the financial magazine *Euromoney* estimated that half of the international banks were "gunslingers," undertaking aggressive overseas banking salesmanship. But borrowing was concentrated among ten to fifteen countries, with middle-income countries benefiting disproportionately from private loan expansion while many low-income sub-Saharan countries suffered both from reduced net transfers and from the falling concessional component of these transfers. Many Western economists heralded the increasingly efficient credit market, where market allocation rose at the expense of government-induced credit. Ruling elites in Zaïre, Zambia, Ghana, and Nigeria were lured by the use of easy bank credit to enhance coalition building while postponing large debt servicing for (perhaps) a future regime. Yet stagnating sub-Saharan Africa soon was on a treadmill, in which growing debt service required expanded borrowing to maintain a given net transfer.

In 1980–82, the expansive phase of international banking in LDCs ended with high real interest rates, partly because the U.S. Federal Reserve Bank tightened monetary policies to counter the expansionary effect of a federal budget deficit of unprecedented size. Weeks notes with irony the sizable U.S. deficits in the 1980s while U.S. administrations supported World Bank and IMF adjustment policies that imposed "fiscally responsible" spending reductions on LDCs. While the U.S. economy enjoyed economic expansion beginning in 1983, even while trade deficits grew, because high interest rates attracted capital inflows to finance the huge import surplus, LDC recession from collapsing commodity markets and prices lasted several years longer. A 5 percentage point rise in interest rates slowed GDP growth by 1 percentage point in the sub-Sahara (and 2 points in Latin America).[20]

Commercial banks' giddy optimism about LDC borrowing turned around in August 1982, when Mexico unilaterally declared its inability to service debts. Thereafter, bankers perceived the chances of LDC debt repudiation, insolvency, and illiquidity to be higher and substantially cut back LDC credit, reviving a joke popular during the Great Depression that characterized private credit as an umbrella that a person is allowed to borrow as long as the weather is fine, but which he has to return the moment it starts raining. Indeed, twenty-seven countries in sub-Saharan Africa (Central African Republic, Liberia, Malawi, Niger, Senegal, Sudan, Togo, Zaïre, and Zambia), the Middle East, Central Europe, Asia, and Latin America initiated debt rescheduling proceedings with their bankers by the end of 1983, representing half of the bank-loan portfolio in LDCs.[21]

The average interest rate for fixed-interest loans (generally subsidized or long-term) rose from 4 percent (1970) to 6 percent (1981) to 7 percent (1986). Between 1971 and 1981, interest rates on floating-interest loans (primarily commercial) increased from 8 percent to 18 percent. The reductions of the average loan maturity from 20 to 16 years and the average grace period from 6 to 5 years from 1970 to 1986 also aggravated the problem of debt service. In the early 1990s, as economic reform in Central and Eastern Europe increased the demand for capital, low-income African borrowers experienced interest-rate shocks, as most of their debt was tied to variable interest rates.[22]

Additionally, from 1980 to 1985, at the peak of LDC debt expansion, loans at bankers' standards to LDCs fell from $47.1 billion to $28.9 billion. Much of this decline resulted from a fall in loans from commercial banks (from $38.4 billion to $15.0 billion) due to the second oil shock and bank overexposure to potential LDC default.[23] The irony for many LDCs is that the commercial-bank debt they assumed in the 1970s to escape IMF discipline compelled them to seek IMF (or World Bank) lending in the 1980s in an even weaker bargaining position. As IMF Managing Director Jacques de Larosière asserted in 1987: "Adjustment is now virtually universal [among LDCs]. . . . Never before has there been such an extensive yet convergent adjustment effort."[24]

During the 1970s and early 1980s, many banks made loans to avert losing business to competing banks. As IMF economist Nowzad argues: "Herd behavior can generate its own momentum." However, one major lender reducing LDC loan exposure, followed by other banks, can precipitate a debt crisis that can become a self-fulfilling prophecy.[25]

The Relationship between Export Growth and Interest Rates

The global debt crisis worsened as interest-rate growth minus export-earnings growth swung from negative to positive in the 1980s. When the noninterest current account is zero, the debt-export ratio will grow without limit if the interest rate on debt exceeds the growth rate in export receipts. LDC commercial borrowing and debt-export ratios ebb and flow with the tide of world financial markets, dependent on DC needs and regulations. In the mid- to late 1970s, as international loans were still underrepresented in bank portfolios, new loans to LDCs exceeded debt-servicing commitments. Yet during the late 1970s, as DC banks expanded aggressively into LDC lending, bank portfolios shifted from too few to too many LDC assets. The sharp rise in world interest rates (from reduced petrodollars, the drying up of LDC lending opportunities, and the massive capital imports of the United States), together with the collapse in LDC export growth in the early 1980s (in Mexico, Brazil, and non-oil LDCs in Africa and Latin

America), brought on the global debt crisis. Indeed, the additional LDC debt burden of $30–35 billion resulting from a two-percentage-point increase in world interest rates almost equals the 1988 annual value of new commercial loans received by LDCs.[26] One offsetting factor was that, in the late 1980s and early 1990s, the World Bank increased concessional lending to the Sub-Sahara through the IDA, which charges interest rates substantially below commercial rates, lengthens the grace period in which interest charges or repayment of principal is required, lengthens the repayment period, and may allow repayment in local, inconvertible currency. Moreover, the Bank's soft loans to the Sub-Sahara have been sizable enough to exceed debt service payment, so the net transfer from the Bank to low-income sub-Saharan Africa is positive and large. Unfortunately, the IMF, African Development Bank, and bilateral lenders did not join the World Bank in averting African net resource transfers (see chapter 5).

South Korea, Taiwan, Singapore, Hong Kong, Thailand, and Malaysia did not face the crises faced by many African countries and Latin American countries such as Mexico and Brazil; their export and GNP growth exceeded interest rates during the 1980s. These selected East and Southeast Asian countries, avoiding the export glut by specializing at a higher level of processing than sub-Saharan countries, encountered no major debt problems because of rapid export expansion, spurred partly by forgoing overvalued domestic currencies (see below) and adjusting exchange rates close to market-clearing rates.[27]

Primary-Product Export Glut

In sub-Saharan Africa in 1989, 89 percent of merchandise exports were primary products.[28] Even countries not experiencing export price booms (like copper exporters Zaïre and Zambia and iron ore exporters Liberia and Mauritania) could borrow because of previous growth, mineral resources, and expectations that mineral prices would eventually rise again. Indeed, LDCs experiencing export booms increased, rather than decreased, their foreign borrowing during the 1970s.

During the 1980s, the adjustment essential to export more than import and produce more than spend required translating government spending cuts into foreign-exchange earnings and competitive gains, usually necessitating reduced demand and wages, real currency depreciation, and increased unemployment, especially at a time when DC income and import-demand growth slowed. Additionally, when many other LDCs go through the same adjustment (including export expansion), the benefit to a given LDC is less. Real non-oil commodity prices fell throughout most of the 1980s (fig. 4.2). By 1985, for example, the pressure on debtor countries to increase export revenues contributed to a glut in primary products and collapse of their prices.

Nyerere observed in 1986, soon after his retirement as Tanzania's head of state, that

> during the last few years of world recession, the fall in commodity prices has been catastrophic; the World Bank has estimated that from 1980 to 1982, the prices of non-oil primary commodities declined by 17 per cent in current US dollar terms. As a proportion of their GDP the result was a 2.4 per cent loss of income for the low income countries of Africa south of the Sahara. Can this kind of thing be regarded as irrelevant to the current economic crisis in Africa?[29]

While the severely indebted middle-income countries' annual export growth, 1982–87, was 4.3 percent, low-income Sub-Sahara's was only 0.6 percent, resulting in export volume and purchasing power in 1987 lower than in 1970. Indeed, from 1980 to 1987, African exports fell 56 percent (from $94.7 billion to $53.2 billion), while those from Nigeria declined 72 percent (from $26.0 billion to $7.3 billion), "a shock of a magnitude," according to Avramovic, "which probably no country has ever sustained in time of peace." Slow export growth, combined with declining terms of trade, exacerbated sub-Saharan Africa's external disequilibrium and reduced imported inputs and capital needed for economic growth during the 1980s. The Sub-Sahara's volume of imports, damaged by foreign-exchange shortages and inadequate trade credit, fell 2.6 percent yearly, 1980 to 1987, while debt arrears and their associated difficulties in obtaining trade financing increased the prices paid for imports.

Tanzania, Ghana, Zambia, Nigeria, and Senegal, under Bank and Fund pressure, reduced real wages by more than 30 percent from the early to mid-1980s, experienced increases in the unemployment rate, and depreciated local currency to increase external competitiveness. Few countries, however, *voluntarily* reduced domestic employment and real wages to return the balance on goods and services account to equilibrium.[30]

Cline's estimate of the impact of exogenous shocks to oil-importing developing countries indicates that, of the $482 billion increase in external debt, 1973–82, the cumulative effect of oil price increases in excess of inflation was $260 billion; real interest rates, 1981–82, in excess of their 1961–80 average was $41 billion; the terms of trade loss, 1981–82, $79 billion; and the export volume loss caused by the world recession, 1981–82, $21 billion.[31]

World Bank economists compare the severely indebted middle-income countries mainly from Latin America and Africa[32] to East and Southeast Asian middle-income countries (MICs) Taiwan, South Korea, Hong Kong, Singapore, Thailand, and Malaysia. First, the Asian MICs treated exogenous shocks in the 1970s and 1980s as permanent and promptly undertook adjustment, thus avoiding excessive foreign borrowing. Severely indebted countries, considering these shocks temporary aberrations, continued with normal levels of expenditure, borrowing externally and postponing adjustment. Second, the Asian countries were less dependent on a few commodity exports and better able to withstand declining commodity prices. During the global recovery beginning in 1982, they expanded manufactured exports rapidly to reduce their debt-export ratios and escape the debt crisis. Third, the Asian middle-income countries followed relatively cautious macroeconomic policies in the 1970s, thus avoiding high inflation. At the same time, they used borrowed external resources to expand capacity by investing in human capital, infrastructure, and other productive investments, while preventing public enterprises from running massive deficits.[33] Finally, exporters in these MICs received close to market-clearing exchange-rate prices for foreign sales, acquired pre-shipment credit for working capital and labor costs, gained from investment in education, training, and infrastructure, and benefited from favorable regulatory environment.[34] Yet overall the growing market shares of Asian MICs in manufacturing as well as in primary products were threats to Africa's attempt to expand exports. Chapter 7 shows that Bank/Fund trade and exchange liberalization programs, together with adjustment lending tied to a short leash, failed to spur sub-Saharan countries to achieve growth and external balance.

The World Bank estimates that the combined terms of trade and interest-rate shocks reduced developing countries' annual GDP growth by more than 3 *percentage points*, 1981–86. LDC total growth, 1980–87, was 2.3 percent yearly (roughly canceled out by population growth), slower than the 5.6 percent annual growth, 1970–79, and the Bank's 1980 forecast of 4.5 to 5.1 percent per annum. Mosley, Harrigan, and Toye's regression equation for twenty-five countries receiving World Bank structural adjustment loans, 1980 to 1987, shows that with Bank financial flows and country compliance with Bank conditions held constant, an increase in the terms of trade has a positive effect on GDP growth rates, a result statistically significant at the 1 percent level.[35]

Commodity price instability increased from the 1950s and 1960s to the 1970s and 1980s for bananas, coconut oil, peanut oil, palm oil, coffee, copra, cotton, maize, tea, wheat, sugar, jute, cocoa, rice, sorghum, and tobacco (but not rubber), major African export and food crops. Africa's exports were hurt by DC stagnation in the early 1980s and the early 1990s. Each 1 percent change in the DCs' business cycle index is associated with a 2.2 percent change in primary commodity prices, affecting Africa substantially, as 80 percent of their exports are primary goods. The OECD's quantity index of imports has a major impact on Africa's economic growth.

The United States, in its attempt to reduce its trade deficit, is not likely to encourage increased exports from LDC debtors. Japan and Germany have always been reluctant to stimulate their economies and are not likely to absorb more exports from debtors. Furthermore, DC food subsidies have inhibited Africa's food growth.[36] As the FAO argues: "The 1980s clearly demonstrated that external factors alone are enough to push the adjustment process completely off course."[37]

Foreign Capital Dependence

Chapter 3 indicates that MNCs play an important role in alliances between domestic political leaders and foreign capital. Roughly four-fifths of Africa's early 1980s commodity trade was handled by MNCs. While their ownership shares in African primary production declined after 1970, their control of processing, marketing, distribution, and services expanded. For vertically integrated goods like bananas and tea, MNCs exercise much control over pricing and contract, buying from their own plantations and selling to their own processors. While market power is weaker with commodities that MNCs buy from independent producers and sell to independent processors, global marketing and financial control still gives MNCs some power to determine supply and price. For example, three conglomerates account for 70 to 75 percent of the global banana market; six corporations, 70 percent of cocoa trade; and six MNCs, 85 to 90 percent of leaf tobacco trade.[38]

Moreover, MNCs can distort intrafirm transfer prices by overstating investment, management, and patents costs, overpricing inputs transferred from another subsidiary, and underpricing outputs sold within the MNC to another country, thus understating earnings and tax liabilities, transferring funds extralegally, or circumventing foreign-exchange controls in Africa. And most African countries lack the personnel and political strength to challenge MNC price fixing.

The World Bank criticizes Africa's high tariff rates. Indeed, my analysis of the economic arguments for and against free trade indicates that although tariffs to protect infant industry sometimes promote growth their adverse effects on resource efficiency mean that their value is more limited than many African policymakers suppose.[39] But African governments often design tariffs to compete against one another to attract MNCs. In Nigeria in the 1960s, the prime motive for establishing foreign manufacturing enterprises was to change a highly competitive market to a monopolistic market in international trade. Ironically, the greatest pressure for increased protection for manufacturing was not from government or domestic producers but from foreign capitalists and their local collaborators.[40]

MNCs in Africa contribute to inequality in several ways. Foreign capital usually enters Africa only if political leaders, civil servants, and private middlemen are rewarded for facilitating the joint venture. Much of this reward is for economically unproductive activity and is paid for by tariff and quota protection, higher consumer prices, or subsidies from tax revenue. In Africa, where direct taxes like income taxes are, as we have seen, not well developed, the tax structure is usually regressive, meaning that people with lower income pay a higher percentage of income in taxes. Any subsidy to inefficiency falls disproportionately on low- to middle-income workers and farmers.

Moreover, MNC-associated enterprises tend to use technology designed for DCs, which have high wages and relatively abundant capital. Estimates based on capital resources available indicate that the appropriate capital stock per person in the United States is 45 times that of Nigeria.[41] Additionally, African capital, foreign-exchange, and labor-cost distortions that make the actual price of capital cheaper than its market rate encourage MNC high-technology, capital-intensive, and import-intensive processes rather than local modification or adaptation. Apart from the potential for patronage and corruption among political leaders and civil servants, there are other reasons for increased inequality. Those who control capital (private capitalists or government officials) receive a lion's share of the income from these processes. Even much of the labor share goes to relatively affluent, high-level personnel and skilled workers. And foreigners constitute a reference for salary and consumption levels for elite Africans, who want to keep up with the Akitoyes and the Abdullahis. Moreover, capital-intensive technology increases unemployment. The emphasis on an inefficient, highly protected, capital-intensive industrial sector with compensation for indigenous intermediaries has increased income discrepancies and external disequilibrium.[42]

When Kenya stressed joint ventures between foreign capital and the government, 1964–70, manufacturing grew no faster than the economy as a whole, partly because Kenya preferred Western capital (allied with African elites) to that of long-time resident Asian business people. Ironically, at the same time the government, the United Nations, and the Development Finance Corporation of Kenya were identifying new industrial projects, the government pressured local Asians to withdraw capital from trade and even industry. Most Asian manufacturing firms were small-scale and labor-intensive, and they had survived (with little protection) in the early 1960s. In contrast, MNCs were usually capital-intensive, used substantial imported inputs, increased external economic dependence, and required high protection.[43]

Although Kenya's policy of joint ventures increased government ownership and income, it had only limited success in the goal of Africanizing staff, decisions, and control. The Economist Intelligence Unit (1985) indicates that although foreigners owned only 42 percent of Kenya's 1976 total issued capital of large-scale manufacturing and service firms, they controlled about 75 percent of these firms through majorities on the boards of directors. Because it views society as a whole, government should use an efficiency criterion that balances profits with wages and savings with consumption, rather than the profit maximization of private enterprise.[44] Yet the Kenyan government, despite overall majority ownership, acquiesced in foreign goals to maximize profits by keeping wages for ordinary workers low.

Such neocolonial-created inequalities in Kenya have not been limited to industry. Kenya's 1960 land concentration was comparable to Latin American inequalities, much higher than the Afro-Asian average. And in the 1960s Africa's newly emerging large capitalist farmers (generally politicians, bureaucrats, or their clients) depended on state-administered foreign capital for credit to buy property in the old "white highlands," while using political pressure to influence public agencies setting farm prices. Thus Kenya maintained its high concentration ratio. In the 1970s, the largest 0.1 percent of the farm owners held 14 percent of the arable land; 2.4 percent held 32 percent of it. While 30 percent of the smallholdings were under 0.6 hectares, the largest farms exceeded 1000 hectares.[45]

The collaboration between Ivorian petty capital and French industrial capital in the late colonial period continued after independence. State ownership in Côte d'Ivoire, the most industrialized francophone African country, rose from 18.2 percent of industrial capital in 1971 to 30.4 percent in 1979, but most was joint ownership with foreign capital. Europeans constituted 6.8 percent of the 1971 urban wage and salary earners but received 32.2 percent of the total wage bill. Ivorian supervisors and managers in industry comprised 5 percent of the total in 1968 and 28 percent in 1974. Foreigners held 56.3 percent of the 1979 total industrial investment, despite limited new foreign investment in the 1970s. But this foreign-led industrialization provided few new jobs, especially for unskilled and semiskilled workers, since manufacturing's capital intensity was high and increasing in the 1970s.[46]

Unstable Foreign-Exchange Rates in the Industrialized Economies

The leading DCs' uncoordinated exchange-rate and financial policies under the world's post-1973 managed floating exchange-rate system (where central banks intervene in the exchange-rate market) resulted in gyrating exchange rates and interest rates. Efforts to set target zones, within which key currencies floated, destabilized capital movements and exchange rates as they inevitably approached zone boundaries. Weeks finds a significant part of Latin American currency instability traceable to dollar instability. This and other contributors to global instability increase external shocks and undermine LDC long-run planning.[47]

Since world markets quote commodity prices in U.S. dollars, its 70 percent appreciation relative to other currencies, 1980–85, increased the real cost of commodity purchases by countries whose currencies depreciated against the dollar. Moreover, when debts are denominated in U.S. dollars, its appreciation increases local and nondollar currency costs of debt service. Conversely, U.S. dollar depreciation increases the dollar value of nondollar debt (some paid by dollar-denominated exports), as exemplified by Indonesia's 1985 debt to the Japanese (¥1,250 billion) that increased from $5 billion to $10 billion in 1988 as exchange rates moved from ¥250=$1 to ¥125=$1. LDCs are limited in their contractual and asset portfolio adjustments to rampant exchange-rate fluctuations.

Overvalued Domestic Currencies

In sub-Saharan Africa, the real effective exchange rate in 1985 was 75 percent above its 1970–72 level (15 percent for IDA-eligible countries), while Asia's effective exchange rate declined 32 percent and Latin America's 37 percent over the same period. In the late 1980s, under Bank/Fund adjustment pressure, a growing number of sub-Saharan countries had more flexible exchange rates. From 1980 to 1987, the debt-distressed sub-Saharan countries reduced their effective exchange rates by 40 percent, while those without this distress had only a 4 percent drop. In Zaïre, the effective exchange rate fell 75 percent in 1983–84.[48]

One indicator of overvaluation, the Sub-Sahara's black market exchange rate vis-à-vis the official nominal exchange rate, appreciated from 1.36 in 1971 to 1.53 in 1980 to 2.10, before falling (often at Bank/Fund insistence) to 1.38 in 1985. Exchange-rate distortions in Africa reduced its export competitiveness while spurring applications for artificially cheap foreign capital and inputs. However, in the late 1980s the World Bank and IMF made devaluation a condition for adjustment loans, offsetting some past inflation, so Africa's real exchange rate in 1987 (relative to 1980) was 96 compared to Asia's 59 and Latin America's 55, narrowing real exchange-rate divergences with other LDC regions.[49]

Overvalued domestic currencies (and international trade and payments restrictions) dampen exports, induce imports, and encourage capital flight from LDCs, exacerbating the current account deficit and external debt problems. Several countries with overvalued currencies in the late 1970s devalued in 1979–82, frequently under foreign and IMF pressure. Under two World Bank structural adjustments, Nigeria devalued the naira 89 percent (from $1.19=₦1 to $0.124=₦1, or ₦0.894=$1 to ₦8.038=$1, as expressed in table 4.3), 1985–90. Other examples of real devaluation include Peru, 30 percent (1978); Egypt, 82 percent (1979); Brazil, 21 percent (1980); Turkey, 33 percent (1980–82); and Argentina, more than 90 percent (1982).[50]

Sub-Saharan Africa's inflation in the 1970s and 1980s was higher than that of its major trading partners. As the sub-Saharan countries resisted nominal devaluation, their currencies became increasingly overvalued.[51]

Foreign Aid Ineffectiveness

Wheeler shows no significant correlation between aid per capita and growth in sub-Saharan Africa in the 1970s. This evidence, while not conclusive, raises questions about the value of aid.[52]

Aid to Kenya helped harmonize the interests of a dependent bureau-

Table 4.3. Average Exchange Rate, 1979–1991 (Naira per United States dollar)

1979	0.603	1984	0.766	1988	4.537
1980	0.546	1985	0.894	1989	7.365
1981	0.614	1986	1.755	1990	8.038
1982	0.673	1987	4.016	1991	8.772
1983	0.724				

Sources: Economist Intelligence Unit, Nigeria: Country Profile, 1990–91 (London, 1990), p. 12; and Economist Intelligence Unit, Nigeria: Country Profile, 1992–92 (London, 1991), p. 11.

cratic and commercial bourgeoisie with foreign capital.[53] Indeed, officials and intermediaries in Kenya, Zaïre, Malawi, and many other African recipient countries depend critically on external assistance for increasing income, dispensing patronage, and controlling state power. Additionally, as this chapter later points out, much aid increasing the incomes of government officials, their clients, and their allies returns overseas through capital flight.

The effectiveness of aid appears to have declined after 1970, when program support (for example, to infrastructure or agriculture) was replaced by project assistance, which entailed more precise foreign monitoring and control over funds, as well as more local personnel and resources committed to projects. Furthermore, each of the eighty-two major donor organizations in Africa in 1980, with their competing requirements, insisted on continual, extensive project supervision and review, so recipient government agencies become more answerable to them than to their own senior policy officials.[54]

Donors frequently recommend and supervise poorly conceived projects. But even when projects are well conceived, officials fail to learn how to manage them because they lack the power to make their own decisions. Morss argues the proliferation of donors and requirements has resulted in weakened institutions and reduced management capacity. Thus aid, whose annual real value dropped from the late 1970s to the 1980s, made limited contributions to Africa's current-account and external debt position.

Because of African states' weaknesses, they lack the indigenous capacity for policy formulation. Multilateral and bilateral donors rarely consider alternative approaches suggested by African governments.

Finance and planning ministry officials in Africa perceive Bank/Fund lending and structural adjustment programs as imposed from the outside. In 1988, one official characterized both agencies as "having taken the role of those who should be designing recovery programs." To most ministry officials participating in World Bank seminars, 1987–88, African countries have only a superficial input into designing SAPs. While many African countries possess much underutilized capacity, their officials charge that the Bank and the IMF impose excessive demands on the administration of the recipient country without enhancing its ability to make decisions on its own economies.[55]

Moreover, in many countries, aid is biased against the poor. In Kenya (1963–76), only 11 percent of development assistance reached the very poor, only a third was directly concerned with rural development, and most of this went to relatively well-off farmers.[56]

Chapters 8 and 9 discuss increased official development assistance (ODA) assistance to debt-distressed sub-Saharan countries as a way of debt relief.

Falling Aid-Loan Ratios

Although OECD countries agreed to a target of ODA as 0.70 percent of GNP, the actual percentage during the 1970s and 1980s was 0.30 to 0.36 percent, with the United States' percentage about one-half to two-thirds as high. In 1988, ODA/GNP was 0.21 percent for the United States and 0.36 percent for the OECD. In 1989, when the United States' percentage was 0.15, Japan, with 0.32 percent, surpassed the United States as the world's largest donor for the first time, with $9.0 billion ODA disbursements compared to the United States' $7.7 billion (although the United States regained the lead in 1990 with $10.9 billion compared to Japan's $9.3 billion). While the OECD target for aid to least developed countries was 0.15 percent of GNP, in 1989 OECD donors achieved only 0.08 percent (and the United States 0.02 percent).[57]

The LCDs' worsening external deficit after 1973–74, discussed earlier, was exacerbated by the fall of the ratio of ODA to commercial loans: from 1.40 in 1970, 0.66 in 1973, 0.55 in 1975, 0.36 in 1978, and 0.23 in 1984, increasing to 0.33 in 1987 mostly because of a fall in private lending. ODA declined sharply in 1982–83 during the DCs' recession, when LDC external debt grew at its fastest rate.[58]

In sub-Saharan Africa, the grant element of loans declined steadily from 46 percent in 1970 to 17 percent in 1979, before rising to 20 percent in 1981–82 and 50 percent in 1987 as loans at bankers' standards declined and commercial interest rates fell. The nominal value of commercial loans to the Sub-Sahara increased steadily from 1970 to 1982, before falling steeply the rest of the 1980s (although multilateral agencies increased their lending after 1982) at the same time debt service of long-term debt and newly acquired short-term debt rose rapidly, reducing the overall net resource transfer from the early to late 1980s (table 2.2).

Meanwhile ODA rose gradually from 1970 through 1980, leveling off through 1983, before increasing to $8,222 million in 1985 (with $1,000 million additional emergency assistance to the drought-stricken Sub-Sahara), $11,066 million in 1987, and $13,329 million in 1988. Because of the United Nations' emphasis on concessional aid to least-developed countries, mostly in sub-Saharan Africa, its ratio of ODA to commercial loans was higher in the 1970s than LDCs and it rose faster and achieved much higher ratios in the 1980s (table 4.4). Still the rising trend in the ratios in the 1980s was not a result of *real* increases in aid but a leveling and decline of commercial loans at bankers' standards.

In the late 1980s, food aid comprised almost half of sub-Saharan

Table 4.4. Ratio of Official Development Assistance (ODA) to Commercial Loans in Sub-Saharan Africa, 1970–1987 (Selected Years)

Year	(1) ODA (Grant and Loan Components) ($ millions)	(2) Commercial Loans ($ millions)	(3) Col. 1 —— Col. 2
1970	1,046	749	1.40
1973	1,538	1,658	0.93
1975	3,216	2,531	1.27
1977	3,528	2,905	1.21
1980	7,126	6,317	1.13
1982	7,311	7,383	0.99
1983	7,122	5,260	1.35
1985	8,222	3,744	2.20
1987	11,066	2,982	3.71

Sources: World Bank (1981a: 162, 165); World Bank (1986a: 85); U.N. Development Programme and World Bank (1989: 75); World Bank (1989a: 251); Giovanni Andrea Cornia, "Economic Decline and Human Welfare in the First Half of the 1980s," in Cornia, Jolly, and Stewart, vol. 1 (1987: 14); World Bank and U.N. Development Programme (1989: 14–16); and OECD (1988a: 240–45).

food imports. Much donated food is expensive to transport and does not match local tastes. But recipients should not treat food aid merely as disposal of surplus but as program or balance-of-payments support. Food aid supplied in bulk can be sold, with proceeds used for financing development projects such as food-for-work rural public works to increase future agricultural productivity.

Sub-Saharan Africa experienced a severe financial squeeze, 1982–85, as all three types of financial flows—export credits, loans, and ODA—fell (in real terms) from 1979–82 to 1982–85. However, the grant element of aid rose, with ODA (especially for IDA-eligible countries) equal to 90 percent of total net flows in 1985–87 (95 percent in 1987) compared to 50 percent in 1980–83. In 1987, 43 percent of the debt of IDA countries was at market interest rates. In the same year in the Sub-Sahara, grants comprised more than one-half of the total gross capital inflows of IDA countries, compared to less than one-fifth for non-IDA countries. The Sub-Sahara's share of net ODA disbursements rose from 23 percent in 1980 to 30 percent in 1987, with multilateral donors (especially the IDA with $1.6 billion, and the European Community with $0.8 billion in 1987) accounting for much of the increase.[59]

Despite the small amount of aid to Africa, for nineteen African LDCs, 1987–88, ODA as a percentage of GNP exceeded 10 percent. Least developed (IDA) countries included Somalia, 32 percent; the Sahel group (Mauritania, Mali, Niger, Chad, Burkina, Senegal, The Gambia, and Cape Verde), 20 percent; Lesotho, 18 percent; Tanzania, 16 percent; Ethiopia, 16 percent; Rwanda, 12 percent; and Sudan, 12 percent. Low-income countries were Mozambique, 31 percent; Zambia, 23 percent; Madagascar, 15 percent; and Zaïre, 12 percent; the only middle-income country was Réunion, with 19 percent. Other countries with more than 10 percent included least-developed South Yemen, 15 percent, and Nepal, 14 percent; low-income Mongolia, 26 percent; El Salvador, 10 percent; and middle-income New Caledonia, 32 percent; Papua New Guinea, 14 percent; and Jordan, 11 percent.[60]

Capital Flight

Many African countries not only have difficulty acquiring new loans but also suffer from the flight of their citizens' private assets, sometimes as large as official external liabilities. Bankers and economists may feel it futile to loan more funds to LDCs if a large portion flows back through capital flight. For Nigeria, the propensity to flee attributable to additional external borrowing, 1976–82, was 0.42, meaning that 42 cents from each dollar lent by foreign creditors leaves the country through capital flight![61] This flight intensifies foreign-exchange shortages and damages the collective interest of the wealthy classes that buy foreign assets. Reversing capital flight will not eliminate the debt crisis, but it can reduce depth burdens and commercial bankers' justification for resisting increased exposure to debtor countries.[62]

Definitions

Which of the domestic holdings of foreign assets (property, equity investment, bonds, deposits, and money) should be classified as domestic capital flight rather than normal capital outflows? Defining capital flight as "resident capital outflow" makes it easier to conceptualize and measure than alternative definitions that characterize it as illegal, abnormal, or undesirable to government or due to overinvoicing imports or underinvoicing exports. Using Erbe's estimates of capital flight as amounts equal to current account balance, net foreign direct investment, and changes in reserves and debt, the largest capital flights, 1976–82, were from Argentina, Mexico, Venezuela, Indonesia, Egypt, and Nigeria (table 4.5), while net flights from Brazil (whose real devaluation in 1980 was substantial), South Korea (whose exchange rate remained close to a market-clearing rate), Colombia, and the Philippines were negative. However, when Erbe estimates capital flight as a percentage of increased debt, 1976–82, the rank order of LDCs with the largest flight percentages was Syria (with 96 percent), Argentina (75 percent), Venezuela (59 percent), Indonesia (44 percent), Nigeria (42 percent), Costa Rica (38 percent), Bolivia (34 percent), Jordan (33 percent), India (33 percent), Mexico (31 percent), Zambia (29 percent), Jamaica (27 percent), Guatemala (22 percent), and Cameroon (20 percent). While Erbe suggests that her method of estimation similar to the World Bank's, identifies countries with the largest flight, she regards her estimates as the lower limit of capital flight.[63]

Most literature on capital flight focuses on Latin America (Argentina, Brazil, Mexico, and Venezuela) and Philippines, with South Korea used as a control, since it experiences little capital flight. The OECD (1982) estimates the $70 billion capital flight from Latin America, 1982, as double the interest portion of the Latin debt-service payment for that year. The Bank of England puts Latin capital flight, 1981–84, at only $80 billion, a mere 25 percent of total Latin debt servicing for the period. The Bank of International Settlements sug-

Table 4.5. Estimates of Capital Flight from Less-Developed Countries, 1976–1982[a]
($ billions)

Argentina	17.2	Jordan	0.6
Mexico	13.5	Zambia	0.4
Venezuela	8.5	Tunisia	0.4
Indonesia	5.2	Papua New Guinea	0.4
Egypt	3.9	Cameroon	0.4
Nigeria	2.7	Jamaica	0.3
India	2.1	Guatemala	0.3
Syria	1.9	El Salvador	0.3
Costa Rica	0.8	Peru	0.1
Bolivia	0.7		

Source: Erbe (1985: 271).
[a]Less-developed countries with more than $100,000 estimated capital flight, 1976–82.

gests that, in 1988, assets held by Latin residents abroad exceeded Latin debts to commercial banks. Chang and Cumby estimate $40 billion flows of capital flight from the Sub-Sahara, 1976–87, so its capital flight assets abroad in 1987 were $20–30 billion, mostly held by Nigerians.[64]

For nine of the fifteen most severely indebted countries, capital flight assets exceeded external debt in 1987. Whenever international capital markets are highly integrated and transaction costs low, private individuals will have strong incentives to circumvent what appear to be arbitrary barriers to capital movements, as even the United States found in the 1960s when interest-equalization taxes and foreign credit restraint programs resulted in eurocurrency and eurobond market expansion to satisfy the offshore demand for funds.[65]

As suggested above, there are many methods of exporting capital illegally, and such forms of capital flight are hard to measure. They include taking currency overseas, sometimes in a suitcase, directly investing black-market money, and false invoicing in trade documents (overinvoicing of imports and underinvoicing of exports).[66]

Causes

Resident capital outflows result from differences in perceived, risk-adjusted returns in source and haven countries. We can attribute these differences to high inflation rates, confiscatory taxation, discriminatory interest ceilings or taxes on residents, financial repression, default

91

on government obligations, overvalued domestic currencies, expected currency depreciation, limitations on convertibility, poor investment climate, political instability, and slow growth in source countries, all exacerbated by the United States' abandoning income taxation on nonresident bank-deposit interest and much other investment income and (in the early 1980s) paying high interest rates. In 1982, Mexico's devaluation and inflation "almost totally wiped out the value of obligations denominated in Mexican pesos." The domestic entrepreneurial energies lost from these policies were substantial.[67]

Since most sub-Saharan countries have low international credit ratings, they rely heavily on domestic borrowing, which, in the absence of sizable domestic capital markets, necessitates new money from the banking system, generating an inflationary effect. However, because government limits imports, inflation does not translate directly into increased imports but into excess liquidity in the domestic market. This excess is channeled into the informal sector or the black market for foreign exchange, where rates are increased by pressure to transfer wealth, at almost any cost, overseas.[68]

In Nigeria, official reluctance to devalue the naira, 1981–83, when inflation was 20 percent per annum, discouraged foreign direct investment, spurred substantial capital flight, and encouraged firms to build up large inventories of imports, often with overinvoicing and concomitant foreign deposits, or to underprice exports, with the difference placed on deposit abroad. Nigeria, having exhausted its official reserves and borrowing limits, had built up its arrears on trade credit to $6 billion by the end of 1983.[69]

The deregulation and globalization of financial markets in the 1980s has largely merged "hot" money, the flow of illegal, underground funds, with mainstream flows. The umbilical cord that connected borrowers to lenders, and the origin with the destination of capital, was broken. Hoogvelt notes the duplicity of banks that make loans to LDCs while receiving deposits from their LDC clients, of debt exchanges arranged to allow those holding fraudulently amassed assets abroad to buy up their country's debt in the secondary markets at greatly discounted prices, and of the Bank/Fund's insistence on states' guaranteeing private debt while privatizing the public sector. On the last, Hoogvelt observes: "The IMF has never instructed [Zaïre's President] Mobutu [Sese Seko] to bring his $5 billion worth of stolen loot back into the country—but they have sacked thousands of public employees."[70]

Indeed, Naylor noted that

recycling had taken a bizarre new twist. An ever growing number of off shore banking and tax havens competed for the increasingly large supply of hot and footloose money fleeing the developing countries. The hot money was then lent through the Euro-banking system funding loans to developing countries in need of hard currency to bolster their foreign exchange positions drained by capital flight.[71]

A Zaïrian Pathology

Zaïre, whose capital flight cannot be tracked statistically, is a blatant example of flight from LDCs desperately needing foreign exchange to resolve debt problems. Thus foreign exchange from smuggling Zaïrian goods, such as diamonds, abroad is so widespread that a neighbor, Congo, became a diamond exporter of some importance in the 1970s and early 1980s without having any diamond deposits! For almost two decades the country has stumbled from one debt crisis to another, lacking the capacity to pay debt service, which was $375–525 million annually after 1985.

For Pierre Dikoba, Mobutu's "loot[ing] the country" explained the torn tin roof, malarial mosquitoes, and the lack of furniture, books, and pictures in the Kinshasa primary school where he taught in 1991. In 1988, U.S. House Foreign Affairs Chair Howard Wolpe asserted: "Literally hundreds and hundreds of millions of dollars have vanished into the hands or bank accounts of the president and his collaborators." Körner and colleagues estimate Mobutu's 1984 overseas wealth at four to six billion dollars, invested in Swiss bank accounts and Western real estate, enough to solve Zaïre's debt crisis. Indeed, if Mobutu (and his allies) had not taken out of the country a large proportion of funds the Zaïrian government borrowed abroad, Zaïre might not have had a debt crisis.[72] In 1977, President Mobutu denounced *le mal zaïrois* (the Zaïrian disease), stating that "everything is for sale, everything is bought in our country. And in this traffic, holding any slice of public power constitutes a veritable exchange instrument, convertible into illicit acquisition of other goods."[73]

Yet since the late 1950s, when U.S. aid to the Sub-Sahara began, Zaïre has been the largest single recipient of aid from the United States, receiving $61 million of its $575 million aid to Africa in fiscal year 1990. Zaïre's pattern in the 1980s was to promise reform, receive external financing based on the promise, then ignore the commitment for reform and begin a new cycle by negotiating new reform programs. Finally, in 1990, as U.S. geopolitical interests changed with the end of the Cold War, the U.S. administration acquiesced to a congressional mandate terminating aid to Zaïre.[74]

How to Reduce Flight

Source countries need robust growth, market-clearing exchange rates and other prices, an outward trade orientation, dependable positive real interest rates, fiscal reform (including lower taxes on capital gains), taxes on foreign assets as high as domestic assets, more efficient state enterprises, sequential market liberalization, supply-oriented adjustment measures, a resolution of the debt problem, and incorruptible government officials.[75] Haven countries can lower interest rates and cease tax discrimination favoring nonresident investment income, while their banks can refuse to accept funds from major LDC debtor countries.

Just listing policies suggests the difficulty of the problem. For Dornbusch, capital flight is the caboose, not the locomotive, meaning that capital flight is symptomatic of the financial repression and economic underdevelopment at the root, rather than the cause, of the debt crisis.[76] We have another vicious circle—low growth, capital flight, and foreign-exchange restrictions that hamper growth.

To reduce capital flight and economic distortions, Bank/Fund reforms emphasize eliminating exchange controls, lowering trade barriers, removing interest-rate ceilings, and abolishing nonprice rationing of loans. Yet even economies devastated by World War II liberalized prices and reconstructed business before removing exchange controls in the late 1950s in Western Europe and in the early 1960s in Japan. Indeed, the Sub-Sahara, in its early reforms, needs to use exchange controls to avoid inflation and foreign-exchange shortages. Exchange-rate liberalization should be a long-term goal rather than an immediate action under structural adjustment. In the next decades, Africa and other LDCs should press for surplus countries to undertake more adjustment, should reduce global financial concentration by encouraging non-Western banks (and other measures, discussed in chapter 9), and should urge the United States to remove tax policies favoring nonresident bank deposits and Switzerland to lift secrecy protection for bank deposits (dubbed Africa's second AIDS epidemic, "acquired Investments Deposited in Switzerland") of African politicians and economic malfeasors facing judicial due process for criminal activity.[77]

Income Distribution Effects

Capital flight involves not only a perverse export of domestic savings and foreign exchange, which are short in poor LDCs, and adverse effects on growth and employment, but also increased income inequality. Owning external wealth is a privilege generally reserved for the richest 5 to 10 percent of the population. Most increased external wealth accumulation of the wealthiest few is made possible by the substantial external debt of the public sector which, after real devaluation, often becomes impoverished. Indeed, private borrowers may acquire foreign assets ostensibly for their project at the same time the public sector is required by foreign creditors to guarantee private debt! African countries service public and guaranteed private debts through taxing earners in local currency to pay those who earn interest in dollars, yen, and deutsche marks; some of these earners are Africans who hold assets abroad. The forced savings to transfer resources required by the debt service are at the expense of depressing real economic activity and real wages.[78]

Conclusion

This chapter analyzed the effect of foreign trade, aid, and investment on debt. African economic domination usually involves economic ties between foreign economic interests and domestic political elites and their allies, who use foreign aid and investment to expand state power. While Africa's rulers incur debt partly to expand patronage, they respond to external pressures on debt crises by reducing social programs, especially those for workers, peasants, and the poor.

An aggravating corollary of these problems is capital flight. Caused by slow growth, overvalued domestic currencies, high inflation rates, the DC aid policies (supporting wealthy capital-fleeing elites), interest rates, and termination of income taxation on nonresident bank-deposit interest, capital flight exacerbates the debt crisis. External debt frequently makes possible the substantial overseas assets of Africa's very rich. Yet Africa's savings to service debt are at the expense of wages and aggregate demand.

Chapters 5 through 9 discuss policies to increase the competitiveness of Africa and reduce its external disequilibrium.

5

World Bank and IMF Adjustment and Stabilization

.

The IMF is our only hope. It is the only institution that can lend money and impose conditions for doing so. No government can do this, nor any bank.
—German IMF Governor Karl Otto Pohl (1982)

Irrespective of the causes of balance of payments difficulties, the Fund generally has insisted on heavy reliance on demand management policies for correcting maladjustments in external payments. Thus, developing countries have been required to curtail demand as a means of adjusting to changes in the external environment—such as the decline in growth of world trade, changes in energy prices, the declines in the availability of finance, soaring interest rates, and exchange rate variations, among others—even though these factors were already constricting their growth.[1]

Throughout most of the post–World War II period, the World Bank emphasized development lending to LDCs, while the International Monetary Fund loaned resources to help DCs and LDCs cope with balance-of-payments crises. In the 1980s, the Bank led DC and multi-lateral-donor coordination of loans to LDCs, increasing its external leverage. Although IMF direct credits to LDCs fell in the mid-1980s, the Fund retained influence not only through cooperation with the World Bank but also because the Bank, commercial banks, and bilateral lenders insisted on IMF approval of country stabilization programs before proceeding with funding.

Since traditional Bank long-term project lending affected only a small part of the economy and neglected the immediate or medium-run priorities of LDCs facing a debt-servicing crisis, in the late 1970s the Bank perceived the need for a new approach, policy-based lending.

The World Bank

In 1975, the World Bank established a "third window" between banking-standard and concessional loans: an interest subsidy account for discount loans for the poorest countries facing oil-price increases.[2] Although the Bank set up a Special Program of Assistance (SPA) in 1983 to ease the debt crisis, by the late 1980s critics, including some U.S. economists and members of Congress, voiced dissatisfaction with the Bank's minimal contribution to debt relief. The leadership of the Bank, while pointing out that 45 percent of its loans were to heavily indebted countries, argued, however, that the Bank's primary role was development lending for poor countries, not financial guarantees for commercial bank loans to middle-income countries.[3]

A late 1987 decision of the World Bank group (including the IDA), the IMF, and bilateral donors concentrated the SPA on low-income debt-distressed sub-Saharan countries. The SPA encompasses (1) increased IDA disbursements ($1 billion in 1988) for adjustment lending and supplemental adjustment credits, (2) IDA reflows and investment income for additional lending to countries with outstanding obligations to the World Bank, but no longer eligible to borrow from it, (3) credits from the IMF's Structural Adjustment Facility (SAF) ($0.4 billion in 1986–87) and Enhanced Structural Adjustment Facility (ESAF) with even more resources, (4) increased cofinancing of adjustment with other donors, and (5) greater debt relief, including cancellation of debt from overseas development assistance loans and concessional rescheduling for commercial debt from or guaranteed by creditor governments.

For SPA, sub-Saharan recipients need to be IDA-eligible, have a debt-service ratio of 30 percent or more in 1988–90, and be undertaking a World Bank or IMF adjustment program. Burundi, Central African Republic, The Gambia, Ghana, Guinea, Guinea-Bissau, Kenya, Madagascar, Malawi, Mali, Mauritania, Mozambique, Niger, São Tomé and Príncipe, Senegal, Tanzania, Togo, Uganda, and Zaïre were eligible in 1988, and Chad, Benin, and Somalia in 1989. A U.N. advisory group recommended that ESAF funds be above currently planned aid programs.[4]

SPA increased the external cash flow of eligible countries on terms suited to the low-income Sub-Sahara. Barriers to growth indicate protracted adjustment, necessitating SPA-type support for much of the 1990s. The World Bank–sponsored consultative group meeting, U.N. Development Program–sponsored roundtable conferences, and other consultative groups are important instruments for coordinating aid.[5]

Beginning in 1988, 10 percent of IDA reflows and investment income went to qualifying countries in proportion to their Bank interest payments. Besides contributions from the multilaterals, some funds are released during debt rescheduling and the EC contributed about one-fifth of the substantially undersubscribed second phase of SPA (1991–93).[6]

In September 1989, the Bank transferred $100 million from net income to establish a Debt Reduction Facility (DRF) to reduce commercial debt and debt-service burdens of the poorest debt-distressed countries, mostly in sub-Saharan Africa. The DRF provides grants to IDA-only countries of as much as $10 million to buy back commercial debt instruments. Since much of the debt of these countries has been discounted by 80 to 90 percent, a small amount of cash should have substantial impact in reducing debt stocks and service. The debt facility is open to countries with a Bank/Fund adjustment program and (in the Bank's judgment) a credible debt-management program.

Niger bought back its commercial bank debt of $108 million at 18 cents per dollar with $10 million DRF and $9.5 million from France and Switzerland in March 1991. The following June, Mozambique received $10 million DRF and $21 million from Sweden, Switzerland, the Netherlands, and France to buy back $308 million commercial debt. As of mid-1991, no other LDC had used the DRF. The Bank observed: "Much of the delay in drawing the resources of the facility is due to the reluctance of banks to participate, in part to avoid setting precedents for other countries [such as Brazil and middle-income countries] where their exposure is larger."[7]

Adjustment Loans

In 1979, the World Bank introduced structural adjustment loans (SALs), no longer tied to specific projects but intended for support of the balance of payments through fifteen-to-twenty-year loans, with three to five years' grace and interest rates only one-half percent above the Bank's borrowing costs (except for a front-end fee on new commitments). In the 1980s, Bank SALs were contingent on the IMF's approving the country for standby credit for balance-of-payments problems. Bank SALs (or SECALs) were complemented by IMF lending, which also included SALs and extended SALs (discussed below) in the late 1980s. In the early 1980s, soon after the SAL began, LDC growth and external balance problems worsened as a result of reduced terms of trade, rising real interest rates, the OECD recession, and other factors discussed in chapter 4.

In the first half of the 1980s, most adjustment lending was to middle-income countries, particularly in Latin America. Since then, the Bank/Fund has been increasingly aware of the chronic nature of adjustment, especially in low-income LDCs. The concept of adjustment has become more protracted and elastic, closely overlapping with development in the Bank's post–1989 publications, though not its policies (see below).

African countries received $0.7 billion in twelve adjustment loans, 1980–82, from the World Bank; $1.5 billion in twenty-four loans, 1983–85; and $3.6 billion in forty-five loans, 1986–88. In 1985, the Bank introduced the Special Facility for Africa (SFA) for DCs to increase their aid to African countries undertaking major reforms. Direct bilateral donors and the World Bank's Joint Program of Action for Sub-Saharan Africa contributed $2 billion to the SFA from mid-1985 to mid-1988 for adjustment financing. Additionally, Bank loans for technical assistance were increasingly oriented toward assisting adjustment.[8]

While SALs accounted for only 9 percent of Bank lending from 1979 to 1983 and had little impact on the most highly indebted countries, SALs comprised 25 percent of lending in 1987, when sub-Saharan Africa received 46 percent of the Bank's adjustment loans, but only 16 percent of SAL value.[9]

External disequilibrium may result from external shocks (unfavorable international economic events). The purposes of structural adjustment are to reduce the external deficit, to promote resumption of rapid growth, and to achieve changes that will prevent future internal or external disequilibrium. Thus, in the 1970s and 1980s, Malaysia adjusted by diversifying crops and raising productivity in response to declining rubber-price prospects, while Tanzania failed to adjust to falling sisal prices. Releases have been delayed in about three-fourths of the Bank's loans because of insufficient progress in fulfilling conditions. When SALs were successful, the Bank tended to have a small number of key conditions and took great care in monitoring programs. Recipient governments had more success when they understood and accepted the SAL, assigned responsibilities clearly, and had an institutional capacity to formulate policy. The World Bank requires government commitment to the SAL, realistic timetables, and flexibility in design and interpretation. SALs have increased the Bank's workload, including investigation, preparation, supervision, and monitoring, but this work is not as substantial as with the project lending of the 1970s.[10]

The major macroeconomic objective of structural adjustment programs (SAPs) is to improve the external balance and domestic fiscal balance; their microeconomic objective is to enhance resource efficiency by removing price distortions, by opening up competition, and by deregulation. ALs (adjustment loans) supporting government programs have medium-term objectives—targets for key macroeconomic (stabilization programs on the demand side) and sectoral variables (supply-side measures, including SALs and SECALs, or sectoral adjustment loans); the Bank also monitors specific government actions over twelve to eighteen months. The Bank tranches loans, meaning that disbursements depend on satisfactory compliance with previous stages of the SAL.[11] For example, Malawi received SAL I, $41 million, in 1981 to undertake price and balance-of-payments reform. SAL II, in 1984, which provided $55 million from the Bank's IDA soft-loan window, was contingent on the successful completion of Bank conditionality (conditions) for SAL I. Conditions for SAL II included removing the fertilizer subsidy to smallholder farmers, decontrolling consumer prices, increasing government revenue, and restructuring state-owned enterprises. SAL III (1986), which approved $40 million (together with Japanese, U.S., and West German financing of $22 million) after SAL II was largely fulfilled, stressed further subsidy removals, tax restructuring, increased industrial export competitiveness, and stimulating private trading in agriculture.[12]

The Bank usually supports broad macroeconomic restructuring before detailed sector reforms, as appropriate macro-policies are essential to improve incentives for tradable-goods production, the choice of production techniques, and assessment of relative profitability. Since countries cannot deal with all economic problems at once, the Bank asks for a series of operations, each supporting specific actions. SECALs, many of which focus on trade reform among highly indebted middle-income countries, account for more operations and dollars spent than SALs. For the low-income debt-distressed Sub-Sahara, the Bank recommends a greater commitment of IDA, other multilateral, and bilateral funds to cofinance SAPs.

The World Bank wanted LDCs to adjust to external disequilibrium by increasing efficiency through improved institutions and policies. External resources do not substitute for reform but allow adjustment at higher levels of consumption and investment than otherwise. SALs were intended to assist adjustment, to help design programs, to provide funds, and to be a catalyst for other external financing (as in Nigeria in 1986–88). With increased experience, the Bank's expectations concerning investment, external balance, production, employment, public-sector resource use, price policies, interest rates, reforms, and policy actions became more specific. SAL agreements indicated that Bank disbursements were contingent on specified measures to be taken by the recipient. Yet excessively detailed conditionality results in game playing by both the Bank and the sub-Saharan country, which may never expect to adhere to such rigorous requirements. Sometimes SAPs prescribe compensating policies to offset spillover effects, but these policies must consider social, political, and economic repercussions. Since many recipients receive assistance from both the Bank and Fund, the two agencies try to work collaboratively, although they often experience conflict.[13]

In 1989 the Bank's Commodity Risk Management and Finance Unit started technical assistance to help LDCs use international financial markets for risk management. The program complements the U.S. Treasury's Financial Technical Assistance Program, launched in 1987, which emphasizes institution building in managing external assets and international capital markets. The Bank's program helps state-owned enterprises (such as oil companies) develop the ability to manage external risks—especially those from commodity price changes.[14]

The IMF

A balance-of-payments equilibrium refers to an international balance on goods and services balance over the business cycle with no undue inflation, unemployment, tariffs and other protection, or exchange controls. The IMF provides ready credit equal to the reserve tranche (the country's original contribution of gold or foreign exchange, or 25 percent of its initial quota) to member nations with payments problems. Members borrowing from the IMF in excess of the reserve tranche agree to certain performance criteria, with emphasis on a long-run international balance and price stability. IMF standby arrangements assure members of the ability to borrow foreign exchange during a specified period up to a specified amount if they abide by the arrangement's terms. Fund conditionality, a quid pro quo for borrowing, includes the borrower's adopting adjustment policies to attain a viable payments position—a necessity for preserving the revolving nature of IMF resources. These policies may require that a government reduce budget deficits through increasing tax revenues and cutting back social spending, limit credit creation, achieve market-clearing prices, liberalize trade, devalue currency, eliminate price controls, or restrain public-sector employment and wage rates. The IMF monitors domestic credit, the exchange rate, debt targets, and other policy instruments closely for effectiveness. Even though the quantitative significance of IMF loans for LDC external deficits has been small even as late as the 1970s and 1980s, the seal of approval of the IMF, often the lender of last resort, is required before the World Bank, African Development Bank, and other bilateral and multilateral lenders provide assistance.

Policies generally shift internal relative prices from nontradable to tradable goods, promoting exports and "efficient" import substitution. While policies generally move purchasing power from urban to rural areas, consumers to investors, and labor to capital, sub-groups within these categories may be affected very differently; moreover, government functionaries who oversee and administer programs still possess discretion in distributing rewards and sanctions. Conditions attached to IMF credits provoke member (especially LDC) discontent, as in Nigeria's anti-SA "riots" in May–June 1989. Furthermore, the long lags from negotiation to commitment to implementation under the 1980s' broader definition of conditionality make evaluation difficult.[15]

Beyond these IMF credit lines are an extended facility, 150 percent of the quota, based on a detailed medium-term program; a supplementary financing facility subsidy account, 140 percent of quota (financed by repayments from trust fund loans and voluntary contributions) to support standby arrangements for eligible low-income LDCs under previous programs; a compensatory and contingency financing facility (CFF), 75 percent of quota, for a temporary shortfall in export earnings or excess costs of cereal imports beyond the country's control; buffer stock financing, 50 percent of the quota, to stabilize export earnings; an oil facility, funds borrowed from oil-exporting countries to lend at competitive interest to LDCs with balance-of-payments deficits; and a subsidy account, contributed by twenty-five DCs and high-income oil exporters that made available interest subsidies to low-income countries during the oil-price peaks of 1980–81 and 1990. To illustrate this account, the IMF's intermediation enabled India to borrow $2.85 billion from Saudi Arabia in 1981 at an interest rate of 11 percent, compared to 18 percent in commercial markets.

Yet between 1983 and 1985, most special funding beyond direct IMF credits dried up, with net annual lending to LDCs falling from $11.4 billion to $0.2 billion. Beginning in 1986–87, the IMF added its SAF. A U.N. advisory group recommended that CFF be restored to its role in the late 1970s of being "a low-conditionality, relatively automatic, and quickly available source of funds for short-term contingency needs." The U.N. group indicated that CFF, which has had an average grant element of 20 percent since 1987, should come from new contributions or IMF gold sales and should be concessional (at IDA rates) when involving low-income Africa.

Additionally, the IMF's ESAF, backed by bilateral donors beginning in 1987, supports borrowing by the Fund's poorest members at 0.1 percent annual interest with five years' grace. ESAF and SALs were financed by recycling the IMF Trust Fund (from the sale of IMF gold) and by Japan and European countries with external surpluses (but not the United States, which had an international deficit and opposed IMF long-term concessional aid). As an example of an IMF funding package, in 1988 the IMF approved $85 million ($35 million as a SAL, $18 million as a supplementary subsidy account, and the rest as standby credit) for Togo, whose export earnings from cocoa, coffee, palm products, and peanuts had declined from 1985 to 1987. Another example of IMF funding was a gradual five-year (rather than the usual 18- to 24-month) Enhanced Structural Adjustment Program, 1990–91/1994–95, showcased in Zimbabwe. This program, which involved devaluing the Zimbabwean dollar and cutting the civil service, was labeled "ESAP's fables" by a local computer programmer.[16]

While the collective vote of the Third World's LDCs and high-income oil-exporters in the IMF, based on member quotas, is 40 percent, LDCs often support DCs in laying down conditions for borrowers so as not to jeopardize the IMF's financial base. But African finance and planning officials feel that Africa has little voice in the Fund or Bank, pointing out that the original post–World War II agreement has not been meaningfully changed.

African borrowers say that IMF conditionality is excessively intrusive. Thus, for example, in 1988, in exchange for IMF lending, Togo relinquished much policy discretion, agreeing to reduce its fiscal deficit, to restrain current expenditures, to select investment projects more rigorously, to privatize some public enterprise, and to liberalize trade. Yet the IMF must be satisfied that a borrower can repay a loan. Lacking adjustment by surplus nations, there may be few alternatives to monetary and fiscal restrictions or domestic-currency devaluation for eliminating a chronic balance-of-payments deficit.

African critics, supported by a commission of twenty diplomats from five continents chaired by former West German Chancellor Willy Brandt, charge that the IMF presumes that international payments problems can be solved only by reducing social programs, cutting subsidies, depreciating currency, and restructuring similar to Togo's

1988 program. According to the Brandt report, the Fund's insistence on drastic measures in short time periods imposes unnecessary burdens on low-income countries that not only reduce basic-needs attainment but occasionally lead to "IMF riots" and the downfall of governments.[17] These critics prefer that the IMF concentrate on results rather than means.

IMF leverage to encourage African austerity in the face of reduced funds and internal political opposition was less in the 1980s than in the 1970s. Yet the World Bank's adjustment loans consolidated IMF conditionality, 1980–91. The IMF became gatekeeper and watchdog for the international financial system, because an IMF standby agreement served as a necessary condition for Bank ALs and commercial bank negotiation. Moreover, the Bank led donor coordination between DCs and multilateral agencies, increasing external leverage. Many African recipients, lacking personnel, abdicated responsibility for coordinating external aid, increasing Bank and donor influence.[18]

The Bank and IMF face the difficulty of making prudent loans to borrowers that private lenders have declared uncreditworthy. The main method of enforcement is the threat of cutoffs of new loans, as setting other conditions for a sovereign borrower is limited.

Since the late 1980s, the IMF, with the World Bank, has played the central role in imposing conditions on Africa, so that the Fund has become more than the lender of last resort, with the Paris Club of official creditors, OECD governments' aid and loans, and commercial bankers linking support to IMF agreement. Through weighted voting, the United States has a substantial influence on quota and loan decisions and can, with the support of the United Kingdom, Japan, France, and Germany, block all critical decisions. The negotiation between the IMF or Bank (backed by the resources and leverage of country donors and DC capital markets) and sub-Saharan governments, who rarely ask for Bank/Fund assistance except in dire difficulties, is hardly one of equals. Many sub-Saharan countries agree to programs merely to acquire Fund/Bank resources or seals of approval for acquiring foreign aid, loans, investment, or debt relief and may not be committed to stabilization conditions or targets. Indeed, Edwards contends that Bank/Fund adjustment programs can best be described as emergency stabilization programs geared toward increasing trade balances in very short periods of time. As Nyerere complains: "When we reject IMF conditions we hear the threatening whisper; 'Without accepting our conditions you will not get any money, and you will get no other money.' " African finance and planning ministry officials perceive the Fund as an intermediary between creditors and debtors. A Fund staff member commented in 1987:

> The Fund is perceived by both creditor and debtor countries as being in the center of the debt issue. Creditors expect the Fund to ensure that debtors play according to the rules of the game by following prudent policies. The rest of the time, however, the Fund is treated with benign neglect. Programs tend to be, at best, negotiated modifications to initial proposals by the Fund or Bank.[19]

A greater stress by the IMF on growth and efficiency in adjustment programs and lesser emphasis on reducing domestic demand and attaining external balance would reduce conflicts with the Sub-Sahara. Furthermore, the recommendations of the IMF would be more credible if it utilized independent experts trusted by both donor and recipient to report periodically on the program's progress. Or the IMF and other agencies might spur creation of an expert international secretariat trusted by both donors and recipients and sensitive to local political, social, and cultural conditions.[20]

The question for an LDC with a major debt problem is not whether to adjust but how to adjust—on their own or with IMF or World Bank assistance and conditions. Streeten asks why borrowing countries do not pursue AL policies on their own without financial incentives if, as the IMF contends, its imposition of loan conditions is in the interest of the borrower. Answer: Borrowers' policymakers may be ignorant and need instruction; may see the relationship in power rather than business terms; may analyze, forecast, and assess administrative and institutional capacity and transitional costs otherwise than does the IMF; and may have objectives, tradeoffs, ideologies, risk premiums, and time preferences (such as an existing government eager to stay in power that emphasizes short-run gains) different from those of the IMF.[21]

Sub-Saharan countries resist Bank/Fund adjustment programs because of genuine doubts that they will work, fear that the Bank/Fund has a narrow concept of structural adjustment, and the perception that vested interests will resist change. Adjustment programs rarely work, because of unilateral and doctrinaire design, insufficient coordination between donors and funding organizations, a lack of adaptation of programs to local goals, and a disregard of terms of trade.[22]

The IMF expanded its role from short-term lending for balance-of-payments purposes (emphasizing the restriction of domestic demand) to greater stress on longer-term growth (encompassing improved allocative efficiency). For example, IMF SALs from 1986 to 1990 provided concessional assistance for medium-term macroeconomic and adjustment programs to low-income countries (especially in Africa) facing unanticipated external shocks or chronic balance-of-payments problems. When the IMF arranges concessional components, recipients can be more flexible on exchange rates, budgets, money supply, and public-enterprise operations.[23]

However, IMF SALs have introduced confusion in role as the IMF, like the Bank, has been taking a longer-term perspective and has added the monitoring of sectoral and microeconomic policies to that of macroeconomic policies. The Bank has evolved from project to sector loans to SALs, increasing its involvement in sectoral and macroeconomic policies. Indeed, since 1979, the Bank has set conditions for recipients' exchange rates, a traditional IMF role. The expanding roles of the Bank and Fund require greater cooperation than before between them, and among them and bilateral agencies.

Since the late 1980s, the IMF has drafted a Policy Framework Program (PFP), amended and agreed on by the Bank and borrowing government, which establishes a joint understanding of the latter's economic situation and policies essential for stabilization and adjustment. Some IMF officials also sent the PFP to bilateral donors for response before setting out a final PFP with the recipient country, so donors are involved without giving or withholding approval of the plans. A PFP is a requirement for a government borrowing under the IMF's SAF or ESAF. Yet many doubt that the PFP's statements of planned reforms are pinpointed enough to be used to coordinate reform or avoid policy conflict.[24]

The Fund/Bank drafted a PFP for Nigeria's Bank SAL for 1989–91 and a 1989–90 IMF ESAF (not drawn on). Beginning in late 1989, the administration of General Ibrahim Babangida abandoned the concept of a fixed five-year plan, introducing a three-year rolling plan for the first time for 1990–92 in the context of a more comprehensive fifteen-to-twenty-year plan. A rolling plan is revised at the end of each year, so estimates, targets, and projects are added for another year. Thus planners would have revised the 1990–92 three-year rolling plan at the end of 1990, issuing a new plan for 1991 to 1993. In effect a plan is renewed at the end of each year, but the number of years remains the same as the plan rolls forward in time. In early 1991, the Bank pledged grants to cover shortfalls in Nigeria's rolling plan.

Internal and External Balances

The following national-income equation shows the relationship between savings, investment, and the international balance on goods and services (that is, exports minus imports of goods and services).

$$\text{Savings} - \text{Investment} = \text{Exports} - \text{Imports},$$

where savings and imports, but not investment and exports, are dependent on national income.

In Africa, the financial institutions (banks, stock and bond markets, mutual funds, social security, pension and provident funds, insurance funds, and government debt instruments) needed to bring savers and investors together are poorly developed. Thus, the leading form of investment in Africa is from savings by firms,[25] ranging from a subsistence farmer clearing land to a joint stock company or proprietorship reinvesting profits in plant, equipment, machinery, buildings, and inventory. Still, the equation indicates that if an economy's savings (refraining from consumption from current income) are not adequate, it can increase investment or capital formation from imports in excess of exports (a current-account deficit), which necessitates borrowing, attracting investment, or receiving grants from abroad (that is, an inflow of capital from abroad).

Internal balance refers to full employment; external balance refers to exports equal to imports. Figure 5.1 shows Keynesian income determination. The upward-sloping line shows Savings (S) minus Investment (I) (net domestic savings). The downward-sloping line shows Exports (X) minus Imports (M) (net exports). The intersection of S − I with X − M indicates net savings and net exports on the vertical axis, and on the horizontal axis, an equilibrium income (Y_E) short of the full-employment level of income (Y_F).

A simple algebraic manipulation changes our equation to the macroeconomic equilibrium where

$$\text{Savings} + \text{Imports (leakages)} = \text{Investment} + \text{Exports (injections)},$$

aggregate demand equals aggregate supply, or expenditures equal income.

Sub-Saharan countries facing a persistent external deficit can (1) borrow overseas without changing economic policies (feasible if the deficit is temporary), (2) increase trade restrictions and exchange controls, which reduce efficiency and may violate international rules but may be tolerated in LDCs, or (3) undertake contractionary monetary and fiscal policies or expenditure-reducing policies (a shift of the (S −

Figure 5.1. Internal and External Balances

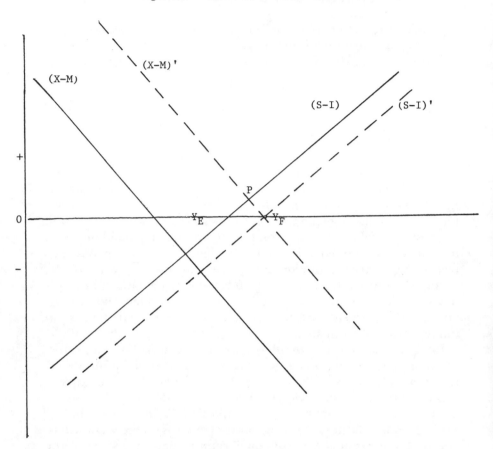

I) curve upward and to the left), which sacrifice internal goals of employment and growth for external balance. Remedy (3), which critics call "leeching" after the nineteenth-century medical practice of using bloodsuckers to extract "unhealthy blood" from the sick, works with sufficient regularity to be considered the creditor community's least-risk choice. An economy, if depressed sufficiently, will at some point reduce its balance-of-payments deficit. And indeed, World Bank evidence for thirty countries, 1980–85, indicates that LDCs undergoing structural adjustment gave up domestic employment and spending objectives to cut their payments deficit.[26] If the deficit is chronic, additional borrowing without policy change only postpones the need to adjust. Although the Bank's publications since 1989 indicate a joining with the ECA and UNICEF consensus to seek growth, stabilization, and adjustment over a longer period, with greater attention to social goals than before, there is no evidence that Bank adjustment programs have changed from requiring improved external balance in the short run (two years or so).[27] Thus Bank or Fund lending is still usually conditioned on (4) expenditure switching through devaluing local currencies. For long-term adjustment, the Bank/Fund prescribes supply-side adjustments through infrastructure, market development, institutional changes, price (including interest rate) reforms, reduced trade and payments controls, and technology inducement to improve efficiency and capacity to facilitate growth with external balance, but these changes take too much time for short-run adjustment.

Consider the intersection of $(X - M)$ and $(S - I)$ in Figure 5.1, corresponding to an external deficit with unemployment. To attain both external or internal balances, the country combines expenditure-switching (depreciating domestic currency) and expenditure-increasing (expansionary monetary and fiscal) policies.

Depreciating the currency—for example, increasing the shilling's (domestic currency) price of the dollar from $Sh15 = \$1$ to $Sh20 = \$1$—results in the country's export prices falling in dollars. If the sums of the price elasticities of demand for exports plus imports are at least roughly equal to one, the country's goods and services balance will improve. Thus net exports $(X - M)$ increase (say) to $(X - M)'$, an international surplus. At the same time the net exports and net savings schedules intersect at a point further to the right (P), corresponding to higher income and employment, but still at less than full employment.

Increasing demand through reduced interest rates or a rising government budget deficit (higher government spending or lower tax rates), an expenditure-increasing policy, lowers net savings $(S - I)$ to $(S - I)'$. The new net savings and net exports schedules intersect at a full employment level of income, Y_F, with a zero balance of goods and services balance, attaining both internal and external balances.

The preceding model of two balances, while oversimplified, shows the cost of using austerity measures—contractionary monetary and fiscal policies—prescribed by the IMF.

Reforms

From 1979 to 1988, more than half of the forty-five sub-Saharan countries adopted macroeconomic reform programs under World Bank auspices to reduce an external disequilibrium, frequently to help countries to adapt to changes in the global environment. These programs were often launched in conjunction with IMF stabilization programs to bring aggregate demand in line with aggregate supply. During the same period, sometimes in overlapping programs, eighteen sub-Saharan countries borrowed to initiate structural adjustment and fourteen did so to support sectoral reforms.

The Bank/Fund position is that "evidence from a wide range of countries suggests that growth is better sustained under policies that minimize price distortion and are outward oriented in the sense of exposing products to international price competition."[28]

In the Sub-Sahara, a relatively high number (more than half) of these World Bank SALs emphasized policy measures related to the exchange rate, agricultural prices, the government budget, and public enterprise.[29] (However, the francophone West African currencies, the CFAF pegged to the French franc, lacked the exchange-rate flexibility of other LDC currencies.)

The Bank ranks the success of LDC adjustment programs high but those in the Sub-Sahara lower. Changes requiring less government spending, restructuring, or institutional changes work best because of less resistance. The policy areas where implementation was most successful involved prices—exchange rates, interest rates, or energy or agricultural prices (to spur incentives for farm output). Additionally, the IMF reports substantial success in reducing price controls (as in Ghana, Malawi, and Pakistan) but less progress in rationalizing industrial tax incentives. The Bank stresses that reforms must continue after the loan disbursement ceases.[30]

The World Bank and IMF, in adjustment programs, have asked African countries to raise producer prices and to liberalize marketing and pricing systems, especially for food crops. Currency devaluations are said to be particularly important in raising export prices and the farmers' share of export value. The Bank and IMF believe that these measures, together with government restraining nominal wage increases in the public sector, raise farm income relative to urban incomes. While most sub-Saharan states set prices and retain a monopsony on export prices, since the mid 1980s Guinea, Malawi, Mali, Niger, Nigeria, Somalia, and Zaïre have either abolished fixed prices or permitted private traders. Concerning all but one of these countries, the Bank/U.N. Development Programme position is that real food and export crop prices rose from liberalization, 1983 to 1986. In Burkina, Ghana, and Madagascar, official farm prices increased faster than inflation, 1980–85, through higher world prices, reduced domestic taxation, or currency devaluation, according to the Bank and the

United Nations. But they state that rapid inflation in Sierra Leone, Somalia, Sudan, and Tanzania continued to erode farmer income and purchasing power through 1985 despite nominal farm price increases. Another indicator of increased agricultural production incentives in the Sub-Sahara was the increase in the nominal protection coefficient (NPC), or producer price divided by maximum price (maximum price being export price less processing and marketing costs), from 0.7 in 1976 to 1.1 in 1987 (although NPCs overstate protection with widespread overvalued domestic currencies in the 1980s). Moreover, the Bank and the United Nations underscore the improvement in agricultural production in the late 1980s. Altogether, this suggests to the Bank/U.N. "that Sub-Saharan Africa can have adjustment with growth, and an improving standard of living, even when the external environment is not favorable."[31]

The Bank and the United Nations, to complete the analysis, need to examine changes in both agricultural terms of trade and export volume. During the period before their analysis, 1977 to 1983, LDC export volume in agriculture increased by 21 percent while its terms of trade fell 30 percent, so export purchasing power fell 15 percent (1.21 volume × 0.703 terms of trade = 0.85). During their period of focus, 1983 to 1990, agricultural export volume rose 45 percent while terms of trade declined 21 percent, so increased export purchasing power from the 45 percent expansion in export volume was only 14 percent (1.45 × 0.787 = 1.14).[32]

Empirical studies indicate a low elasticity of supply in the short run for agricultural goods but a high long-run elasticity unless foreign-exchange shortages, inadequate infrastructure (transport, communication, power, health, education research and extension services), managerial scarcity, weak financial institutions, and a lack of technology limit growth. Government measures to stimulate output with farm price decontrol will not work when, as in Argentina in the 1940s, farmers feel the more favorable prices would not be permanent.[33]

A *single country* exporting agricultural goods would often be a price taker with substantial scope in expanding export receipts as it faces an infinitely elastic demand curve alongside a long-run elastic supply curve. However, as indicated in chapter 4, a single-country analysis suffers from a fallacy of composition: What is true for one country is not necessarily true of numerous African and other poor LDCs under pressure from Bank/Fund adjustment programs to expand agricultural and other primary-product exports. As these LDCs expanded supply, relative prices fell substantially. Primary-product export growth reduced terms of trade, thus decreasing export purchasing power, 1977–83, and only increasing this power slightly, 1983–90. The high DC effective rate of protection also blocks technologically feasible primary-product processing and light industry, tightening the export noose blocking export expansion as an engine of growth for sub-Saharan Africa and many other low-income countries. Widespread currency devaluations under Bank/Fund adjustment programs also spur export expansion in primary products, suggesting that the export trap, rather than anti-farm bias, may be the impulse supporting African and LDC resistance to devaluations.

Sixteen adjustment programs, more than half the programs (outside the CFA franc zone), tried to reform the exchange rate. African ministry officials at World Bank policy seminars in 1987–88 argued that market exchange rates (auctions and interbank markets) depersonalize and depoliticize exchange rates. Modified auctions, like the Régime d'Importations Libéralisées in Madagascar, can increase confidence in the banking system by eliminating corruption in foreign-exchange allocation. To work, auctions need to be more than a temporary expedient, monopolies must be controlled, and foreign exchange must be adequately funded. In Zambia in the late 1980s, where the auction was underfunded, funds were earmarked for specific sectors, and credit availability was delayed, excess demand for foreign currency was not eliminated. In Nigeria and Ghana, however, the foreign-exchange auction caused the gap between the free and the official market tiers to narrow during the late 1980s. Additionally, more efficient foreign-exchange rationing resulted in more productive use of resources.[34]

Transitional problems result in inflation and shortages before consumers switch to domestic replacements for foreign food and consumer goods, before export and import replacement industries expand capacity in response to more favorable prices, and before buyers of imported inputs and capital goods can shift to domestic suppliers. In light of these problems, some economists suggest a dual exchange rate, with the first a near market rate (for example, Sh20 = \$1) used to reduce controls, spur exports and import substitutes, and increase efficiency; and the second, perhaps the old rate overvaluing domestic currency (for instance, Sh 10 = \$1) set to dampen short-run inflationary pressures from price-inelastic foreign goods like food, industrial inputs, and capital goods (or their domestic substitutes shifting to exports) or to maintain foreign-exchange commitments for foreign corporations repatriating interest and dividends.[35] Additionally, earlier we suggested a dual rate to prevent booming natural-resource exports that appreciate domestic currency from making other exports

112

more costly in foreign currencies, thus increasing foreign competition and unemployment.

The debt crisis worsened public finances, since debtor governments usually assumed private and financial-sector external liabilities. Moreover, the fall in external capital flows required increased internal financing of the deficit, resulting in increased inflation, output stagnation, and declining private investment. Crisis countries like Ghana, Nigeria, Tanzania, Zambia, and Senegal relied heavily on implicit taxes on financial intermediaries to finance the deficit domestically.

In the 1970s and early 1980s, these sub-Saharan money markets have been highly oligopolistic even when domestic banks and lenders have been important, as in Ghana, Nigeria, and Tanzania. Government financial repression, with ceilings on interest rates, the domestic price of foreign currency, and other financial prices, reduced the size of the financial system and economic growth.

The motive for African financial restriction was to encourage those financial institutions and instruments from which the government can expropriate seigniorage (i.e., can claim resources in return for controlling currency issue and credit expansion). The state favored and protected an oligopolistic banking system whose reserve requirements and obligatory holdings of government bonds enabled government to tap savings at low interest rates. Authorities suppressed private bond and equity markets through transactions taxes, special taxes on income from capital, and inconducive laws because of the difficulty of extracting seigniorage from private assets. The state imposed interest-rate ceilings to stifle private-sector competition in fund raising. Imposing these ceilings, foreign exchange controls, high reserve requirements, and restrictions on private capital markets increased the flow of domestic resources to the public sector without higher taxes, inflation, or interest rates.

Banks engaged in nonprice rationing of loans, facing pressure for loans to those with political connections but otherwise allocating credit according to transaction costs, all of which left no opportunity for charging a premium for risky projects. The Sub-Sahara's financially repressive regimes, uncompetitive markets, and banking bureaucracies not disciplined by market and profit tests encouraged the adoption of inefficient lending criteria. Countries that eschewed taxes on financial intermediation for borrowing internally at market rates, such as Colombia, Indonesia, South Korea, Turkey, and Thailand, avoided rescheduling and maintained access to foreign capital in the 1980s.[36]

The World Bank/IMF position assumes that profits are a reliable indicator of public-sector efficiency and that small-scale enterprise (especially the informal sector of petty traders, artisans, repairpersons, and cottage industrialists) can play an important role in industrial restructuring. But the Bank-sponsored liberalization in Zambia in 1985–87 virtually destroyed small-scale industry, as only a few large concerns had the resources to buy foreign exchange at auction or to borrow from banks at decontrolled interest rates. Moreover, most informal activities arose from a lack of formal-sector employment or the need to supplement formal-sector wages insufficient to support a family on even the most basic diet. An extensive study of the informal sector in Dar es Salaam, Tanzania, during 1987–88 indicates that more than three-fourths of the enterprises were started during Tanzania's stagnation period, 1980–87. The number of self-employed women increased from 7 percent in 1971 to 66 percent in 1987. Two-thirds of the women began their activities because their husbands' wages were insufficient for survival. The bulk of activities were very small-scale, such as making or selling items like tea, pastries, porridge, soup, kerosene, flour, and so forth, hardly indicating a vibrant entrepreneurial class ready to expand employment opportunities. Most income earned was for food consumption, not capital accumulation. A number of women left skilled or semiskilled occupations as instructors, nurses, and accountants, specialties emphasized by the World Bank as needing expansion, for jobs in the informal economy. The study also found children dropping out of school to assist their parents, contributing to a falling primary enrollment rate in the 1980s. Many felt that they no longer needed to attend once they could read or write, since they would end up with unskilled informal-sector jobs anyway.[37]

Some African countries have established intrinsically unviable activities, building capacity far in excess of market needs and management capabilities. Sub-Saharan industrial policy must recognize the small domestic markets, the limited (often falling) import capacities due to debt crises, the limited industrial capabilities, and the necessity of receiving appropriate DC technological transfers without substantial MNC domination. The Sub-Sahara should not overestimate the high productivity possible with imported, capital-intensive high technology, but it needs to stress learning by doing. The small-scale sectors need to be encouraged, even in the export sector. Africa's comparative advantage is in goods with simple production technology, protected by high transport costs, using domestic materials, or based on local resources such as agro-based industries, textiles, paper, wood, cement, simple metal products, and some chemicals. Nigeria, with a large resource endowment, and Zimbabwe, with advanced capabilities, might be exceptions.[38] Yet Africa's slow expansion in labor-intensive

114

manufacturers and low-level processing exports results partly from the highest DC protection in commodities in which LDCs can best compete.

Public enterprise in the early 1980s contributed 15 percent of GDP in sub-Saharan Africa, compared to 12 percent in Latin America and 3 percent in Asia. World Bank- and IMF-sponsored adjustment programs in twenty-six sub-Saharan countries, 1980–88, stressed rehabilitation, divestiture, privatization, market-clearing prices, improved efficiency, and improved accounting and auditing systems of public enterprises, contributing to a slower expansion of the public sector in the 1980s than in the 1970s. Aggregate 1987 country profit rates for SOEs ranged from 1.4 percent in Zambia to −4.3 percent for The Gambia, a median of −0.6 percent for twenty-one countries, meaning a deterioration of capital resources, even though SOEs frequently enjoy monopoly privileges. For sub-Saharan Africa, net financial flows from government to public enterprises were 10 to 15 percent of government fiscal deficits in the late 1980s, or up to 1 percent of GDP. The investments and operating losses of public enterprises accounted for at least 15 percent of domestic and external borrowing. In Benin, SOEs received 45 percent of domestic credit and a large percentage of external financing. Public firms that borrow heavily from domestic banks and fail to service their debt weaken the banking system and crowd out other borrowers.[39] Many sub-Saharan countries restrict the entry of new firms and rarely close down inefficient firms, thus defeating the market's creative destruction, by which an industry's old, high-cost producers are replaced by new, low-cost enterprises.[40] Yet public firms' losses sometimes result not from inefficiency but from the necessity to perform social functions, including provision of output at prices less than the market.

Conclusion

The major macroeconomic goals of Bank/Fund structural and sectoral adjustment and IMF stabilization programs are an international balance-of-payments equilibration and an internal government budgetary balance. Microeconomic objectives, primarily from World Bank adjustment programs, are to improve resource allocative efficiency through increasing competition and reducing state intervention in prices. In the 1980s, the World Bank led donor coordination of loans to Africa, while the IMF, despite substantial reductions in lending, 1980–86, retained influence through the World Bank and commercial banks approving loans contingent on an IMF standby arrangement. By 1987, the Bank, the IDA (the Bank's soft-loan window), the IMF, and bilateral donors put more emphasis on special assistance to least-developed debt-distressed sub-Saharan countries.

Reform programs under Bank/Fund auspices have had only limited success. First, the Bank and Fund conducted a single-country analysis, failing to consider how simultaneous export expansion by numerous LDCs, experiencing high export concentration and responding to adjustment pressures, can increase supply and depress price. Second, the Bretton Woods twins neglected the effects of external shocks such as declining terms of trade. Third, the World Bank and IMF did not anticipate the domination of foreign-exchange auctions by only a few large companies. Fourth, the Bank/Fund overlooked inflation, due to a low elasticity of supply of output, expanding as a result of adjustment. Fifth, the IMF and Bank underestimated the way the transition to trade, exchange-rate, and capital-market liberalization can exacerbate inflation, domestic budget deficits, and current-account deficits (see chapter 7).

The case studies of five African countries in the next chapter suggest that during periods no longer than a decade, Bank/Fund programs, while sometimes enhancing these countries' ability to service their debts, rarely increased investment rates or restored external equilibrium.

6

Case Studies of World Bank and IMF Adjustment Programs

■

When did the IMF become an International Ministry of Finance?
When did nations agree to surrender to it their power of decision
making?
—Tanzanian President Julius K. Nyerere (1980)

The new SAL soon revealed itself as the offspring of Janus, smiling
with one face as it delivered welcome foreign exchange, frowning with
the other as it insisted on the performance of politically dangerous
and administratively complex tasks.
—Mosley, Harrigan, and Toye

This chapter examines Bank/Fund adjustment programs in five sub-
Saharan countries—Tanzania, Zambia, Ghana, Nigeria, and Senegal—in the 1980s and early 1990s. Understanding the problems that
specific countries encounter when adjusting internally and externally
should help us with our critical assessment in chapter 7.

Tanzania

In 1967, six years after independence, President Nyerere's Arusha
Declaration announced the nationalization of manufacturing enterprises, which were under control of the National Development Corporation (NDC), a holding company for state-owned industries. Most
expropriated property was owned by Asians or other foreign interests.
NDC's surpluses, as well as the gains of the nationalized banking and
financial institutions, increased substantially beginning in 1967. In the
first few years, industrial enterprise management and organization

117

did not change much, as NDC had management contracts or partnerships with multinational corporations (MNCs), often former owners. In the 1970s, public-sector employment increased rapidly, overhead costs rose, profits declined, and industrial concentration increased.[1]

In rural areas, Arusha launched *ujamaa* (literally, "familyhood"), implying communal village production units. Ujamaa socialism encouraged collective efforts, avoided wide wealth disparities, and nationalized land. The ruling party, TANU (the Tanganyika African National Union, subsequently the Chama Cha Mapinduzi, or CCM), pressed for a major state role in establishing "ujamaa villages," which would use existing technology but benefit from economies of a larger labor force.[2] From 1967 to 1976, the percentage of the rural population living in these villages increased from zero to 91.3 percent.[3] Another landmark was the 1974–76 "villagization," a resettling of peasants into larger villages, which facilitated rural collectivization and the extension of bureaucratic clientelism into the village.

Tanzania's bureaucracy grew rapidly after the 1967 Arusha Declaration and 1972 "decentralization," which increased central government personnel in the regions. The total established posts in the Tanzania civil service rose from 65,708 to 295,353 (a 349 percent increase), 1966–80. From 1966 to 1976, *total* economic growth increased 4 percent yearly, wage employment 3 percent, and civil service employment 13 percent.[4]

After Arusha, state officials controlled channels of access and distribution in the economy, giving officials from the national to village level many opportunities for capricious and corrupt dealings, with large MNCs on down to petty traders. Corruption especially damages socialist regimes like Tanzania by undermining their egalitarian principles of income redistribution, poverty reduction, and majority rule. Amin laments: "Austerity, the revolutionary effort to use new and less costly methods, has not resisted the appetites of the new bureaucracy."[5]

Nyerere, ten years after the Arusha Declaration, observed that most Tanzanians were poor, many had lower standards of living than in 1967, inequality was high, and the country was neither socialist nor self-reliant. He pointed out:

> I am a very poor prophet. In 1956 I was asked how long it would take Tanganyika to become independent. I thought 10 to 12 years. We became independent 6 years later! In 1967 a group of the youth who were marching in support of the Arusha Declaration asked me how long it would take Tanzania to become socialist. I thought 30 years. I was wrong again: I am now sure it will take us much longer.[6]

In 1983, Nyerere, asked to name his greatest achievement, responded: "I think I would still give the same answer: that we have survived."[7]

Tanzania was hurt economically in the 1970s by rising oil prices (1973–75), the disbandment in 1977 of the East African Community (with Kenya and Uganda), and the Uganda war and occupation (1978–80), with their widespread shortages. Shivji contends that, while these factors were significant, the most important cause of Tanzania's economic crisis was the inability of the state class to increase (or even maintain) the transfer of resources from the peasants through taxes and unfavorable prices. Peasants had begun to resist this exploitation by switching from cash to food crops or operating on the black market.

Ujamaa socialism and egalitarianism increasingly collided with the actions of the state class, with its mushrooming racketeering, embezzlement, and accumulation. To workers and peasants, economic liberalization meant their paying for social services, while the state class was untouched and the saboteurs of ujamaa were being rehabilitated.[8]

While Tanzania rejected an IMF accord in 1981, including the removal of subsidies for maizemeal, events in the next five years, including the continuing breakdown of social benefits and decline in living standards under ujamaa, made the country receptive to IMF market reform. Supporters of liberalization were emboldened after an ambitious government plan for export and food self-sufficiency, the National Economic Survival Program, failed in 1982 after one year. As socialist rhetoric cooled and a defensive Nyerere admitted the validity of individual property and private enterprise, supporters of Bank/Fund programs, such as the Chamber of Commerce, the Department of Economics at the University of Dar es Salaam, and some bureaucrats and traders, dominated the debate on economic policy, limited to the affluent and educated classes. From 1982 to 1986, the political leadership undertook adjustment, implementing wage cuts, introducing school fees, cutting public-sector employment, increasing maizemeal and farm producer prices, removing gasoline subsidies, allowing the use of foreign exchange by exporters (or black-market operators), and devaluing the shilling, but opposing privatization and greater accountability for the nationalized sectors. Beginning in 1985, new President Ali Hassan Mwinyi and his allies, in opposition to ruling party Chairman Nyerere, dominated the closed debate, arguing for IMF adjustment programs that they claimed to be mere extensions of the previous liberalization. In 1986, following petroleum shortages, the country encountered difficulties in obtaining interna-

119

tional credit, the piling up of cash crops from lack of transport, severe water shortages, and an increased incidence of cholera and AIDS. A five-year fall in export purchasing power and the lack of major donor support also helped contribute to the failure of internal economic reforms.

In 1986, the Tanzanian government signed an IMF accord for $65.4 million standby credit for 1986–88. Nyerere's support by the time of the IMF agreement legitimized the program for most Tanzanians. The government agreed to substantial devaluation, removal of maize flour and fertilizer subsidies, price and foreign-exchange decontrol, public-sector layoffs, liberalized imports, curbs on monetary expansion, domestic credit ceilings, reduced income-tax rates, public-sector enterprise reforms, reduced government spending, private competition in wholesaling and retailing, long-run contracts for farm land leases, and other market-oriented changes that the leadership had rejected in 1981. In 1987, Tanzania received $42.5 million in structural adjustment loans from the IMF in tandem with $147.0 million concessional aid from the IDA, with forty years to repay at no interest charge. By 1987, state-owned enterprises (SOEs) in sisal, livestock, timber, shipping, bicycles, domestic appliances, trade, and general foods were sold to private entrepreneurs; many workers in SOEs were retrenched; and many foreign firms returned to control factories and plantations.

The late 1980s also saw the culmination of the scaling back of state-delivered universal primary education, free health services, and free clean water for all, which were features of the egalitarian socialist ideology of the 1970s. Western (even Nordic) donors reduced their support for education by more than 50 percent from the 1970s to 1980s. By 1990, many primary schools lacked desks, books, or chairs, and poor parents had no funds for school fees. And the depressed industrial economy could not absorb the school graduates, most of whom disdained farm work. Moreover, the health budget fell from per capita spending of $3 in 1973 to less than $1 in 1988. Even expenditures on established programs such as child immunization and tuberculosis control were cut back.[9]

The IMF stressed devaluation and foreign-exchange decontrols to improve the external balance and agriculture's relative domestic prices. However, Tanzania experienced many of the same difficulties undermining devaluation's positive effect on adjustment that are mentioned in chapter 7, such as rising input costs, continuing inflation, and low short-run trade elasticities.

The annual growth of GDP per capita, 1985–88 (in constant 1985 prices), was −0.6 percent, a continuation of the decline before IMF adjustment. Even the depressed demand from this negative growth failed to bring about external adjustment, as Tanzania's current-account deficit remained at $375 million from 1985 to 1988 and increased to $426 million in 1990. Consumer prices, increasing at more than 30 percent annually in 1984–85, rose at about the same yearly rate from 1986 to 1990.[10] Real minimum wages, which were 52 in 1980 (1970 = 100), fell to 23 in 1986 and to 17 (an additional one-fourth) in 1988. The government removed the subsidy on maizemeal, the major urban staple, when first adopting IMF structural adjustment in 1986, so the price shot up 450 percent (from Sh2.5 to Sh13.75 per kilogram) and the maizemeal purchased daily on a minimum wage dropped from 8 to 2 kilograms. By 1988, maizemeal had increased so much in price that a minimum-wage worker would use all of his income to purchase 1.3 kg. of maize meal daily, roughly 40 percent of the caloric requirement of a family of five. But the amount spent on food on average for a family of six in 1988 was eight times the minimum wage. With increased input prices and reduced credit, most peasants, while slightly better off than minimum-wage workers, had to seek casual labor to supplement farm income. Many rural women, major food producers, had to find outside work to purchase hoes, fertilizers, salt, sugar, clothing, and even staple foods; children, too, increasingly entered the wage labor force, or assisted a parent in self-employment in the informal sector, thus reducing school attendance. Many rural women weaned their infants much too early in order to return to remunerative work.[11]

In the 1960s and 1970s, Tanzania was the only sub-Saharan African country to use a progressive income tax to redistribute income to low-income classes. The IMF condition that Tanzania reintroduce excise taxes at the expense of income taxes made the tax system more regressive, increasing disposable income concentration.[12]

The IMF found domestic allies (political leaders, bureaucrats, business people, economists, intermediaries, and speculators benefiting from economic liberalization) who argued that economic recovery involved pain for the bulk of the population. Cooperating with IMF adjustment allowed these allies and their clients to avoid such pain and protect major interests from reform. Moreover, the IMF's allies were disproportionately represented among the emerging economically prosperous group allied to foreign capital and controlling a large share of imports and exports. This local nouveau riche and foreign bourgeoisie gained at the expense of the poor, peasants, and working classes, who not only lacked voice but were generally even unaware of the political debates and struggles. Tanzanian bureaucrats and business people were able to achieve secured ownership title deeds, open to the resourceful with funds, at the expense of villages and individual peasants. Land ownership, concentrated in the hands of a few people, provided preferred access to financial credit.

Reintroducing school fees and the cutback of public hospitals reduced these services for the poor. The state sector, worn down by the pressure of international donors and heavily penetrated by their domestic allies, conceded to liberal reforms and extracted benefits from them. The state bourgeoisie used statism and one-party government to consolidate itself as a class, and the masses had little access to organizations outside of the state to stop this bourgeoisie.[13]

For most Tanzanians, the replacement of ujamaa socialism in the 1970s by the economic liberalism of the 1980s "meant rehabilitating the former saboteurs while making the working and peasant classes pay for education, water, health, and medical care." The populace, whose cultural expression in the 1960s centered on party-led activities, increasingly sought expression outside the party. The state, lacking popular support, increasingly resorted to coercion, breaking the trade unions, closing the University of Dar es Salaam in 1990, and expanding paramilitary repression, including the July 1986 killing of four unarmed workers at the state-owned Kilombero Sugar Factory who were part of a demonstration of thousands of workers protesting the government's pay arrears.

In the 1980s, state funds could be used not only privately, as in the 1970s, but also for private accumulation; economic liberalism rationalized acquiring resources at the expense of the majority of the population. The absence of an ideological consensus in the 1980s meant that people increasingly had to resort to bribes for transactions with the bureaucracy. Indeed in mid-1991 the U.S. Agency for International Development (USAID) suspended Tanzanian aid, which, according to the former USAID director in Dar es Salaam, "had not gone to the poorest" but "had lined the pockets of . . . elites," supporting local importers buying "products abroad for virtually nothing with 'under-the-table' payments to the Treasury."[14]

Ghana and Zambia

Throughout the 1970s the Bank/Fund and other external agencies tried to persuade reluctant governments like Ghana and Zambia to adjust economically. Zambia negotiated standby arrangements with the IMF in 1978 and 1981, undertaking devaluation, reducing budget deficits, freezing wages, and decontrolling prices. But not until 1979–80 did the Bank implement policy-based (adjustment) lending. In the early 1980s, Zambia and Ghana recognized their foreign-exchange (and domestic economic) crises as chronic and received IMF standby credits in 1983 as last resorts to reverse their deteriorating economic performances.

Birmingham, Neustadt, and Omaboe considered Ghana at independence (1957) the most prosperous black African country. But Ghana's annual real GNP per capita growth was −0.3 percent from 1950 to 1960, −0.3 percent from 1960 to 1970, and −3.2 percent from 1970 to 1981, while its investment fell 3.1 percent yearly in the 1960s and 4.3 percent annually in the 1970s. Ghana's increased income inequality and continuing decline in GNP per capita meant steadily increasing poverty rates.

Soon after independence in 1964, Zambia was one of the most prosperous countries in the Sub-Sahara, but with wealth based on one export, copper, and thus highly vulnerable to external price changes. Moreover, Zambia had a yearly GNP per capita growth, 1965–83, of −1.3 percent, the decline having begun with the collapse of copper, cobalt, and zinc prices in the 1970s. With 1970 as 100, commodity terms of trade fell to 46 in 1975 and 29 in 1985, while export purchasing power plummeted to 41 in 1975 and 15 in 1985! By 1985, the World Bank had reclassified Zambia from a middle-income to low-income country.[15]

Ghana's large public investments in the first half of the 1960s were inefficient, as unparalleled growth in investment-income ratios contributed to little increase in income. Moreover, Ghana faced continuing balance-of-payments problems during the 1960s and 1970s, largely because of an increasingly overvalued cedi that discouraged export volume expansion, especially in cocoa. Other problems Ghana encountered included poor economic management, inefficient public enterprises, large budget deficits, black markets for exports, imports, and foreign exchange, and returning emigrants expelled from Nigeria. Additionally, before 1983, Ghana had the highest price distortion among noncommunist LDCs. reducing productivity, protecting inefficiency, and discouraging resource mobility, thus diminishing growth and savings and creating product and resource shortages. Furthermore, Ghana's terms of trade declined 1.1 percent annually, 1970–84.[16]

Both Ghana and Zambia emphasized industrialization, increasing the share of manufacturing in GDP steadily through the mid-1970s. The drastic cut in the 1975 price of copper reduced Zambia's foreign exchange for imported inputs, while currency overvaluation, falling cocoa exports, and rising import costs contributed to Ghana's fall in industrial output of 12.8 percent, 1977–82. Exchange-rate, tariff, and interest-rate policies favored investment in consumer-oriented, import-dependent, capital-intensive industries, which contributed to the debt crisis of the early 1980s that gave impetus to reform programs in both countries.[17]

Since independence, Zambia's economy has been dominated by copper, comprising more than 80 percent of export earnings. From the mid-1960s through the mid-1970s, Zambia invested much in infrastructure and directly productive investment, while undergoing a high degree of controls and a high propensity to import (especially capital goods) and discriminating against agriculture. Copper prices collapsed in 1975; even increased foreign borrowing could not stave off a chronic recession.

Added to this, South Africa destabilized landlocked Zambia militarily and economically (including disrupting transport links) for providing offices for the African National Congress and joining with neighbors to bypass South Africa in regional economic integration. ECA estimates that the nine Southern African Development Coordination Conference (SADDC) states—Angola, Botswana, Lesotho, Malawi, Mozambique, Tanzania, Swaziland, Zambia, and Zimbabwe—lost $60 billion GDP (or one-fourth), 1980–88, from South Africa's destabilization.[18]

Chairman Flight Lieutenant Jerry J. Rawlings, who was installed by Ghana's Armed Forces Revolutionary Council in June 1979, handed over power to a new civilian government headed by a little-known diplomat, Dr. Hilla Linman, three months later. On 31 December 1981, an armed forces coup against Linman, by then discredited by a worsening economic crisis, installed Rawlings as Chairman of the Provisional National Defence Council (PNDC). Rawlings, who had proclaimed a "revolutionary government," soon realized the danger of inaction toward a stagnating economy and, in 1983, accepted IMF conditionality as part of his "common sense revolution." To placate critics, his government pointed out that the agreement emphasized structural factors (not spending reduction) and multiple exchange rates, which allowed import surcharges and export bonuses. During the adjustment programs, strikes and mass protests were few, as labor, intellectuals, and dissidents feared the PNDC government, which detained, molested, and even murdered opponents of adjustment.

In 1983, Ghana increased taxes, raised prices of essential goods, and devalued the cedi; the IMF agreed to loan Ghana $400 million, while the IDA, the World Bank's soft-loan window, provided a $65 million grant. Ghana began Economic Recovery Program I (ERP I), 1984–87, featuring three IMF standby arrangements (which created debt-servicing problems in 1987–89); ERP II, 1987–89, relied on IMF SAPs (and an extended fund facility) and World Bank aid. ERP I, which removed the binding import constraint, was supported by bureaucrats and capitalists, who hoped to use the IMF to consolidate their power and crush the radicals in the workers' movement. The ERPs instituted a surcharge on nonessential imports and a bonus to exporters, intro-duced monetary and fiscal discipline, removed price distortions on oil and other goods, increased capital formation, curtailed some public enterprises, and rehabilitated cocoa, timber, gold, transport infra-structure, and other key sectors.

When Ghana's central bank devalued the cedi, which, despite rapid inflation, had only been changed once during the previous decade, from C1.15 = $1 in February 1973 to C1.75 = $1 in August 1978), it shifted the free-market rate in a dual-exchange system to C30 = $1 (December 1983), C60 = $1 (October 1985), C90 = $1 (January 1986), and C228 = $1 (September 1988), a nominal fall of the cedi of 99 percent in ten years.[19]

Initially, Ghana and Zambia received little assistance from the IMF, World Bank, or bilateral donors to support structural adjustment. Later in the 1980s the Bank and Fund, with meager Zambian collabo-ration, conducted an analysis for Zambia, establishing the framework, guiding the negotiations, and becoming virtually a de facto finance ministry in Zambia. Still, the fact that Zambia received little financial aid from DCs, even by 1985, contributed to its 1984–85 SECAL col-lapse. Zambia's debt service and capital outflow far exceeded inflow from overseas while export earnings were stagnant or even falling, 1983–87. Ghana, however, had greater commitment and competence, jointly formulating Bank/Fund adjustment strategy.[20]

Both Zambia and Ghana adopted foreign-exchange flexibility, liber-alized trade, provided incentives for exports, increased farm producer prices, cut budget deficits, lowered government borrowing, reduced subsidies, encouraged private enterprise, achieved market interest rates, and reorganized debt servicing and arrears, thus attracting new assistance from the IMF, the Bank, and country donors by the mid-1980s.[21] The Bank and Fund hailed Ghana's adjustment as a success while Zambia abandoned its agreement with the IMF in 1987, reintro-ducing fixed exchange rates, price controls, and food subsidies.

For Ghana, devaluation gave a fillip to steadily increasing cedi cocoa prices, 1984–91, which spurred rising cocoa export earnings (in cedis)

125

in the mid- to late 1980s. One-third of the increased annual cocoa exports from 1983 to the late 1980s resulted from higher producer prices attracting output previously smuggled abroad. Ironically, while the Bank/Fund trumpeted Ghana's success in devaluing to expand cocoa exports, their *dollar* prices and revenues both fell steadily from 1983 to 1991 (excluding weather fluctuations). Moreover, Ghana's current account worsened (while IMF debt service was about one-fourth of 1987–89 export proceeds) and exports were still dominated by cocoa (which comprised 50 to 75 percent of earnings) and gold in the 1980s, even as export concentration declined.[22]

Zambia continued to face depressed copper prices while undertaking IMF standby borrowing and Bank adjustment programs. Furthermore, Zambia's copper and industrial sector relied heavily on imported inputs, whose prices skyrocketed with depreciation, while Ghana's cocoa exports had a low import content. Indeed, by 1985, Zambia's real imports were 25 percent of 1974 levels and gross investment was 10 percent of GDP, compared to 29 percent in 1974. Real GDP per capita had fallen 35 percent, 1974–85.[23]

Ghana's inflation rate fell from 122 percent in 1983 to 40 percent in 1984 (following liberalization) and 10 percent in 1985, but rose to 25–40 percent, 1986–1991—annual rates more than those in the 1970s. Reform released hoarded consumer goods, reallocated scarcity rents from distributors to producers, and increased food availability, especially through the mid-1980s. Manufacturing expanded in the late 1980s, and timber, sawmilling, and non-cocoa exports increased after 1990, when an Export Finance Company provided financing. Ghana's oligopolistic firms gained from the foreign-exchange auction, while other producers encountered a cost-price squeeze. Transport vehicles, 80 percent of which were out of service in 1983 for lack of spare parts and gasoline, began running again as the market replaced state action by rationing imports and other inputs. Reforms were aided by rising public spending, more efficient transport and communication, and an overflowing market.

From 1984 to 1988, Ghanaian GDP per capita grew modestly,[24] investment rates increased, the capacity to import rose, and urban-rural per capita income discrepancies probably declined as price de-control and rising farm export prices redistributed income from industry to agriculture. Moreover, real wages declined, unemployment rose (accelerated by substantial public-sector layoffs, especially from the lowest-paid grades), petty retail traders (often women) were hurt from reduced margins, and urban income inequality widened in the four to six years after the adoption of the IMF adjustment. Despite protest from labor unions about the effect on the cost of consumer goods, Ghana widened the distance between the two exchange rates in 1985 and 1986. Dual rates maintained some price distortions, postponed resource adjustments, and spurred people to acquire foreign exchange cheaply in one market and sell it expensively in another. In the late 1980s, the Ghanaian government undertook a more comprehensive adjustment program to continue and deepen the reforms.[25]

Ghanaian cocoa producers benefited from improved (cedi) prices relative to food, 1983–88, and the easing of the labor shortage by Ghanaian workers returning from Nigeria. In response to rising producer prices, cocoa farmers rehabilitated plants or planted anew, which expanded pod capacity, with a three- to six-year lag. But Ghana was not able to reverse its fall in food output per capita during ERP I; poor (non-cocoa) northern farmers and southern female food farmers were damaged most. Furthermore, under the macroeconomic recovery programs, 1983–89, Accra substantially cut government capital and recurrent spending, especially in agriculture, while foreign net financing fell short of estimated targets by more than one-third. Farm income per capita (outside cocoa) dropped, governmental capability fell, and infrastructure (including roads to transport cocoa exports) remained in poor condition. If roads are impassable, railways poor, and ports congested, exports of cocoa will not respond much to rising cedi prices. In early 1990 Chairman Rawlings admitted that, despite the international acclaim concerning Ghana's recovery program, "we know what a struggle it still is to make ends meet."[26]

For Zambia, the prices of world copper remained low (falling, 1983–86) and its short-run supply was inelastic. Copper export receipts fell from 1983 to 1986 in dollar terms. During this period debt servicing was almost as high as export receipts!

After Zambia undertook a Bank-sponsored SAP in 1985, traditional exports expanded, albeit from a low base, and industrial capacity utilization increased through 1986. In December 1986, after riots in the Copperbelt (just southwest of Zaïre's Shaba, formerly Katanga, province), President Kenneth Kaunda, already incurring heavy political costs from continuing austerity, rescinded his announcement of the removal of maizemeal subsidies and price controls. In 1987, controlled goods sold only on the black market, budget deficits increased, copper prices fell further, external debt ($5.7 billion) was four times GDP, and the decade-long decline in GDP per capita continued. In May 1987, the government restored state intervention, reversing all major reforms, such as foreign-exchange auctioning, interest rate and price decontrols, and liberalized trade. Lusaka was in arrears to the Bank, which suspended its loan disbursement straightaway. In response, the government instituted a "Growth from Own Resources" program, as external financial flows dried up.[27]

From its beginning in 1985, the foreign-exchange auction worked poorly in Zambia, as 100 firms, of which 99 were foreign owned, captured 90 percent of the underfunded donor-dependent foreign-exchange market. Indeed, the Bank of Zambia even initially rejected bids for foreign exchange for tire imports by indigenous firms manufacturing rubber sandals. Many factories operated at a fraction of capacity, with some eventually closing down because of growing shortages of foreign exchange (and rising imported input prices). The kwacha (Zk), generally under a crawling peg vis-à-vis a basket of DC currencies when not lurching downward, depreciated 55 percent against the dollar, 1983–85, and 94 percent, 1983–89, placing intolerable pressures on the budget and, indirectly, on the money supply, provoking capital flight, and raising annual consumer price increases from 12 percent in 1982 to 20 percent, 1983–84, to 48 percent, 1985–88, and more than 100 percent, 1989–90. Local non-copper exporters, encountering cost-inflated input prices and receiving no assistance from government, failed to respond to the spur of depreciation. Indigenous import-substitute manufactures, facing trade liberalization, fell after 1985; while a depreciating kwacha provided added protection, few local firms found domestic sources that could meet specifications for inputs previously bought overseas. Moreover, many small-scale farms, facing a high cost of borrowing, the removal of input subsidies, and rising input prices, could not survive the enormous transformation of the late 1980s; large-scale foreign-owned farms emerged, taking advantage of economies of dealing with politics and the public bureaucracy. Furthermore, industrial MNCs, with access to hard currency having substantial purchasing power in Zambia, expanded during the period, increasing their oligopolistic domination. Many parastatals, which had not been able to cover costs at controlled prices without subsidies, were subsequently compelled to survive or sink under Fund/Bank conditions; many could not successfully compete against the market power of global companies.[28]

Zambia's high industrial concentration was associated with great income inequality. In the 1970s, Zambia had the highest income inequality in the Sub-Sahara, an inequality that increased with negative growth in the 1980s, thus increasing poverty rates substantially. In monitoring price liberalization, the Zambian government tried to intervene to improve equity at the expense of efficiency but was reproved by the IMF, which opposed interference with the free market mechanism.[29]

In the 1980s, the Zambian government encountered mounting unrest over worsening living standards, especially for workers, who faced falling real wages and increased unemployment. In 1989, after Kaunda's United National Independence Party (UNIP) won the 1988 election, the government devalued the kwacha twice, announced reductions in maize subsidies, removed price controls, and raised interest rates, boosting the cost of living and incurring protests and strikes, which contributed to the closure of the University of Zambia. In late 1989, the government's recovery program was approved by the Fund, which resumed lending. In the next two years, opposition to adjustment and the one-party government of Kaunda intensified, inspiring his *volte face* in calling for multiparty elections in October 1991. Zambia Congress of Trade Unions (ZCTU) Chairman Frederick Chiluba became president, using a new broom to sweep away corrupt parastatal chief executives. Just before the election, the IMF, World Bank, and bilateral lenders suspended lending to Zambia for its refusal to decontrol the price of maizemeal, failure to comply with other IMF conditions, and interest arrears to the Bank.[30]

Adjustment programs have been inefficacious in the wake of prolonged stagnation and poor economic management, as in Zambia. IMF and Bank resources could not offset the hardships caused by price decontrol, subsidy removal, and foreign exchange auctions.[31] In both Ghana and Zambia in the mid-1980s, IMF structural adjustment distributed income to commercial farmers and away from (especially low-income) workers.[32]

Nigeria

Nigeria conducted a national debate for four years during President Shehu Shagari's last months in office (1983) and the military governments of Major-General Mohammed Buhari (1983–85) and Major-General Ibrahim Babangida (1985–86)—years that began a steady decline in the terms of trade during the 1980s (table 4.1) and saw a large negative net resource transfer. The populace had expressed several objections to Nigeria's taking an IMF loan: (1) domestic firms would not be able to compete as well if Nigeria relaxed import controls, (2) devaluation would raise the naira cost of imported food, capital, and industrial inputs, (3) reducing fuel subsidies would increase transport and production costs, (4) an open door to foreign investment would undermine local industries and indigenous technology, and (5) the IMF's short-term loan would make Nigeria more dependent.[33] The announcement of the Fifth National Development Plan, 1986–90, which embodied spending reductions to respond to the crisis, coincided with the coup overthrowing Buhari in August 1985.

In 1986, President Babangida, who had conducted a year-long dialogue with the Nigerian elites and publics, rejected IMF terms for borrowing. The Babangida government skillfully played the World Bank against the IMF for public relations gains, securing standby approval from the IMF but rejecting its conditions, while agreeing to impose similar terms "on its own" approved by the Bank. In October 1986, the Bank, with Western commercial and central bank support, delivered $1,020 million in quickly disbursed loans and $4,280 million in three-year project loans.

The federal government received three-fourths of its current revenue from oil, whose prices fell during most of the 1980s. By continually reducing real public spending between 1983 and 1988, especially for capital, imports, civil service and armed forces salaries, consumer subsidies, and parastatals, many of which were sold off, the federal government decreased its deficit substantially. In 1986–87, under a World Bank SAP, Nigeria slashed the budget deficit even more and tightened monetary policy. But during 1988, when the poor 1987 harvest put pressure on food prices and opposition to austerity mounted, the government doubled the budget deficit and lifted the wage freeze, and the Central Bank of Nigeria eased monetary policy. In late 1989, food supplies grew and the central bank tightened monetary policy through 1991.[34]

Rapid inflation, 20 percent yearly between 1973 and 1980 and more than 20 percent per year between 1980 and 1984 as measured by the consumer price index, dropped to 5.5 percent in 1985, 5.4 percent in 1986 (years of good harvests), and 10.2 percent in 1987, before rising to 38.3 percent in 1988 and 50.5 percent in 1989 and falling abruptly to 7.5 percent in 1990 and 9.5 percent in 1991.[35] The political leadership responded to deteriorating world prices and increasing external debts by lurching from austerity to fulfill Bank/Fund conditions to inflationary policies to retain domestic support, but failed to satisfy either external or internal players.

Despite several debt reschedulings, Nigeria's debt overhang still dampened investment and adjustment in the late 1980s (until the second half of 1989). Nigeria, with years of austerity and stagnation, could not afford to reduce consumption but had to cut investment to effect an external transfer. Large payments acted as a tax on investment, since a share of returns goes to creditors. Substantial debt servicing often meant slowing economic growth to avoid an import surplus. Without concessional funds, rescheduling only postponed external crises.[36] Nigeria could not increase both consumption and investment until world oil prices rose in late 1989 and the early 1990s.

Nigeria, with only $408 million in official development assistance, received $1.09 aid receipts per capita, ranking the lowest among LDCs (1988), compared to Israel, $282.07 (high-income); Jordan, $108.95; Senegal, $78.85 (middle-income); and Zambia, $63.73; Bangladesh, $14.62; Pakistan, $13.32; Indonesia, $9.34; India, $2.58; and China, $1.84 (low-income). This aid was 0.4 percent of Nigeria's GNP, compared to 2.4 percent for low-income countries and 1.0 percent for middle-income countries. However, in 1989, when the World Bank reclassified Nigeria as low-income and IDA-eligible, aid trebled, with Japan and the United Kingdom the major donors, and the grant element of aid rose to 55 percent.[37] But in 1991, Nigeria was not eligible for the Bank Special Program of Assistance (SPA) or Toronto terms for reducing official debt (see chapter 8).

Under two World Bank structural adjustment programs (1986–88 and 1989–91), the Nigerian government tried to eliminate inefficient state intervention and obtain budgetary relief through abolishing agricultural commodity marketing boards and liberalizing cash-crop exports. These measures, together with devaluation, increased the naira prices of export crops, especially cocoa. The state also privatized many public enterprises by selling equity to private investors, while restructuring other parastatals to improve efficiency. The federal government encouraged private investment, allowed foreign ownership in most manufacturing, and liberalized and speeded up administrative procedures for new investment.[38]

The Babangida government, which came to power during depressed oil prices in August 1985, undertook a SAP, 1986–88. In September 1986, the government introduced a second-tier foreign exchange market (SFEM), sold on auction for a near-equilibrium price and used for trade transactions, export earnings, and import requirements. Under SFEM, the second-tier naira depreciated 66 percent to ₦1 = $0.64 and declined further in value through July 1987, when the two tiers were merged. Nigeria abolished its producer price controls (by the Prices, Productivity, and Incomes Board), 30 percent import surcharge, and import licensing system; reduced its import prohibition list substantially; and promoted exports (through fiscal and credit incentives and by allowing exporters to retain foreign currency) when adopting the SFEM. While this liberalization opened the way for an IMF agreement and debt rescheduling, the military government declined to use the $475 million IMF standby funds. Meanwhile the naira continued depreciating, especially after the relaxing of financial policy early in 1988. The effect of the SFEM in breaking bottlenecks, together with the reduction of food price increases, dampened inflation in 1986, but the easing of domestic policy in 1988 accelerated inflation. Real interest rates were negative, and capital flight and speculative imports resumed. But in 1989, the government again unified foreign-exchange markets, depreciating (but not stabilizing) the naira and reducing the external deficit. Manufacturing firms increased their reliance on local inputs and raw materials, firms relying on domestic resources grew rapidly, capacity utilization rose (though still below 50 percent), and non-oil exports grew from $0.6 billion in 1986 to $0.9 billion in 1988 (yet merely 12 percent of export value, only at 1970s levels, and dominated by cash crops like cocoa). Large firms benefited from the foreign-exchange auction and enjoyed higher capacity use than smaller ones. But domestic industrial firms undertook little investment or technological improvements, despite dramatically reduced labor costs.[39]

Real wages fell 65 percent in the 1980s, amid a statutory wage freeze (1982–88), salary cuts in the public sector in 1985, falling terms of trade, the SAP's distribution of income from wage earners to property owners and large farmers, and reduced health, education, and social spending. The central trade union body, the Nigeria Labour Congress (NLC), whose leaders were detained and threatened with sedition charges in 1987 and suspended by the government in 1988, resisted adjustment policies that reduced employment and real wages; it proposed alternative adjustment policies and spearheaded the protest against falling income and consumption among low-income groups. The military government banned opposition newspapers, deeply cut educational support, inspected university course content (after 1986), forbade partisan politics by university teachers (beginning in 1989), intermittently closed universities, detained and dismissed university critics, and killed tens and arrested hundreds of students and academics while squashing strikes, demonstrations, and political opposition. Discontent with falling incomes and declining social programs contributed to often vociferous domestic unrest, such as fundamentalist Muslim riots in Kaduna state 1987, strikes and riots in April 1988 in response to the World Bank insistence on reduced gasoline subsidies, student hostility to government economic policies in May–June 1989, the second attempted coup d'etat (May 1990) against Babangida, and

Muslim-Christian fighting in the north in early 1991. Furthermore, in 1991, the NLC protested the mere doubling of the minimum wage from 1981 in the face of a tenfold increase in general prices.[40]

The Nigerian government agrees with the views of scholars such as Dudley, Kilby, and Peace, that workers represent the interests of a privileged few; thus the state is justified in repressing unionization, bargaining, and labor protest to facilitate Bank-sponsored adjustment programs that support the general welfare. However, as I argue elsewhere, the belief that there was a "labor aristocracy" in Nigeria in the 1960s and 1970s was based on the average annual wages of workers, which were several times income per capita, rather than on average *income* of worker *households*, which is no more than that of the average household in Nigeria. Jamal and Weeks's data indicate that the household income of workers in the 1980s relative to that of Nigeria generally had fallen since the 1970s.[41]

Nigeria's negative growth and balance on current and capital account deficit, 1980–87, included the early period of the World Bank structural adjustment program. The modest recovery, 1988–91, and external surplus, 1989–91, largely resulted from rising oil prices rather than structural adjustment. Moreover, worker and peasant incomes continued to erode, and non-oil export shares failed to increase, even after economic growth resumed in 1988.

Nigeria's severe debt crisis in the mid- to late 1980s was magnified by the sizable trade deficit, 1981–83, and the bunching of debt payments in the mid- to late 1980s. From 1984 through 1986, debt service/exports equaled 33 percent, falling by 60 percent from 1986 to 1987 from debt rescheduling by the Paris (official) and London (commercial) Clubs of creditors in late 1986. Subsequent rescheduling and improved external balances increased the secondary market for Nigerian debt from $0.25 in mid- 1990 to $0.42 in the second quarter of 1991.[42]

The Nigerian adjustment program contained several flawed premises. First, the effort at reducing real wages, while narrowing the gap between urban wage earners and rural, probably did not reduce overall income inequality, as the major split was between small peasants, informal-sector workers and operators, the bulk of wage earners, and the unemployed, on the one hand, and the rest of the population, on the other, and not between affluent urbanites and poor farmers.[43] Second, firms too small to buy foreign currency at the public auction were compelled to buy from concentrated sellers at monopoly prices. Third, clients of leading officials had privileged access to loans and inputs essential for the acquisition of public enterprises by private individuals. Emphasis on gradual privatization of public-sector firms, as well as liberalizing entry into activities previously restricted to the public sector, would have worked more efficaciously than the extensive sale of state-owned firms to private individuals. Finally, the Bank neglected the political constraints in undertaking adjustment; indeed, at some point Nigeria might have chosen default over the onerous conditions of the Bank SAL and IMF standby approval.

Senegal

From independence in 1960s to late in the decade, Senegal's average living levels increased, as the peanut economy expanded. However, from 1965 to 1989, Senegal's real growth rate was negative. Economic retrenchment prevailed during the six years following the 1968 withdrawal of the French peanut price subsidy, and strong export prices for peanut oil and phosphates, 1974 to 1978, temporarily ensured Senegal's international creditworthiness. However, drought and disease struck the peanut crop in 1978 (reducing GDP per capita 26 percent that year) and again when petroleum prices peaked, 1979–81. From the 1960s through the mid-1980s, the government monopsony agricultural marketing board [*Caisse di Péréquation et de Stabilisation des Prix* (CPSP)] set peanut oil, cotton, and phosphate producer prices low to transfer a surplus to industry. From 1967 to 1985, the state appropriated CFAF 135 billion in constant 1980 prices (about $448 million) from peanut producers and CFAF 13 billion from cotton farmers. Smallholder farmers lost CFAF 98 billion and consumers of vegetable oil, sugar, and imported rice paid CFAF 58 billion during the same period. Such agricultural taxation, with net resource flows to agro-industries and traders, slowed export and economic growths, especially hurt by the second oil shock, 1970–81. By 1986, peanut oil prices were only 40 percent of their average nominal price of the 1970s; in 1989 the real price fell further, although recovering to a nominal price in 1990 higher than the average during the 1970s.

Until the late 1960s, low primary-product export revenues provided subsidies to rural elites, lucrative profits for French oil-processing firms, and sufficient state revenue for a growing civil service. In the 1970s, political strength shifted to an urban-based national bourgeoisie, who used the state to expand infrastructure and advance the interests of private and numerous state-owned enterprises (SOEs) in industry over farmers and foreign capitalists. Government also provided economic services to farmers, emphasizing cooperatives, marketing agents, subsidized farm inputs (like seeds and fertilizer), and seasonal credit for smallholders credit. In the late 1970s the rural and urban clientalist systems lost their importance, being replaced by SOEs and international institutions (MNCs and aid agencies).

In late 1979, in the midst of falling terms of trade, the Senegalese government concurrently approached the Bank and Fund for assistance and policy dialogue. Then it announced its first major adjustment plan, the Medium-Term Economic and Financial Recovery Plan (EFRP), 1980–84, which provided a framework for Bank SAL I in 1982. Neither the Bank SAP nor the 1983 IMF standby agreement, which emphasized privatization, higher agricultural prices, and stricter investment criteria, was completed in 1983 because of government opposition to Bank insistence on removing fertilizer subsidies, Bank concern with a low benefit-cost ratio in an investment project in peanut storage, and the sharp drop in peanut export prices and incomes. From 1980 to 1983, the budget deficit remained high, the current account deficit was 15 to 25 percent of exports, and inflation increased to 11 percent yearly in 1983, a level maintained through 1985.[44]

In 1984, the government prepared a long-term plan, Economic Adjustment Plan in the Medium and Long Term (PAML), designed to cover policy from 1985 to 1992. As part of the plan, government implemented the Nouvelle Politique Agricole (New Agricultural Policy, or NAP) for agricultural adjustment and reform. While NAP objectives were to increase cereals self-sufficiency from 50 percent in the mid-1980s to 80 percent in 2000, privatize farmer support activities, and diversify farm output through irrigating crops outside the peanut belt, farmers did not diversify and agricultural productivity failed to increase in the late 1980s. Bank SECALs in agriculture and industry after 1984, an IMF SAF and ESAF in 1986–88, and Bank SALs in 1986–87 and 1989–90, which emphasized redirecting resources from protected industry and peanut cultivation to maize, rice, and other cereals, decontrolling agricultural prices, cutting farm taxes, privatizing farm marketing, and eliminating fertilizer and rice subsidies, received little popular support.

During the late 1980s, agricultural export prices fluctuated substantially around a falling trend, so exports grew slowly and the debt-service ratio increased (to 23 percent in 1987, achieved only by substantial arrears, as the scheduled ratio was 37 percent). Spending (especially investment) reductions under IMF auspices increased economic stress and dried up patronage, threatening the existing coalition of elites that maintained the multiparty democracy established by the first elected president, Leopold Sedar Senghor, during the prosperity of 1976. Strikes by students and teachers in response to the 1980 austerity spurred Senghor to step down from the presidency in 1981, being succeeded by the previous prime minister, Abdou Diouf. But economic stress continued, with university cutbacks provoking unrest in the late 1980s, to which Diouf responded by closing the university for the academic year, 1987–88. Subsequent student uprisings broadened to a political challenge to Diouf, whose 1988 reelection victory was regarded by opposition parties as massive fraud. The April 1989 border clashes with Mauritania and the withdrawal of The Gambia from the Senegambia Confederation in August 1989 added to the pressures on the Diouf administration. The shrinking economic benefits in the 1980s under adjustment and reform threatened the patronage network of the Parti Socialiste (PS) machine, creating adversaries from the former ruling coalition of economic interests.

But inflation dropped (consumer prices increased less than 5 percent annually from 1987 through mid-1991) and the current-account deficit decreased in the late 1980s. Growth estimates from the Economist Intelligence Unit, together with population estimates from the Population Reference Bureau, indicate real GDP growth per capita at a fraction of 1 percent yearly, 1986 to 1990.

Senegal rescheduled official debt with the Paris Club 1981, 1982, 1983, 1985, and 1986, and renegotiated private debt under London Club auspices in 1984. However, in 1987, the Paris Club rejected Senegal's request for a three-year debt rescheduling, granting only eighteen months instead. During the late 1980s, Senegal's access to private financial markets fell; nevertheless, the Paris Club rescheduled $145 million of Senegal's debt in 1990. Moreover, Senegal benefited from net aid flows in excess of debt service of $50 per capita in 1981–87, flows dependent on compliance with Bank/Fund conditions. By the early 1990s, Senegal, a middle-income country, rescheduled Paris Club debts on Toronto terms, previously reserved only for low-income countries (less than $580 GNP per capita in 1991, based on 1989 data) that were debt distressed. These terms, agreed to by the 1988 economic summit of the G7 in Toronto, involved a menu of choices for rescheduling between extended maturities (with reduced present debt value of 15 percent and 14 years' grace period, chosen by the United States and Japan), partial writedowns, or reduced interest rates (both decreasing debt present value by 33 percent). However, creditors reduced Senegal's aid and lending in the early 1990s, as the IMF had withheld its "seal of approval," contingent on Senegal's eliminating rice subsidies and restructuring its agricultural production. Senegalese political leaders, citing widespread DC crop subsidies, resented IMF pressures to abolish subsidies to rice producers.[45]

Attaining Objectives

The next sections examine lessons from Tanzanian, Zambian, Ghanaian, Nigerian, and Senegalese adjustments, with more general issues delayed until chapter 7. Traditionally, the IMF focuses on macroeconomic objectives (external balance, government balance, and inflation), while the World Bank emphasizes microeconomic goals (prices and markets). Yet, when policies are being prescribed, microeconomics cannot be separated from macroeconomics, especially on foreign-exchange prices. In practice, the distinction between the Bank and Fund has been blurred since the late 1980s, as the Bank does not institute adjustment programs unless the IMF approves standby credit. Moreover, after the late 1980s, the two institutions undertook joint programs.

Keynes, in 1944, envisioned an IMF oriented toward stimulating demand for rapid economic growth. In practice, the IMF and its officers, who ingest a fear of inflation with their mothers' milk, have emphasized international price stability and a sound climate for the banking industry. For the IMF, the major macroeconomic objectives of stabilization and structural adjustment programs are improving the external balance and domestic fiscal balance. As FAO contends: "An important aspect of [IMF] loans and their associated policies is that they do not present a growth package as such, . . . [but] their primary role is to serve as a balance-of-payments support."[46] In other words, the IMF, which reflects the views of the United States and other large shareholders, does not focus on economic development but on correcting external-account deficits. Since IMF loans are short-term (one to two years) and supply-side (structural) changes take years, IMF programs almost always require demand restraint, with contractionary monetary and fiscal policies (spending reductions and slow growth in the money supply).[47]

The Bank's microeconomic objectives, on the other hand, are enhancing resource efficiency by removing price distortions, opening up competition, and deregulation. Since the Bank has been slicing up adjustment loans into smaller and smaller elements and since the release of each slice (or tranche) is dependent on the performance of certain conditions, the Bank, in practice, has a planning horizon almost as short as the Fund's. Indeed, the Bank increasingly front-loads conditionality, so key conditions are fulfilled in advance of the release of any part of the loan, as in the reform and stabilization before Tanzania's 1988 and 1989 SECALs.[48] And while post-1988 publications of the Bank, increasingly on the defensive in international fora, have recognized growth and income distribution as goals of long-term structural adjustment, the Bank's goals, as expressed in adjustment programs, are similar to those of the Fund.

In the 1980s, the World Bank led donor coordination of loans to Africa, while the IMF, despite substantial reductions in lending, 1980–86, retained influence through coordination with the Bank. By 1987, the Bank, the IDA (the Bank's soft-loan window), IMF, and bilateral donors put more emphasis on special assistance to least-developed debt-distressed sub-Saharan countries. The five African case studies suggest that, during periods of five to ten years, Bank/Fund programs, while sometimes enhancing these countries' ability to service their debts, rarely increased investment rates or restored external equilibrium. Hutchful explains reasons for Ghanaian state policies, both before and during Bank/Fund adjustment programs, 1983–91, which he believes reduced the welfare of the general population: "State interest in Ghana has been conceived and elaborated to a large degree autonomously of and in conflict with not only the popular interests of labour and the peasantry but also with those of external and domestic capital, to which developmentalist rhetoric (and formal investment laws) otherwise pay lip-service."[49]

Income Distribution

While the Bank/Fund gives lip service to income distribution and basic needs, in practice, as with Ghana, Zambia, and Tanzania, the Bank and IMF subordinate poverty reduction to the unfettered working of the free market system. The Bank and Fund lack systematic studies of the effects of adjustment on poverty and income inequality; for example, the Bank-sponsored study on 1987–88 Ghanaian poverty by Boateng, Ewusi, Kanbur, and McKay (1990) examines a point in time but makes no comparisons across time.

People who own property, hold an influential position, and have a good education are in the best position to profit as growth proceeds. Thus a society with high income inequality is likely to remain so or become more so, whereas one with small disparities may be able to avoid large increases in inequality. It simply may not be possible to grow first and redistribute later, because early social and economic positions may have already fixed the distribution pattern. Benefiting the poor requires policies—such as agrarian reform, enhancing access to provide resources (credit, fertilizer, and extension advice), improving labor market functioning, and sustaining health and educational services—that maintain or increase the poor's assets.[50]

Elsewhere I show that in Africa children from upper classes and established business families use the advantages of their parents— property, influence, and status—to acquire education, training, capital, experience, and concessions and to become disproportionately successful in economic activities, especially business. Wealth and position facilitate the possession of greater opportunities like better information, superior education and training, and a lower discount of future earnings. African elites use power and wealth to acquire education and investment opportunities to maintain their families' high-status positions.[51]

Chapter 7 discusses designing adjustment programs to protect the most vulnerable parts of the population.

The Planning Horizon

While the crises in Ghana, Zambia, and Senegal developed over at least a decade, stabilization takes at least that long. Zambia had too little time to stabilize, let alone restructure, its economy. Liberalizing and privatizing, while probably an appropriate goal, work more effectively if planned over a longer period. Zambia faced major political opposition to eliminating food subsidies and increasing farm prices, tasks less daunting if part of a long-range plan. Except for 1988, Zambia's GDP per capita fell every year from 1984, the beginning of Bank SECALs, to 1990.

A U.N. advisory group recommended that the World Bank refinance hard loans to Zambia (which accounted for 46 percent of its debt) and Tanzania (where World Bank funding comprised 67 percent of total debt) at IDA (concessional) terms. This World Bank financing should be additional resources and not IDA replenishment, the group stated.[52] Converting hard to soft loans is discussed further in chapter 8.

The Comprehensiveness of Liberalization

The theory of the second best states that if economic policy changes cannot satisfy *all* the conditions necessary for maximizing welfare, then satisfying one or several conditions may not increase welfare. This theory indicates that liberalizing one price while other prices are still repressed may be worse than having all prices distorted. As Nove put it, "To change everything at once is impossible, but partial change creates contradictions and inconsistencies."[53] Few sub-Saharan countries are likely to possess the combination of factors that helped Ghana's adjustment, 1983–88. Ghana's high degree of economic distortion provided scope for more gains from "getting prices right," especially from raising cocoa producer prices, which in 1976, at 22 percent of export prices, was the lowest in the world.[54]

Ghana's adjustment program focused on a relatively few policy instruments, concentrated primarily in agriculture.[55] Commercial agriculture, which requires fewer wage and outside price changes, may gain more from liberalization than industry does. Cocoa in Ghana exemplifies this, as does agricultural reform in China since 1979. China decontrolled (and increased) prices for farm commodities, virtually eliminated their compulsory deliveries to the state, reduced multi-tiered pricing, relaxed interregional farm trade restrictions, encouraged rural markets, allowed direct sales of farm goods to urban consumers, and decollectivized agriculture, instituting individual household management of farm plots under long-term contracts with collectives and allowing farmers to choose cropping patterns and non-farm activities. From 1979 to 1986, China's 2.2 percent annual growth in foodgrain output per capita (not even as rapid as gains in oilseed, livestock, and cotton output) was among the fastest in the world, and faster than its 0.3 percent growth, 1954–77 (using a five-year moving average to reduce distortions from weather fluctuations from both series). China's industrial reform, plagued by inconsistencies from partial change, was much less successful.[56]

Trade Liberalization

Multinational corporations invest overseas because of international imperfections in the market for goods, resources, or technology. The MNCs benefit from monopoly advantages, such as patents, technical knowledge, superior managerial and marketing skills, better access to capital markets, economies of large-scale production, and economies of vertical integration (that is, cost savings from decision coordination at various production stages).[57] Successful trade liberalization and exchange-rate equilibration usually require the domestic ability to produce inputs previously bought overseas. Ghana was a fortunate exception in that its increased volume of cocoa exports resulting from cedi depreciation relied largely on inputs already produced internally. In contrast, Zambian exporters suffered from liberalization because domestic industry lacked the capability of producing inputs previously purchased abroad. Moreover, as the preference for them declined during liberalization, indigenous firms in Zambia found it increasingly difficult to compete with well-established foreign firms with oligopolistic power.

Chapter 7 contains a more general discussion of trade and exchange-rate liberalization, including the sequencing of these reforms.

Privatization

The stress on privatization began with the appointment in 1981 of a leading New York banker, A. W. Clausen, as World Bank president, who was succeeded in 1986 by Barber B. Conable, a former academic and member of the U.S. Congress, and in 1991 by Lewis Preston, a New York banker. The emphasis was not just an extension of the domestic economics of American President Ronald Reagan and British Prime Minister Margaret Thatcher to Western-dominated multilateral aid and lending programs; it was also an LDC response to the failure of public enterprises to match expectations. In February 1986, Babacar N'Diaye, president of the African Development Bank, criticized the private sector for performing inefficiently and claimed that it needed a more conducive environment for growth. Yet, as Stewart argues, the Bank's focus should be on substituting local private ownership for public ownership or reforming parastatals, rather than on wholesale privatization. Even the World Bank's *World Development Report, 1983* contends, "the key factor determining the efficiency of an enterprise is not whether it is publicly or privately owned, but how it is managed." If entry barriers are removed, the report states, there is no presumption that the private sector has better management. Moreover, Bank/Fund analyses in mid-1980s indicated that public enterprises can perform well with competition, managerial autonomy and accountability, hard budget constraints, and firm size commensurate with technical and managerial skills.[58]

The transition from centrally managed state enterprises to a liberal, privatized economy is politically and technically difficult. Prices masked by controls inevitably rise. Forcing inefficient firms to close is likely to be unacceptable where labor is not mobile. Pent-up demand for imports may hurt the balance of payments. Skilled people are usually lacking.[59] Moreover, government may require parastatals to achieve social objectives, such as setting quality standards, investing in infrastructure, producing social goods for low-income earners, controlling sectors vital for national security, wresting control from foreign owners or minority ethnic communities, rescuing bankrupt firms in key sectors, avoiding private oligopolistic concentration, raising capital essential for overcoming indivisibilities, producing vital inputs cheaply for the domestic market, capturing gains from technological learning, and creating other external economies that private firms would overlook. To illustrate, Nigeria's abolition of the government Cocoa Marketing Board and licenses for marketing cocoa in 1987 resulted in poor quality control and fraudulent trading practices, which adversely affected the reputation of Nigerian cocoa. The government subsequently incurred substantial costs reintroducing inspection procedures and marketing licenses.[60]

Moreover, the effectiveness of creating market incentives and deregulating state controls presupposes a class able and willing to respond by innovating, bearing risk, and mobilizing capital. While significant groups of indigenous entrepreneurs have emerged in Kenya, Nigeria, and Côte d'Ivorie, the private sector in Tanzania, Ghana, and Zambia, for example, is much more limited. Additionally, some regimes have restricted the commercial and industrial enterprises of such visible minorities as the Asians in East Africa.

Even where privatization is desirable, government may want to proceed slowly to avoid a highly concentrated business elite being created from newly privatized firms falling into a few hands, as was true during indigenization. It would be ironic if two goals of privatization—improvements of efficiency and competition—were sabotaged because of creation of new oligopolies from a limited number of buyers. Moreover, the fact that the private sector may lack the requisite business skills and experience means that an emphasis on providing private competition to the private sector and a gradual reduction of the relative size of the public sector may be preferable to abrupt privatization. To quote a publication of the World Bank/IMF: "The rationale for privatization is most straightforward and least controversial where a public enterprise is engaged in a purely commercial activity and is already subject to competition."[61]

While Ghana's reform of state-owned enterprises (SOEs) was to enhance their competitiveness and management responsibility, re-structuring failed to modify management or corporate boards, criteria for management promotion and pay, or rules for allocating capital between SOEs. Indeed, existing managers, many of whom should have been discharged, oversaw enterprise divestiture, viewing work-force retrenchment and restructuring as unrelated activities, disproportionately laying off production workers and retaining administrative and clerical staff, and sometimes, in the absence of guidelines for work-force requirements, reporting no redundant staff.[62]

Fine-tuning of Monetary Policy

The IMF cannot expect an LDC such as Zambia to fine-tune monetary policy to absorb efficaciously a shock such as a kwacha depreciation of more than 90 percent in six years. The banking system, often limited in its ability to regulate the money supply to influence output and prices in DCs, is even less effective in sub-Saharan Africa. Zambia's money market is externally dependent, poorly organized, fragmented, and cartelized. Zambia's banking system, highly dependent on international transactions, cannot control the money supply easily because of the variability of foreign-exchange assets. Tanzania, Zambia, Ghana, and Nigeria lacked the ability to avoid inflation rates of more than 20 percent annually during at least part of their SAPs, a factor that the Bank/Fund needs to recognize in its adjustment programs and targets.

Ironically, Senegal, Côte d'Ivoire, Cameroon, Congo, Gabon, Benin, Burkina, Central African Republic, Mali, Chad, Niger, Togo, and Equatorial Guinea were more likely to have a problem opposite to that of inflation—a depressed economy from deficient aggregate demand. The franc-zone economies that pegged their CFAF to the French franc (CFAF50=Fr1) operated in a straitjacket. In the mid-1980s, when the strong dollar increased import costs and non-franc denominated external debt service, some francophone African financial ministers called for a float against the French franc, but French officials were adamantly opposed. Being a franc-zone member prevented Senegal from devaluing or using expansionary monetary and fiscal policies to stimulate growth and employment.[63]

Conclusion

The studies of five African economies indicate that, with the possible exception of Ghana, Bank/Fund adjustment did not result in an economic turnaround. Indeed, the societies experienced inflation, falling real wages, elite consolidation, corruption, growing concentration, reduced social services, political repression, riots, and strikes and had little protection from external shocks. These countries, most of which had been in desperate plight by the early 1980s, would probably have faced many of these problems even if they had undertaken adjustment on their own. Moreover, they probably could not have acquired the funds they needed had they not also agreed to Bank/Fund policy reforms. Yet, even if you grant the need for liberalization, the sequences recommended by the Bank and Fund were often counterproductive and many of their policies were ill conceived.

7

A Critique of World Bank and
IMF Adjustment Programs

■

The very institutions that in the past 25 years have contributed to
the deprivation of the poor through their growth-oriented policy
prescriptions are also the ones promoting themselves as champions
of peasant rights, "basic needs" and environmental sustainability. Yet,
the economic programmes they currently support in Africa are aimed
at further ensuring Africa's ability to repay its debts to the rich nations,
not to strengthen Africa's independent development. These programmes are essentially based on theft, deceit and intimidation. Theft,
because international transfers from the poor to the rich are rapidly
increasing. Deceit, because the poor are always told that development
is just around the corner, if they would only tighten their belts for a
short while. Intimidation, because conditionally keeps the poor countries under constant pressure: "If you do not do it our way, we will
cut you off from further loans and aid."
—Fantu Cheru

To regard nutrition, health services and education as the fruits of
development to be deferred until after high production, is self-de-
feating. Only the well-nourished, healthy and literate can consistently
and increasingly be efficient, productive workers. To see access to
pure water, reduction of women's work-load and child survival as
goals for after economic recovery is to ensure that there will be, at
best, delayed and stunted recovery.
—Reginald Herbold Green

Premises of Adjustment
and Stabilization Programs

Adjustment lending (AL), a phenomenon of the 1980s and early
1990s, accounted for 3.3 percent of the World Bank's total lending in

1980 but gradually increased to 25 percent in 1987. Between 1980 and 1987, although 46 percent of the Bank's adjustment loans were to sub-Saharan Africa, the value of its borrowing comprised only 16 percent of ALs, 24 percent of SECALs, and 6 percent of agricultural sectoral lending, two-fifths of which went for financing a single import of fertilizers for Nigeria. The Bank and Fund have linked their limited agricultural lending to policy changes, including agricultural research, privatization, and removing price controls. Yet the growth in the Sub-Sahara's real agricultural output, 1980–85, was −0.7 percent annually, compared to 2.9 percent yearly, 1970–79.[1]

Adjustment lending has elicited criticisms within and outside the Bank and Fund, Concerns include (1) insufficient coordination and diplomacy among the recipient country and its creditors (including the Bank, which presses for lower tariffs to promote domestic competition while the Fund advises on avoiding tariff reductions to maintain public revenues), (2) too little analysis of the effect of the lending on the Bank's portfolio, (3) too much policy dominance by the Bank and Fund, (4) lack of emphasis on reform, (5) overoptimistic assumptions about the international environment and commercial bank lending, (6) neglect of external factors, such as oil shocks and deteriorating terms of trade, (7) too little attention to the impact of adjustment on poverty and on spending for nutrition and education, (8) inadequate program design, (9) poor program implementation, (10) insufficient adaptation to local conditions, (11) the secrecy of the recipient country's letter of intent with the Bank/Fund, reducing internal political dialogue, and (12) too little consideration of how conditionality may undermine a political leadership's legitimacy. On the last point, critics charge Bank/Fund staff with too much emphasis on LDC leaders' political will or courage, reducing the politics of adjustment to an exercise in *machismo*.

African finance and planning officers want the Bank and Fund to place priorities on employment, growth, reducing income inequality, and maintaining health and educational programs, rather than reducing government budget deficits, restructuring parastatals, removing food subsidies, liberalizing international trade, improving exchange rates, and encouraging exports. Because structural adjustment redistributes income, it involves careful political management. African countries need a more gradual approach to adjustment to avoid debilitating consequences and to minimize domestic social costs of adjustment. Countries need flexibility, protection for minimum social services, and public support, including a perception that costs and benefits are distributed fairly. Political leaders must consult all interested parties (not just ministers, high-ranking government servants, and planners) in designing the adjustment program. According to finance and planning officers, the Bank and Fund need to rely more on local research institutions and chambers of commerce and industry for policy analysis. As Avramovic argues, "Adjustment and development programmes should be prepared, and seen to be prepared, by national authorities of African countries rather than by foreign advisers and international organizations. Otherwise commitment will be lacking."[2]

The history of colonialism and neocolonialism in Africa indicates how little experience Africans have had in directing their own economic plans and technical adaptation and progress. Technical change can be viewed as a prolonged learning process based on experience and problem solving. Each successive piece of capital equipment is more productive, since learning advances are embodied in new capital goods.[3] Africans must be in charge of their planning and development for them to capture technological learning gains for sustained economic growth.

When designing programs, policies to solve a problem in one area may create difficulties elsewhere. A devaluation may decrease the trade deficit but raise local-currency costs and the budget deficit. Exchange-rate decontrol may provide " 'absolution' to the racketeers who hoarded foreign currency," a complaint under Tanzania's adjustment.[4] Tariff reductions, as in Nigeria, Ghana, Zambia, Morocco, and Thailand in the 1980s, increased efficiency but reduced revenue and raised short-term unemployment. A reduced current-account deficit may conflict with import liberalization and efficiency.

Stabilization programs tend to become ineffective before attaining their aims, experiencing the worst of employment losses associated with demand restraint and renewed external crises linked to demand expansion. These programs generate a stop-go policy cycle that emanates from weak capabilities, strong societal pressures, and insecure political leaders who target short-term goals and reserve long-term adjustment for their successors.[5]

An Overseas Development Institute study indicates that the principal components of Fund/Bank programs have been demand-reducing measures through repressed consumption by way of income and social-spending reduction. Indeed, Stewart shows that 99 percent of IMF programs in the Sub-Sahara, 1980–84, applied limits on credit expansion, and 91 percent, restraint on central government expenditure.[6] Additionally, sub-Saharan governments object to the Fund's market ideology (preoccupation with price and public-enterprise reforms) and neglect of external determinants of stagnation and instability. Moreover, with the income elasticity of tax revenue low in the Sub-Sahara, IMF austerity usually curtails spending, especially anti-poverty and long-term investment programs. In their Declaration of Uruguay, 27–29 October 1988, the seven largest Latin American countries contended: "The conditionality of adjustment programs, sector lending, and restructuring agreements often entails measures that are inadequate and contradictory, making the economic policies more difficult in an extremely harsh economic climate."[7]

The linking of government and commercial bank support to IMF agreements with debtor countries has increased the pressure on low-income countries to acquiesce to IMF terms. Yet in October 1987 the IMF announced a $65 million standby agreement with Costa Rica in which it did not require the government to reach an agreement with private banks concerning its arrears.[8] Unfortunately this break in IMF, World Bank, commercial bank, and official donor solidarity is rare. A further reducing of the linkage between Fund/Bank agreements and official and commercial creditors in low-income sub-Saharan Africa would increase Africa's options.

Stein argues that World Bank/IMF recommendations fail to analyze how the existing African economic structure embodies attributes earlier supported by the Bank or Fund. For example, the Bank, as the largest donor, wrote the appraisal supporting the $250 million externally financed Mufundi Pulp and Paper Mill in Tanzania in December 1978; the project experienced substantial cost overruns and has many features, such as import substitution and high foreign-exchange- and capital-intensity, that the Bank now opposes. Furthermore, the Bank/Fund recommended privatization and foreign investment, even though these policies implied the growth of MNCs, major contributors to capital-intensive import-substitution production and high industrial concentration, which the Bank now condemns. Finally, international capital has often demanded measures that distort the market.[9]

The Politics of Lending and Adjustment

The case studies in chapter 6 showed how the funds from adjustment lending and the distribution of benefits from Bank/Fund stabilization and restructuring influenced the shifts of power within sub-Saharan countries. For example, in Tanzania in the late 1980s, President Mwiyi, some economists, business people, and bureaucrats supported Fund/Bank liberalization reforms from which they subsequently benefited.

Bank reform programs emphasize reducing government intervention to set prices and shelter inefficient sectors. The Bank, however, is limited because its division of labor with the Fund places the price it considers the most important to liberalize, the exchange rate, under Fund jurisdiction. However, the Bank "radicals," who share some views of the Latin American structuralists (see below), stress that the objective of supply-oriented SAPs is to raise export supply elasticity to enable the Marshall-Lerner condition (sufficiently high trade elasticities for the current-account balance to improve with domestic currency devaluation) to operate.

Bank conditionality offers opportunities for borrowers to cheat because the Bank usually specifies tens of conditions, whose fulfillments may not be achieved for several years. Since surely not all of the 100-plus conditions for Thailand during its 1983 SAL mattered, the overloaded administration, which had discretion in choosing priorities, could use the program to favor certain individuals and departments and evade or deemphasize some unwanted conditions. While Bank documents argue that limiting conditionality to a smaller number of concerns would enable the Bank to take a stricter position of fulfillment, Bank politics results in a SAL becoming "a 'Christmas tree' decorated with enough conditions to please everyone."[10]

The Bank did not anticipate the global debt crisis of 1982 or the sudden cessation of commercial bank lending to the Sub-Sahara in the late 1980s. After 1982, the Bank was more open to using SALs to persuade a reluctant government to embrace policy reforms. The power relationship between the Bank and recipient, rather than the severity of the recipient's economic disease, principally determined conditionality. The countries (mostly sub-Saharan) with the weakest bargaining strength were more likely to accept more heavily conditioned loans than better placed bargainers, such as Brazil, the Philippines, and South Korea. Thus, those least in need of reform medicine swallowed it most readily, while those most in need, by the Bank's criteria, swallowed little at all.

A clearer surrender to political pressure from the United States was the Bank's $1.25 billion loan to Argentina in 1988, despite the absence of an IMF stabilization program, to enable the country to reduce its debt to U.S. commercial banks. Additionally, before 1991, the United States also pressured the Bank to tolerate much slippage of conditionality fulfillment by Kenya and the Philippines. In Bangladesh, a loan officer of the Bank bowed to intense pressure from its executive board to meet country targets, however unpromising the government's potential performance and whatever the negotiating position of the recipient government.[11]

In the 1980s, IMF conditions were quantified and precise and the consequences of failure to meet conditions non-negotiable and serious, resulting in a suspension of further lending until reinstatement by the IMF Board. In contrast, Bank conditionality became increasingly soft, with little penalty for poor compliance. One strategy that borrowers use is to negotiate an ambiguous condition (such as "prepare a satisfactory programme of action for the sugar sector," for Mauritius in 1984–85); at assessment they receive the benefit of the doubt from the Bank. Indeed, the Bank has not worked out any method for assessing the impact of adjustment lending. During the decade, 1980–90, the Bank refused the release of a second or third loan tranche only to Senegal (1982) and Argentina (1989). Most negotiations between the Bank and recipient center on when, not whether, after evaluation the subsequent tranche will be released.

Are reforms sustained after Bank adjustment programs are completed? Krueger, a sometime World Bank insider, contends that a Bank program tips money and political power within the country toward those benefiting from liberalization. However, empirical evidence indicates, except for the shift to a flexible exchange-rate regime, the overwhelming majority of policy reforms lasted no longer than the Bank program—an unsurprising finding, given the looseness of conditions and assessment and the Bank's eschewing the strategy of organizing the gainers or compensating the losers from reform.

In the late 1980s, LDCs successfully pressured the Bank toward increasing its lending in excess of the growing debt-service payment received, but the Bank refused to admit the policy change, since it has a policy against allowing fresh loans to countries in arrears on its past loans. For such a transfer to take place, the Bank has to perform a ritual dance, where-by a third party pays off the Bank's arrears, knowing that the forthcoming Bank lending will allow the third party to be promptly repaid.[12]

Trade, Exchange Rate, and Capital Market Policies

Although price controls, exchange-rate misalignments, and government budget deficits contributed to Africa's external crisis, the immediate freeing of markets and contraction of spending will not resolve the disequilibrium. Many sub-Saharan governments feel that the Bank and IMF focus only on demand reduction. After 1981, the IMF emphasized shock treatment for demand restraint in the low-income Sub-

Sahara, rarely provided financing for external adjustments, and cut programs from three years to one year, applying Reaganomics internationally. One year is not enough for adjustment. Demand restrictions, inflation deceleration, and currency depreciation do not switch expenditures to exports and import substitutes or expand primary production quickly enough to have the desired effect on prices and trade balance. Studies indicate, even in DCs (for example, the United States, 1985–88), the current-account improvement from devaluation usually takes about two to five years, usually beginning with a worsening trade balance in the first year. The time for adjustment is due to the lags between changes in relative international prices (from exchange-rate changes) and responses in quantities traded. Lags involve time for recognition, decision (assessing the change), delivery, replacement (waiting to use up inventories and wear our machines), and production.[13] Even after 1988, despite increased emphasis of SAPs on productive capacity and long-term sectoral change, in practice African countries still face unrealistically short adjustment times, resulting in severe economic disruption and excessive hardship for the poor.

The IMF has stressed devaluation and foreign-exchange decontrols to improve the balance of trade, increase domestic prices and terms of trade for agriculture, and reduce shortages of foreign inputs, along with market interest rates to improve capital allocation. Green supports African states' complaints that World Bank or IMF adjustment programs fail to consider sub-Saharan market imperfections. However, government frequently creates market imperfections through policies of financial repression, encouraging financial institutions and instruments from which the state can expropriate seigniorage (or claim resources in return for controlling currency issue and credit expansion). Government favors and protects an oligopolistic banking system whose reserve requirements and obligatory holdings of government bonds enable the state to tap savings at zero or low interest rates. Authorities suppress private bond and equity markets through transactions taxes, special taxes on income from capital, and inconducive laws because of the difficulty of extracting seigniorage from private assets. The state imposes interest rate ceilings to stifle private sector competition in fund raising.

Imposing these ceilings, foreign-exchange controls, high reserve requirements, and restrictions on private capital markets increases the flow of domestic resources to the public sector without higher taxes, inflation, or interest rates. Banks engage in nonprice rationing of loans, facing pressure for loans from those with political connections but otherwise allocating credit according to transaction costs, all of which leave no opportunity for charging a premium for risky (and sometimes innovative) projects. Overall, these policies also encourage capital-intensive projects and discourage capital investment.

Africa's financially repressive regimes, uncompetitive markets, and banking bureaucracies not disciplined by market and profit tests may encourage the adoption of inefficient lending criteria. The high arrears, delinquency, and default of many African (especially official) banks and development lending institutions result from failure to tie lending to productive investment, neglect of marketing, delayed loan disbursement and unrealistic repayment schedules, misapplication of loans, ineffective supervision, apathy of bank management in recovering loans, and irresponsible and undisciplined borrowers, including many who (for cultural reasons or misunderstanding government's role) fail to distinguish loans from grants. Thus Nigeria's highly oligopolistic money markets, financial repression (of interest rates and exchange rates), government loans boards lacking accountability, and sluggish expansion in response to improved prices in export and import-substitution industries prevented timely adjustments to financial and exchange-rate changes.[14]

Yet even though it helped to create these market imperfections, government cannot immediately decontrol all prices and liberalize foreign-exchange and capital markets. Although devaluation raises import prices, the demand for foreign exchange may not be restrained, as relaxing foreign-exchange licenses and import restrictions spurs the use of foreign inputs and probably increases capital flight in the short run. Indeed, substantial devaluation may generate hyperinflation, as the domestic currency experiences a free fall that expectations make irreversible (Zambia in 1985–87 and Sierra Leone in 1986–87).

The effect of devaluation (say, from C90=$1 to C228=$1) on the trade balance depends on demand and supply elasticities, considered by critics to be low in African agriculture, especially over a one- to two-year period. The elasticity of demand for African primary products like tea, coffee, sugar, and cocoa is so low that increasing the output of agricultural exports to undertake Bank/Fund-sponsored adjustment might result in reduced revenues from increased output. On the supply side, African farmers have little short-run (one year or less) but substantial long-run elasticity (0.3–0.9) for cash crops, as farmers choose to allocate labor and land variously to commercial output, subsistence commodities, black-market activity, nonfarm work, or leisure. Supply response would be at least a year or two for cotton and tobacco and between five and six years for tree crops such as coffee, tea, cashews, and sisal in Tanzania. Cost-induced inflationary pressures due to devaluation (from economic interests fighting to maintain income and consumption shares) should reduce output expansion. Inadequate infrastructure, such as poor transport for Ghanaian cocoa, limits supply increases, slowing export response to higher cedi prices for a given dollar price of cocoa. Still, most African countries no longer oppose devaluation but want more control on its size, timing, structure (such as single versus multiple exchange rates), and accompanying policy measures.[15]

When IMF conditions require devaluation and an improved trade balance to extend further credit in a year or so, African countries have little choice in adjustment. While it is sufficient for the sums of the export and import demand elasticities to be at least one for devaluation to improve the trade balance, actual short-run African elasticities often appear much below necessary and sufficient levels. Most African finance ministers are elasticity pessimists, doubting that devaluation will improve the trade balance, certainly not in the short run, over which period empirical studies suggest that elasticities are perverse, even in the industrialized countries. In any event, governments rarely know the "correct" market rate or how exchange-rate changes will affect income and trade variables that feed back to affect the equilibrium price of foreign exchange. Finally, African countries remove balance-of-payments deficits quickly not from exchange-rate changes (and expenditure switching) but from reduced import demand due to a fall in real income (or a depressed economy).

Trade liberalization in the midst of stabilization, even if politically possible, may perpetuate a government budget crisis. As Mosley, Harrigan, and Toye argue, given labor and resource immobility, early liberalization of external trade and supply-side stimulation in "one glorious burst" result in rising unemployment, inflation, and capital flight and the subsequent undermining of adjustment programs. This trade-reform failure is consistent with second-best theory, which indicates that removing one distortion in a highly distorted economy may reduce overall welfare.

Mosely, Harrigan, and Toye and FAO suggest the following trade, exchange, and capital market liberalization sequence: (1) liberalizing imports of critical capital and other inputs, (2) devaluing domestic currency to a competitive level, while simultaneously restraining monetary and fiscal expansion to curb inflation and convert a nominal devaluation to a real devaluation, (3) promoting exports through liberalizing commodity markets, subsidies, and other schemes, (4) allocating foreign exchange for maintaining and repairing infrastructure for production increases, (5) removing controls on internal interest rates to achieve positive real rates, and expanding loans agencies to include farmers and small business people, (6) reducing public sector deficits to eliminate reliance on foreign loans at banking standards without decreasing real development spending, and reforming agricultural marketing to spur farmers to sell their surplus, (7) liberalizing other imports, rationalizing the tariff structure, and removing price controls and subsidies to the private sector, and (8) abandoning external capital-account controls.

The eighth step recognizes the necessity of reforming internal capital markets before liberalizing international capital movements. However, neither Bank/Fund recommendations nor implementation bore much relationship to this eight-stage sequence. In most cases, the Bank asked for liberalizing trade early without limiting the imports that it should be applied to. For example, the foreign-exchange requirements associated with trade liberalization, the major component of the Bank's first SAL in Kenya (1980), became unsustainable, so liberalization had to be abandoned. Additionally, import liberalization preceded agricultural export expansion based on commodity market liberalization, price decontrol, and export promotional schemes. On the other hand, Ghana, under a Bank SECAL beginning in 1983, allocated foreign exchange through an auction, and the goods eligible for entry to the auction expanded over time in line with the increased supply of foreign currency.

Recipients should implement IMF demand-reducing programs before the Bank's supply-increasing ones. If countries begin with supply reforms, which take a longer time, the lack of demand restraint will contribute to inflation and an unmanageable current-account deficit. Still, adjustment loan recipients also need to avoid excessive initial demand restraint that depresses the economy; simultaneous devaluation, as in stage 2, could avoid this contractionary effect.[16]

Inflationary Financing

Large budget deficits, creating inflation at less than full employment, were major sources of external imbalance and macroeconomic instability. Countries that increased expenditures when commodity prices boomed or when external funds were readily available, such as Nigeria in the 1970s, could not easily reduce spending when external funding later fell. Many countries that had received substantial adjustment loans and reduced their budget deficits in the early 1980s suffered growing shortfalls in the late 1980s when the loans dried up (or, as in Zambia and Malawi, the terms of trade fell). As noted earlier, several sub-Saharan countries experienced inflationary pressures as a result of relying on expanded domestic financing to replace external funds. Inflation, in turn, reduces access to international borrowing and makes structural adjustment difficult.[17]

Persistent inflationary financing may, however, be less disruptive than losing political support through demand-reducing financial policies and resistance to wage and price increases. African governments, such as Ghana in the early 1980s, preferred the diffused and ambiguous unpopularity of allowing rising prices and foreign-exchange shortages to the risk of taking more sharply focused countermeasures that could provoke the opposition of powerful interest groups.

When communication between economic groups is poor, several classes or economic interests may overestimate their strength and make excessive money demands that can be worked out only through inflation. Such a process may reduce tension that could otherwise result in revolution or war. Many African heads of state or ministers of labor averted a political strike or mass discontent by granting inflationary wage increases. Nigeria's General Yakubu Gowon temporarily forestalled political rebellion by awarding Adebo Commission recommendations for general wage increases in 1971 and Udoji Commission salaries to accommodate high-level civil servants and military officers in 1974 (although inflation, worker grievances, and military discontent contributed to the 29 July 1975 coup that overthrew him). The political threat of conflict may be so great that government has little choice but to tolerate political inflation.[18] Moreover, inflation gains additional momentum once workers, consumers, and business people expect it to continue and once major segments of the economy have a vested interest in sustaining it.

Reductions in Social Spending

How do the effects of structural adjustment programs on income and government spending influence inequality, poverty rates, and basic needs attainment? Past DC adjustment suggests that SALs would contract income and social spending, thus contributing to high rates of malnutrition, infant mortality, and illiteracy. Figure 7.1 shows a highly positive correlation between the United States' infant mortality (an indicator of sanitation and clean water facilities, since infants are especially susceptible to waterborne diseases) and unemployment rates, suggesting that poverty and unemployment reduce health care, nutrition, and sanitation and raise infant mortality. In the Sub-Sahara, adjustment to the debt overhang and stagnation of the 1980s reduced (or slowed the growth rate of) nutrition, infant survival, life expectancy, and primary school enrollments.

A UNICEF study of eighteen sub-Saharan countries indicates that rising debt was accompanied by falling GDP per capita, 1980–85, in 72 percent of the countries, declining government expenditures per person in 60 percent, and falling shares of both health and education in 47 percent.[19] To adjust, the Sub-Sahara had to reduce its external deficit substantially between 1982 and 1986 (in the midst of declining terms of trade and poor export prospects) by cutting back imports (because of adjustment programs and falling real income) and government spending.[20]

Between 1980 and 1984, twenty-six of twenty-seven sub-Saharan countries with IMF-supported adjustment programs reduced govern-

Figure 7.1. Infant Mortality Rate and Unemployment Rate in the United States, 1915–1967

Source: Brenner (1973: 149).

Note: Fluctuations in infant mortality rate per 1,000 live births under 1 day matched with those in rate of unemployment index/inverted for the United States, 1915–67.

ment spending as a share of GDP. During 1984 to 1988, twenty-three sub-Saharan countries undertook programs to increase revenue and decrease expenditure as a part of Bank/Fund-sponsored adjustment, while six made other government finance reforms, including increasing *relative* civil service wages (as in Ghana and Uganda), reducing aggregate real wages, and setting ceilings for recurrent and capital expenses, transfers, and subsidies.[21]

Most sub-Saharan countries failed to maintain the physical infrastructure built in the 1960s; they reduced expenditures on social services and subsidies, cut back public-sector employment, and experienced reduced real wages and increased unemployment. Average annual growth in private consumption per capita was negative during 1982–85 in the Sub-Sahara and in all low-income and highly indebted countries receiving adjustment lending. Only manufacturing exporters (mostly from Asia) receiving adjustment loans had a positive growth (2.2 percent yearly 1982–85) in consumption per capita.[22]

The numerous cuts in living standards in sub-Saharan countries undergoing adjustment usually hurt the poor and disadvantaged disproportionately. Low-income households adjusted with increased labor, self-production, reserve use, debt, or (with the paucity of public assistance) income transfers within the clan. Even IMF Managing Director Michel Camdessus stated, "Too often in recent years it is the poorest segments of the population that have carried the heaviest burden of economic adjustment." In rare instances where the less privileged have political power, such as the Malaysian Malays, stabilization programs, food subsidies, and exemption from credit restrictions prevented severe damage to them.[23]

Pinstrup-Anderson shows how macroeconomic adjustment in Brazil, Botswana, Chile, Ghana, Jamaica, Peru, the Philippines, Sri Lanka, Zimbabwe, South Korea, and Uruguay in the early 1980s generally reduced health spending, child nutrition, and average calorie consumption for the poor. In many countries (such as South Korea, Sri Lanka, Botswana, and the Philippines in table 7.1), adjustment slowed down improvements in indicators like infant mortality. For Uganda, experiencing SA in 1982, maizemeal prices rose 180 times and wages only 11 times, 1972–85, so that nutritional levels deteriorated among the poor, except for rural people who produced food for their own consumption. In Zambia, real food subsidies declined 62 percent during adjustment, 1980–85. During Chile's adjustment in the earlier 1980s, average calorie consumption fell for all except the richest 20 percent, contributing to increased inequality. Zaïre's adjustment to reduced copper demand and declining terms of trade in the 1970s affected real minimum wages, in 1982 only 3 percent of their 1970 level![24]

Adjustment to balance aggregate demand and supply often depressed the economy. Reduced growth and weakened financial positions adversely affected social programs for the poor. In many African countries, annual real health and educational spending in the mid- to late 1980s was only one-quarter to one-half that of a decade before.

Food prices increased, unemployment rose, and real wages fell as Africa decontrolled agricultural and industrial prices. Compared to 1980, real nonagricultural wages dropped considerably during stabilization and adjustment programs (most with the Bank/Fund)—in Tanzania by 40 percent to 1983; in Zambia, 33 percent to 1984; in Malawi, 24 percent by 1984; in Kenya, 22 percent by 1985; in Zimbabwe, 11 percent by 1984; in Mauritius, 10 percent by 1985; and in Swaziland, 5 percent by 1983. During the same period, open unemployment appears to have increased in all these countries.[25]

The ratio of education and health to total government expenditures

Table 7.1. Malnutrition among Preschool Children and Infant Mortality Rates for Selected Developing Countries in the Early 1980s

Country	Percentage of Preschool Children Malnourished		Infant Mortality Rate (per thousand)	
	Period	Percentages for First and Last Adjustment Year	Period	Rates for First and Last Adjustment Year
Brazil	n.a.	n.a.	1982–64	65–73
Botswana	1982–84	25–31	1981–86	68–65
Chile	1982–84	8.8–8.4	1981–84	27–20
Ghana	1980–84	35–54	1970s–80s	86–107
Jamaica	1978–85	38–41	n.a.	n.a.
Peru	1980–83	42–66	n.a.	n.a.
Philippines	1981–85	18–22	1981–84	62–58
Sri Lanka	1979–82	6.1–9.4	1978–80	37–34
Zimbabwe	1982–84	20–20	n.a.	n.a.
South Korea	n.a.	n.a.	1979–81	38–36

Source: Per Pinstrup-Anderson, "The Impact of Macroeconomic Adjustment: Food Security and Nutrition," in Commander (1989: 91), citing Giovanni Andrea Cornia, "Economic Decline and Human Welfare in the First Half of the 1980s," in Cornia, Jolly, and Stewart, vol. 1 (1987: 11–47).

Note: N.a. = data not available.

for the twenty-one AL recipients fell from 21 percent during 1978–81 to 20 percent in 1982–86, affecting nutrition, school enrollment rates, and literacy. Countries with the most adjustment reduced their share of social expenses the most. Between 1980 and 1985, social indicators for low-income sub-Saharan Africa showed no progress. Life expectancy at birth increased from 46 to 48 years, but infant mortality rates remained at 126 per thousand and the average daily calorie consumption fell from 2,060 to 1,911. The FAO estimate of per capita calorie intake as a percentage of daily requirements fell by 1 percent for fifteen recipients of adjustment loans from 1978–81 to 1982–85. Ghana suffered a decline from 79 percent to 72 percent; Zambia, from 96 percent to 92 percent; and Malawi, from 108 percent to 105 percent.

The effect of adjustment varies among the population. Retrenched civil servants and employees may be victims of structural adjustment and stabilization—laid off because of austerity measures or production shifts. Low-income and vulnerable groups hurt by reductions in social programs or price shifts include the urban working class, small farm holders, rural landless laborers, lactating and pregnant women, infants, the disabled, and the aged, but some political leaders and bureaucrats may gain from access to resources and information on shifting opportunities, commercial and industrial business people from decontrol and privatization, and commercial farmers from higher food prices.[26]

Economists with the Bank/Fund argue that the required reforms were consistent with good economic management, as African countries would have needed to adjust their economies regardless of whether the IMF or Bank was involved. Yet the Sub-Sahara suffered a substantial fall in bilateral and IMF credits and import capacity in the 1980s, decreasing the options available for external and internal balances.[27] The fiscal straitjacket prevented African governments from designing programs that could emphasize longer-term adjustment while reducing short-run damage to social programs.

Investment Rate Reductions

A debt overhang indicates outstanding debt so large that investment will be inefficiently low without new money or debt reductions. People's expectations of future debt burdens reduce the incentives for investment and domestically initiated adjustment, and future growth becomes less attractive as higher proportions have to be transferred abroad. When future repayments are large, these obligations act as a tax on investment because a share of returns goes to creditors. A high-debt country invests at less than the most efficient level and overconsumes or engages in capital flight.[28]

Many African countries, having endured years of austerity and stagnation, cannot afford to reduce consumption to effect an external transfer, and thus they shift the burden to investment. The Sub-Sahara's gross domestic investment as a percentage of GDP fell from 23 percent in 1979 to 15 percent in 1989; the gross savings rate declined from 20 percent to 13 percent. Indeed, except for Ghana, 1984–90, which had started with a low investment rate base in the 1960s and 1970s, Bank/Fund adjustment programs contributed to reduced investment rates in sub-Saharan Africa, thus wiping out the investment gains of the 1970s.[29]

The Agricultural Sector

Agriculture, with 62 percent of the labor force and 19 percent of GDP in LDCs, accounts for 71 percent of the labor force and 34 percent of GDP in sub-Saharan Africa. It is important for macroeconomic performance directly and, through raw materials, labor, and product demand, for the industrial sector.[30] IMF adjustment programs to depreciate domestic relative to foreign currency, to free farm prices, and reduce revenues of official marketing boards not only cut price distortions but also expanded farm incomes, prices, and employment opportunities, thus attracting some urban workers, facing declining real wages, back to the rural areas, especially in Ghana. While empirical studies indicate a low short-run elasticity of supply (that is, little percentage change in quantity supplied in response to a 1 percent change in price) in African agriculture, the elasticity in the long run, where the farmer can vary the hectares devoted to a given crop, is high.[31]

Sub-Saharan adjustment increased agricultural income inequality. Agricultural export expansion, higher farm producer prices, and reduced food subsidies benefited landed classes and affluent commercial farmers disproportionately and had little impact on smallholders producing food for subsistence, whose output expansion was limited by lack of labor, land, credit, or appropriate technology. But adjustment usually reduced the surplus that monopsony marketing agencies (often controlled by political leaders and their clients) captured at the expense of agricultural classes generally—landlords, cultivators, and farm workers.[32]

Samora Moises's FRELIMO government in Mozambique and Robert Mugabe's ZANU government in Zimbabwe tried to shift the terms of trade from industry (under the previous white supremacist policies) to agriculture. Zimbabwe's 1982 IMF agreement resulted in a wage freeze and real wage decline, substantial food price increases, and reduced health expenditures, 1982–84. The Ministry of Health found that the percentage of underweight children less than six years old in rural areas rose from 18–22 percent in 1982 to 48 percent in 1984. The Zambia Basic Needs Report in the early 1980s outlined how reduced recurrent allocations after adjustment discouraged a rural woman with a sick child from walking 15 kilometers to the nearest health center, as the woman knew the center was frequently out of drugs.[33]

A study by Lele of the World Bank's approach to agricultural development castigated the shift away from integrated rural development, with its emphasis on supply interventions such as infrastructure, credit, research and extension, to private sector initiatives and adjustment programs. This shift, she argues, is

> flawed by its inadequate recognition of the variety of causal factors underlying past growth (or decline), of the likely effects of price-based policy reforms on aggregate supply responses, and of the complementary, non-price micro-economic actions needed to ensure that the policy reform process was sustainable beyond the short term, and that it was harmonized with underlying development realities and long-term goals.[34]

Indeed, Cleaver, a Bank project economist, argues that farm prices have a minor role relative to state agricultural services in affecting agricultural growth. Ghai and Hewitt de Alcántara indicate that adjustment programs reduced spending for infrastructure and vital farm inputs (seed, fertilizer, and, in the case of Zambia, foreign exchange for jute bags to collect grain for harvest), adversely affecting small farmers (except in Ghana and Zimbabwe).[35]

State Centralization

Accords between a sub-Saharan government and the Bank/Fund force the state to monitor closely the financial flows essential to reverse external imbalances and reduced living standards. To deal with the Bank/Fund, the state needs to improve its analytical, planning, and data-gathering capabilities, provide technical assistance and training, reform state-owned enterprises, and privatize public enterprises.

Stein's study indicates that IMF structural adjustment lending in Tanzania in the late 1980s reinforced the post-Nyerere strategy of state centralization and production, including state monitoring of parastatal enterprises operating on a commercial basis.[36] Moreover, those in control of the state protected those sectors containing their (and allies') vital interests during negotiations with the IMF and subsequent implementation of the AL. Polyani's 1944 words apply to the IMF, World Bank, and their liberal African allies in the 1990s: "Even those who wished most ardently to free the state from all unnecessary duties, and whose whole philosophy demanded the restriction of state activities, could not but entrust the self-same state with the new powers, organs and instruments required for the establishment of *laissez-faire*." Ironically, for adjustment policies to be successful, the Bank/Fund must strengthen the capacity of the African state.[37]

The Structuralist Critique

Beginning in the 1950s, U.N. Economic Commission for Latin America (ECLA) economists criticized IMF orthodox premises that external disequilibrium was short-term, generated by excess demand, requiring primarily contractionary monetary and fiscal policies and currency devaluation. ECLA economists emphasized the necessity for long-run institutional and structural economic change—accelerating the growth of export earnings, improving the external terms of trade, increasing the supply elasticity of food output through land reform, reducing income inequality, and expanding the industrial sector and antimonopoly measures before shorter-run financial and exchange-rate policies would be effective.

The new structuralist critique of the late 1970s and 1980s also stressed the long-run transformation of the economy. Critics viewed the Latin American payments crises as resulting from a long-term structural crisis in export supply and wanted IMF programs to stress these long-run changes and avoid austerity programs.[38]

Martens argues that the World Bank and IMF should stress meeting policy objectives (such as reduced debt or reduced current-account deficit), not policy instruments (such as changes in the exchange rate, tariffs, or budget deficit). If the country does not attain its objectives, the Bank and Fund would then examine the policy instruments used,[39] an approach consistent with longer-run structural transformation.

In sub-Saharan Africa, the IMF and Bank need to adopt a medium- to long-term perspective on economic restructuring. While the IMF's

1983 SAP in Ghana facilitated relatively quick adjustment in the previously distorted producer price of cocoa, the SAP in Zambia at the same time resulted in no movement toward internal or external adjustment because Zambia's major export, copper, was continuing to receive declining world (and producer) prices. The Bank/Fund should have used structural adjustment for helping Zambia diversify its export and import-substitution sectors, so that a more diversified Zambia would be less vulnerable to fluctuating world prices in the long run.

The UNICEF Critique

To avoid heavy social costs, UNICEF urges "adjustment with a human face," including Bank/Fund adjustment programs emphasizing the restoration of LDC growth while protecting the most vulnerable groups, as well as growth-oriented adjustment, such as expansionist monetary and fiscal policies and Bank/Fund loans sufficient to avoid a depressed economy. The empowerment and participation of vulnerable groups—the landless, the urban poor, and women—are essential to improve policies and protect these groups and children, especially the undernourished.[40]

Criticisms by the ECA/OAU

The Lagos Plan, the Abuja Statement, and the ECA Alternative SAP

The ECA's Conference of Ministers formulated state goals and plans at Rabat, Morocco, in March 1979, resulting in their adoption the next month in Monrovia, Liberia, by the Assembly of Heads of States and Government of the OAU. On 29 April 1980, in Lagos, Nigeria, this assembly adopted the Lagos Plan of Action (LPA) to implement the Monrovia Strategy. The Plan's goals of improving income distribution, eradicating poverty and unemployment, democratizing development, promoting increasing national self-reliance, accelerating self-sustained development, and speeding up regional economic integration are generally incontrovertible. But the policy emphases of the ECA/OAU's "socialist" (actually statist) Lagos Plan were detailed comprehensive planning, large parastatal firm expansion, capital-goods and heavy-industry development, increased state intervention in peasant price-setting, and an introverted development strategy,[41] approaches the Bank criticizes with some merit.

In 1982, the ECA's Adedeji stressed that, on economic and political matters, the international community must give Africa the respect of sovereign states on economic and political matters, stating that

> if Africa is to develop the necessary self-confidence to pull its economy out of the shadows of backwardness and underdevelopment, it is essential that our partners-in-development respect our priorities, perceptions, goals and strategies. It also means that the provision of financial and technical assistance from such partners must reflect those African priorities and goals. It is only by so doing that the ghost of the suspicion, that the African economy is being manipulated by outside powers with a view to frustrating the achievement of national and regional economic objectives, can be laid to rest.[42]

Africa's economic growth in the 1980s, after the adoption of the Lagos Plan, was negative. While more than thirty countries adopted Bank/Fund adjustment programs, few of these programs contributed to Africa's long-term development objectives. For the ECA, the reasons were orthodox financial, credit, exchange-rate, and trade prescriptions that had little validity in Africa's poorly structured economies.

In 1986, ECA/OAU indicated to the U.N. General Assembly Special Session that Africa's fundamental problem was a "vicious interaction between excruciating poverty and abysmally low levels of productivity in an environment characterized by serious deficiencies in basic and social infrastructure, most especially the physical capital, research capabilities, technological know-how and human resource development that are indispensable to an integrated and dynamic economy."[43] The next year, inspired by the U.N. Programme of Action for Africa, the ECA, with financial support from the U.N. Development Programme and consultation with economists and government and international organization officials in Africa and elsewhere, embarked on a search for an African alternative to SAPs. The ECA recognized that rescheduling debt in the early to mid-1980s merely postponed debt-service payments without reducing the debt's present value. Accordingly, in 1987 the ECA's Abuja (Nigeria) statement addressed debt relief, calling for lower interest rates on existing debts, longer repayment and grace periods, conversion of bilateral debts into grants for low-income countries undertaking structural adjustment, repayment of debt in local currency, and conversion of debt into equity.[44]

For the ECA,

> the major transitional adverse social consequences of structural adjustment programmes are: declining per capita income and real wages; rising unemployment and underemployment; deterioration in the level of social

services as a result of cuts on social public expenditures; falling educational and training standards; rising malnutrition and health problems; and rising poverty levels and income inequalities . . . Many African governments have had to effect substantial cuts in their public social expenditures such as education, health and other social services in order to release resources for debt service and reduce their budget deficits. From the point of view of long-term development, the reduction in public expenditures on education . . . necessitated by stabilization and structural investment programmes, has meant a reversal of the process, initiated in the early 1960s, of heavy investment in human resources development. . . . Today, per capita expenditure on education in Africa is not only the lowest in the world but is also declining. . . . Thus, Africa may begin the next millennium with a greater proportion of its population being illiterate and unskilled than it did at the beginning of the post-independence era in the 1960s. . . . All indications are to the effect that structural adjustment programmes are not achieving their objectives.[45]

The ECA objected to the World Bank's and IMF's adjustment programs emphasizing deregulating prices, devaluing domestic currency, liberalizing trade and payments, promoting domestic savings, restricting the money supply, reducing government spending, and privatizing production. These programs, ECA argued, fail in economies like those of Africa with a fragile and rigid production structure not responsive to market forces.

Africa's rigidities have resulted in drastic cuts in domestic spending, which retard structural adjustment. Restrictive credit policy in Africa reduces investment and output, especially of social service and essential goods, and accelerates inflation. Increased interest rates encourage speculative rather than productive activities, reduce capacity utilization, and accentuate shortages of critical goods. Indiscriminate export promotion undermines food self-sufficiency and contributes to undesirable environmental degradation. Devaluation does not improve African international payments balances because of resource immobility, low demand elasticities, capital flights, and inflationary impetus from increased prices of imported inputs. Liberalizing trade leads to greater external dependence and is not feasible in the face of DC protection against African exports. Doctrinaire privatization policies required by the World Bank and IMF fail to consider the weak private sector in Africa, its substantial externalities, and the empirical evidence that public-sector efficiency is comparable to that in the private sector, given firms of the same size. The recommendation for more reliance on prices disregards Africa's market imperfections and structural rigidities.

Finally, reducing budget deficits has an adverse impact on the welfare of Africa's poorest by decreasing spending on education, health, sanitation, water supply, and other social services. The ECA argued that trade, price, and fiscal balances cannot be ends in themselves, especially in the short run. Structural adjustment programs must be consistent with spurring long-term growth and reducing poverty in Africa.[46]

The ECA called for a holistic alternative to failed Bank/Fund structural adjustment programs, with an emphasis on increased growth and long-run capacity to adjust. A series of meetings in early 1989 with senior officials of central banks and ministries of finance and economic planning culminated with the adoption of the African Alternative Framework to Structural Adjustment Programmes for Socio-Economic Recovery and Transformation (AAF-SAP) by ministers of finance and economic planning in Addis Ababa, 10 April 1989. AAF-SAP's main thrusts were integrating SAPs and long-term development, designing programs for the characteristics of specific countries, considering human dimensions, democratic decision-making and planning, and inter-country cooperation in planning, implementing, and monitoring national programs.[47]

The ECA contended that excessive outward development, a predominantly subsistence economy, narrow production base, weak intersectoral links, capital shortages, lack of entrepreneurship, low level of technological application, neglect of the informal sector, degraded environment, urban bias, market fragmentation, and weak institutions were major contributors to Africa's underdevelopment. Also, the Commission pointed out, economic management suffered from inadequate institutions, poor accountability, short-term planning, and unfavorable external factors. For the ECA, these factors meant that the African economy had a built-in tendency to generate crises from within and assimilate peril from abroad.[48]

Major ECA goals were to reduce mass poverty and immiseration, to provide the poor access to land and other factors of production, to create employment opportunities, and to improve wealth distribution. Africa must stop emulating DC consumption patterns, replacing them with indigenous consumption, and thus reduce imports, especially of luxury items. While ECA conceded that Africa should expand exports where they have a comparative advantage, the commission called for increasing technological internalization, financial autonomy, and intra-African trade and integration (including a reaffirmation of an African Economic Community, which the Lagos Plan had envisioned by the beginning of the twenty-first century).[49]

The ECA's list of policy instruments, while ambitious, was short on specifics. Agrarian policies included land reforms, enhancing women's role in the food sector, increasing agriculture's share of investment, improving rural financial institutions, strengthening agricultural research and extension, subsidizing fertilizers and other farm inputs, guaranteeing minimum prices for food crops managed through strategic food reserves, increasing credit for food production, attaining food self-sufficiency, and creating rural industries and cooperatives. Policies to increase allocative efficiency comprised improving governmental efficiency, privatizing selective industries, realigning consumption patterns with indigenous production possibilities, and minimizing military and other nonproductive spending. Programs to enhance local enterprise included emphasizing small-scale industries and encouraging private entrepreneurship. Fiscal policy instruments encompassed enlarging the tax base, switching expenditures to increase social spending, subsidizing the supply of essential commodities, banning certain luxury items, levying high tax rates on conspicuous consumption, and strengthening science and technology. The ECA's domestic capital and financial policies were aimed at maintaining capital more effectively, allocating credit (using subsidized interest rates) to priority sectors, and liberalizing financial institutions. Policies to increase African economic integration consisted of harmonizing intra-African financial cooperation and reducing African duplication of production capacity. International trade and exchange policies included encouraging capital repatriation, increasing the share of foreign exchange for vital inputs into agricultural and industrial production, undertaking multiple exchange rates to rationalize resource flows, diversifying exports and domestic production, promoting exports, limiting debt servicing to levels consistent with rapid growth, providing incentives for processed exports, and removing DC trade barriers. Finally, the ECA stressed the importance of facilitating mass participation in decision making and promulgating self-help programs.[50]

The ECA emphasized adjustment programs as primarily the responsibility of Africans, who may set up programs in partnership with outside agencies, rather than having these agencies do the formulating, designing, implementing, and monitoring. Democratization encourages the population to accept sacrifices implied by the programs. Moreover, those designing national programs must regularly consult with various ministries, the planning agency, the public sector, private sectors, local authorities, private associations, and so forth. The media and interest groups, not just government, need to be involved in publicizing the program. African policymakers want multilateral agen-

167

cies such as the World Bank and IMF to support the programs that African governments design under alternative SAPs and to stop viewing correct policy as a matter of "macho-political will."[51]

Thus, the ECA feels that conventional structural adjustment programs are inadequate in addressing the real causes of Africa's deep-seated economic problems, including the adverse international economic factors. Indeed, Executive Secretary Adedeji argued that structural adjustment "has produced little enduring poverty alleviation and certain [of its] policies have worked against the poor." According to the ECA, Africa needs a human-centered alternative development strategy that considers a unique production and consumption structure.[52]

While much of this ECA emphasis is sensible, the ECA's continuing stress on detailed control by the state—in the face of lack of data, inability to redistribute income through tax revenue, and shortages of highly prepared managers and professionals to conceive, examine feasibility of, start, keep on schedule, amend, and evaluate investment projects—impedes efficiency and egalitarianism. For effective planning, African states must transcend mere lip service to their constituencies and enter wide consultation with consumers, workers, business people, farmers, other interest groups, regions, and ethnic communities.

Empirical Evidence

IMF (and Bank) adjustment programs seek to restore viability to the balance of payments and maintain it in an environment of price stability and sustainable rates of growth. As the previous chapter points out, the World Bank's own studies indicate that Bank/Fund adjustment programs have been successful.

The ECA has criticized the World Bank view that agricultural and total output growths since the mid 1980s have shown encouraging signs, especially among countries undertaking economic reforms under IMF or Bank SAPs. According to the ECA, countries identified by the Bank and UN as weak adjusting countries (without strong economic reforms) had a positive rate of GDP growth of 1.2 percent annually, 1980–87, compared to strong adjusting countries' yearly −1.5 percent and nonadjusting countries' 3.1 percent per annum.[53] Parfitt argues that two of the states classified as strong adjusters, Zaïre and Nigeria, did not have strong Bank/Fund SAPs, 1986–87; Tanzania should not be classified as a strong reformer because of consistent opposition to SAPs before 1986; and Mali, Sierra Leone, Somalia, and Sudan should be identified by the Bank as strong, not weak, adjusters, because they operated successful programs throughout the 1980s.[54] Analysts need to evaluate the success of adjustment by empirical studies, some of which are summarized below.

Loxley finds little evidence that IMF programs restored growth and external balance or spurred bank credit inflows in the 1970s, as only five of twenty-three sub-Saharan African countries reached growth targets; thirteen of eighteen, inflation targets; and eleven of twenty-eight, trade targets. For Gylfason, the economic performance of thirty-two LDCs signing IMF standby agreements, 1977–79, was not significantly better than ten other LDCs.[55]

King and Robinson use the World Bank's *World Debt Tables* (1984) to compare LDCs rescheduling and not rescheduling debt, 1976–81. They find that reschedulers attained desired outcomes of slower import and debt-service growths but had undesirable slower export (with a three-year lag) and GNP growths, as well as reduced foreign-exchange inflows due to increased risk.[56]

Adjustment programs resulting in switching expenditure from foreign to domestic sources are supposed to improve the external balance while increasing growth. A World Bank study of fifty-four LDCs receiving adjustment lending during 1980–87 indicates that more than half of the recipients improved their current account; however, their average growth was slower than before despite being significantly higher in the short run (though no more sustained) than non-recipients'. Also recipients' export growth and import decline were faster than others', although some recipients' import reduction resulted from lack of foreign exchange. Moreover, while recipients' social indicators were generally higher than others', recipients' calorie intake stagnated or declined during the 1980s, a trend worse than other LDCs experienced. Furthermore, as indicated in chapter 2, UNICEF found in 1980–85, during a period when sub-Saharan African Bank/Fund adjustment program recipients reduced social spending, that child welfare in the Sub-Sahara declined.[57]

The Bank also measures the net change in performance of countries receiving adjustment loans (ALs) in the three years before to the three years after receiving ALs and compares this change to countries not receiving these loans. Among sub-Saharan Africa and low-income countries generally, current-account balances and debt-service ratios improved faster, growth was slower, and inflation faster among recipients than the comparison groups. Middle-income countries receiving ALs, however, had faster growth (though faster inflation) than the comparators. For both low-income and middle-income countries, the burden of adjustment fell heavily on investment.

However, the twelve sub-Saharan countries (including Ghana, Kenya, Malawi, Zambia, and Côte d'Ivoire) that received more than three adjustment loans grew faster than comparators. Among the thirty countries receiving 1980–85 ALs, manufacturing exporters— Brazil, South Korea, the Philippines, Thailand, Turkey, Morocco, Uruguay, Yugoslavia, and Pakistan—had the greatest improvement, while low-income (especially sub-Saharan) countries had the least improvement.

IMF studies suggest that demand-restraining monetary and fiscal policies reduce growth until the long lags associated with exchange-rate, interest-rate, resource-allocation (such as increasing agricultural producer prices), and other market reforms stimulate growth. The 1987 real exchange rate of countries undergoing Bank adjustment depreciated on average by about 40 percent from their 1965–81 levels. Changes in exchange rates and interest rates improved resource allocation and restructured the economy toward exportables and import substitutes, stimulating investment and growth.[58]

Commander's study finds commercial (especially export and import-replacement) farmers, their wage labor, and traders benefiting from exchange-rate and other adjustments. Public-sector employees, domestic-goods producers, and informal-sector workers tend to be hurt by adjustment.[59] Moreover, as indicated before, real wages dropped and unemployment increased in Tanzania, Zambia, Ghana, and Nigeria during the 1980s.

UNCTAD maintains that the economic performance of the twelve least-developed countries with consecutive SAPs throughout the 1980s did not differ significantly from least-developed countries as a whole. Additionally, Africa's overall annual GDP growth during the period was only 0.4 percent, a low rate "largely influenced by the poor performance of countries with strong adjustment programs." Moreover, the ECA's analysis of World Bank data indicated that Africa's GDP growths, investment rates, budget deficits, and debt-service ratios fell after structural adjustment programs. Furthermore, Faini, de Melo, Senhadji, and Stanton's study of ninety-three LDCs undertaking adjustment before 1986, controlling for initial conditions and external factors, finds no evidence of a statistically better (or worse) performance for Bank/Fund loan recipient countries.[60]

Stewart uses World Bank data to ask whether Bank/Fund policies restore external equilibrium and internal balance (including a growth of investment, public expenditure, and imports), as well as long-term development. When she uses World Bank categories, she finds no difference in the fall in GNP per capita, 1980–87, between sub-Saharan countries undergoing strong Bank/Fund adjustment programs and those with weak programs. Additionally, during the period, real domestic investment and export earnings fell, the fiscal deficit remained large, debt continued to accumulate, and the current account did not improve, despite falling imports, in sub-Saharan countries undertaking adjustment. When Stewart deplores that "after undergoing tough programmes, many countries found themselves with reduced real income, increased poverty, deteriorating social conditions, reduced growth potential and often with no significant improvements in their external accounts," she is describing the situation in Nigeria (before the 1989–91 oil price recovery), Zambia, and Tanzania. She concludes that, irrespective of the cause, Bank/Fund policies did not meet their short-run objectives and were undermining growth potential, 1980–87.[61]

Mosley, Harrigan, and Toye and FAO criticize methods for evaluating Bank/Fund adjustment programs. Comparing performance before and after adjustment, though useful and informative, has a strong static bias, FAO points out. The questions to ask are: How would the economy have performed without the policy reforms? How does this performance compare with the actual performance? Moreover, comparing adjusting to non-adjusting countries ignores the conditions when adjustment policies were initially implemented, the different economic and political characteristics of the countries, and the different policies.[62]

Mosley, Harrigan, and Toye reject comparing LDC World Bank AL recipients with LDC nonrecipients; the results will be misleading because recipients are not representative of LDCs generally. For example, perhaps only the most desperate countries apply for Bank ALs, or the Bank may eliminate from consideration economies that are too weak to undergo programs. For this reason, Mosley et al.'s comparisons were based on selecting nonrecipient countries with similar characteristics to 1980–86 recipients. To illustrate, Côte d'Ivoire was paired with Cameroon, Kenya with Tanzania, Malawi with Zimbabwe, Senegal with Sierra Leone, Pakistan with Egypt, and Thailand with Malaysia. Another problem, the linkage of Bank ALs to other finance programs, such as an IMF stabilization agreement, was disentangled by regression analysis, which holds other influences constant.

Although both AL recipient and control groups grew more slowly in the early 1980s than in the late 1970s, the AL group had a significantly worse growth experience than the control group. Among the

AL-assisted countries in which compliance with policy conditionality was high, growth was even more unfavorable compared to the relevant control group. While the standard deviations were large, the AL countries had a greater fall in investment rates (from cutting the government development budget, from the multiplier effect in lowering aggregate domestic demand, and from the lesser constraints on spending on consumer import goods compared to project aid), but a more substantial improvement in current-account balance, a lesser decline in real export growth, and greater reduction in real import growth than non-AL countries (with all differences here and subsequently significant at the 5 percent level).[63]

Mosley, Harrigan, and Toye's regression-based results, which examine growth in all AL countries, in sub-Saharan countries, and in middle-income countries (with time lags varying from zero to two years) as a function of financial flows, compliance with Bank conditionality, and extraneous variables (weather and terms of trade), are consistent with their paired comparisons. Bank financial flows are negatively correlated but compliance with Bank conditions positively correlated with growth, so overall Bank program effects are nil (or perhaps negative, since the negative money effect is immediate, while the positive compliance effect, from price-based and other reforms, is lagged at least a year and uncertain to materialize). The authors explain the surprising negative effects of money flows by showing that they reduce pressures for policy reform and appreciate the real dollar price of domestic currency (as in "Nigerian disease," discussed earlier). The same study finds that Bank financial flows have a strong negative effect and compliance with Bank reform a strong positive impact on export growth in the immediate period, but the relationships are reversed for a longer period (one or two years); the net effect of Bank programs on export growth is negative in the same and next years but positive two years hence. IMF standby credit, while positively related to middle-income countries' growth, is negatively correlated with sub-Saharan growth. Both weather and terms of trade improvement have a positive effect on growth.[64]

FAO, which examines the critical period after 1981–83, divides LDCs into healthy adjusters, who reduced internal and external deficits without jeopardizing growth, so savings and export earnings rose; unhealthy adjusters, who decreased the external deficit by restricting imports and investment, thus threatening the long-term capacity to expand; and deteriorators, whose internal and external deficits increased. Deteriorators appreciated their currencies in real terms, unhealthy adjusters' currencies did not change, and healthy ones depreciated currencies, resulting in the most success in improving their trade balances. Income distribution shifts following devaluation (for example, from urban to rural residents) sometimes contributed to a recession, at least in the short run.

All three country categories experienced a severe fall in their commodity terms of trade in the 1980s, but among sub-Saharan countries, only the healthy adjusters (Botswana, Burkina, Madagascar, Mauritania, and Mauritius) expanded export volume enough to maintain or increase their export purchasing power. Nigeria, whose oil prices plummeted, experienced a fall in both commodity terms of trade and export purchasing power, 1980–87. The deceleration or decline in export purchasing power weakened the Sub-Sahara's financial ability to compensate for the average food-production declines by importing low-priced food.

While savings rates declined from the 1970s to the 1980s, they recovered substantially after 1981–83 in the healthy adjusters, while falling uninterruptedly among unhealthy adjusters and deteriorators, with a collapse in savings in Africa. After the mid-1980s, Africa's trade balance was reduced to its lowest levels relative to GDP since the early 1970s, while Latin America's came close to a balance. LDC import and investment rates declined during the depression of 1981–83, afterward recovering unevenly and contributing to growth in the healthily adjusting Latin American countries but not recovering in any major African country grouping.

Agriculture helped to mitigate the worst effects of the 1981–83 recession, partly by generating a positive net balance for debt servicing. The agricultural sector's long-run declining share of GDP, which accompanied economic growth, was arrested during the stagnation of the 1980s. In this decade, all sub-Saharan countries showed a decline in agricultural terms of trade except Burkina (cotton, shea nut, peanut, and sesame exports), Mauritius (sugar, tea, and molasses), and Senegal (cotton, peanuts, and fish products). In Africa, debt-service payments on agricultural loans comprised only 5 percent of the total, 1984–88, although agriculture accounted for 36 percent of GDP. Indeed agriculture, which had favorable terms for borrowing, transferred $0.6 billion net resources to Africa, while industry's contribution was a negative $1.5 billion.[65]

While the World Bank indicates Bank/Fund adjustment programs are effective, independent empirical studies fail to show the success of Bank/Fund adjustment. Instead, these studies, taken as a whole, show that the record of growth, external balance, and social indicators of sub-Saharan countries with strong Bank/Fund adjustment programs was no better than those with weak or no adjustment programs. Moreover, Bank/Fund programs reduce investment and social spending. The Bank could argue that sub-Saharan Africa would have no better record with adjustment programs organized by national planners. Turning this statement on its head, many African leaders see no evidence that national planners do any worse than did the Bretton Woods twins, but at least national adjustment plans provide indigenous people with experience and learning benefits. Perhaps in desperation more African leaders may surmise that default (or a less confrontational alternative, such as pressure for debt writedowns, writeoffs, and rescheduling) is less costly than any feasible Bank/Fund conditions. Chapters 8 and 9 indicate some strategies that sub-Saharan countries can explore for resolving the debt crisis when full payment is too costly.

Designing Pro-Poor Programs

Studies of the 1980s show that Bank/Fund structural adjustment and macroeconomic stabilization programs rarely restored growth and balance-of-payments equilibrium or reduced poverty rates in sub-Saharan Africa. However, the Bank and IMF can minimize damage to anti-poverty programs by funding programs that compensate the most vulnerable portions of the population. On compensation, IMF Managing Director Michel Camdessus points out:

> The first [conviction] is that adjustment does not have to lower basic human standards. . . . My second conviction is that the more adjustment efforts give proper weight to social realities—especially the implications for the poorest—the more successful they are likely to be. . . . People know something about how to ensure that the very poor are spared by the adjustment effort. In financial terms, it might not cost very much. Why? Because if you look at the share of the poorest groups in the distribution of these [adjusting] countries' income, it is a trifling amount. . . . Unfortunately it is generally "everyone else," and not the poverty groups, that is represented in government.[66]

Mosley, Harrigan, and Toye are correct in observing that statements such as this by Camdessus "almost certainly exaggerate the extent to which the Fund at the operational level has moved or will move away from this traditional brief," that is, the required internal changes for restoration of a sustainable macroeconomic recovery.[67] The IMF lacks a program to address borrowing countries' concerns for redistributing

174

income or to compensate those most vulnerable to adjustment programs.

The World Bank Social Dimensions of Adjustment Projects (SDA) attempts to find policy instruments to achieve economic development and poverty reduction, with emphasis on short-term compensation where adjustment programs have immediate costs for identifiable groups. In Ghana, the Program of Action to Mitigate the Social Costs of Adjustment (PAMSCAD), beginning in 1988, provided limited funds for public works, food-for-work projects, and retrenched public-sector workers rather than projects to offset declining health care and potable water, malnourishment among women and children, and adjustment costs by the poorest classes. The Bank also encouraged compensatory programs in Guinea, Guinea-Bissau, and Senegal. But PAMSCAD, subject to the political constraints that Camdessus mentions, provides too little assistance for the poor and near-poor hurt by adjustment. In 1989, a Bank internal memorandum cited the lack of a general program to mitigate the social costs of adjustment.[68]

Tsikata warns that the redistributive impact of Ghana's adjustment programs

will strike at powerful vested interests—rentiers and patrons whose opportunities come under threat as these measures bite. That such interests fight back to regain their ascendancy is only to be expected, and the recovery efforts will only be sustained if their political patronage no longer provides the protection they enjoyed in the past. That is why the politics of stabilization is so often also the politics of destabilization, as a government determined to effect these transformations will face attempts to overthrow it. Ghana has had its full share of such destabilization effects and perhaps the best testimony to the role of the vested interests in these attempts has been the extent of external financial resources as well as external political backing they have received even from quarters in which the economic reforms have been applauded. It is possible such "reforms" could be carried out in a manner that restores the pre-eminence of the vested interests which would firmly sustain the neo-colonial order. But quite simply, in our view, unless the neo-colonial state is transformed or is transforming there can be little hope for sustained recovery for Africa's economies much less hopes of attaining development.[69]

Evidence suggests that Bank/Fund adjustment programs are initially likely to worsen the condition of the poor. Adjustment programs should not merely compensate for poverty increases, as just discussed, but should be redesigned to protect the income and social services of the poor. The poor are highly represented among urban workers, petty traders and artisans, informal-sector workers, small farmers, tenants, landless workers, and single heads of households, as well as the old, infants, pregnant and lactating mothers, the ill, the handicapped, and the unemployed.

According to case studies, poor women, whose working day is longer than that of men, have virtually no spare time. Planners should design adjustment programs so that poor women, who bear much of the stress of adjustment as both household managers and members of the labor force, do not lose.[70]

Most LDCs cannot support an income transfer, except for some upper-middle countries, such as Brazil and Turkey. For example, in Kenya, Tanzania, Ethiopia, and Sudan, where the majority of the population lives close to subsistence, welfare payments to bring the population above the poverty line would undermine work incentives and be prohibitively expensive.

Sub-Saharan countries need programs to target the rural and urban poor whose purchasing power falls with food price decontrols. Low-income buyers of food may suffer malnutrition or even die during the transition. In the 1980s, Zambia, Brazil, Bolivia, Peru, the Dominican Republic, Tunisia, Egypt, and Poland faced riots during food-price decontrol. To reduce the adverse effect on the urban poor, government can increase the producer price for essential food crops slowly, reduce *general* food subsidies to provide more funds to target the poor, and maintain or even increase funds for nutritional foodgrain consumed by the poor. Subsidizing or distributing cheaper food (sorghum or poor-quality rice) that higher income groups do not eat can benefit the poor. Another strategy is to target programs for the poorest groups, such as development in rural areas where most poor live, and health and nutritional programs for expectant and nursing mothers and children. Other programs include food-for-work programs, labor-intensive projects (with a positive employment effect), and targeted public expenditures (such as food and health care) for the especially vulnerable.[71]

Conclusion

The goals of World Bank adjustment loans and supplementary IMF stabilization lending, especially in the 1980s, have been to improve internal and external balance and allocative efficiency. While the Bank programs have medium- to long-term objectives, program continuation has been based on satisfying short-run Bank/Fund conditions (usually the current-account balance, spending contraction, and price stability), which are regarded by African borrowers as excessively intrusive and frequently a political threat. African politicians and ministers, as well as outside analysts, increasingly criticize Bank/Fund intervention, which does not enhance growth, basic-needs attainment, equality, or external balance. The Bank and IMF need to stress conditions consistent with long-term growth and international balance and include funds to compensate the poor as part of adjustment and stabilization programs.

The ALs of the 1980s offered the Sub-Sahara external resources and support for improving efficiency and strengthening institutions, but not enough for adjustment with growth, income distribution, basic-needs attainment, or even external equilibrium.[72] Despite a 1989 World Bank report stressing nutrition, education, health care, the environment, and grass-roots democracy, the Bank-led rolling plan for Nigeria in the early 1990s, SAP II in Tanzania (1989/90–1991/92), and other programs continue the earlier emphases on short-run external equilibration, reduced social expenditures, and privatization (with foreign capital collaboration).[73] International and sub-Saharan policy changes, as discussed in chapters 8 and 9, are necessary for adjustment programs to attain long-range goals of growth, income redistribution, and external balance.

8

The Brady Plan, Toronto and Trinidad Terms, and Debt Exchanges

.

Forgive us our debts.
                    —**Matthew 6:12**

We have been too profligate in encouraging private lending to Third World countries where the chances for repayment were minuscule. Insisting on payment from countries that can't pay doesn't do you much good and earns you a lot of ill will.
                    —**Congressman Henry J. Hyde (Illinois)**

As banking developed from the seventeenth century on, so, with the support of other circumstance, did the cycles of euphoria and panic. Their length came to accord roughly with the time it took people to forget the last disaster—for the financial geniuses of one generation to die in disrepute and be replaced by new craftsmen who the gullible and the gulled could believe had, this time but truly, the Midas touch.
                    —**John Kenneth Galbraith**

This chapter examines policy approaches for DCs and multilateral agencies to reduce the debt overhang that inhibits the growth and external balance of LDCs, especially in sub-Saharan Africa. Although in the 1970s and early 1980s creditors took a case-by-case approach to the debt crisis, by the mid- to late 1980s, several policymakers advocated global debt relief plans. We begin discussion by examining six influential and widely discussed plans: that of U.S. Secretary of the Treasury James A. Baker, III in 1985; the Toronto Terms, by the Group of Seven (G7) Economic Summit (of leading industrialized nations) in 1987; that of U.S. Secretary of the Treasury Nicholas Brady in 1989; the Trinidad Terms, proposed by then British Chancellor of the Exchequer John Major at the meeting of Commonwealth finance ministers in 1990; the proposal by Netherlands' Minister for Development Cooperation Jan Pronk to a U.N. Conference on the Least Developed Countries in Paris in 1990; and the Egypt-Poland Terms proposed at the Paris Club during the Persian Gulf War in 1990.

The Baker Plan

In the early 1980s, the U.S. government had no strategy besides declaring that debtors should pay the full interest due to American banks. However, by 1985, Washington had realized the limitations that the debt crisis placed on LDC (especially Latin American) growth and on demand for U.S. exports. Peruvian President Garcia's 1985 U.N. speech posing the problem as "democracy or honoring debt" forced U.S. political leaders to focus on tradeoffs. Some U.S. bankers and Treasury officials feared a debtors' cartel. In response, at the 8 October 1985 IMF-World Bank meeting in Seoul, Secretary of the Treasury Baker unveiled a U.S. proposal that emphasized expanded lending rather than debt writeoffs and writedowns. The plan called for the Inter-American Development Bank, IMF credits and "new techniques" of "enhanced surveillance" (the inspiration for the IMF's beginning structural adjustment lending in 1986–87), World Bank SALs, contributions from trade-surplus countries like Japan, and additional commercial bank lending, to help the highly indebted middle-income countries. Baker provided for the IMF to continue to coordinate new bank lending, but with some centralization, so as to avoid the free-rider problem, in which individual banks could benefit by new loans from other banks. The initiative called for multilateral development banks to provide $3 billion and commercial banks $7 billion annually (2.5 percent of previous exposure each year) to the LDCs that, with the later inclusion of Costa Rica and Jamaica, became the "Baker Seventeen" (see table 1.2). Countries receiving funds were not to sacrifice growth, as the package of budget restraint, tax reform, liberalized trade and foreign investment, the privatization of some state-owned enterprises, and setting public-sector prices closer to the market would promote efficiency without making contractionary financial policies necessary. The IMF, though under pressure from the U.S. Federal Reserve Board and Treasury and a Mexican threat of debt repudiation, contributed only $1.7 billion to a $12 billion dollar "growth-oriented" package of adjustment and structural reform, which was to include $6 billion from commercial banks. Baker stressed longer-term structural adjustment, not short-term balance-of-payments stabilization. But the Baker initiative did not address how to go from the initial lending package to subsequent inducements for voluntary capital flows. Also, the approach does not help the poorest countries, and its terms do not consider past management performance. Moreover, Latin American debtors considered the new resources inadequate and asked for a reduction of the interest-rate spread over the Eurodollar London rate or LIBOR (virtually a risk-free interest rate) and a ceiling on debt-service payments.[1]

Brazil's moratorium on debt payments in early 1987 drove secondary market prices for debt down and restrained new-money packages. In response, in September 1987, Secretary Baker called for a "menu approach," tailoring bank participation to individual bank interests. The approach included bonds for new money, debt-equity conversion, and exit bonds. The rapid DC growth, 1986–88, which reduced international interest rates relative to 1981–82, was a positive sign, but the continuing fall in commodity prices was negative. Private banks loaned less than the Baker target (two-thirds of $21 billion for 1985–87), least-developed countries received no new-money packages, and multilateral banks disbursed about 60 percent of the target, only a modest increase above previous levels. Eleven of the seventeen Baker countries had negative capital flows from the IMF, 1985–87. A limited amount of structural reform (reduced tariffs, privatization) took place, especially in Latin America. In Latin America, those countries with larger foreign resource transfers had faster growth, 1986–88.

The Baker Plan, which stressed saving U.S. banks at the expense of the IMF, the World Bank, multilateral banks, and Japanese creditors, was vastly underfunded, emphasized middle-income countries in financial trouble, and neglected addressing the debt burden of the world's poorest countries. These countries, including India, Bangladesh, and the low-income Sub-Sahara, adversely affected by external shocks or growth deceleration, had reduced borrowing, not so much by choice but by necessity (because of low creditworthiness).[2]

The plan did, however, forestall a major writeoff of Third World debts that threatened the nine major U.S. banks in the early 1980s. Latin American debtors ceased threatening to form a cartel. This lessened the concerns of top creditor banks about LDC default and gave them time to reduce gradually their exposure to LDC borrowers. Baker also reduced the vulnerability of money-center banks by enlisting the Bank/Fund and DC lenders in the effort to reduce bad debts. Indeed, in the next few years the Bretton Woods-official donor-commercial bank policy and lending cartel strengthened its sanctions against unilateral LDC default. The insistence of the World Bank, bilateral lenders, banks, and export credit agencies on IMF approval of macroeconomic stabilization (usually involving credit and budgetary restraints) left LDC borrowers few other funding sources. Furthermore, the Baker initiative made time available for the U.S. Federal Reserve and bank regulators to support U.S. money-center banks through measures such as increased reserve requirements.[3]

Thus, by 1987, Huizinga could say that "bank stock prices to a large extent already reflect the low quality of developing-country loans. Thus no major U.S. bank goes under if it gets a return on its developing-country debt that is consistent with developing-country prices observed in the secondary market."[4] More importantly, the Baker Plan's averting a possible debtors' cartel and widespread unilateral LDC default enabled the top creditor banks to reduce their LDC-debt exposure, so they could boycott reschedulings and new-money packages and insist on LDC full servicing while no longer fearing their own collapse. Ironically, the major money-center banks' new-found immunity from LDC defaults contributed to the death of Baker's efforts to spur increased bank lending to LDCs.

Toronto Terms

In Venice in June 1987, the heads of government of the G7 agreed to reduce interest rates and extend repayment maturities to twenty years and grace periods to ten years for "countries facing specially difficult situations," primarily in sub-Saharan Africa. In 1988, the Paris Club rescheduled the debt of Somalia, Mozambique, Malawi, Niger, and Guinea-Bissau to twenty-year maturities, with ten years' grace.[5]

Since Venice terms were still little more than an empty gesture, the G7 in Toronto agreed in June 1988 to reschedule concessional debt, canceling it at least in part, with the balance to be repaid with a twenty-five-year maturity including fourteen grace years, and to ask the Paris Club to define rescheduling options for nonconcessional debt to be adopted at the Bank/Fund annual meetings in Berlin in October 1988. Eventual Toronto terms included a "menu" of the following three supposedly equivalent rescheduling options for low-income debt-distressed countries with an acceptable ongoing Bank/Fund adjustment program: (1) partial writedowns (forgiveness of one-third the eligible debt service plus rescheduling the remainder at market interest rates, with a fourteen-year maturity with eight years' grace (and market interest rates), (2) longer terms (rescheduling eligible debt service at market interest rates, but with a twenty-five-year maturity), and (3) rescheduling of debt at lower interest rates (3.5 percentage points below or one-half market rates, whichever provides the smaller reduction), with repayment maturity of fourteen years and eight years' grace. At Toronto, the United States agreed for the first time to allow other creditors to apply concessional interest rates for reschedulings, but the U.S. chose option (2), inferior to the other options. As of late 1990, Toronto terms for the Sub-Sahara had been distributed relatively evenly among the three options.

Western bankers advising the U.N. Secretary-General recommended that the Paris Club provide multiyear rescheduling agreements for debt-distressed African countries, in which no interest and principal were to be paid for three years. After that, interest rates were to be written down to IDA levels.

Since Toronto terms apply only to debt maturing within eighteen months of the consolidation period, the reduction in actual debt service was only about $100 million annually in 1989–90. The terms do not apply to Nigeria or most middle-income sub-Saharan countries. Since 36 percent of consolidations used option (2), the reduced present value of future debt obligations was 15–20 percent, not the 30–33 percent corresponding to options (1) or (3). If creditors apply the same mix of options as in 1989–90, the total indebtedness of low-income sub-Saharan countries from 1989 through 2000 will be reduced by just more than $2 billion, debt-service savings will be $310 million, and the present discounted value of debt-service savings will be less than $1.85 billion, a mere saving of 2.5 percent of debt service yearly, an amount that would only slightly reduce the debt overhang.[6]

The Brady Plan

By the 1980s, commercial banks no longer deemed most balance-of-payments financing compatible with their fiduciary obligations, so net commercial credit to LDCs continually fell, becoming negative between 1983 and 1989. On 10 March 1989, U.S. Treasury Secretary Brady presented a plan for debt, debt-service reduction, and new-money packages on a voluntary and case-by-case basis, relying on World Bank, IMF, and other official support. The Brady Plan asked commercial banks to reduce their LDC exposure through voluntary debt reduction or writeoffs whereby banks exchange LDC debt for cash or newly created bonds partly backed by the IMF or the World Bank, or debtor countries convert or buy back debt on the secondary market.[7] (Some governments, such as France, where the export credit agency's legal requirements prohibit writedowns of debt or lower interest rates, can make up the equivalent in increased gross flows.) While the IMF and World Bank are to set guidelines on debt exchanges, negotiations of transactions are to be in the marketplace, according to Brady.[8]

Debtor countries prefer debt reduction to new money, which enlarges debt and constrains growth. Debt overhang acts as a tax on investment and income increases. In the early 1980s, when financial flows dried up, many debtors needed trade surpluses to service debt.

The IMF and Bank were to set aside $12 billion (one-fourth of policy-based lending) for discounted debt buybacks, with $12 billion matching funds from the Bank and $4.5 billion from the Japanese government; thus total Brady Plan government or multilateral resources were to be $28 billion, 1990–92. In early June 1989, Mexico was the first country to benefit from the plan, receiving $3 billion from World Bank and Inter-American Development Bank cofinancing and $2 billion from the Japanese to issue conversion bonds, which could purchase debt with a $10 billion face value for a secondary market price of $5 billion (that is, 50 percent of face value). Moreover, fortunately for Mexico, the IMF and Bank did not make resources conditional on Mexico's coming to an agreement with commercial banks.[9]

However, replacing commercial bank debt with Bank/Fund funds reduces flexibility for recipients, as debt to the IMF and Bank, which require first claim on debt servicing, cannot be rescheduled. Still, the increase of IMF quotas by 50 percent in May 1990 made more short-term funds available for debt reduction.[10]

The highly indebted "Baker Seventeen" countries are not homogeneous. During the late 1980s, oil producers Mexico, Venezuela, Nigeria, and Ecuador needed external finance to offset a terms-of-trade decline more rapid than that of other primary producers. But official aid to the highly indebted countries did not increase, 1989–90, except for Bolivia, Nigeria, Jamaica, the Philippines, and Costa Rica.

DC commercial banks have faced increasing constraints on lending in the early 1990s, with slower DC growth, a perception of low creditworthiness of debtor countries, difficulties of implementing reform programs, increased regulatory and competitive pressures of banks, the effect of depressed secondary market prices of LDC loans on bank share prices, the reluctance of U.S. and Japanese banks to increase exposure to highly indebted LDCs, the riskiness of new-money approaches, and the free-rider problem of banks collecting full interest due without contributing to fresh-money loans (see below). Furthermore, commercial banks concentrated loan arrangements on Brazil and Mexico rather than on sub-Saharan Africa and other low-income debtors. As a result, the financing gap in the Sub-Sahara (Nigeria excepted) widened in the early 1990s.[11]

Debt-reduction measures include the exchange of foreign debt against domestic assets (debt-equity conversions), which can contribute to accelerating inflation and higher interest rates if assets acquired by the creditor are private but guaranteed by government. The exchange of discounted foreign debt for another foreign asset requires that the new asset be more secure and that its probability of servicing be larger than that of the old debt.

Buying back a debt at a discount with foreign exchange is not feasible for most LDC debtors, who have little foreign currency available. Few creditors have been willing to reduce interest rates on existing debt instruments. Attracting reflows of flight capital may require higher risk premiums and high real interest rates. Moreover, reflows may be put in highly liquid form rather than in investment in expanding productive capacity.[12]

Trinidad Terms

In September 1990, British Chancellor Major proposed the following terms for low-income debt-distressed countries: (1) rescheduling of the entire stock of debt in one stroke instead of renegotiating maturities only as they fall due at fifteen-to-eighteen-month intervals, (2) increasing the debt cancellation from one-third to two-thirds of outstanding debt stock, (3) capitalizing all interest payments at market rates on the remaining one-third debt stock for five years and requiring phased repayment with steadily increasing principal and interest payments tied to debtor-country export and output growth, and (4) stretching repayments of the remaining one-third debt stock to twenty-five years with a flexible repayment schedule. The present value of the debt stock of the eligible (poorest) sub-Saharan countries would be reduced by $18 billion (rather than $2 billion under Toronto terms) or $34 billion if all low-income African countries were eligible. Mistry indicates that the Trinidad terms "represent a significant departure from business-as-usual by a weighty creditor country."[13]

The G7 nations at their July 1991 London summit and the Paris Club nations meeting the following September failed to adopt Trinidad terms, largely because of U.S. and Japanese objections. In response, in October 1991 at the Commonwealth conference in Harare,

Prime Minister Major announced that Britain would unilaterally cancel, at Trinidad terms, bilateral debt of the poorest nations worth $17.7 billion, an effort especially benefiting Zambia, Tanzania, Zaïre, and Mozambique.[14]

The Pronk Proposal

A few days after Major's proposal at Trinidad, Dutch Cooperation Minister Pronk proposed to a U.N. Conference on the Least Developed Countries that creditor governments cancel all debt owed them by least-developed debt-distressed countries in return for their commitment to implement sound economic policies. Under the Pronk proposal, debt stock held by the poorest sub-Saharan countries would be reduced by $40 billion, and scheduled annual debt service by $3–4 billion. The proposal would be easy to administer, prompting Mistry to remark that "for that reason . . . it is likely to be eschewed by the Paris Club which prefers its solutions to be complicated, often to the point of incomprehensibility."[15]

Egypt-Poland Terms

In June 1990, the U.S. government announced the Enterprise for the Americas Initiative, which included reducing part of the $12 billion official debt owed the U.S. by Latin American countries undergoing Fund/Bank reforms. In 1990, during the Persian Gulf War, the U.S. government extended generous terms to two middle-income countries, canceling $6.7 billion in military debt owed by Egypt (a "debt for war" swap) and 70 percent of the $3.8 billion U.S. government debt of Poland (favored because of the large Polish-American communities in Chicago and other politically crucial northern cities), thus allowing both to evade bitter IMF prescriptions. Mistry sees no economic explanation for the Paris Club's "desultory foot-dragging over the debt crises of Africa and Latin America," whose countries are subject to a Bank/Fund short leash, while finding more than $13 billion for the European Bank for Reconstruction and Development for Central Europe and concluding agreements with Egypt and Poland at terms more generous than Toronto terms. For Mistry, this piecemeal approach, including Secretary of State Baker's using U.S. influence to help Egypt get an IMF-approved stabilization agreement essential to permit other DCs to reduce Egyptian debt, involved an "embarrassing ad hoc improvisation when G-7 decides to favour debtor countries for some expedient political reasons (e.g., Poland and Egypt) and, by the same token, to punish others using the Damoclean sword of debt as a tool for foreign policy leverage)." These selective initiatives should set precedents for sub-Saharan and other poor-country debt writeoffs but instead impart chaos to international debt management.[16]

Canceling Debt

A debtor unilaterally repudiating debt must weigh this default against the likelihood of exclusion from international markets and other economic sanctions. But the debtor may be able to avoid sanctions when the lender agrees to or initiates debt reduction or cancellation or the conversion of loans to grants.

Should DCs or multilateral agencies use concessional aid for debt relief or cancellation? Most large debtors are middle-income countries, and *not* among the poorest states. Thus UNCTAD (1978) emphasized widespread debt renegotiation to cancel or reschedule debts of least-developed (largely overlapping with IDA-eligible) countries. Concentrating concessional debt relief on sub-Saharan African and other least-developed countries would follow a similar precedent on other concessional aid.

From 1978 through 1990, fourteen OECD countries canceled more than $2 billion of concessional debt (mostly under Paris Club auspices), about one-fifth of concessional loans to IDA-eligible countries in the Sub-Sahara. Sweden, Canada, the Netherlands, Belgium, the United Kingdom, the Federal Republic of Germany, Denmark, Norway, and Finland were major contributors to debt forgiveness to the Sub-Sahara. OECD nations also gave recipients concessional aid to buy commercial bank debt instruments at heavily discounted prices. Many aid and debt-reduction programs provided by official creditors tended to help commercial banks disproportionately. As discussed below, debtors using aid for buying bank discounted debt instruments do not help the debtor country unless the donor restricts use of the aid to a buyback. Moreover, debt relief that comes from DCs' existing aid budgets does not increase resource transfers to LDCs. While concessional debt service saved in 1987 was only $5 million a year, these savings increased over time, as cancellations reduced the growth in the stock of consolidated debt.[17]

From 1987 through 1990, France, Canada, Germany, Japan, and the United States converted $2 billion in nonconcessional loans to grants for sub-Saharan countries, mostly under Paris Club auspices. Included was the United States' forgiving twenty-three sub-Saharan food and development loan recipients $425 million in 1990 ($200 million for Zaïre and $175 million for Kenya, neither a good performer in economic reform or human rights) and $325 million in 1991.[18] A U.N. advisory group comprising mostly Western commercial and investment bankers recommended that bilateral agencies retroactively convert ODA to grants for all debt-distressed countries (especially least-developed countries) in Africa.

Since 1985, creditor governments and agencies have gradually increased ODA to sub-Saharan Africa, while multilateral agencies (especially the IDA) have increased their aid even more rapidly. Indeed, many Bank/Fund programs of adjustment loans involved cofinancing with IDA and bilateral donors. Assistance to Africa grew while aid to Asia and Latin America remained roughly stagnant or even fell.[19]

Rescheduling Debt

Between 1980 and 1987, $30 billion of debt-service obligations were rescheduled, involving more than half (24) of the sub-Saharan countries and reducing scheduled debt-service payments by $10 billion, or 57 percent of the total. The Sub-Sahara, which had a tenth of LDC debt, accounted for 17 percent of debt consolidation from LDCs to Paris Club official creditors in 1986 and 3 percent of LDC debt consolidation to London Club commercial creditors in 1986. Much of the sub-Saharan current debt service originated as export credits or guarantees. The Paris Club rescheduled nonconcessional debt in 1987–88 at reduced interest rates or at market rates with an eighteen-year maturity, including eight years' grace. The long gestation lag for constructing infrastructure or creating externalities suggested rescheduling that provides longer maturities and grace periods than were previously provided.

While all Toronto options reduced debt servicing in the short run, lower interest rates provided the largest immediate relief but at the expense of higher debt service in the middle run (10–15 years), and extending terms increased debt servicing in the long run, that is, more than fifteen years. Nonconcessional Paris Club debt accounted for only one-third of the total debt servicing of the sub-Saharan countries whose debt was rescheduled in 1988. Debt reductions were obstructed under Paris Club rules, which required debtor governments to seek parallel treatment from non-Club (Soviet and Arab) creditors. Furthermore, some creditor governments were financing the debt write-downs by reducing other parts of their aid budgets. Thus, the Toronto-Berlin menu is not a full solution.[20]

In 1989, twelve sub-Saharan countries rescheduled debt at the Paris Club under Toronto terms. The Sub-Sahara's savings on interest payments came to about $50 million or 2 percent of total debt service in 1989, slowing the debt buildup and establishing the principle of concessional rescheduling of official bilateral claims. Additionally, forgiveness of bilateral development assistance loans at the Paris Club through 1989 amounted to $5–6 billion or 8 percent of the Sub-Sahara's 1989 outstanding debt. In rescheduling countries, investment rose while consumption initially fell and eventually stabilized, while in nonscheduling countries investment fell dramatically.[21]

In early 1990, the Club offered rescheduling over a period of fifteen years (five years longer than the previous period) for lower middle-income countries Congo, Morocco, El Salvador, and Honduras.[22] Later in 1990, the Paris Club rescheduled official bilateral debt for seventeen low-income sub-Saharan countries and Senegal with long maturities (twenty-five years) and reduced interest rates. More than $5 billion was consolidated under Toronto terms from October 1988 through September 1990, resulting in a cash-flow savings of $100 million annually and $5 billion in total.[23]

World Bank economist Selowsky warns lenders to distinguish between debt reduction for countries that have undertaken sound monetary and fiscal policies and those that have not and to set priorities to determine which countries should be helped by debt relief. DCs have rescheduled middle-income sub-Saharan countries on a case-by-case basis, while trying to increase commercial lending. Under Paris Club arrangements of the late 1980s, debt accumulating at commercial rates of interest doubled roughly every seven years. Even for the less-impaired sub-Saharan countries, interest rates on rescheduled debt were below market rates. For countries with immediate prospects for creditworthiness, DC export credit agencies should renew coverage. Paris Club members will need to re-evaluate a few times in the 1990s, probably making additional debt concessions as Africa's position further deteriorates. The debt Laffer curve suggests that it makes little sense to charge commercial interest rates on arrears and rescheduled payments.[24]

Paris Club nations cancel and reschedule only official bilateral debt (39.5 percent of sub-Saharan debt stock in 1990) owed over a period of fifteen to eighteen months. One alternative would be to reschedule the entire stock of debt for low-income African countries at one time.[25]

Multilateral institutions, whose debts receive preferred status, held 25 percent of sub-Saharan debt stock (see the next chapter). The next five sections of this chapter examine ways to contend with the sub-Saharan commercial debt problem.

Commercial Bank Lending

As indicated, net commercial credit to LDCs continually fell in the 1980s. In the late 1980s, commercial banks reduced balance-of-payments financing, instead offering financial instruments more tailored to the banks' regulatory, accounting, and tax situation. Yet the debt from this earlier period was still substantial, so 23.5 percent of 1990 sub-Saharan debt was owed to private creditors (compared to 43 percent in 1980) and 12.0 percent to short-term (mostly commercial) financing. In 1989, Nigeria accounted for 35 percent of the $34 billion long-term debt to private creditors, as well as 48 percent of both the $8.2 billion scheduled debt-service payments and $4.2 billion actual payments. Similarly, Benin, Mozambique, and Niger had a disproportionate share of debt owed to private creditors in 1989.

One approach, the market-based "menu" approach—buybacks, debt-equity swaps, debt exchanges, and exit bonds—allows commercial banks and debtor countries to fine-tune instruments case-by-case. However, buybacks and debt-equity swaps actually increased banks' short-term financing requirements. Moreover, creditors have used the menu mainly for major Latin American debtors, with little application to Africa. Two sub-Saharan exceptions are Nigeria and Côte d'Ivoire, where banks have designed legal features to spur their full participation in new-money arrangements and to reduce free riding. In 1988, 250 creditor banks contributed on a prorated basis to new money for multiyear rescheduling agreements (MYRAs). Banks not participating (free riders) were not to receive interest payments from the new resources made available.[26]

Debt-Equity Swaps

Debt-equity swaps involve an investor exchanging at the debtor country's central bank the country's debt purchased at discount in the secondary market for local currency, to be used in equity investment.[27] From 1982 to 1991, the active market for the swapping or selling of commercial bank claims on LDCs grew rapidly. Usually, with a swap, a DC commercial bank (Citicorp led here) sells an outstanding loan made to a debtor-country government agency to an MNC, which presents the loan paper to the debtor's central bank, which redeems all or most of the loan's face value in *domestic currency* at the market exchange rate. The investor, by acquiring equity in an LDC firm, substitutes a repayment stream depending on profitability for a fixed external obligation. Yet many bankers doubt that a country that lacks foreign exchange for debt service would make exchange available for repatriating corporate income.

After 1985, when Chile and Mexico introduced debt conversion to reduce external claims, swaps on the secondary market grew rapidly. The annual value of debt conversions increased from $773 million in 1984 to $2,088 million in 1985 to $2,236 million in 1986 to $8,188 million in 1987 to $22,358 million in 1988. Debt-equity swaps accounted for $773 million in 1984, $1,843 million in 1985, $1,522 million in 1986, $3,335 million in 1987, and $9,205 million in 1988.[28]

Debt Buybacks

In 1989 the World Bank established an IDA Debt Reduction Facility (DRF) for the poorest debt-distressed countries, which Niger and Mozambique used in 1991. Commercial banks, however, are reluctant to participate in the DRF, partly to avoid setting precedents for larger commercial debtors.

Who benefits from a self-financed debt buyback? Krugman and Obstfeld argue that a heavily indebted country loses from buying back part of its own debt on the secondary market. The market price of debt rises as the outstanding debt falls and vice versa, meaning that "the average market value of a troubled sovereign debt is always greater than its marginal value. . . . The debtor purchases its debt at its post-buyback average value, the market price. But the resulting reduction in expected payments to creditors is the debt's marginal value, which is always below the market price," meaning that the market price of the remaining debt rises when a country buys back part of its debt.[29]

To see why countries lose from buying back their own debt, let us discuss how the secondary-market price of debt is determined. Assume Nigeria has a debt with a face value of $32 billion, which is the amount Nigeria promised to repay lenders when it first borrowed the funds. Nigeria's debt sells on the secondary market at a discount relative to face value, as no one knows how much of the $32 billion owed by Nigeria actually will be repaid. Suppose Nigeria is expected to pay the face value $32 billion with probability 0.125, $8 billion with probability 0.125, and $4 billion with probability 0.75, or $4 billion plus $1 billion plus $3 billion, adding to $8 billion, a fair measure of expected value, that is, what Nigeria expects to pay and its creditors expect to receive. The price of a debt claim with face value $1 is $8 billion divided by $32 billion, or 25 cents per dollar of face value.

Now assume that Nigeria were to buy back $8 billion of its debt on the secondary market for 25 cents per dollar face value or $2 billion, financing its purchase by reducing consumption or spending central-bank reserves. Whereas before the buyback Nigeria's expected repayments were $8 billion, afterward they are: 0.125 probability to pay the reduced face value $24 billion, 0.125 probability to pay $8 billion, and 0.75 probability to pay $4 billion, or $3 billion plus $1 billion plus $3 billion, totaling $7 billion, which divided by the remaining $24 billion debt equals 29.17 cents on the dollar. The price of Nigeria's debt rises by 4.17 cents per dollar because the total payout, which is unchanged where the expected value is less than 100 percent, is now divided up among a smaller pool of claimants.

This price increase harms Nigeria, which will not actually be able to purchase its debt at the initial price of 25 cents on the dollar but will need to pay the post-buyback price of 29.17 cents on every dollar of debt it purchases. The reason is that each debt holder knows that Nigeria's buyback will raise the secondary market price of the debt, and no one will sell at a lower price when he can hold on to his debt and gain the full capital gain. Thus, Nigeria will be forced to pay the full post-payback price of 29.17 cents on every dollar of debt it purchases.

Holdouts make a capital gain of 29.17 cents minus 25 cents, or 4.17 cents per dollar. Creditors who sell will do so only at the post-buyback price, the same price they could get by holding on to their debt until after the buyback. Nigeria's extra payments after the buyback are $7 billion, so the buyback reduces expected payments by $8 billion minus $7 billion, or $1 billion. Nigeria paid for this benefit by using internal savings to pay for the debt it bought. Its payout was $0.2917 \times \$8$ billion $= \$2.33$ billion, so its net gain is $1 billion $- \$2.33$ billion $= -\$1.33$ billion, a poor outcome from its perspective.

Ironically, commercial banks that sell their claims at a discount on the secondary market receive no benefit, while existing holders of commercial bank claims on debtor countries who do not participate in debt exchanges receive a higher secondary-market asset price (or higher future repayment stream). Debtors would receive more benefit and commercial bank holders less benefit from debt exchanges if a debt reduction consortium (for example, under World Bank or U.N. Development Programme auspices, as discussed in chapter 9) were to buy all or part of the commercial bank debt of the Sub-Sahara and forgive a portion of the debt. Some DCs provide tax and regulatory support for buyers of debt on the secondary market by aid, charitable, or environmental agencies (for example, debt for development or nature, discussed in the next chapter).[30]

Other Debt Exchanges

Other types of conversions include debt-debt conversions, in which foreign currency debt is exchanged for obligations in domestic currency, informal debt conversions by private companies and citizens, exit bonds for creditor banks wishing to avoid future concerted lending, and direct buybacks by the debtor. A debtor country can offer to settle arrears with individual banks by trading debts for long-term bonds, with a long grace period and an amortization period of twenty-five to thirty-five years. While most debt conversions involved Latin American countries, especially Argentina, Brazil, Chile, Mexico, Uruguay, Venezuela, and Costa Rica, in 1991 the Philippines and Nigeria agreed to debt exchanges with commercial bank creditors.[31]

An exit bond is a buyback financed by future cash flows. Debtor countries invite banks to bid to exchange their loans for bonds with a future stream of interest payments on a reduced principal (say) fully secured by U.S. Treasury securities. The African Development Bank proposed that this type of securitization be explored in Africa.[32]

DC governments can provide tax and regulatory support for commercial banks engaging in concessional debt exchanges and donations of claims to aid or charitable organizations. These organizations would use the local currency to support programs in the debtor country.[33] Indeed, a U.N. advisory group recommended that, when commercial banks dispose of their claims on sub-Saharan Africa at a steep discount, bilateral donors should consider providing aid to debtor countries to purchase these claims.[34] However, debtor-country policy should be against debt-equity swaps or debt buybacks for debt reduction (as discussed in the previous section), except for handling private debt or privatizing a public-sector firm.[35]

Concerted Action

Debt reduction is the restructuring of debt to reduce expected present discounted value of the debtor's contractual obligations. Contrary to Brady Plan premises, general commercial debt reduction (encompassing other than the largest debtors) is not workable without multilateral coordination. Bilateral arrangements are subject to free-rider problems, where nonparticipating banks benefit from increased creditworthiness and value of debt holdings. Banks are willing to reduce LDC debt, but only if their competitors do likewise.[36]

The solution lies in concerted debt reduction, where all banks owed a debt participate jointly on a prorated basis. For debt relief, just as in U.S. bankruptcy settlements (under Chapter 11 of the Bankruptcy Reform Act of 1978), concerted efforts are more effective than individual deals by creditors with debtors, and rebuilding of debtor productive capacity more effective than legalistic solutions.[37]

Debt reduction can improve creditor welfare, as a large debt overhang can worsen debtor economic performance and diminish the creditor's expected returns. Just as in bankruptcy, decentralized market processes rarely result in efficient debt reduction, since each individual creditor is motivated to press for full payment on its claims, even if collective creditor interests are served by reducing the debt burden. The bankruptcy settlement cuts through the problem of inherent collective inaction and enforces a concerted settlement on creditors. Bankruptcy proceedings (under U.S. law) force individual creditors to give up some legal claims, reducing the contractual obligations of debtors, and thus preserving debtor capacity to function effectively and thereby service as much of the debt as possible. The debt overhang prevents countries from returning to the loan market; the most effective way to revive lending is to reduce the debtor's debt-servicing burden. We should apply the lesson of bankruptcy to sovereign debt overhang, even though debtor LDCs face a liquidity rather than a solvency problem. A major objective in debt reorganization is to reverse investment and productivity declines resulting from poor creditworthiness. Debt reduction may be the only feasible alternative, as banks, lacking incentives, are becoming increasingly resistant to new-money packages, and debtors lack incentives to undertake tough reform measures designed to increase future debt-servicing payments abroad. DCs can best support moderate political leaders by reducing debt so that debtor countries have an incentive to undergo reform and offer long-term benefits to their publics.

Before 1989, major creditors undertook insufficient joint action to attain success in debt reduction. From 1989 to 1991, to avoid damaging precedents for other LDC debtors, creditors only cooperated in working out debt-reduction packages with selected large debtors, such as Mexico and Venezuela. Moreover, banks providing debt reduction insisted that other creditors provide new moneys, to prevent free riding (see below). Furthermore, as in Nigerian debt relief, creditors provided a sweetener through submarket interest rates on reduced debt and new loans. But as of 1991, commercial banks failed to organize debt-reduction schemes among sub-Saharan debtors (other than Nigeria), despite recognition that Côte d'Ivoire, Sudan, Congo, Zambia, and Tanzania cannot fully service their debts on normal market terms.[38]

The meager debt-reduction record among sub-Saharan and other smaller commercial debtors is intrinsic to the way banks bargain with debtor countries. Bargaining with the smaller LDC debtors will fail unless creditors undertake concerted agreements to reduce debt. Insistence on voluntary, piecemeal arrangements between individual debtor and bank creditor will frustrate a comprehensive settlement of LDC debt overhang.[39]

The inherent barrier to voluntary schemes with small debtors is that the nonparticipating creditor who holds on to its original claims (which will rise in value) will be better off than those participating in collective debt reduction. *Creditor participants pay the cost of debt reduction, while all creditors share the benefits.*

Creditors made little attempt to address the problems of debtor countries other than the largest debtors, or small countries like Mozambique facing South African–supported destabilization and potential famine, as settlement with most others provides a harmful precedent for agreements with large debtors. Moreover, banks realize that official lenders, who have important stakes in maintaining global political and economic stability, have an incentive to reduce debt. Commercial bankers look to the World Bank, the IMF, bilateral donors, and multilateral regional banks as sources of funds substituting for fresh bank lending in the next few years.

Moreover, U.S. regulatory oversight of banks is based on book value rather than the market value of bank assets and liabilities. Some American banks would fail to be in compliance with regulations on capital adequacy if they used market value. The United States needs to revise its banking rules to remove penalties from banks assessing their discounted assets at close to market value.

Additionally, as shown by the hypothetical example of Nigeria buying back its own debt, LDC debtors do not benefit from debt exchanges without some inducement; indeed, support for these exchanges has frustrated comprehensive arrangements. With these exchanges, small but influential minorities in debtor countries benefit while the countries generally lose. Furthermore, big banks, with heavy LDC debt exposure relative to equity, have a motivation to wait. Smaller banks cut their losses and make side deals, while large banks reap advantages from the concessions of smaller banks, especially those with substantial net deposits in the interbank market. If official agencies supported debtor countries, even when they fail to reach negotiated agreements with banks, debtor countries' bargaining power would increase relative to banks.[40]

Direct Foreign Investment

Other options for acquiring external financing include increased foreign direct investment (FDI) and reflows of flight capital (mainly for Nigeria). FDI flows to Africa were less than $500 million annually, 1988–90, comprising about 5 percent of net flows and modest compared to other LDC regions. Investment inflows have been concentrated in a few sectors, such as oil and mining, and in a few countries, like Nigeria, Gabon, and Kenya.[41] DC investors perceive the risk of investment in the Sub-Sahara as high, because of political instability, inadequate skills, a lack of infrastructure, and inconducive policies toward foreign capital.

DC Trade

Trade policies by the United States, Canada, Europe, and Japan reduced the export potential of Africa and other LDCs. Chapter 4 has shown that the DCs' effective rate of protection on processing and manufacturing is much higher than the nominal rate suggests. And David Henderson, Head of the OECD's Economics and Statistics Department, observes that "for the first time in economic history the impetus to trade liberalization is not coming from the industrial countries which profess to accept liberal norms, but rather from countries whose past tradition had been to reject them."[42]

Several studies suggest that LDCs have a comparative advantage in exporting such manufactured goods as textiles, processed foods, and light consumer goods. The 1974–79 Tokyo Round and subsequent trade negotiations under the General Agreements on Tariffs and Trade (GATT) generated cuts in U.S. tariffs (although not in quotas and other nontariff barriers) on consumer goods and textiles but few reductions for processed foods. At the same time, the Japanese reduced tariffs against textiles, where they had been traditionally more competitive, as well as nontariff barriers (NTBs) against processed goods, while retaining tariffs against consumer goods and processed foods. European Community and Canadian tariff protection extended to consumer goods, textiles, and processed foods. Just before the Tokyo Round, the United States had an 11.6 percent effective tariff rate across manufacturing industries, compared to 15.9 percent for Japan, 15.2 percent for the EC, and 20.6 percent for Canada. The United States, Canada, and Japan retained NTBs on textiles, consumer goods, and processed foods but (unlike the EC) not on other areas of manufacturing, except for Japan's barriers against high-technology and research-and-development-intensive manufacturing.[43]

In 1974, DCs introduced new NTBs such as the Multifiber Arrangement (MFA) and increased restrictions in 1978, 1982, and 1986. The MFA allows bilateral agreements—often arising from economic pressures brought by rich countries—and unilateral ceilings on any product category to limit "disruptive" textile and clothing imports. While the NICs like South Korea, Taiwan, and Singapore have been the chief losers under MFA, low-income countries have also been affected, including Nigeria, subject to U.S. textile quotas since 1991. Even little Mauritius was forced to conclude a "voluntary" export restraint agreement, restricting its textile exports to the European Community even though exports from Mauritius comprise less than 0.1 percent of the EC's textile imports.[44]

Other disturbing developments have been trade restraints—trigger price arrangements, antidumping duties, industrial subsidies, and other NTBs—introduced since the 1970s. In 1987, DC use of NTBs affected about 25 percent of nonfuel imports from LDCs, compared to 21 percent of those from other DCs. Beginning in 1989, the Super 301 provision of the U.S. Omnibus Trade and Competitiveness Act, which directed the president to identify unfair traders, threatened trade sanctions against LDCs for trade, foreign-exchange, and investment restrictions. Indeed, international trade agreements with the U.S. and other DCs represent attempts to reregulate markets in response to changing economic and political conditions. In 1990, the net producer subsidy equivalents for the United States were 44 percent in wheat, 49 percent in rice, and 62 percent in milk; for the EC, 46 percent for wheat, 60 percent for rice, and 69 percent for milk; and for Japan, 99 percent for wheat, 87 percent for rice, and 85 for milk.[45] Moreover, the Uruguay Round of GATT trade negotiations (1986–92) made little progress in reducing DC agricultural subsidies and high effective rates of protection against LDC processing and manufacturing.

Since the late 1960s, the DCs have adopted a generalized system of tariff preferences (GSP), whereby tariffs on selected imports from LDCs are lower than those offered to other countries. Under the GSP of the European Community's Lomé Conventions (beginning in 1975), fifty-one (now sixty-six) anglophone and francophone African, Caribbean, and Pacific (or ACP) countries received preferred access to EC markets for certain products and funding by the EC's European Development Fund, the largest single source of concessional aid to the Sub-Sahara. EDF aid consists of support for essential imported inputs and, despite inadequate funding, Stabex concessional assistance to stabilize export earnings, including grants to least-developed, land-locked, or island countries. ACP countries have expressed concern about the expanded conditionality and slow disbursement of aid, the increased linkage of EC support to Fund/Bank ALs, and the EC non-tariff barriers that dilute export access.[46]

In 1985, the GSP covered 22 percent of the total value of merchandise from LDCs in the EC, 12 percent in the United States (with low-income countries accounting for only 0.5 percent), and 7 percent in all OECD countries. U.S. legislation (starting in 1975) excluded OPEC countries, Central and Eastern Europe, goods with a low percentage of value-added in LDCs, countries with total exports or commodities with exports to the United States in excess of a certain assessed value, textile and apparel goods subject to quota agreements, watches, certain steel articles, electronic articles, and footwear. Indeed, the United States' GSP actually shifted LDC exports to products that ran contrary to long-run competitive market forces. New U.S. GSP legislation in the 1980s increased protection against LDCs and hurt heavily indebted countries' attempts to expand exports. GSP benefits have, thus, been modest, but expanding the schemes could make for more rapid industrial export growth in the Sub-Sahara and other LDCs.[47]

Conclusion

The Baker Plan, unveiled in September 1985, emphasized expanded lending by the IMF, the World Bank, the Inter-American Development Bank, Japan and other large surplus nations, and commercial banks for middle-income countries. However, in practice official bilateral and multilateral funds fell short of the Baker proposal, and banks became increasingly reluctant to provide new moneys to debtors, especially from the Sub-Sahara. The Toronto terms, adopted by the Paris Club in 1988, consisted of creditor government rescheduling with a choice between writedowns, extended maturities, and submarket interest rates offered to primarily low-income countries, but they applied only to debt maturing close to the time of rescheduling. In March 1989, the U.S. Secretary of Treasury presented the Brady Plan, which asked commercial banks to reduce their LDC exposure through voluntary debt reduction, whereby banks exchange LDC debt for cash or newly created bonds partly backed by the IMF or the World Bank, or for debtor countries to convert or buy back debt on the secondary market. Yet commercial creditors have not been willing to undertake voluntary writedowns or writeoffs for small debtors. Although debt reduction is in the interest of creditors generally, voluntary reduction has been limited because of the free-rider problem, whereby nonparticipating banks benefit from the increased value of their debt claims at the expense of participating banks. Banks will reduce African debt only if their competitors do likewise. Debt reduction will work only with concerted action, where all banks and other creditors participate jointly on a prorated basis. In 1990, the British finance minister, Major, proposed the generous Trinidad terms, canceling the debt stock of two-thirds of the debt-distressed low-income sub-Saharan countries and rescheduling the remaining debt at more favorable terms. In 1991, Prime Minister Major, irritated when the G7 failed to agree to Trinidad terms, announced the terms for Britain's poorest borrowers. However, the rest of the G7, especially the United States, did little to reduce sub-Saharan Africa's debt overhang.

9

Resolving the Debt Crisis

.

Is it reasonable to expect debtor countries to shoulder the burden of adjustment if it may be demonstrated that it was, in substantial part, policies in industrial countries which caused the debt problem in the first place?

—Graham Bird

It is not an accident that a less compassionate policy at home and a so-called hard-headed approach abroad have been revived at the same time. The idealism born out of adversity during the Second World War seems to have spent itself; and a new arrogance and indifference born out of plenty seem to be in the ascendant.

—I. G. Patel

It is dangerous to permit capitalism's compulsive tendencies to enforce financial discipline during crisis to overpower the system's broader interests in growth, prosperity, and politico-economic integration. The Marshall Plan, coupled with the West's economic expansion and political integration during the post–World War II period, is a great testament to the enlightened self-interest of generosity in matters of debt and reconstruction.

—Robert Devlin

Debt overhang and the interrelated stagnation and poverty have had a debilitating effect on the welfare of the Sub-Sahara's population. This chapter examines the ethics and cost of aid and the strategies attempted by DCs, commercial banks, multilateral agencies, and African states to resolve the debt crisis, before concluding with a sketch of debt, development, and democracy in Africa.

What effect does writing by academics have on the policies of banks, states, and international financial institutions? Stanley Fischer, World Bank Vice President and Chief Economist, in an introduction to the proceedings of a Bank-organized conference in 1989, argued that "frank and open debate does not take place in official and banking circles. . . . Official agencies operate on the basis of an agreed-upon strategy, and none of them could openly confront the existing strategy without having an alternative to put in place." In the debt crisis, solutions adopted, such as the Baker Plan, Toronto Terms, and Brady Plan, were "not based directly on any of the many earlier proposals. The public debate helps describe the ingredients for and the menu of possible solutions: the official processes pick and choose their own recipes."[1] The goal of this chapter is to contribute to the debate about the range of ingredients and menus.

Lifeboat Ethics

Some scholars argue that studies indicating limited resources for global economic development discourage aid by OECD countries to desperately poor countries like those in sub-Saharan Africa.[2] Hardin maintains that foreign aid *should* be denied to the poorest countries as a way of ensuring the survival of the rest of the human species. Since the Sub-Sahara's economic plight is worse than that of any other world region, Hardin's "lifeboat ethic" would eliminate aid to the Sub-Sahara.

Hardin sees the developed nations as a lifeboat with a load of rich people. In comparison,

> the poor of the world are in other, much more crowded lifeboats. Continuously . . . the poor fall out of their lifeboats and swim for a while in the water outside, hoping to be admitted to a rich lifeboat, or in some other way to benefit from the "goodies" on board.[3]

Hardin sees only three options for the passengers on the rich lifeboat, filled to perhaps 80 percent of its capacity:

1. Take all the needy aboard so that the boat is swamped and everyone drowns—complete justice, complete catastrophe.

2. Take on enough people to fill the remaining carrying capacity. However, this option sacrifices the safety factor represented by the extra capacity. Furthermore, how do we choose whom to save and whom to exclude?

3. Admit no more to the boat, preserve the small safety factor, and assure the survival of the passengers. This action may be unjust, but those who feel guilty are free to change places with those in the water. Those people willing to climb aboard would have no such qualms, so the lifeboat would purge itself of guilt as the conscience-stricken surrender their places.

This ethical analysis aside, Hardin supports the lifeboat ethic of the rich on practical grounds: the poor (that is, the Sub-Sahara) are doubling in numbers every 23 years, the rich (DCs) every 144 years. During these 144 years, the 3-to-1 ratio of those outside to those inside the rich lifeboat will increase to 57 to 1.[4]

Hardin's premises about population growth are faulty. He expresses concern that some of the "goodies" transferred from the rich lifeboat to the poor boats may merely "convert extra food into extra babies."[5] However, while food production grew more slowly than population in the Sub-Sahara, 1965–88, food output has grown faster than population in developing countries as a whole in every decade since World War II. Moreover, although population has been rising in the Sub-Sahara, the increase has been because of falling mortality rates, not greater fertility (which instead has been dropping slowly). Furthermore, if aid to LDCs increases GNP, fertility rates do not rise but decline.[6]

In addition, Hardin's lifeboat metaphor is flawed. In contrast to Hardin's lifeboats, which barely interact, nations in the real world interact intensely through trade, investment, military and political power, and so on. His metaphor is not realistic enough to be satisfactory. Hardin must admit that the rich lifeboats are dependent on the poor lifeboats for many of the materials and products of their affluence. Furthermore, the rich lifeboats command a disproportionate share of the world's resources. Indeed, one seat on the lifeboat (that is, access to a given amount of nonrenewable resources) can support thirty times the population from the Sub-Sahara as from DCs. Limits-to-growth theorists would argue that it is North Americans, not Africans, who most endanger the stability of the lifeboat. The average American, for instance, consumes 390 times as much energy per capita as the average Ethiopian.[7] Nor does Hardin acknowledge that the carrying capacity of the planet, unlike that of the lifeboat, is not fixed but increases with technical progress. Technical assistance can enhance sub-Saharan output without hurting the DCs. Finally, Hardin's rich lifeboat can raise the ladder and sail away. In the real world, we should not abandon the poor in sub-Saharan Africa, especially when we note that its receipt of U.S. aid costs only 0.07 percent of U.S. GNP or $13.50 per capita annually.[8]

External flows to indebted countries are sharply down; the resources that these countries need, while substantial in relation to their present capital formation, would require virtually an imperceptible increase in contributions from DCs' resources. Indeed, concessional debt relief and other aid is only a small fraction of 1 percent of the GNPs of the

DCs; the additional share for the U.S. is less than one-tenth of what Americans spend for tobacco products.[9]

In this final chapter, after discussing the increased global competition for funds, we summarize proposals concerning how to reduce debt overhang and restore growth and external balance of LDCs, especially in sub-Saharan Africa. Small increases in spending by DCs and multilateral agencies for the IDA-eligible Sub-Sahara (for example, a doubling of existing commitments, so the United States provides $27 per capita yearly in 1989 dollars) can provide the margin essential for ruling elites to have the luxury of a fifteen-to-twenty-year planning perspective. Elites would have sufficient funds to spend to retain the support of previously antigrowth and antiegalitarian allies while investing in higher-return (and longer-run) policies and projects that benefit the majority of the population—peasants and low-income workers.

Global Competition for Funds

In 1991 at the United Nations, Africa demanded reparations from the West for slavery, colonialism, and neocolonialism. Africa wants a kind of Marshall Plan, including a writeoff of its total foreign debt.[10]

In the 1990s, as Germany integrated its eastern states and OECD capital flowed to Central Europe and the former Soviet Union, Africa and other LDCs faced increasing competition for global financial resources. Writing down the 1989 external debt of $101 billion for 120 million people of Central Europe, to say nothing of the $60 billion for 291 million people of the former Soviet Union, diverted resources from sub-Saharan Africa, with $174 billion of debt for 427 million people. To be sure, OECD Aid Ministers and Heads of Aid Agencies stated, in their 1989 Policy Statement on Development Cooperation in the 1990s: "Member governments recognize the importance of the fundamental political changes in Central Europe and will support the important process of economic reform in these countries. This will not diminish their determination to give high priority to development co-operation with the third world." Indeed, most OECD members have stressed that aid to Central Europe, Russia, Ukraine, and other former Soviet republics should be additional to aid to LDCs. But OECD publics are likely to be more demanding in assessing sub-Saharan and other recipients' human-rights record, geopolitical importance, and past use of concessional funds. Low-income Africa competes for funds in a capital-short world and would need greater returns on capital to meet higher real interest rates on nonconcessional loans.[11]

International agencies (the G7, the EC, the World Bank, and the IMF) and U.S. humanitarian lobbies need to keep the food and development needs of sub-Saharan Africa before the world community. In May 1991, in the wake of the Persian Gulf war, the Paris Club wrote down Egypt's debts to foreign government debts by one-half, or $7 billion. Total U.S. military and economic aid to sub-Saharan Africa ($1,421 million) was only 39 percent of the $3,621 million assistance to higher-income Israel (with 4.6 million people) and 56 percent of the $2,539 million to middle-income Egypt.[12] Donors, such as the United States, could switch several middle-income recipients from aid to loans at or near bankers' standards, thus freeing more concessional funding for sub-Saharan Africa.

In April 1991, African-American members of the U.S. Congress and African political leaders met in Abidjan, Côte d'Ivoire, to discuss African development and human rights and promised to meet annually. The Congressional Black Caucus pressed for an increase in U.S. ODA for sub-Saharan Africa from $800 million in 1991 to $1,000 million in 1992, and, in the aftermath of Washington's canceling Polish, Israeli, and Egyptian debts, urged cancellation of official sub-Saharan debts.[13] While the Black Caucus failed to reach its aid objectives in 1991, it has the potential to lead efforts for raising U.S. assistance to Africa later in the 1990s.

Debt Conversion

Recipient countries may avoid sanctions by getting donor countries to arrange debt conversions. Bilateral lenders should divide debt into nonperforming and performing parts and compute the value of the debt as if it included the performing part only.[14] Debt that is not to be collected should be converted to concessional aid. Additionally, creditors as a whole, who hold debt highly discounted in the market, benefit by writing off some existing debt, thus moving debtors back to a higher point for the expected value of the debt on their debt Laffer Curve.

Debt Cancellation

According to Sachs, an LDC facing a substantial debt overhang in the early 1990s might be better off defaulting on a portion of its debt than undertaking austere domestic adjustment or timely debt servicing. About twenty countries undertook such unilateral action in the 1980s.

There may simply be no IMF adjustment program for full debt servicing that makes the LDC better off than forgoing the program by partially suspending debt payments. Any IMF program may be too tight relative to other options for the debtor government.

Sachs maintains that the best strategy for the IMF (or other international agencies) would be a program based on partial and explicit debt relief, which can serve as a carrot for political turnaround. Cline doubts, however, that these agencies can use debt relief as a "policy bribe" in exchange for economic reform. Indeed, creditor sanctions on debtor behavior are very ineffective. The IMF's Joshua Greene admitted that assessing African debt for rescheduling is so hopeless that it would be simpler to forgive the entire debt.[15] My view is that the Bank/Fund needs to encourage widespread debt renegotiation to cancel or reschedule debts, especially of IDA-eligible countries.

Debt Rescheduling

Twenty-eight of the forty sub-Saharan African countries rescheduled their official and private debts, 1980–90, a total of 113 times.[16] Nevertheless, sub-Saharan arrears on interest obligations totaled $10 billion at the end of 1990, the same as debt-service payments that year.[17]

Results of a World Bank rescheduling model indicate that DCs will need to increase real financial flows and the grant component of aid for the Sub-Sahara to resume normal debt-servicing capacity in the mid- to late 1990s. Partial forgiveness and lower interest rates are more concessional than extending terms under late 1980s' Paris Club practices, which entails both additional concessionality and more rescheduling.

Debt-for-Nature Swaps

While DCs contribute disproportionately to carbon dioxide, methane, and nitrous oxide omissions that exacerbate global warming, LDC emissions are also a problem. LDC leaders argue that DC interest in resolving the debt problem and the environmental crisis provides an opportunity to connect the two issues. Sub-Saharan countries might repay debt in local currency, with (say) half the proceeds made available to an international environmental fund that spends to protect the local environment and the remaining local-currency payments made available for population or development projects. Bigman suggests that the G7 and other industrial countries use a tax on fossil fuels to finance the environmental fund and an environmental protection corps of young DC volunteers serving for one year.[18]

Inevitably, growth in Africa will increase environmental pressures. The prevailing environmental problems are desertification (from irregular rainfall and overuse), deforestation (reduced forest and woodland cover, deteriorating soil protection, and fuelwood shortages), contamination and loss of groundwater, and urban and water pollution (especially from inadequate sewerage treatment and industrial discharges).[19]

Environmental stress increases with population growth. Reducing government expenditures to cope with the debt crisis also reduces resources, especially imports, available for accelerating economic growth, cutting environmental degradation, or slowing population growth. The purchase of African debt by a DC nongovernmental organization (NGO) in exchange for local currency to be spent promoting the environment, a debt-for-nature swap, can enhance the African environment without compelling African states to divert resources from growth. In 1987–91, organizations promoting the environment purchased sub-Saharan debt in Zambia, Ghana, and Madagascar worth a face value of $6 million and total LDC sovereign debt with a face value of $98 million.[20]

Debt-Equity Swaps

Although IDA-eligible sub-Saharan countries generally benefit little from arrangements to reduce private bank claims, Nigeria, Côte d'Ivoire, Benin, and Mozambique, with sizable commercial debt, would gain substantially from reducing bank debt. However, Dornbusch argues that the U.S. government has been "obscene in advocating debt-equity swaps and in insisting that they be part of the debt strategy." According to him, the U.S. Treasury has made these swaps a dogma, and the IMF and World Bank, against their staffs' advice, have simply caved in.[21] Debt writeoffs and writedowns must be part of a concerted multilateral effort.

Coordinating Debt Reduction

While the World Bank and IMF have, as of late 1991, shown little interest in coordinating concerted debt reduction for smaller debtors, a wider Debt Reduction Consortium (DRC) can amalgamate consultative groups (CG) chaired by the Bank, the Paris Club, London Club, and roundtables chaired by the U.N. Development Programme. As former World Bank official Percy Mistry indicates, the focus for debt relief should be shifted from the Paris Club to another organization, such as the CG, where debtor countries have a better opportunity to present their case and creditors a wider perspective on the debt question.[22] The DRC, which would meet for a period of several months initially and periodically thereafter, can assist creditors in establishing an international facility for concerted action to reduce interest rates to debtors, provide technical guidance concerning levels of debt reduction, and expedite concerted bank participation in debt-reduction packages. A multilateral debt-conversion facility under DRC leadership could systematically securitize a large amount of debt more rapidly and cheaply than could private market channels. The consortium's roles would be to help structure negotiations and to provide most of the increased credit.

To avoid a "blank check" for writing off continually increasing debt, the DRC should evaluate the progress of LDC debtors' adjustment programs on the basis of long-term growth and external balance. Given the inability of Bank/Fund loans and programs to relieve the external disequilibrium of the sub-Sahara and to enable it to learn from experience, the DRC should assess the repayment potential of programs designed by the debtor countries themselves (with international agencies providing economic and technical personnel on request).

The major shareholders must insist that the IMF not permit commercial banks and other creditors to restrain the Fund from disbursing moneys to debtor nations before their final agreement with creditors. The IMF, World Bank, multilateral development banks, the Paris Club, official export credit agencies, and commercial banks should tolerate LDC borrowers arrears with other lenders, especially with recalcitrant banks that refuse to join concerted debt rescheduling. The IMF and other official agencies can isolate holdout banks and undermine free riding by making sure that nonparticipating banks receive no payment and that participating banks receive a premium over the secondary market price of debt in the future.[23]

Emphasis on IDA-Eligible Countries

The low cost of assistance, such that relatively small amounts can avoid substantial deprivation, suggests that donors should emphasize reducing the debt burden (and increasing funds) for the low-income Sub-Sahara and IDA-eligible countries. With the breakup of the Soviet Union and the transformation of Central Europe, the United States can afford to direct its foreign policy and economic assistance more toward IDA-eligible countries (twenty-nine of forty-seven in the Sub-Sahara and six others) or fledgling democracies rather than toward Cold War allies—Egypt, South Korea, Honduras, Zaïre, and Kenya. As Lancaster points out, "Cancellation of the debt of [Zaïre and Kenya in 1990–91] raises questions about the U.S. commitment to a case-by-case approach to debt relief, sends their governments (and others) the wrong signals about the importance of economic reform, and discredits administration promises of providing debt relief only to the deserving." The U.S. can now justify aid by stressing "core values" abroad, such as democracy, human rights, and economic reform.[24]

To be consistent with its own and its allies' past policies, the United States needs to extend Egyptian-Polish or even the more concessional Trinidad terms to IDA-eligible countries and provide funding for the Bank/Fund to reduce conditionality and give concessional aid to debt-distressed countries. These changes require a substantial increase in U.S. aid as a percentage of GNP from its 0.15 percent in 1989 (the lowest of the eighteen OECD countries and less than one-half of the OECD average of 0.33 percent). Fifty-six percent of the United States' aid budget went to middle-income countries, and 44 percent to low-income countries, with 17 percent of the U.S. total to least-developed countries and 11 percent (not completely overlapping) to sub-Saharan Africa. Among OECD countries, the percentage of the aid budget directed to low-income countries was 56 percent, while the least-developed countries received 25 percent and the Sub-Sahara 30 percent.

Admittedly, the United States has a strong interest in a prosperous and democratic Latin America, mostly comprising middle-income countries; however, the Sub-Sahara needs to receive increasing *real* aid to help stop the precipitous decline in living standard from continuing through the early 1990s. An increase in U.S. aid to 0.30 percent of GNP in 1991 would have increased aid to $15.5 billion in 1989 prices, roughly a 100 percent real rise; moreover, maintaining middle-income and other LDC real resources constant, while increasing funds to the least-developed countries, would increase their U.S.-assisted real resources sevenfold. Alternatively, for the Sub-Sahara, a doubling of U.S. aid/GNP plus a doubling of the percentage of U.S. aid going to the Sub-Sahara would result in an increase in U.S. sub-Saharan aid from $823 million in 1989 to $3,317 million in 1991 (in 1989 prices). Increasing the rest of the OECD's contribution to the Sub-Sahara one and one-half times (from 0.35 percent to 0.53 percent percent of GNP) would increase their aid from $9,380 million in 1989 to $14,647 million in 1991 (in 1989 prices). The $17,964 million total aid for 1991 (in 1989 prices), together with an (optimistic) assumption of comparable growths in loans at banking standards (mostly from bilateral and multilateral sources) and foreign investment, would provide the foreign financing that World Bank economists Husain and Underwood expect the Sub-Sahara to need annually to cover investment for a 1 percent annual per capita growth plus actual debt-service payments (25 percent of exports, with scheduled payments 39 percent).[25]

Among severely indebted LDCs, the United States and other OECD countries need to redirect aid to low-income countries, especially those that are IDA-eligible. Western bankers advising the U.N. Secretary-General recommended that the Paris Club provide multiyear rescheduling agreements, three years long for debt-distressed African countries, in which no interest and principal are to be paid for three years. After that, interest rates are to be written down to IDA levels.[26] Moreover, DC official creditors can have a major role in writing debt down or off, as IDA-eligible Africa owes the majority of its debts to governments and multilateral lending institutions such as the Bank and Fund that receive concessional funds from DC governments.

I propose several changes in the relationship between the Bank/Fund and bilateral aid agencies and the debt-distressed LDC governments. First, these agencies should insist that the LDC governments asking for adjustment assistance, and not the donor agency, lead submission of the adjustment programs. This would enhance the adaptability of policy instruments to the country's specific economic and social conditions, and it would help the LDC appropriate gains from learning by doing. Like fast-growing late-nineteenth-century Japan, the contemporary LDC government may want to hire foreign experts to assist the planning under local government direction[27] (or donor agencies could budget funds for hiring foreign help).

Second, donor agencies should not place conditions on the direction of national economic policies but should determine lending by the financial management and debt-servicing capacity of the borrowers. This study indicates that Bank/Fund policy-based conditionality has had little success and in some instances has been counterproductive. As discussed in chapter 7, the Bank/Fund's policy advice on the sequential advance toward liberalization has frequently been flawed. For example, the Bank's insistence on removing trade protection before promoting exports and liberalizing internal commodity markets, or on decontrolling external capital before reforming internal capital markets, contributed to an increased current-account deficit and capital flight. Economic policy cannot be uniform; it is dependent on indigenous goals and institutions. Local political leaders must make national economic policy and bear responsibility for its outcome.

Third, the donor agencies and borrowers should exchange information and views on economic policy. In providing advice, the donor agencies would be able to draw on their management experience in LDCs. To reduce borrower-lender frictions and help borrowers learn how to administer projects, this exchange must be a dialogue rather than a mere policy veto by lenders.[28]

African aid recipients, such as Mozambique, are concerned about the demands of economic assistance programs on scarce professional, technical, and administrative cadres. Wuyts laments: "The real braindrain takes place out of both public and private sector employment towards employment with donor agencies. Salaries in the latter sector are often set in dollars and therefore remain insulated against exchange rate devaluations" during adjustment programs.[29] Donor agencies, such as the Bank/Fund and most OECD countries, that add new programs and requirements impair the capacity of the state to manage public expenditures. On the other hand, aid that increases the financial, technical, and administrative capacity of existing domestic programs and ministries is more likely to enhance the recipient's planning effectiveness.

In 1991, the World Bank, the African Development Bank, and the U.N. Development Programme established the African Capacity Building Foundation (ACBF) "to put Africa more in control of its economic future" by strengthening local institutions and skills in public policy analysis and development management.[30] Foundations of this type can lapse into instruments for donor control. If this is avoided, the ACBF would be consistent with the emphasis in this study on LDC governments preparing their own adjustment and reform programs.

Multilateral Debt Reduction

Twenty-eight percent of sub-Saharan Africa's debt-service payments in both 1989 and 1990 was on multilateral debt. The World Bank projects 34 percent of these payments to multilateral agencies in 1991. Both the Bank and Fund receive preferred treatment and were substantially serviced in 1989 and 1990 (see table 9.1).[31] But from 1984 through 1990, while the Bank was putting at least $84 million a year *into* the Sub-Sahara, the Sub-Sahara was making net transfers to the IMF of at least $4.5 *billion* a year. As Mistry puts it: "At a time when the Fund is exerting considerable—many Africans would argue too much—influence over the course of economic policies and directions in African countries it has actually been extracting resources from these countries at an unconscionable rate rather than contributing positively to them." While the IMF's function is to provide emergency financing until a country corrects its external account, Mistry asserts that "sub-Saharan Africa is a fundamentally different situation in which the general normative argument does not apply. . . . The Fund was quite wrong in getting as heavily involved in sub-Saharan Africa as it did with inappropriate upper-tranche facilities on the erroneous assumption that it was dealing with a temporary crisis of liquidity."[32] The IMF (and particularly its more powerful shareholders, such as the United States) opposed expanding contributions of concessional resources, such as SAF and ESAF resources, unless prospective recipients subjected themselves to tough IMF discipline. The Fund puts its own debt collection ahead of the interests of the country it is ostensibly helping. Moreover, the IMF's argument that the small amount of concessional funds recommended would be inflationary is spurious.

The Fund needs a "zero net transfer" policy during the early 1990s,

Table 9.1. Scheduled and Actual Debt-Service Payments of Sub-Saharan Africa, 1989 ($ millions)

Payment due to	Amount due	Amount paid	Paid as percentage of amount due
Official	10,203	4,869	48
Multilateral	4,206	3,604	86
Bilateral	5,997	1,265	21
Private	7,994	2,305	29
Total	18,197	7,174	39

Source: World Bank, vol. 1 (1991b: 89).

Note: Payments on short-term debt and private nonguaranteed debt are not included. Payments to the IMF are included.

by providing concessional resources to the Sub-Sahara.[33] IMF policy of safeguarding resources is consistent with refraining from extracting resources from sub-Saharan countries, if the IMF can raise concessional resources from its major shareholders and provide a one-time emission of SDRs (about $6.5 billion) to write off the debts owed it by low-income debt-distressed countries. To his credit, IMF Managing Director Camdessus, though loath to relax IMF conditionality, in October 1991 advocated Trinidad terms for poor countries and proposed that the Paris Club "go the extra mile" to grant Nigeria and lower-middle income countries debt relief on Egypt-Poland terms.

Breaking Up the Policy Cartel

The *Economist* asserts that "the Fund in its new form [primarily a development lender, not a financier of short-term imbalances to maintain the fixed exchange-rate system] must be, above all, in harmony with the Bank. Why not merge them?" For the *Economist,* eventual merger should be the goal.[34] Such a merger would be unfortunate, however, as the Bank provides more concessional funds for the Sub-Sahara, the Bank's consultative group is more concerned with debtor-country interests than the Fund, and the Bank's net transfers *to* the Sub-Sahara partly offset the Fund's net resource flow *from* the Sub-Sahara. Merging would increase the stranglehold that the Fund's philosophy of tough conditionality has placed on Africa.

Mosley, Harrigan, and Toye refer to the Fund and Bank as a "managed duopoly of policy advice."[35] The Fund's "seal of approval" in the form of a stabilization program obstructs the economic development of sub-Saharan debtors. Requiring the IMF's seal of approval before the Bank, OECD governments, or commercial banks will arrange debt writeoffs and writedowns creates a monopoly position leaving debtors little room to maneuver. In reality international policy enforcement is cartelized, with OECD governments, especially the United States, the EC, and Japan, largely determining policy through their control of the Bank and Fund and their regulation of commercial banks. Sub-Saharan debtors would benefit from the strengthening of independent financial power within the world economy—Middle Eastern or East Asian banking, U.N. Development Programme and UNCTAD funding for debtors, EC and Japanese positions independent of the United States, and a disassociation of commercial bank, World Bank, bilateral, and even African Development Bank lending from IMF approval.[36]

Outward-oriented Policies

While South Korea, Taiwan, Hong Kong, and Singapore, which comprised less than 2 percent of LDC population, accounted for 54 percent of total LDC manufactured exports, sub-Saharan Africa, with 11 percent of the LDC population, had 1 percent of total manufactured exports in the late 1980s.[37] Given the slow growth of exports, many sub-Saharan governments tried to industrialize and improve their international balance of payments by import substitution. Replacing imports with domestic production, as an exception to resource allocation by comparative advantage, can be justified on the grounds of increasing returns, external economies, technological borrowing, and internal stability. However, as I show elsewhere,[38] such arguments for protection are more limited in effect than many LDC policymakers suppose. Studies indicate that most LDCs have carried import substitution to the point at which gains to local industrialists are less than losses to consumers, merchants, input buyers, and taxpayers. Indeed, Africa's import substitution has generated self-reliant but socially wasteful technology that would have been written off with lower protection rates.

Inward-looking policies have been costly to African states, increasing their dependence on just a few exports and on the protection and monopoly power of foreign capital. Moreover, protection reduces the domestic-currency price (naira or shilling) of foreign exchange, thus discouraging exporters. Import restrictions increase local demand for import-competing sectors' production and use of domestic resources, increasing the price of domestic inputs and the foreign-exchange (dollar) price of domestic currency, thus reducing exports. Indeed, DeRosa argues that this fall in exports matches the protection-induced fall in imports in the Sub-Sahara. The mean tariff, customs surcharge, surtax, stamp tax, other fiscal charges, and tax on foreign-exchange transactions in sub-Saharan countries are 33 percent of value. Since nontariff barriers (quantitative restrictions, foreign-exchange restrictions, minimum price systems, and state trading monopolies) affect 81 percent of tariff line items, the total protective and exchange-rate distortions caused by the Sub-Sahara's import barriers are substantial. DeRosa estimates that sub-Saharan Africa loses 15 to 32 percent of its potential export revenue because of import protection.[39] Emphases on export expansion activities have the following advantages: (1) competitive pressures tend to improve quality and reduce costs, (2) information provided by DC users can improve export technology and product quality, (3) cost economies develop from increased market size, and (4) increased imports of productive inputs result from the greater availability of foreign-exchange earnings.[40]

DC Policies

Yet DeRosa and other Bank/Fund liberalizers fail to realize that Africa's emphasis on import substitution instead of export expansion is a result of an export trap: declining export purchasing power is due to rapid LDC primary-product export growth and a DC tariff structure biased against LDC expansion in primary-product processing and light manufactures (chapters 4 and 8). For African industrial export expansion to be successful, DCs must reduce protectionist policies. If DCs had dropped manufacturing tariffs on Africa in 1989 by 5 percentage points, an IMF simulation model estimates the following effects:[41]

	1990	1991	Average 1992–95
current account balance / export	+1.0%	+0.8%	0.0%
debt / export	−9.2%	−11.3%	−9.5%
debt service / export	−1.5%	−1.7%	−1.4%
real GNP	+1.2%	+1.6%	+1.6%
export volume	+2.6%	+3.4%	+3.3%
import volume	+3.0%	+4.1%	+4.5%

Part of the challenge for DCs, especially in GATT negotiations, is to identify policies promoting growth internationally, but also strengthening domestic political constituencies' support of trade liberalization.

The United States, although not a surplus nation, bears some responsibility for the low level of global economic activity in the 1980s and early 1990s. U.S. policies in the early 1980s, including tight monetary policy, high interest rates affecting global rates, and no tax collection on foreign capital, dampened the demand for LDC exports and attracted an excessive capital outflow from LDCs to the United States. Moreover, since 1973, increased unemployment rates and trade deficits (exacerbated in the 1980s) increased domestic pressure in the United States for protection.

Keynes's view at Bretton Woods in 1944 was that, when international disequilibrium occurs, the IMF should place the burden of monetary and fiscal policy adjustment on surplus nations. The asymmetry of monitoring deficit countries but not surplus countries reduces the growth of the world economy, especially the African periphery. The IMF, United States, and European deficit countries should pressure Japan and Germany to expand financial policies through monetary ease and increased government spending, thus reducing the frequency and severity of recessions in Africa and requiring less painful disinflation and spending reductions in Africa.

Debt, Development, and Democracy

The Carter Presidential Center's *Africa Demōs* estimated in 1992 that slightly more than half of the forty-six sub-Saharan African countries were democratic or strongly or moderately committed to democratic change.[42] With scanty press coverage of Africa, many people have overlooked the political upheavals in the Sub-Sahara, which since 1989 have been as revolutionary as in Central Europe and the former Soviet Union.

USAID announced in 1990: "Within each region of the world, allocation of A.I.D. funds to individual countries will take into account their progress toward democratization. This will place democracy on a comparable footing with progress in economic reforms and the establishment of a market-oriented economy."[43] Some in the U.S. Congress, however, prefer linking aid to the promotion of U.S. exports abroad, especially construction projects.

In an address delivered in July 1991, IMF Managing Director Michel Camdessus deplored the viewpoint "that countries that have recently introduced democracy lack the maturity to manage rigorously [and] that we must facilitate their task by closing our eyes to the abandonment or temporary suspension of the adjustment process."[44] While World Bank economists Fischer and Husain think that LDCs not undertaking Bank/Fund reform and adjustment should carry their debt burden until they attain the political will, African finance ministers complain that the Bank/Fund neglects the political constraints that operate in countries undertaking adjustment. How does the Bank or Fund expect to persuade African officials to implement adjustment programs that tarnish their prestige as political leaders?[45]

For vastly different reasons, in a statement published in late 1990, the Africa Leadership Forum, OAU, and ECA, jointly representing recipient countries, also rejected donor's biases toward multiparty democracies.

> Increasingly there is a tendency of donor countries to introduce a new political conditionality in addition to the existing economic conditionalities for aid and concessionary resource flows to Africa. This new conditionality is unacceptable. Multipartyism is being used as one of the criteria for certification for aid. Yet, multipartyism is no guarantee for democracy. African countries must ensure genuine democracy and popular participation which should be self-induced and sustained rather than externally imposed.[46]

Are economic adjustment and reform compatible with democratization? Sandbrook's survey of thirty-nine sub-Saharan states shows that authoritarian regimes have no better record on development or integration than liberal democratic regimes, findings generally confirmed by Diamond, Linz, and Lipset.[47] Since other empirical research on Africa's limited democratic experience is sparse, we will use evidence from LDCs generally.

Lal contends that "a courageous, ruthless and perhaps undemocratic government is required to ride roughshod over . . . newly-created special interest groups." Democratic governments are viewed by Lal as the source of irrational economic policies to placate interest groups. As a World Bank study points out, transitional democratic systems have been remarkably unsuccessful in implementing IMF adjustment programs. Indeed, authoritarian systems appear to be especially successful, the study contends, in controlling rapid inflation in polarized environments. Yet the Bank argues, in opposition to Wilson, that overall political liberties contribute to economic development.[48]

Stedman and Hakim report that in 1982–87, under existing civilian rule, the opposition candidate won seven of eight Latin American presidential elections, primarily because of debt crises and adjustment programs. Although the winning candidates called for higher wages, great social spending, price controls, domestic protection, and sometimes debt suspension or default, no winner ameliorated the economic crisis. Indeed, the Acapulco Summit Meeting of Latin American Presidents in 1987 stated: "The economic crisis undermines democracy in the region because it neutralizes the legitimate efforts of our people to improve their living standards."[49]

Haggard and Kaufman, examining twenty-five African, Asian, and Latin American countries from 1978 to 1986, find no difference be-

215

tween the macroeconomic policies of established democratic and authoritarian governments, but countries undergoing transitions to democracy pursued more expansionary central-bank credit and expenditures policies than before and after the transition and compared to established regimes. Established governments gave more discretion to national monetary authorities and economic ministries than did countries changing regime types.

Hirschman agrees, observing that

> when a civilian, democratic government first comes into power after a long period of repressive military rule, it is normal for various, newly active groups of the reborn civil society—particularly the long-repressed trade unions—to stake substantial claims for higher incomes. . . . New inflationary and balance-of-payments pressures are of course likely to result from the granting of such demands. . . . [I]nflation can nevertheless be a useful mechanism in this situation: it permits newly emerging or re-emerging social groups to flex their muscles, with inflation acting as a providential safety valve for accumulated social pressures.

In Nigeria, the repression and control of partisan and ethnic-regional politics under military rule, 1966–79, gave way to demands for increased patronage, income shares, and social spending during the Second Republic, 1979–83. Indeed, in 1979–80, the ports lacked the capacity for imports such as cement going to government agencies controlled by politicians distributing benefits to contractors and other clients. South Korea, though, attained high growth, current-account surpluses, and financial stability before democratic transition, increasing policy flexibility after 1988. As in Korea, coalitional strategies that limit mass appeal and dampen expectations contribute to greater domestic financial and external economic stability. However, in establishing stabilization and adjustment programs, fledgling democratic governments can emphasize the failure of outgoing governments. Moreover, *new* democratic governments, like new authoritarian regimes, provide a fresh supply of ministerial energy and popular credit, facilitating economic reforms; a new broom sweeps the cleanest.[50] Still, regime instability may continue unless the new government can resist an externally imposed economic stabilization that undermines its legitimacy.

While Africa had fewer open elections than Latin America, heads of state feared that economic mistakes might hasten their removal through irregular power transfers such as coups, assassinations, and military takeovers. The strongest opposition comes from vested interests (mainly upper and middle classes) threatened by privatization, currency devaluation, farm price decontrol, and other reforms. Measures helping the poorest third rarely contribute to ruling-class sustainability, except where the poor's interests overlap with those of the middle deciles. Indeed, Nelson's study of seven Muslim-majority countries—five Middle Eastern states plus Pakistan and Turkey—showed the most populous group, the peasantry, not to be a part of any politically dominant coalition, and organized labor to be a part of one in only three of the seven.[51]

In designing adjustment programs, the IMF cannot neglect domestic political pressures, especially in sub-Saharan Africa when economies are facing declining terms of trade and export purchasing power, as in Nigeria (1983–85) and Zambia (1983–91). In 1987, President Kaunda, who lost the IMF "seal of approval" by restricting debt servicing to 10 percent of export earnings in the face of Zambia's 70 percent obligation, asked the multilateral agencies, "Which is a better partner for you in the long run, a nation which devotes all of its resources to paying the debt and, therefore, grinds to an economic and political halt, or a stable nation capable of sustaining the repaying of its entire debt?"[52] In the early 1990s, the response of the World Bank, the United States government, and several other major Bank shareholders was to promote not only democratic elections but also opposition parties advocating economic liberalization and reform. In 1991, just before the election, DCs and the Bank/Fund supported the eventual electoral winner, opposition party Zambia Congress of Trade Unions, which stressed debt repayment, by suspending loans to the Kaunda government.

Economic adjustment and falling foreign capital flows hurt the disadvantaged most. While Africa's political elites incurred debt partly to expand patronage, they responded to pressures from debt crises by slashing spending for the poor and working classes. The international community and the Sub-Sahara can probably reduce the distress of the poorest groups by increasing the adjustment time horizon to, say, ten to fifteen years, so that political elites have time to plan more stable structural changes. Spurring African leaders to undertake political and economic reform requires DCs to write down debt, liberalize trade, and increase aid, at least to countries such as Nigeria, Côte d'Ivoire, Tanzania, Senegal, Namibia, Ghana, Cameroon, Uganda, Benin, Gabon, Guinea, Togo, Malawi, and Burkina, if not to Sudan, Somalia, and Zaïre, where political conflict or blatant corruption precludes even minimally effective capital utilization.

What if the DC policy and lending cartel (governments, commercial banks, and the Bank/Fund) should refuse to provide funds to low-income sub-Saharan African countries without their undergoing IMF-type conditionality? Then, the Sub-Sahara, while recognizing the immense short-run cost, may have no choice but to default on debt payments and undertake adjustment programs by itself, while joining with other LDCs to undermine the cartel's policy and funding stranglehold.

But I am hopeful that DC governments will contribute leadership in assisting the Sub-Sahara while favoring Africans' directing their own planning. To be sure, DC help provides no guarantees, but inaction probably means continuing growth of poverty and malnutrition in Africa. While the immediate cost of response by rich countries is negligible, the breathing space might enable some African political leaders to focus on long-range planning and investment to improve the welfare of its masses.

Notes

■

Introduction: Africa's Economic Crisis

1. Sub-Saharan Africa, or the Sub-Sahara, is often called simply "Africa" herein. It comprised 557 million (or 82 percent) of the continent's population in 1991 (Population Reference Bureau 1991).

2. Ghai (1991: 2).

3. World Bank, vol. 1, *Analysis and Summary Tables* (1990c); World Bank, vol. 2, *Country Tables* (1990c); and Mistry (1991: 3, 36).

4. Andrew Kiondo, "The Nature of Economic Reforms in Tanzania," in Campbell and Stein (1992: 41–45).

5. Martin A. Klein, "Presidential Address," presented to the annual African Studies Association meeting, St. Louis, 25 November 1991; and "The World Bank and Education in Africa," *CAFA Newsletter,* no. 2 (Fall 1991): 2–12, with quotes from pp. 2, 6.

6. UNICEF (1985: 21).

7. IMF, *World Economic Outlook,* various issues.

8. Economist Intelligence Unit, *Country Profile, 1989–90:* 17, 37; Economist Intelligence Unit, *Quarterly Economic Review of Zambia,* No. 1 (1986): 33–37; Economist Intelligence Unit, *Ghana, Country Profile, 1989–90:* 15–17; Nafziger (1988a: 52); World Bank (1988a: 10–11); and Stein (1991).

9. UNICEF (1989); and Harsch (1989: 47).

10. Central Europe includes Poland, Czechoslovakia, Hungary, Romania, Bulgaria, and the former Yugoslavia.

1. The Third World External Debt Crisis

1. Harry Huizinga, "The Commercial Bank Claims on Developing Countries: How Have Banks Been Affected?" in Husain and Diwan (1989: 129–40).

2. Rudiger Dornbusch, "International Debt and Economic Instability," in Federal Reserve Bank of Kansas City (1986: 63–86); Sachs (1989: 87–104); "Debt Breakthrough," *Wall Street Journal,* 30 December 1987, pp. 1, 4; Robert Guenther and Douglas R. Sease, "Citicorp's Chief Comes under Fire as Earnings Remain Disappointing," *Wall Street Journal,* 21 June 1990, pp. 1, 8; Fred

R. Bleakly, "Citicorp's Ability to Raise New Capital May Be Hurt by Moody's Downgrades," *Wall Street Journal,* 28 January 1991, pp. A-3, A-4; Devlin (1989: 4–5, 231–32); Sewell, Tucker, and contributors (1988: 231); Buiter and Srinivasan (1987: 412); John T. Cuddington, "The Extent and Causes of the Debt Crisis of the 1980s," in Husain and Diwan (1989: 18); Huizinga, "Commercial Bank Claims", p. 130, *IMF Survey,* 25 January 1988, p. 17, and 12 December 1988, p. 385; World Bank, vol. 1 *Analysis and Summary Tables* (1989b: 17); and William Darity, Jr., "Is to Forgive the Debt Divine?" in Weeks (1989: 234), who contends that "the yields required by investors to purchase big bank bonds were so high at the start of 1988 that they were approaching the characteristics ascribed to junk bonds."

Secondary market debt price generally rose from 1989 to 1991 for countries, such as Mexico, Brazil, Argentina, Chile, Venezuela, Nigeria, and the Philippines, undertaking market-based debt exchanges (see chapter 8). "The IMF and the World Bank," *Economist,* 12 October 1991, pp. 23–24.

3. McKinnon (1984); Guttentag and Herring (1985); Darity, "Is to Forgive the Debt Divine?" pp. 235–36; and Bruce Morrison, "Facing the Reality of the Debt Crisis," in Weeks (1989: 197–98).

4. Nowzad (1990: 9–13); Kenen (1989: 436–37); Kreinin (1987: 418); World Bank (1982a: vii); and Cuddington, "Extent and Causes of the Debt Crisis," p. 17.

5. OECD (1989: 58, 62); *IMF Survey,* 6 January 1990, p. 12; World Bank, First Supplement (1990b: 1); and World Bank, vol. 1, *Analysis and Summary Tables* (1990b: 130).

6. Charles Humphreys and John Underwood, "The External Debt Difficulties of Low-Income Africa," in Husain and Diwan (1989: 47).

7. Stijn Claessens and Ishac Diwan, "Liquidity, Debt Relief, and Conditionality," in Husain and Diwan (1989: 213–25).

8. Ranis (1987: 189–99); and O'Donnell (1987: 1157–66).

Starney confessed in early 1988 that the interest moratorium was a mistake, causing Brazil to lose chances for interest rate reductions that other debtor countries received. Huizinga, "Commercial Bank Claims," pp. 134–35.

9. Peter Truell, "Latin American Nations Take Action on Debt," *Wall Street Journal,* 21 March 1990, p. A-3; and Campbell and Loxley (1989: 8).

10. IMF (1989b: 99); and World Bank and U.N. Development Programme (1989: 4). See Bulow and Rogoff (1990: 31–42), for a dissenting view.

11. Sewell, Tucker, and contributors (1988: 233–34).

12. Ibid.; and Humphreys and Underwood, "External Debt Difficulties," pp. 98–99, 102.

13. Husain and Diwan (1989: 2); Humphreys and Underwood, "External Debt Difficulties," p. 45; and World Bank, vol. 1, *Analysis and Summary Tables* (1989b: 5, 42–45).

14. Sutcliffe (1984: section 13).

15. Mohsin S. Khan, "Comment, in Husain and Diwan (1989: 209).

16. Richard O'Brien, "Roles of the Euromarket and the International Monetary Fund in Financing Developing Countries," in Killick (1982: 148–50).

17. Nafziger (1988a: 61–63); Commander (1989: xii); Cuddington, "Extent and Causes of the Debt Crisis," pp. 15–18; Pastor (1987: 249–62); and Stanley Fischer, "Foreword," in Husain and Diwan (1989: v–vi).

18. Rogoff (1990: 4); OECD (1989: 47–51); and World Bank (1989c: 164–65).

19. Husain and Diwan (1989: 1).

20. Husain and Underwood (1992: 27).

21. World Bank, vol. 1, *Analysis and Summary Tables* (1990b: 120–21).

In 1991, Cameroon, Gabon, Zimbabwe (middle-income countries) and Ethiopia and Uganda (low-income countries), listed in table 1.8, were not considered severely indebted, while unlisted low-income Burundi, Comoros, Equatorial Guinea, Guinea-Bissau, and São Tomé and Príncipe were. Among the severely indebted, only Burundi, Ghana, and Kenya did not reschedule from 1984 to 1991. See Table 1.2 for the list of middle-income severely indebted countries in 1989 and 1991.

22. Cuddington, "Extent and Causes of the Debt Crisis," p. 16; and Stephen O'Connell, "Comment on Humphreys and Underwood," in Husain and Diwan (1989: 67).

23. World Bank and U.N. Development Programme (1989: 12–16); and World Bank, Vol. 1, *Analysis and Summary Tables* (1990b: 126, 130).

24. IMF (1988: 122–32); Sachs (1988: 17–26; World Bank (1988c: 258–59); OECD (1989: 164–65); Husain and Diwan (1989: 2); Cuddington, "Extent and Causes of the Debt Crisis, p. 20; Husain and Underwood (1992: 24); and Sachs (1985: 523–64).

25. OECD (1989); World Bank (1989b: 164–65, 190–91); World Bank and U.N. Development Programme (1989: 18); Husain and Underwood (1992: 24); and World Bank, 2 vols. (1990b).

26. Official support for export credits to LDCs fell precipitously after the onset of the debt crisis in the early 1980s. The flows of new commitments of medium- and long-term credits from rich-country ECAs to LDCs were: $81.6 billion in 1981, $85.5 billion in 1982, $67.5 billion in 1983, $55.7 billion in 1984, $51.7 billion in 1985, $47.8 billion in 1986, $51.6 billion in 1987, and $44.7 billion in 1988. The flows to low-income countries were $12.1 billion in 1985, $11.9 billion in 1986, and $10.3 billion in 1987, and rising to $12.8 billion in 1988. Some ECAs provided comprehensive debt relief under the auspices of organizations like the Paris Club. Johnson, Fischer, and Harris (1990).

27. Humphreys and Underwood, "External Debt Difficulties," p. 49.

28. Ibid., pp. 50–51.

29. OECD (1988b); World Bank (1981b: 60); and World Bank (1988a: 79).

30. OECD (1988b: 72); and Sonko (1988).

31. Husain and Diwan (1989: 2); and Barry Eichengreen and Richard

Portes, "Dealing with Debt: The 1930s and the 1980s," in Husain and Diwan (1989: 69–86).

32. Devlin (1987: 91–93; and Diaz-Alejandro (1984: 382).

2. The Great Descent: Stagnation and External Deficits

1. Not surprisingly, in 1971–73, after the chronic external deficits of the United States contributed to the collapse of the Bretton Woods adjustable peg system (fixed domestic price of international reserves but with price adjustments from time to time to address chronic payments imbalances), the U.S. President's Report (1973: 125) argued: "Deficit countries would . . . be unable to restore equilibrium unless surplus countries at least followed policies consistent with a reduction of the net surplus in their payments positions." Yet the U.S. monetary authorities have had little sensitivity to LDC debtors who (unlike the United States) cannot induce foreign central banks to finance persistent international deficits.

2. Nyerere (1986: 387).

3. FAO (1991: 90).

4. Mills (1989: 7–9).

5. Nurkse (1944).

6. UNICEF (1985: 21).

7. UNICEF (1989); and Giovanni Andrea Cornia, "Economic Decline and Human Welfare in the First Half of the 1980s," in Cornia, Jolly, and Stewart, vol. 1 (1987: 11–47); and Reginald Herbold Green, "The Human Dimension as the Test of and a Means of Achieving Africa's Economic Recovery and Development: Reweaving the Social Fabric, Restoring the Broken Pot," in Adedeji, Rasheed, and Morrison (1990: 3).

8. Giovanni Andrea Cornia and Frances Stewart, "Country Experience with Adjustment," in Cornia, Jolly, and Stewart, vol. 1 (1987: 112); and Per Pinstrup-Anderson, Maurice Jaramillo, and Frances Stewart, "The Impact on Government Expenditure," in Cornia, Jolly, and Stewart, vol. 1 (1987: 73–74).

9. Nafziger (1990: 301–9) explains how the equation is derived from the national accounts equation, as well as the sources of investment in Africa and other LDCs.

10. Reisen and Van Trotsenburg (1988: 22–23).

11. Devlin (1987: 81); J. M. Keynes, "The German Transfer Problem," in American Economic Association (1950: 161–69); World Bank, vol. 2, *Country Tables* (1990b); and Reisen and Van Trotsenburg (1988: 24–26).

12. Since the last quarter of 1985, the United States has been the world's largest net debtor. Economists do not know how to fit this U.S. debt period into a balance-of-payments stage theory. Because of the widespread use of the

dollar for international payments and reserves, global companies and central banks sometimes have accumulated dollar assets even when the United States has a persistent deficit in its balance on goods and services. Foreigners may eventually discontinue providing credit to the United States, which would have to reduce consumption to increase savings and reduce its foreign debt.

An example of the advantage of being the kingpin in the international currency system is the United States' unilateral action in the late 1960s and early 1970s to suspend the gold exchange standard, detaching the dollar from gold to avoid painful internal adjustment—an action not open to less dominant countries. Indeed, in the 1970s, inflation in the United States and DCs radiated out to the LDCs through trade links. See Cline and associates (1981).

The United States' net foreign liabilities (or net debt) at the end of 1989 totaled $675 billion, 13 percent of GNP and almost six times Brazil's. Japan, the largest creditor, with $292 billion (10.7 percent of GNP), and Germany, with $254 billion (19 percent of GNP), fit the balance-of-payments stage theory. "Economic and Financial Indicators," *Economist,* 15 December 1990, p. 99.

13. World Bank (1981b: 49–63; Nafziger (1983: 136–37); World Bank and U.N. Development Programme (1989); and John T. Cuddington, "The Extent and Causes of the Debt Crisis of the 1980s," in Husain and Diwan (1989: 27–28).

14. Robert S. Greenberger, "U.S. Aid to Africa Slips as White House Sets Priorities for Post-Cold War '90s," *Wall Street Journal,* 19 March 1990, p. A-11.

15. Mills (1989: 9).

16. Robert E. Wood, "The International Monetary Fund and the World Bank in a Changing World Economy," in MacEwan and Tabb (1989: 307–9); and OECD (1990b: 42).

17. World Bank and U.N. Development Programme (1989: 84).

18. World Bank and U.N. Development Programme (1989: 13); Cuddington, "Extent and Causes of the Debt Crisis," pp. 18–19); World Bank, First Supplement (1990a: 1); John Sinclair, "Africa and Structural Adjustment: A Personal Perspective," in North-South Institute (1988: 38); and Mistry (1991: 19–27).

19. OECD (1990b: 7).

20. Myrdal, vol. 2 (1968: 895–900).

21. Nafziger (1988a); Stephen O'Connell, "Comment on Humphreys and Underwood," in Husain and Diwan (1989: 67); and Acharya (1981a: 16–19).

22. Killick (1978).

23. Patel (1964: 329–49); and Hance (1967).

24. Heilbroner (1963).

25. When a country's commodity terms of trade shift greatly, growth in GNP in constant prices does not accurately reflect changes in purchasing

power. The volume of imports that can be bought with a given export volume rises if the terms of trade increase and falls if they decrease, indicating that the Sub-Sahara's growth, 1965–89, is overstated. World Bank (1980a: 160–61). Africa's substantial fall in the terms of trade, from 1965 to 1989 (see fig. 4.1), indicates (roughly) a purchasing-power adjusted growth of −0.2 percent, 1965–89.

Moreover, since growth is overstated as countries modernize, increasing the proportion of goods and services produced for the market, the Sub-Sahara's overall growth during this period may be slower than indicated. Nafziger (1990: 22–33).

26. ECA (1985); and Adedeji (1989: 1), based on a speech from 1985.

27. U.N. General Assembly (1986).

28. U.N. Inter-Agency Task Force (1988).

29. Harsch (1989: 47); World Bank and U.N. Development Programme (1989: 2–6); and Camdessus (1991: 2).

30. U.N. General Assembly (1991: 3).

31. Nafziger (1988a: 21–30); Nyerere (1977); IMF (1986); and Jamal and Weeks (1988: 271–92).

32. Obasanjo and d'Orville (1990: 3); World Bank (1984); Thandika Mkandawire (Executive Secretary of the Council for the Development of Economic and Social Research in Africa (CODESRIA), Dakar), "Crisis and Adjustment in Sub-Saharan Africa," in Ghai 1991: 81); and ECA (1983).

33. Kirkpatrick and Diakosavvas (1985: 326–42); and Adedeji (1989: 2).

34. Patricia Daley, "The Politics of the Refugee Crisis in Tanzania," in Campbell and Stein (1992: 115).

Goliber (1989: 10–11) estimates 4 million refugees in Africa in 1988, with Mozambique and Ethiopia each the source of 1 million and Angola, Sudan, and Somalia dividing 1 million into roughly equal shares. Ironically the main asylum countries, Ethiopia, Sudan, Malawi, Somalia, and Zaïre, included three source countries. Adedeji, Rasheed, and Morrison (1990: xiii) indicate that Africa, with 5 million in 1990, had more refugees than any other continent.

Richard Sandbrook estimates that 4.5 million people died from internal wars in sub-Saharan Africa (excluding South Africa and Namibia), 1960–87. "Economic Crisis, Structural Adjustment and the State in Sub-Saharan Africa," in Ghai (1991: 104).

35. Hans Singer, "The Role of Food Aid," in Pickett and Singer (1990: 178–81).

36. J. Ay, "Agricultural Output per Agricultural Worker," Rome: FAO, June 1989, in Nafziger (1990: 136).

37. Paulino (1986).

38. Jamal (1988: 657–70).

39. Jagadish Shukla, "The Effect of Climate Changes on the Sahel," presentation to a Department of Biology seminar, Kansas State University, 19 September 1991.

3. Ruling Elites and External Disequilibria

1. Shivji (1991: 81).

2. Nkrumah (1970).

3. Sklar (1979: 531–52).

4. For a discussion of how colonialism and post-independence neocolonialism shaped Africa's ruling elite, see Nafziger (1988a: 35–64).

5. Sklar (1979: 531–52).

6. Ibid.

7. Jamal and Weeks (1988: 271–92); Reginald Herbold Green, "The Human Dimension as a Test of and a Means towards Africa's Economic Recovery and Development," in Adedeji, Rasheed, and Morrison (1990: 4); Lecaillon et al. (1984); Nafziger (1988a); and Bienen and Diejomaoh (1981).

8. Communication during discussion following my lecture on "Nigerian National Integration and Economic Development," to the Nigerian Section, Soviet Academy of Science, 24 May 1978.

9. World Bank (1981a).

10. Vengroff and Farah (1985: 75–85); Cleaver (1985); and Acharya (1981b: 16–19).

11. Nyongo (1984: 3–30); and Bates (1981). For an analysis of how those dominating the state intervened in the market to support their and their clients' interests at the expense of Africa's poor, peasants, and workers, see Nafziger (1988a: 140–56).

12. Ayub and Hegstad (1987: 26–29); Kohli and Sood (1987: 34–36; and Park (1987: 25–27).

13. Donald B. Kessing, "Manufacturing in East Africa," in Meier and Steel (1989: 81–86).

14. Robert Millward, "Measured Sources of Inefficiency in the Performance of Private and Public Enterprises in LDCs," in Cook and Kirkpatrick (1988: 143–61).

15. Heller and Tait (1983: 44–47).

16. Central Bank of Nigeria, *Annual Reports and Statements of Accounts* (Lagos, 1960–80) (annual); Nigeria, Office of Statistics, *Digest of Statistics* (Lagos, 1960–80) (quarterly); and Ogbuagu (1983: 241–66).

17. Bukuku (1988).

18. Heller and Tait (1983: 163–68; and IMF (1986: 16).

19. Short (1983: 30–36); John Nellis, "Performance of African Public Enterprises," in Meier and Steel (1989: 219–25); and World Bank Staff, "State Ownership in Ethiopia," in Meier and Steel (1989: 225–29).

20. Nkrumah (1973: 191), based on a 1964 speech.

21. Mills (1989: 14–18).

22. Richard Sandbrook, "Economic Crisis, Structural Adjustment and the State in Sub-Saharan Africa," in Ghai (1991: 106–9); and Mamdani (1988: 1166).

23. World Bank and U.N. Development Programme (1989: 10).

24. Schatz (1978: 47).

25. Schatz (1984: 45–57).

26. World Bank (1986b: 72).

27. Reginald Herbold Green, "Articulating Stabilisation Programmes and Structural Adjustment," in Commander (1989: 43); and Nafziger (1977: 132–36).

28. Tanzi (1987: 205–42); Perry (1980: 89–93); Tait, Grätz, and Eichengreen (1979: 123–56); and Chelliah, Baas, and Kelly (1975: 187–205).

29. Wagner (1958).

30. This includes taxes raised from national, regional, state, and local governments.

31. Goode (1962: 157–71); and Tanzi (1966: 156–62).

32. Rolph van der Hoeven, "External Shocks, Adjustment, and Income Distribution," in Weeks (1989: 31).

33. Pechman and Okner (1974); and Tanzi (1966: 156–62).

34. Kaldor (1963: 23).

35. Ogbuagu (1983: 241–66).

36. Falola and Ihonrbere (1985: 108).

37. Collier and Lal (1986); and Livingstone (1981); and Mosley, Harrigan, and Toye, vol. 1 (1991: 152).

38. Hyden (1980).

39. Roemer (1985: 234–52).

40. Nafziger (1983); and Paul Collier, "Oil and Inequality in Rural Nigeria," in Ghai and Radwan (1983: 191–217).

41. Nafziger (1983: 136–37); Central Bank of Nigeria, *Annual Report and Statement of Accounts for the Year Ended 31st December 1970* (Lagos, 1970); Central Bank, *Annual Report, 1973;* Central Bank, *Annual Report, 1983;* and Central Bank, *Annual Report, 1985.*

42. Collier, "Oil and Inequality," pp. 191–217.

43. Bienen and Diejomaoah (1981).

44. "Third Time Lucky," *Economist,* 11 August 1990, pp. 22–26.

45. World Bank (1986b: 72); Nafziger (1983: 152–53); and Collier, "Oil and Inequality," pp. 191–217.

46. Nafziger (1988: 152–59); and Nancy C. Benjamin and Shantayana Devarajan, "Oil Revenues and the Cameroonian Economy," in Schatzberg and Zartman (1986: 161–88).

47. Forrest (1986: 4–26).

48. Flora Lewis, "Oil Crisis of '73 Wreaking Economic Havoc," *Kansas City Times,* 22 November 1988, p. 7. See Evans (1986: 10–23).

Botswana, like Cameroon, avoided much of the reverse Nigerian syndrome, even reducing public spending as a percentage of GDP during the diamond boom following 1983. Richard Sandbrook, "Economic Crisis, Structural Adjustment, and the State," p. 102.

4. External Trade, Aid, Investment, and Debt

1. Simonsen (1985: 120); Dornbusch and Fischer (1986: 836–41); Cline (1984: 1); Sachs (1985: 526); and John T. Cuddington, "The Extent and Causes of the Debt Crisis," in Husain and Diwan (1989: 16–24).

2. G.E.A. Lardner, "Beyond the Neocolonial Nexus: Inheritance, Implementation, and Implications of the *Lagos Plan of Action*," in Adedeji and Shaw (1985: 35–46).

3. ECA (1985).

4. Economist Intelligence Unit, *Quarterly Economic Review*, 1989, and *Country Profile, 1989–90*.

5. IMF (1986: 215–17); IMF (1989b: 107–9, 142); and IMF (1990: 146, 181).

6. Lancaster and Williamson (1986).

7. U.N. Development Programme and World Bank (1989: 7); Lancaster and Williamson (1986); Wangwe (1980: 1033–59); Ali and Pitkin (1991: 5); and U.N., *Yearbook of International Statistics* (New York, 1973–85).

8. Lancaster and Williamson (1986); and Richard Sandbrook, "Economic Crisis, Structural Adjustment and the State in Sub-Saharan Africa," in Ghai (1991: 102).

9. Harsch (1989: 50).

10. The LDCs' commodity terms of trade rose from 100 in 1971 to 178 in 1980 (although declining to 141 in 1990), contributing to a decreasing goods and services balance in the 1980s. Calculated from IMF (1989b: 98, 102); IMF (1990: 139, 141).

11. IMF (1991: 114); IMF (1987: 68); U.N. (1949); Prebisch (1962: 1–22; first published in Spanish in 1950); and Singer (1950: 473–85). Nurkse (1961) also contributed to these ideas.

12. Nafziger (1990: 396–99).

13. Spraos (1985).

14. Kindleberger (1956).

15. World Bank (1981a); and Mills (1989: vii–2).

16. Nafziger (1986: 19–21).

17. World Bank (1991b: 234–35).

18. Chenery and Strout (1966: 679–733); Kindleberger and Herrick (1977: 296–98); Meier (1980: 331–34); World Bank and U.N. Development Programme (1989: 15–16); World Bank (1989c: 226–27); Nafziger (1990: 403–4); World Bank (1987: 136–38); World Bank (1981b: 23); World Bank (1988c: 16–17); and World Bank (1991c: 234–35).

19. Krueger (1987: 169); Rahimibrougerdi (1988); Nowzad (1990: 9–11); Cavanagh et al. (1985: 25); Erbe (1985: 274); and FAO (1991: 87).

20. Mistry (1991: 2); and World Bank (1991a: 4).

21. Devlin (1989: 9–81); John F. Weeks, "Losers Pay Reparations, or How the Third World Lost the Lending War," in Weeks (1989: 48); *Wall Street Journal*, 12 March 1976, p. A-7; World Bank, vol. 1 *Analysis and Summary Tables*

(1990b: 70–82); Bill Paul, "A Bank Loan Officer Mindful of the Past Becomes Tightfisted," *Wall Street Journal,* 12 March 1976, pp. 1, 25; "Tracking the Lead Bank: Who's Competing Hardest," *Euromoney,* August 1979, pp. 12–30; and Hays (1977: 49).

22. World Bank (1988c: 260–61); and Ishrat Husain and Saumya Mitra, "Future Financing Needs of the Highly Indebted Countries," in Husain and Diwan (1989: 205).

23. World Bank (1986b: 56).

24. Robert E. Wood, "The International Monetary Fund and the World Bank in a Changing World Economy," in MacEwan and Tabb (1989: 305); and *IMF Survey,* 23 February 1987, p. 50.

25. Nowzad (1990: 11–12).

26. Simonsen (1985: 120); Cuddington, "Extent and Causes of the Debt Crisis," pp. 20–21, 30–31; Helmut Reisen, "Public Debt, North and South," in Husain and Diwan (1989: 118); World Bank, vol. 1, *Analysis and Summary Tables* (1990c: 4); and Karen Lissakers, "Background to the Debt Crisis: Structural Adjustment in the Financial Markets," in Weeks (1989: 68–73).

27. Cuddington, "Extent and Causes of the Debt Crisis," pp. 20–21; and Nafziger (1990: 401–2). For similar policies in Meiji Japan, see Nafziger (1986: 19–21).

28. World Bank (1991b: 235). Real world prices for numerous primary commodities (including bauxite, uranium, sugar, peanuts, cotton, coffee, tea, and cocoa) peaked in the mid- or late 1970s, with prices of the last three tropical beverages falling 11 percent yearly, 1982–90.

29. Nyerere (1986: 389).

30. IMF (1991: 111); IMF (1987: 66); Mistry (1991: 4–5); World Bank (1985: 62–63); Rudiger Dornbusch, "International Debt and Economic Instability," in Federal Reserve Bank of Kansas City (1986: 71–75); Sachs (1988: 20); Charles Humphreys and John Underwood, "The External Debt Difficulties of Low-Income Africa," in Husain and Diwan (1989: 46); Cuddington, "Extent and Causes of the Debt Crisis," p. 27; and IMF (1989a: 102); and Avramovic (1991: 16–17); with quotation from p. 16.

31. Cline (1984: 13).

32. Algeria, Bahamas, Barbados, Belize, Botswana, Cameroon, Cape Verde, Colombia, Cyprus, Djibouti, Dominican Republic, Egypt, El Salvador, Fiji, Gabon, Greece, Grenada, Guatemala, Jamaica, Jordan, Lebanon, Malta, Mauritius, Oman, Panama, Papua New Guinea, Paraguay, Portugal, Romania, St. Vincent, Seychelles, Solomon Islands, Swaziland, Syrian Arab Republic, Tonga, Trinidad & Tobago, Tunisia, Turkey, Western Samoa, Yemen Arab Republic, Yugoslavia, and Zimbabwe.

33. Fischer and Husain (1990: 24).

34. World Bank (1988a: 38).

35. Ibid., p. 2; and Mosley, Harrigan, and Toye, vol. 1 (1991: 208–17).

36. Goreux (1980); Wheeler (1984: 1–23); Gilbert (1990: 77–99); World

Bank (1991a: 22–26); World Bank (1989c: 151, 195; and Husain and Mitra, "Future Financing Needs," p. 204.

37. FAO (1991: 113).

38. ECA (1983).

39. World Bank (1981a); and Nafziger (1990: 390–400).

40. Kilby (1969).

41. Stewart (1974: 80–93).

42. Nafziger (1990: 226–35); and Langdon (1980).

43. Leys (1974).

44. Nove (1983).

45. Squire (1981); Leys (1974); and Holtham and Hazlewood (1976).

46. Mytelka (1984: 149–73); and Young (1982).

47. Weeks, "Losers Pay Reparations," p. 44; and Khatkhate (1987: vii–xvi).

48. World Bank Staff, "Recent Adjustment Programs," in Meier and Steel (1989: 123–27).

49. World Bank and U.N. Development Programme (1989: 20–21).

50. Erbe (1985: 274).

51. World Bank and U.N. Development Programme (1989: 20).

52. Wheeler (1984: 1–23).

53. Leys (1974).

54. Morss (1984: 465–70).

55. Mills (1989: 9–10); and Mosley, Harrigan, and Toye, vol. 1 (1991: 110).

56. Ghai, Godfrey, and Lisk (1979).

57. OECD (1988a: 36, 206); OECD (1990a: 188, 232); Nafziger (1990: 356–58); and *IMF Survey*, 30 July 1990, p. 232.

58. ODC (1982: 225–46); and IMF (1988: 96–109).

59. World Bank and U.N. Development Programme (1989: 12–17).

60. OECD (1988a: 221).

61. The concept of propensity to flee is from Cuddington (1986).

62. Lessard and Williamson (1987); and Williamson and Lessard (1987).

63. Robert Cumby and Richard Levich, "On the Definition and Magnitude of Recent Capital Flight," in Lessard and Williamson (1987: 27–67); and Erbe (1985: 271–74).

64. Naylor (1989: 330–31); Bank of International Settlements, *Annual Report, 1988* (Geneva, June 1989), pp. 135–36; Hoogvelt (1990: 121–122; and Chang and Cumby (1990).

65. Bulow and Rogoff (1990: 37); and Cumby and Levich, "Definition and Magnitude of Recent Capital Flight," pp. 27–67.

66. Erbe (1985: 269).

67. Williamson and Lessard (1987), with quotation from p. 21.

68. Rolph van der Hoeven, "External Shocks, Adjustment, and Income Distribution," in Weeks (1989: 30–31).

69. Lessard and Williamson (1987: 213); and World Bank (1985: 64).

70. Hoogvelt (1990: 117–27), with quotation on p. 126.

71. Naylor (1989: 59).

72. Edward T. Pound, "Zaïre's Mobutu Mounts All-Out PR Campaign to Keep His U.S. Aid," *Wall Street Journal,* 7 March 1990, p. A-4; Joe Davidson, "In Zaïre, Corrupt and Autocratic Rule, Backed by U.S., Has Led Straight to Ruin," *Wall Street Journal,* 17 December 1991, p. A-11; and Erbe (1985: 268–69), citing Peter Körner et al., *Im Teufelskreis der Verschuldung, Der Internationale Währungsfonds und die Dritte Welt* (Hamburg, 1984), p. 137.

73. Lemarchand (1979: 237–60).

74. Robert S. Greenberger, "U.S. Aid to Africa Slips as White House Sets Priorities for Post–Cold War '90s," *Wall Street Journal,* 19 March 1990, p. A-11; and Lancaster (1991: 9).

75. Williamson and Lessard (1987: 28–58).

76. Rimmer de Vries, as part of a panel of respondents to contributors in Lessard and Williamson (1987: 188).

77. *Africa Research Bulletin (Economic Series)* 28 (15 October 1991): 10550.

78. Lessard and Williamson (1987: 136–37); and World Bank (1985: 64).

5. World Bank and IMF Adjustment and Stabilization

1. Group of Twenty-four, "The Role of the IMF in Adjustment with Growth," *IMF Survey,* Supplement (10 August 1987), para. 21.

2. Sanford (1988: 787–96).

3. "World Bank Gives Debtors Conditions for More Lending," *Wall Street Journal,* 1 July 1988, p. 19; and Walter S. Mossberg, "World Bank's Conable Runs into Criticism on Poor Nations' Debt," *Wall Street Journal,* 21 June 1988, pp. 1, 24.

4. U.N. (1988: 45–47).

5. World Bank and the U.N. Development Programme (1989: 14–16); and Charles Humphreys and John Underwood, "The External Debt Difficulties of Low-Income Africa," in Husain and Diwan (1989: 45, 52–53, 57); and World Bank, vol. 1, *Analysis and Summary Tables* (1989b: 31, 41–49).

6. *Africa Research Bulletin (Economic Series),* 15 March 1991, p. 10280.

7. Mistry (1991: 30); and Avramovic (1991: 4).

8. Simon Commander, "Prices, Markets and Rigidities: African Agriculture, 1989–88," in Commander (1989: 228–43); and Malathi Jayawickrama, Benoit Morin, and William F. Steel, "World Bank Lending in Support of Adjustment in Sub-Saharan Africa, 1980–88," in Meier and Steel (1989: 128–38).

9. Khan (1987: 26–27); Omotunde E. G. Johnson, "The Agricultural Sector in IMF Stand-by Arrangements," in Commander (1989: 19); Richard E. Feinberg, "An Open Letter to the World Bank's New President," in Feinberg and contributors (1986: 14–18); and Simon Commander, "Prices, Markets, and Rigidities," p. 229).

10. World Bank (1988a: 64–65; and Paul Streeten, "A Survey of the Issues and Options," in Commander (1989: 4–5, 8).

11. World Bank (1988a: 56–57).

12. Mosley, Harrigan, and Toye, vol. 1 (1991: 213–23).

13. World Bank (1988a: 12–14, 68–73).

14. World Bank, vol. 1, *Analysis and Summary Tables* (1989b: 12).

15. Mary Sutton, "Introduction and Summary of Companion Volume," in Killick (1984: 3); Manuel Guitian, "Economic Management and International Monetary Fund Conditionality," in Killick (1982: 73–104); Thomas M. Callaghy, "Toward State Capability and Embedded Liberalism in the Third World: Lessons for Adjustment," in Nelson and contributors (1989: 129); and Miles Kahler, "International Financial Institutions and the Politics of Adjustment," in Nelson and Contributors (1989: 144–45).

16. U.N. (1988: 45–47); Grubel (1981: 531–33); Richard E. Feinberg, "An Open Letter," pp. 14–18; World Bank (1988c: 141); Marcel Massé, "The Role of External Actors in Promoting Development and Change in Africa," in North-South Institute (1988: 24–25); Streeten, "Survey of Issues and Options," pp. 16–17; *IMF Survey,* 8 February 1988, p. 33, 4 April 1988, p. 110, 19 August 1988, p. 273, and 26 September 1988, p. 302; and Andrew Meldrum, "ESAP's Fables," *Africa Report* 36(3) (November/December 1991): 56–60.

17. Independent Commission on International Development Issues (1980: 215–16); and Mills (1989: 10).

18. John Loxley, "The IMF and World Bank Conditionality and Sub-Saharan Africa," in Lawrence (1986: 96–103); ECA (1985); and John F. Weeks, "Losers Pay Reparations, or How the Third World Lost the Lending War," in Weeks (1989: 57).

19. Sebastian Edwards, "Politics in Highly Indebted Countries," in Sachs (1989a: 249); Stiles (1990: 960); Jeffrey D. Sachs, "Conditionality, Debt Relief, and the Developing Country Debt Crisis," in Sachs (1989a: 277–78); Parfitt and Riley (1989: 27–28), including Nyerere quote; and Mills (1989: 9–10), including IMF staff quote.

20. Parfitt and Riley (1989: 17–18).

21. Streeten, "Survey of Issues and Options," pp. 16–17.

22. Mills (1989: 11).

23. U.N. (1988: 45–47); Grubel (1981: 531–33); Richard E. Feinberg, "An Open Letter," pp. 14–18; World Bank (1988c: 141); Massé, "Role of External Actors," pp. 24–25; Streeten, "Survey of Issues and Options," pp. 16–17; and *IMF Survey,* 8 February 1988, p. 33, 4 April 1988, p. 110, 19 August 1988, p. 273, and 26 September 1988, p. 302.

24. Massé, "Role of External Actors," pp. 25–27; Mosley, Harrigan, and Toye, vol. 1 (1991: 53–54); and Lancaster (1991: 39–40).

25. U.N. (1987), as summarized in Nafziger (1990: 305–8).

26. World Bank (1988a: 1–3); and John F. Weeks, "Losers Pay Reparations," p. 61.

27. Stein and Nafziger (1991: 173–89).

28. Meier and Steel (1989: 15).

29. World Bank and U.N. Development Programme (1989: 20).

30. World Bank (1988a: 60–62).

31. World Bank and U.N. Development Programme (1989: 21–31), with quote on p. 31.

32. Calculations from IMF (1991: 156, 160), and earlier issues.

33. Ajay Chhibber, "The Aggregate Supply Response: A Survey," in Commander (1989: 66); and Tony Addison and Lionel Demery, "The Economics of Rural Poverty Alleviation," in Commander (1989: 72–75).

34. World Bank and U.N. Development Programme (1989: 20); and Mills (1989: 13–14).

35. Kaldor (1988: 1093–95).

36. William R. Easterly, "Fiscal Adjustment and Deficit Financing during the Debt Crisis," in Husain and Diwan (1989: 91); Fry (1988: 7–18, 261–335); McKinnon (1973); Shaw (1973); and Nafziger (1990: 341–43).

37. Tripp (1989: 601–23); Stein (1991); and Nafziger (1988b: 147–48).

38. Sanjaya Lall, "Achieving a More Ideal Structure," in Meier and Steel (1989: 93–98).

39. World Bank and U.N. Development Programme (1989: 25–26).

40. Schumpeter (1947: 81–86).

6. Case Studies of World Bank and IMF Adjustment Programs

1. Andrew Kiondo, "The Nature of Economic Reforms in Tanzania," in Campbell and Stein (1992: 32); Silver (1985); and Hyden (1980).

2. Hyden (1980).

3. Mapolu (1984).

4. Bukuku (1988).

5. Freund (1981: 483–500); Markovitz (1977); and Amin (1965).

6. Nyerere (1977).

7. Issa G. Shivji, "The Politics of Liberalization in Tanzania: The Crisis of Ideological Hegemony," in Campbell and Stein (1992: p. 60).

8. Ibid., pp. 52–55.

9. Campbell and Stein (1992: 14–27); Kiondo, "Nature of Economic Reforms," pp. 32–40; Shivji, "Politics of Liberalization," p. 56; Howard Stein, "Economic Policy and the IMF in Tanzania: Conditionality, Conflict, and Convergence," in Campbell and Stein (1992: 66–80); Horace Campbell, "The Politics of Demobilization in Tanzania: Beyond Nationalism," in Campbell and Stein (1992: 86); and Z. M. Roy-Campbell, "The Politics of Education in Tanzania: From Colonialism to Liberalization," in Campbell and Stein (1992: 134–40).

10. IMF, *International Financial Statistics,* November 1991, pp. 514–16.

11. Shivji, "Politics of Liberalization," pp. 77–79; Horace Campbell, "Politics of Demobilization," pp. 93–94; Ulla Vuorela, "The Informal Sector, Social

Reproduction, and the Impact of the Economic Crisis on Women," in Campbell and Stein (1992: 103–9); Tripp (1989: 610–12); and Vali Jamal, "The Demise of the Labor Aristocracy in Africa: Structural Adjustment in Tanzania," in Weeks (1989: 188).

12. Nafziger (1988a: 105); and Shivji, "Politics of Liberalization," p. 79.

13. Campbell and Stein (1992: 25); and Kiondo, "Nature of Economic Reform," pp. 40–45.

14. Shivji, "Politics of Liberalization," pp. 48–53, source of the quote on saboteurs; Campbell, "Politics of Demobilization," pp. 94–95; Africa Watch (1991a: 109–14); and *Africa Research Bulletin (Economic Series)* 28 (15 September 1991): 10584, source of the last quote.

15. Birmingham, Neustadt, and Omaboe, vol. 1, *The Economy of Ghana* (1966); Nafziger (1988a: 72–73); World Bank (1983: 174); World Bank (1987: 202); Venkatash Seshamani, "Zambia," in Adedeji, Rasheed, and Morrison (1990: 104–8); Thomas M. Callaghy, "Toward State Capability and Embedded Liberalism in the Third World: Lessons for Adjustment," in Nelson and contributors (1989: 125–27); Igor Karmiloff, "Zambia," in Riddell (1990: 299).

16. Teal (1986: 267–82); World Bank (1983); World Bank (1988a: 77–78); and Simon Commander, John Howell, and Wayo Seini, "Ghana, 1983–87," in Commander (1989: 108).

17. William F. Steel, "Recent Policy Reform and Industrial Adjustment in Zambia and Ghana," in Meier and Steel (1989: 152–55).

18. ECA (1989b).

19. Rothchild (1991: 6–7, 13); Naomi Chazan, "The Political Transformation of Ghana under the PNDC," in ibid., pp. 28, 44; Richard Jeffries, "Leadership Commitment and Political Opposition to Structural Adjustment in Ghana," in Rothchild (1991: 161); Africa Watch (1991b); Commander, Howell, and Seini, "Ghana, 1983–87," pp. 109–11; J.L.S. Abbey, "Ghana's Experience with Structural Adjustment: Some Lessons," in Pickett and Singer (1990: 35); John Toye, "Ghana's Economic Reforms, 1983–87: Origins, Achievements and Limitations," in Pickett and Singer (1990: 46–59); John Toye, "Ghana," in Mosley, Harrigan, and Toye, vol. 2 (1991: 155–59); and Eboe Hutchful, "From 'Revolution' to Monetarism: The Economics and Politics of the Adjustment Programme in Ghana," in Campbell and Loxley (1989: 103).

20. John Loxley and Roger Young, "Stabilization and Structural Adjustment: Some Lessons from the Experiences of Ghana and Zambia," in North-South Institute (1988: 11–14); and Callaghy, "Toward State Capability and Embedded Liberalism," pp. 121–27.

21. Steel, "Recent Policy Reform and Industrial Adjustment," pp. 152–55).

22. Economist Intelligence Unit, *Ghana: Country Profile, 1991–92* (London, 1991), pp. 19–39; IMF, *International Financial Statistics* (November 1991): 248–51; and Kapur et al. (1991: 27), who use a Gini-Hirschman index to measure concentration.

23. Loxley and Young, "Stabilization and Structural Adjustment," pp. 8–

10; Economist Intelligence Unit, *Ghana, Country Profile, 1989–90,* p. 10; and ECA (1985).

24. World Bank Staff, "Removing Price Controls in Ghana," in Meier and Steel (1989: 180–82); Steel, "Recent Policy Reform and Industrial Adjustment," pp. 155–59; and Lancaster (1990: 124); and IMF, *International Financial Statistics,* November 1991, pp. 248–51.

Figures from the Economist Intelligence Unit, *Ghana: Country Profile, 1991–92,* London, 1991, p. 14, adjusted by either the Population Reference Bureau or the World Bank's *World Development Report,* indicate negative per capita growth. However, *International Financial Statistics,* November 1991, pp. 248–51, whose population growth rates are conservative, indicates an annual real GDP per capita growth of 1.9 percent. Since I am critical of the effectiveness of Fund/Bank reforms, I am granting a modest (rather than negative) growth.

25. ECA (1985); *African Economic Digest* (18 January 1986), p. 5; John Toye, "Ghana's Economic Reforms," p. 58; Nafziger (1988a: 72–73); and World Bank (1988a: 77–78).

26. Commander, Howell, and Seini, "Ghana, 1983–87," pp. 107–26; Toye, "Ghana's Economic Reforms," pp. 58–65; J.L.S. Abbey, "Ghana's Experience," p. 35; and Baffour Ankomah, "Ghana's Reform Programme: How Long Will It Be before the Patient Is Cured?" *African Business,* March 1990, pp. 11–13.

27. World Bank (1988a: 84).

28. Economist Intelligence Unit, *Zambia: Country Profile, 1989–90* (London, 1990), pp. 17, 37; Economist Intelligence Unit, *Quarterly Economics Review of Zambia, 1986,* no. 1 (1986), pp. 33–37; Economist Intelligence Unit, *Ghana, Country Profile, 1989–90* (London, 1990), pp. 15–17; Economist Intelligence Unit, *Zambia: Country Profile, 1991–92* (London, 1991), pp. 1–21; Nafziger (1988a: 52); Stein (1991); Seshamani, "Zambia," pp. 113–18; and Bright Okogu, "Structural Adjustment Policies in African Countries; A Theoretical Assessment," in Onimode (1989: 40).

29. Nafziger (1988a: 22, 28); and Seshamani, "Zambia," pp. 104–20.

30. Economist Intelligence Unit, *Zambia: Country Profile, 1991–92* (London, 1991), pp. 3–8; and *Africa Research Bulletin* (*Economic Series*) 28 (15 October 1991): 10548.

31. World Bank (1988a: 66).

32. Loxley and Young, "Stabilization and Structural Adjustment," pp. 11–14.

33. Parfitt and Riley (1989: 53–58).

34. U.N. (1990: 30).

35. Economist Intelligence Unit, *Nigeria: Country Profile, 1990–91* (London, 1990), pp. 16–17; and Economist Intelligence Unit, *Nigeria: Country Report: 1991,* no. 3 (London, 1991), p. 5.

36. Stijn Claessens and Ishac Diwan, "Liquidity, Debt Relief, and Conditionality," in Husain and Diwan (1989: 213–25).

37. World Bank (1990d: 128, 216–17); and Economist Intelligence Unit, *Nigeria: Country Profile, 1991–92* (London, 1991), pp. 45.

38. U.N. (1990: 30).

39. World Bank Staff, "Impact of Adjustment Policies on Manufacturing in Nigeria," in Meier and Steel (1989: 139–42); Callaghy, "Toward State Capability and Embedded Liberalism," pp. 126–27; Economist Intelligence Unit, *Nigeria: Country Profile, 1990–91* (London, 1990); and U.N. (1990: 30–31).

40. Rimmer (1990: 6); Yusuf Bangura and Björn Beckman, "African Workers and Structural Adjustment," in Ghai (1991: 139–65); Economist Intelligence Unit, *Nigeria: Country Profile, 1990–91* (London, 1990), pp. 16–17; Economist Intelligence Unit, *Nigeria: Country Report, 1991*, no. 3 (London, 1991), p. 7; U.N. (1990: 30–31); Africa Watch (1991a: 41–52); and *Africa Demōs* (2)1 (November 1991): 5, 12.

41. Nafziger (1983: 78–90); Dudley (1972: 133); Kilby (1969: 301–2); Peace (1979: 11–12; Jamal and Weeks (1988: 271–79); and Yusuf Bangura and Björn Beckman, "African Workers and Structural Adjustment," pp. 139–65.

42. Economist Intelligence Unit, *Nigeria: Country Profile, 1991–92* (London, 1991).

43. Jamal and Weeks (1988: 273–79).

44. Delgado and Jammeh (1991: 1–20); Prosper Youm, "The Economy since Independence," in Delgado and Jammeh (1991: 21–30); and Pierre Landell-Mills and Brian Ngo, "Creating the Basis for Long-term Growth," in Delgado and Jammeh (1991: 47–58).

45. Lucie Colvin Phillips, "The Senegambia Confederation," in Delgado and Jammeh (1991: 175); Simon Commander, Ousseynou Ndoye, and Ismael Ouedrago, "Senegal, 1979–88," in Commander (1989: 145–74); Economist Intelligence Unit, *Senegal, The Gambia, Guinea-Bissau, Cape Verde Country Report*, no. 3 (London, 1991), pp. 1–23; Population Reference Bureau (1991); and Mistry (1991: 16–17).

Senegal was also hurt by the closure of the Bank of Credit and Commerce International (BCCI), S.A., for a period in 1991. While the Western press emphasized BCCI's illegal transactions, such as those involving cocaine, heroin, and opium exports from Asia and Latin America to Europe, BCCI Senegal was highly involved in lending to legitimate businesses like CPSP and several other parastatals. Its financing of letters of credit for major Sengalese exporters needing credit overseas was sorely missed while BCCI was closed down.

Many of the sixteen African countries with $20 billion total deposits in BCCI were hurt when some of its banks were closed in 1991. At the beginning of that year, Nigeria had deposits of $584 million; Cameroon, $200 million (including one-third of its international reserves); Zimbabwe, $159 million; and Zambia, $86 million. Cameroon experienced a government budget crisis, even delaying payments to government workers and civil servants. The bank froze the letters of credit of many exporters and importers, while also blocking at least part of the deposits of business people, farmers, and consumers. The reduced demand, creating a negative multiplier effect, even adversely affected petty traders. Carol Forman, "BCCI Debacle Leaves an African Country All the More Troubled," *Wall Street Journal,* 6 August 1991, pp. A-1, A-12.

46. FAO (1991: 89).

47. Stewart (1990: 3).

48. Mosley, Harrigan, and Toye, vol. 1 (1991: 45).

49. Hutchful, "From 'Revolution' to Monetarism," p. 126.

50. Morawetz (1977: 41); Adelman and Morris (1973); and FAO (1991: 112).

51. Nafziger (1988a); and Nafziger (1977).

52. Gerald K. Helleiner, "Summary of the U.N. Secretary-General's Advisory Group Report on Financial Flows for Africa," in North-South Institute (1988: 31–32).

53. Nove (1983: 168).

54. Nafziger (1988a: 143).

55. Commander, Howell, and Seini, "Ghana, 1983–87," pp. 125.

56. Nafziger (1990: 141–43, 448–51); and China, State Statistical Bureau, *Statistical Yearbook of China* (Beijing), various annuals.

57. Kindleberger (1974: 267–85).

58. Keith Marsden and Therese Belot, "Impact of Regulations and Taxation on Private Industry," in Meier and Steel (1989: 163–68); Stewart (1990); World Bank (1983: 50); Park (1987: 25–27; Ayub and Hegstad (1987: 26–29); and Kohli and Sood (1987: 34–36). Nafziger (1990: 446–47) summarizes the Bank/Fund's studies of determinants of public enterprise performance.

59. Mills (1989: 14–18).

60. Hackett (1990: 776).

61. World Bank and IMF (1990: 83).

62. Davis (1991: 987–1005).

63. Economist Intelligence Unit, *Senegal, The Gambia, Guinea-Bissau, Cape Verde Country Report,* no. 3 (London, 1991), pp. 1–23; and Economist Intelligence Unit, *Côte d'Ivoire Country Profile, 1991–92* (London, 1991), p. 8.

7. A Critique of World Bank and IMF Adjustment Programs

1. Simon Commander, "Prices, Markets and Rigidities: African Agriculture, 1989–88," in Commander (1989: 229–31).

2. Avramovic (1991: ii).

3. Arrow (1962: 154–94); and Nafziger (1990: 259–60). Nafziger (1986: 1–26) analyzes how important self-directed development was for late nineteenth-century Japan.

4. Andrew Kiondo, "The Nature of Economic Reforms in Tanzania," in Campbell and Stein (1992: 34).

5. Sachs (1989a: 31); Mills (1989: 21–23); J.L.S. Abbey, "Ghana's Experience with Structural Adjustment: Some Lessons," in Pickett and Singer (1990: 37); Thomas M. Callaghy, "Toward State Capability and Embedded Liberalism in the Third World: Lessons for Adjustment," in Nelson and contributors (1989: 130); Miles Kahler, "International Financial Institutions and the Politics of Adjustment," in Nelson and contributors (1989: 141); and Lancaster (1991: 39).

6. Commander, "Prices, Markets and Rigidities," pp. 228–29; and Stewart (1990: 4).

7. *IMF Survey,* 14 November 1988, p. 354.

8. Devlin (1989: 230).

9. Stein (1991).

10. Mosley, Harrigan, and Toye, vol. 1 (1991), with quotation on p. 43.

11. Ibid., pp. 1–165.

12. Ibid., pp. 65–177; and Krueger (1974: 291–301).

13. Grubel (1981: 349–88).

14. Reginald Herbold Green, "Articulating Stabilisation Programmes and Structural Adjustment: Sub-Saharan Africa," in Commander (1989: 36); Khan (1987: 26–27); Omotunde E. G. Johnson, "The Agricultural Sector in IMF Stand-by Arrangements," in Commander (1989: 19); Richard E. Feinberg, "An Open Letter to the World Bank's New President," in Feinberg and contributors (1986: 14–18); and Commander, "Prices, Markets, and Rigidities," p. 229.

15. Reginald Herbold Green, "Articulating Stabilisation Programmes and Structural Adjustment," in Commander (1989: 36; Godfrey (1985: 32); Ajay Chhibber, "The Aggregate Supply Response: A Survey," in Commander (1989: 56); Bond (1983: 703–26); John Loxley, "The Devaluation Debate in Tanzania," in Campbell and Loxley (1989: 13–36); and Campbell and Stein (1992: 20–22); and Erbe (1985: 268–75).

16. Mosley, Harrigan, and Toye, vol. 1 (1991: 110–16); and FAO (1991: 101–3).

17. World Bank (1988: 38–39).

18. J.L.S. Abbey, "Ghana's Experience," pp. 36–37; Hirschman (1963: 192–223); and Nafziger (1990: 337–38).

19. Per Pinstrup-Anderson, Maurice Jaramillo, and Frances Stewart, "The Impact on Government Expenditure," in Cornia, Jolly, and Stewart, vol. 1 (1987: 74–78).

20. Commander, "Prices, Markets and Rigidities," pp. 231–34.

21. World Bank and the U.N. Development Programme (1989: 23).

22. World Bank (1988a: 29–30).

23. Paul Streeten, "A Survey of the Issues and Options," in Commander (1989: 9); Camdessus quotation from James P. Grant, Executive Director of UNICEF (1989: 17–18).

24. Per Pinstrup-Anderson, "The Impact of Macroeconomic Adjustment:

Food Security and Nutrition," in Commander (1989: 91–96); and Pinstrup-Anderson, Jaramillo, and Stewart, "The Impact on Government Expenditure," pp. 83–85.

25. Ralph van der Hoeven, "External Shocks, Adjustment, and Income Distribution," in Weeks (1989: 30–31).

26. ECA/OAU (1986: 4); and World Bank (1988a: 47).

27. World Bank (1988a: 1–2, 11–12, 33–34, 58).

28. Stijn Claessens and Ishac Diwan, "Liquidity, Debt Relief, and Conditionality," in Husain and Diwan (1989: 213–25).

29. World Bank (1981a: 147); World Bank (1991b: 221); Mosley, Harrigan, and Toye, vol. 1 (1991: 196–98); and Thandika Mkandawire, "Crisis and Adjustment in Sub-Saharan Africa," in Ghai (1991: 81).

30. World Bank (1989a: 277); World Bank (1989c: 168–69); and World Bank (1988c: 282–83).

31. Dharam Ghai and Cynthia Hewitt de Alcántara, "The Crisis of the 1980s in Africa, Latin America and the Caribbean: An Overview," in Ghai (1991: 31–32); Cleaver (1985); Ghatak and Ingersent (1984).

32. Robert Bates, "The Reality of Structural Adjustment: A Sceptical Appraisal," in Commander (1989: 222–26); and FAO (1991: 97).

33. Parfitt and Riley (1989: 33); and Davies and Saunders (1987: 3–23).

34. Lele (1990: 1209).

35. Cleaver (1985); Mosley, Harrigan, and Toye, vol. 1 (1991: 93–95); Ghai and de Alcántara, "The Crisis of the 1980s," p. 32.

36. Callaghy, "Toward State Capability and Embedded Liberalism," pp. 116–17; Stein (1991).

37. Polyani (1944: 140–41); and Richard Sandbrook, "Economic Crisis, Structural Adjustment and the State in Sub-Saharan Africa," in Ghai (1991: 101).

38. Mary Sutton, "Structuralism: The Latin American Record and the New Critique," in Killick (1984: 19–67); Jennifer Sharpley, "Kenya, 1975–81," in Killick, Bird, Sharpley, and Sutton (1984: 164–216); and de Oliveira Campos (1964: 129–37).

39. André Martens, "Structural Adjustment in the Sahel: Beyond the Point of No Return?" in North-South Institute (1988: 15–21).

40. Giovanni Andrea Cornia, Richard Jolly, and Frances Stewart, "An Overview of the Alternative Approach," in Cornia, Jolly, and Stewart, vol. 1 (1987: 131–46); and Frances Stewart, "Alternative Macro Policies, Meso Policies, and Vulnerable Groups," in Cornia, Jolly, and Stewart, vol. 1 (1987: 147–64).

41. OAU (1980); and Lancaster (1990: 123).

42. Adedeji (1989: 5), a speech delivered in 1982.

43. ECA/OAU (1986: 4).

44. ECA (1987).

45. ECA (1989a: 24).

46. ECA (1989a: 16–20, 36–38; and Cook and Kirkpatrick (1988).

47. ECA (1989a: i–iii).

48. Ibid., pp. 1–8.

49. Ibid., pp. 9–15.

50. Ibid., pp. 26–46.

51. Ibid., pp. 49–53; and Mills (1989: 2).

52. ECA (1989a: 21–25); and Rothchild (1991: 14).

53. ECA (1989a: 21–25), criticizing World Bank and U.N. Development Programme (1989).

54. Parfitt (1990: 134–35).

55. John Loxley, "The IMF and World Bank Conditionality and sub-Saharan Africa," in Lawrence (1986: 96–103); and Gylfason (1987).

56. Robin A. King and Michael D. Robinson, "Assessing Structural Adjustment Programs: A Summary of Country Experience," in Weeks (1989: 110–15).

57. Loxley, "The IMF and World Bank Conditionality," pp. 96–103; and Giovanni Andea Cornia, "Economic Decline and Human Welfare in the First Half of the 1980s," in Cornia, Jolly, and Stewart, vol. 1, *Protecting the Vulnerable and Promoting Growth* (1987: 11–47); Cornia, "Adjustment Policies, 1980–1985: Effects on Child Welfare," in Cornia, Jolly, and Stewart, vol. 1 (1987: 63); and World Bank (1988a: 2–4).

58. World Bank (1988a: 18–36).

59. Commander, "Prices, Market, and Rigidities," p. 239.

60. ECA (1989a: 21–25); UNCTAD (1991: 8); and Faini et al. (1991: 957–67).

61. Stewart (1990: 33–34).

62. FAO (1991: 115).

63. Mosley, Harrigan, and Toye, vol. 1 (1991: 181–207).

64. Ibid., pp. 208–32.

65. FAO (1991: 115–149).

66. Quoted in Grant (1989: 18–20).

67. Mosley, Harrigan, and Toye, vol. 1 (1991: 54).

68. Streeten, "Survey of the Issues and Options," pp. 16–17; World Bank (1988a: 29–49); Parfitt (1990: 131); Rothchild (1991: 12); John M. Nelson, "The Politics of Pro-Poor Adjustment," in Nelson and contributors (1989: 102); FAO (1991: 114); and J.L.S. Abbey, "Ghana's Experience," p. 39).

69. Tsatsu Tskikata, "Ghana," in Adedeji, Rasheed, and Morrison (1990: 161).

70. Gaiha (1989: 57); and FAO (1991: 111–12).

71. World Bank (1988c: 6); Streeten, "Survey of the Issues and Options," 11–12); and Nelson, "Politics of Pro-Poor Adjustment," p. 105.

72. Huang and Nicholas (1987: 22–24).

73. World Bank (1989a); Lovejoy et al. (1992: chapter 3); and Stein and Nafziger (1991: 173–89).

8. The Brady Plan, Toronto and Trinidad Terms, and Debt Exchanges

1. For the full text of the Baker Plan, see Kuczynski (1988: 209–16).

2. Sachs (1988: 17–26); Buiter and Srinivasan (1987: 414); Ranis (1987: 189–99); Rahimibrougerdi (1988: 51); Gerald K. Helleiner, "Summary of the UN Secretary-General's Advisory Group Report on Financial Flows for Africa," in North-South Institute (1988: 30); and William R. Cline, "The Baker Plan and Brady Reformulation: An Evaluation," in Husain and Diwan (1989: 176–86).

3. See John F. Weeks, "Losers Pay Reparations, or How the Third World Lost the Lending War," in Weeks (1989: 41–63); Karin Lissakers, "Background to the Debt Crisis: Structural Adjustment in the Financial Markets," in Weeks (1989: 67–73); and Paul M. Sacks and Chris Canavan, "Safe Passage through Dire Straits: Managing an Orderly Exit from the Debt Crisis," in Weeks (1989: 75–87), for elaboration.

Kevin Phillips, "Web of Corruption Surrounds Bush Presidency," *Kansas City Star* (7 April 1992), p. B-7, asserts that in 1988, Baker "approved policies that permitted U.S. banks to avoid having to write off a portion of their hefty loans to Brazil. Baker himself was a prime beneficiary of this policy, because stock in New York's Chemical Bank, where he had a large chunk, quickly rose 40 percent."

4. Harry Huizinga, "The Commercial Bank Claims on Developing Countries: How Have Banks Been Affected?" in Husain and Diwan (1989: 129).

5. World Bank and the U.N. Development Programme (1989: 18–19); and Charles Humphreys and John Underwood, "The External Debt Difficulties of Low-Income Africa," in Husain and Diwan (1989: 45, 51–53).

6. Lancaster (1991: 43–44); U.N. (1988a: 45–47); Helleiner, "Summary of the U.N. Secretary-General's Advisory Group Report," p. 31; Mistry (1991: 16–18); World Bank, vol. 1, *Analysis and Summary Tables* (1990b: 93–94); and Stephan Haggard and Robert Kaufman, "The Politics and Stabilization and Structural Adjustment," in Sachs (1989a: 264–66).

7. Huizinga, "Commercial Bank Claims on Developing Countries," pp. 129–132.

8. World Bank, vol. 1, *Analysis and Summary Tables* (1989b: 24).

9. Cline, "Baker Plan and Brady Reformulation," pp. 187–91); World Bank, vol. 1 *Analysis and Summary Tables* (1989b: 21).

10. FAO (1991: 6).

11. World Bank, vol. 1, *Analysis and Summary Tables* (1989b: 12).

12. Ishrat Husain and Saumya Mitra, "Future Financing Needs of the Highly Indebted Countries," in Husain and Diwan (1989: 199–209).

13. Mistry (1991: 18).

14. *Africa Research Bulletin* (*Economic Series*) (15 November 1991): p. 10572. In July 1991, the Abidjan Round Table of parliamentarians from Africa

and DCs urged Trinidad terms for Nigeria, Côte d'Ivoire, and Congo, a recommendation not yet accepted in 1991.

15. Mistry (1991: 18–19); and Lancaster (1991: 51).

16. Mistry (1991), quoted from pp. 3, 6, and 37; FAO (1991: 7); and Lancaster (1991: 52–54).

17. Humphreys and Underwood, "External Debt Difficulties of Low-Income Africa," p. 45; World Bank and the U.N. Development Programme (1989: 18); and IMF (1990: 77); and World Bank, vol. 1, *Analysis and Summary Tables* (1989b: 24, 44).

18. IMF (1990: 53); FAO (1991: 7); and *Africa Research Bulletin* (*Economic Series*), 15 October 1991, p. 10550; Humphreys and Underwood, "External Debt Difficulties of Low-Income Africa," pp. 51, 57; Husain and Underwood (1992: 29); and Lancaster (1991: 45).

19. U.N. (1988).

20. World Bank, vol. 1, *Analysis and Summary Tables* (1989b: 51–59).

21. World Bank, vol. 1, *Analysis and Summary Tables* (1989b: 5, 20).

22. FAO (1991: 6–7).

23. Husain and Underwood (1992: 29).

24. World Bank and U.N. Development Programme (1989: 18–19); Humphreys and Underwood," External Debt Difficulties of Low-Income Africa," pp. 45, 51–53; Marcelo Selowsky, "Comment," in Husain and Diwan (1989: 257); U.N. (1988a: 45–47); and Helleiner, "Summary of the U.N. Secretary-General's Advisory Group Report," pp. 30–31.

25. World Bank, vol. 1, *Analysis and Summary Tables* (1991b: 99); and Husain and Underwood (1992: 29).

26. Husain and Underwood (1992: 29); and Michel H. Bouchet and Jonathan Hay, "The Rise of the Market-Based 'Menu' Approach and Its Limitations," in Husain and Diwan (1989: 146–51).

27. Stijn Claessens and Ishac Diwan, "Market-Based Debt Reduction," in Husain and Diwan (1989: 271).

28. World Bank, vol. 1, *Analysis and Summary Tables* (1989b: 18).

29. The example below follows a format similar to Krugman and Obstfeld (1990: 663–67); other material is from their pp. 678–79. This source is excellent on market-based debt exchanges.

30. Humphreys and Underwood, "External Debt Difficulties of Low-Income Africa," pp. 55–57.

31. World Bank, vol. 1, *Analysis and Summary Tables* (1989b: 18); Devlin (1989: 275); and World Bank, vol. 1, *Analysis and Summary Tables* (1991b: 35–42).

32. Claessens and Diwan, "Market-Based Debt Reduction," p. 271; and U.N. (1988).

33. Humphreys and Underwood, "External Debt Difficulties of Low-Income Africa," p. 46.

34. U.N. (1988).

35. Jeffrey Sachs, "Efficient Debt Reduction," in Husain and Diwan (1989: 251).

36. Sachs (1989b: 87–104).

37. Sachs, "Efficient Debt Reduction," pp. 239–40; and Dell (1991: 139).

38. World Bank, vol. 1, *Analysis and Summary Tables* (1991b: 35–42).

39. Sachs, "Efficient Debt Reduction," pp. 241–46.

40. Bresser Pereira (1989); and Sachs, "Efficient Debt Reduction," pp. 246–50.

41. Husain and Underwood (1992: 30).

42. David Henderson, "Speech to the Institute for International Economics," *IMF Survey*, 17 May 1991, pp. 13–16.

43. Ray (1989: 80–83).

44. Nafziger (1990: 403); and Parfitt and Riley (1989: 46).

45. *IMF Survey*, 21 December 1988, pp. 386–89; World Bank (1987: 136–37); Ray (1989: 145–46); and UNCTAD (1991: 152).

46. Parfitt and Bullock (1990: 104–16).

47. World Bank (1986b: 142–43); World Bank (1981b: 28–30); and Ray (1989: 86–91, 188–95).

9. Resolving the Debt Crisis

1. Stanley Fischer, "Foreword," in Husain and Diwan (1989: v).

2. See Nafziger (1990: 172–75) for a summary of limits to growth by the Club of Rome's team of scholars at MIT (Donella H. Meadow et al.), Herman E. Daly, and Nicholas Georgescu-Roegen.

3. Hardin (1974: 561–68).

4. The doubling time and ratios are based on 1991 population growth figures in Population Reference Bureau (1991).

5. Hardin (1974: 561–68).

6. Nafziger (1990: 181–212).

7. See World Bank (1991c: 212–13); energy consumption per capita (kilograms of coal equivalent) in DCs as a whole is seventy-one times that of sub-Saharan Africa as a whole.

8. Computed from OECD (1989); and World Bank (1990c).

9. Sewell, Tucker, and contributors (1988: 242).

10. "Africa to Seek Compensation," *Wall Street Journal*, 12 February 1991, p. A-9.

11. Development Assistance Committee (DAC) (1989: 11–12) (including quotation); World Bank, vol. 1, *Analysis and Summary Tables* (1990b: 105–7); OECD (1990b: 11–12); and Wheeler (1990: 11–12).

12. Sewell et al. (1988: 244).

13. "More Aid to Africa Pledged," *Kansas City Star*, 20 April 1991, p. A-11; and "World Wire," *Wall Street Journal*, 22 April 1991, p. A-6.

14. Daniel Cohen, "How to Cope with a Debt Overhang: Cut Flows Rather

than Stocks," in Husain and Diwan (1989: 229–35); and Eduardo Borensztein, "Comment," in Husain and Diwan (1989: 235–37).

15. Jeffrey D. Sachs, "Conditionality, Debt Relief, and the Developing Country Debt Crisis," in Sachs (1989a: 279); Devlin (1989: 233) and William R. Cline, "Latin American Debt: Progress, Prospects, and Policy," in Edwards and Larrain (1989: 45); and Greene (1991).

16. World Bank, vol. 1, *Analysis and Summary Tables* (1990b: 103).

17. World Bank, vol. 1, *Analysis and Summary Tables* (1991b: 124); OECD (1989: 43–45, 65–69); and Harry Huizinga, "The Commercial Bank Claims on Developing Countries: How Have Banks Been Affected?" in Husasin and Diwan (1989: 129–143).

18. Bigman (1990: 33–37).

19. African Development Bank and ECA (1988: 29–98).

20. World Bank, vol. 1, *Analysis and Summary Tables* (1991b: 51–52).

21. Rudiger Dornbusch, "Discussion," in Williamson (1990b: 324).

22. Lancaster (1991: 55–56); and Mistry (1991: 15).

23. Sachs (1989b: 87–104); Devlin (1989: 203, 237–38).

24. Lancaster (1991: 45).

25. OECD (1990a: 140–89); IMF (1991: 2); OECD (1990b: 228–29); and Husain and Underwood (1992: 26–27).

26. Rogoff (1990: 5); U.N. (1988a: 45–47); and Gerald K. Helleiner, "Summary of the U.N. Secretary-General's Advisory Group Report on Financial Flows for Africa," in North-South Institute (1988: 31).

27. Avramovic (1991: 19); and Nafziger (1986: 1–26).

28. Avramovic (1991: 19).

29. Marc Wuyts, "Mozambique: Economic Management and Adjustment Policies," in Ghai (1991: 231).

30. Avramovic (1991: 19); and *World Bank News*, 14 February 1991, p. 13.

31. World Bank, vol. 1, *Analysis and Summary Tables* (1990b: 89); and World Bank, vol. 1, *Analysis and Summary Tables* (1991b: 126).

32. Mistry (1991: 20).

33. Ibid., pp. 19–27.

34. "The IMF and the World Bank," *Economist*, 12 October 1991, p. 48.

35. Mosley, Harrigan, and Toye, vol. 1 (1991: 54–55).

36. Broadening the U.N. Security Council permanent membership to include, among others, LDCs such as India, Brazil, and Nigeria would increase diplomatic pressure to address debt and other economic issues important to developing countries.

On 5 June 1991, the OAU established the African Economic Community, with an ultimate goal an African Common Market in the first quarter of the twenty-first century. I am skeptical concerning its immediate economic benefits, because of the failure of so many past LDC and African attempts at economic integration (see Nafziger [1990: 411–13]). Nevertheless, the long-run (beyond 2000) potential of the AEC to increase the international bargaining power and industrial potential of Africa is substantial.

37. World Bank (1988c: 244–45).

38. Nafziger (1990: 390–400).

39. DeRosa (1991: 42–45).

40. Fransman (1986: 75–93).

41. IMF (1990: 74–76). Erzan and Svedberg (1991: 97–151) indicate that sub-Saharan countries in the early 1980s saw lower trade-weighted average tariffs than LDCs generally. Among LDCs, sub-Saharan countries benefit more from: (1) EC associate status, (2) DC preference toward least-developed countries under generalized system of preferences (GSP) schemes, and (3) lower DC tariff rates on mineral fueld, ores, and metals (which comprised 69 percent of the Sub-Sahara's exports in 1985) than from agricultural products competing with temperate products, and manufactures.

42. *Africa Demōs* (Atlanta) 2(2) (February 1992): 11.

43. U.S. Agency for International Development (1990: 3).

44. "Managing Director's Address: A Viable Economic System is a Priority for Emerging Democracies," *IMF Survey* (29 July 1991): 227.

45. Mills (1989: 21–23); Fischer and Husain (1990: 27); and André Martens, "Structural Adjustment in the Sahel: Beyond the Point of No Return?" in North-South Institute (1988: 15–21).

46. Africa Leadership Forum, OAU, and ECA (1990: 40).

47. Sandbrook (1985); and Diamond, Linz, and Lipset (1988).

48. Lal (1983: 33); World Bank (1991a: 50, 132–34); and Wilson (1991), whose study of thirteen LDCs indicates a negative relationship between political liberalization and economic growth.

49. Louellen Stedman and Peter Hakim, "Political Change and Economic Policy in Latin America and the Caribbean in 1988," in Weeks (1989: 166–74; and Acapulco Summit Meeting (1987).

50. Stephan Haggard and Robert R. Kaufman, "Economic Adjustment in New Democracies," in Nelson and contributors (1989: 57–77); Laurence Whitehead, "Democratization and Disinflation: A Comparative Approach," in Nelson and contributors (1989: 85–86); Hirschman (1986: 17); and Mosley, Harrigan, and Toye, vol. 1 (1991: 146).

51. Joan M. Nelson, "The Politics of Pro-Poor Adjustment," in Nelson and contributors (1989: 100–105); and John Waterbury, "The Political Management of Economic Adjustment and Reform," in Nelson and contributors (1989: 40–46).

52. Venkatash Seshamani, "Zambia," in Adedeji, Rasheed, and Morrison (1990: 120).

Glossary

.

Commodity terms of trade—The price index of exports divided by the price index of imports. For example, if export prices increase 10 percent and import prices 22 percent, the commodity terms of trade would drop 10 percent, that is, 1.10 / 1.22 = 0.90. Also called *net barter terms of trade*.

Concessional lending—Loans that have at least a 25 percent grant element. The grant element of the loan depends on how much lower the interest rate is than commercial rates, the length of the grace period in which interest charges or repayments of principal are not required, the length of the repayment period, and the amount of the repayment that is in local inconvertible currency. To calculate the grant element, compare the present value of the net income stream forthcoming from the loan to that of a loan tendered at bankers' standards.

Conditionality—Conditions that the International Monetary Fund or World Bank sets for lending.

Convertible currency—A currency that may be freely used in international transactions by citizens of any country.

Cost-push inflation—Price increases, notwithstanding constant or dropping demand, due to higher costs in imperfectly competitive markets.

Current account balance—An international balance comprising exports minus imports of goods and services, plus net grants, remittances, and unilateral transfers received (see table 2.3).

Debt—External debt stock owed to nonresidents and repayment in foreign currency, goods, or services.

Debt Laffer curve—An upside-down "U" curve expressing the expected value of the debt as a function of the amount of debt.

Debt service—The interest and principal payments due in a given year on external debt.

Debt-service ratio—The ratio of a given year's debt service to exports of goods and services.

Deficit countries—Countries with negative international balances on goods and services.

Economic growth—The rate of growth of GNP per capita.

External economies (or externalities)—Cost advantages rendered free by one producer to another.

Eurocurrency—U.S. dollars and other convertible currencies deposited in off-

245

shore banks, that is, banks accepting deposits denominated in a currency other than that of the bank's country of residence. Eurocurrency is a misnomer, since the currency trades not only in Europe but also in non-European centers such as Singapore, Hong Kong, Nassau, and Bahrain.

Export purchasing power—Same as income terms of trade.

Formal sector—Government sector and firms with ten or more employees in the private sector.

GDP (gross domestic product)—A measure of the total output of goods and services in terms of income earned within a country's boundaries. GDP includes income earned by foreign residents and companies, even it is transferred abroad, and excludes income earned abroad by a country's residents and companies.

GNP (gross national product)—A measure of total output of goods and services in terms of income earned by a country's residents. GNP includes income by the country's residents abroad and excludes income earned domestically by foreign residents.

GNP per capita—GNP divided by the population.

Grant element—*See* Concessional lending.

IDA-eligible countries—Countries poor enough to be eligible for International Development Association concessional loans.

IMF reserve tranche— The 25 percent of a country's contribution or quota to the IMF that is in gold or foreign convertible currency.

Immiserization—Falling average economic welfare.

Import substitution—Domestic production replacing imports.

Income terms of trade—The commodity terms of trade times export volume. For example, if the commodity terms of trade should drop 10 percent while export volume increased by 22 percent, the income terms of trade would increase by 10 percent, that is, $0.90 \times 1.22 = 1.10$.

International balance of (merchandise) trade—Exports minus imports of goods.

International balance on goods and services—Exports minus imports of goods and services (see table 2.3).

Laffer curve—*See* Debt Laffer curve.

London Club—Forum for developing countries to renegotiate or restructure debts to commercial bank creditors.

Monopsony—A market in which there is only one buyer of a product.

Neocolonialism—The economic, political, and military process by which industrialized countries maintain the former colony as a controlled source of raw materials, markets, and investment after the granting of formal independence.

Net barter terms of trade—*See* Commodity terms of trade.

Offshore bank—*See* Eurocurrency.

Oligopoly—A market with few sellers making interdependent pricing decisions.

Parastatal enterprises—Public corporations and statutory boards owned by the state but responsible for day-to-day management to boards of directors, some of whom are appointed by the state.

Glossary

Paris Club—Multilateral forum for developing countries to renegotiate or restructure debts to governments and officially guaranteed export creditors.

Percentage point—Measure used to express changes in economic growth and other rates of change. For example, if a policy change, such as a reduced tariff or an IMF loan, increases economic growth from 2 percent to 3 percent, growth rises 50 percent (1/2) but by only 1 percentage point.

Price elasticity of demand—The absolute value of the percentage change in quantity demanded, divided by the percentage change in price. Values of more than one are elastic; of less than one, inelastic.

Primary products—Food, raw materials, and organic oils and fats.

Real economic growth—Inflation-adjusted growth in GNP per capita (usually expressed per annum).

Stabex—European Community scheme to stabilize primary-product export earnings from fifty-eight African, Caribbean, and Pacific countries.

Sub-Saharan Africa—The continent of Africa, except Arabic Northern Africa (Egypt, Libya, Tunisia, Algeria, Morocco, and Western Sahara) and the Republic of South Africa.

Surplus—Output minus wages, depreciation, and purchases from other units.

Surplus countries—Countries with positive international balances on goods and services.

Total economic growth—The rate of GNP growth.

Bibliography

■

Books, Monographs, and Articles

Acapulco Summit Meeting of Latin American Presidents, 1987. "Final Communique." 30 November.

Acharya, Shankar N. 1981a. "Perspectives and Problems of Development in Sub-Saharan Africa." *World Development* 9 (February): 16–19.

———. 1981b. "Development Perspectives and Problems in Sub-Saharan Africa." *Finance and Development* 18 (March): 16–19.

Addison, Tony, and Demery, Lionel. 1987. "Alleviating Poverty under Structural Adjustment: Is There Room for Maneuver?" *Finance and Development* 24 (December): 41–43.

Adedeji, Adebayo, ed. 1981. *Indigenization of African Economies.* London: Hutchinson.

———. 1989. *Towards a Dynamic African Economy: Selected Speeches and Lectures, 1975–1986.* London: Frank Cass.

Adedeji, Adebayo; Rasheed, Sadig; and Morrison, Melody, eds. 1990. *The Human Dimensions of Africa's Persistent Economic Crisis.* London: Hans Zell Publishers.

Adedeji, Adebayo, and Shaw, Timothy M., eds. 1985. *Economic Crisis in Africa: African Perspectives on Development Problems and Potentials.* Boulder, Colo.: Lynne Rienner.

Adelman, Irma, and Morris, Cynthia Taft. 1973. *Economic Growth and Social Equity in Developing Countries.* Stanford: Stanford University Press.

African Development Bank and ECA. 1988. *Economic Report on Africa, 1988.* Abidjan and Addis Ababa, March.

Africa Leadership Forum, Organisation of African Unity, and Economic Commission for Africa. 1990. *Report on the Brainstorming Meeting for a Conference on Security, Stability, Development and Cooperation in Africa.* Addis Ababa: 17–18 November.

Africa Watch. 1991a. *Academic Freedom and Human Rights Abuses in Africa.* New York: Human Rights Watch.

———. 1991b. "Academic Freedom in Nigeria." *Association of Concerned African Scholars Bulletin,* no. 34 (Fall): 21–25.

Agbese, Pita Ogaba. 1990. "The Impending Demise of Nigeria's Forthcoming Third Republic." *Africa Today,* 37(3): 23–44.

Bibliography

Ahluwalia, Montek S.; Carter Nicholas, G.; and Chenery, Hollis B. 1979. "Growth and Poverty in Developing Countries." *Journal of Development Economics* 6 (September): 299–341.

Allen, V. L. 1972. "The Meaning of the Working Class in Africa." *Journal of Modern African Studies* 10 (July): 169–89.

Ali, Ridwan, and Pitkin, Barbara. 1991. "Searching for Household Food Security in Africa." *Finance and Development* 28 (December): 3–6.

American Economic Association. 1950. *Readings in the Theory of International Trade*. Homewood, Ill.: Richard D. Irwin.

Amin, Samir. 1965. *Trois expériences africaines de développement: le Mali, la Guinée, et le Ghana*. Paris: Les Editions de Minuit.

Arrow, Kenneth, 1962. "The Economic Implications of Learning by Doing." *Review of Economic Studies* 29 (June): 154–94.

Aspe, Armella, Pedro. 1990. "The Renegotiation of Mexico's External Debt." *IDS Bulletin* 21 (April): 23–26.

Avramovic, Dragoslav. 1991. "Africa's Debts and Economic Recovery." North-South Roundtable. Abidjan, Côte d'Ivoire. 8–9 July.

Ayub, Mahmood A., and Hegstad, Sven O. 1987. "Determinants of Public Enterprise Performance." *Finance and Development* 24 (December): 26–29.

Bates, Robert H. 1981. *Markets and States in Tropical Africa: The Political Basis of Agricultural Policies*. Berkeley: University of California Press.

Bienen, Henry, and Diejomaoh, V. P., eds. 1981. *The Political Economy of Income Distribution in Nigeria*. New York: Holmes & Meier.

Bigman, David. 1990. "A Plan to End LDC Debt and Save the Environment Too." *Challenge* 33 (July/August): 33–37.

Bird, Graham, ed. 1989. *Third World Debt: The Search for a Solution*. Aldershot, England: Edward Elgar.

Birmingham, Walter; Neustadt, I.; and Omaboe, E. N. 1966. *A Study of Contemporary Ghana*, vol. 1. *The Economy of Ghana*. Evanston, Ill.: Northwestern University Press.

Boateng, E. Oti; Ewusi, Kodwo; Kanbur, Ravi; and McKay, Andrew. 1990. *A Poverty Profile for Ghana*. Social Dimensions of Adjustment in Sub-Saharan Africa. Working Paper No. 5. Washington, D.C.: World Bank.

Boissière, M.; Knight, John B.; and Sabot, Richard H. 1985. "Earnings, Schooling, Ability, and Cognitive Skills." *American Economic Review* 75 (December): 1016–30.

Bond, Marian E. 1983. "Agricultural Responses to Prices in Sub-Saharan African Countries." *International Monetary Fund Staff Papers* 30 (December): 703–26.

Bransford, S., and Kucinski, Bernardo. 1989. *The Debt Squads*. London: Zed Books.

Brenner, M. H. 1973. "Fetal, Infant, and Maternal Mortality during Periods of Economic Instability." *International Journal of Health Services* 3 (2): 145–59.

Bresser Pereira, Luiz Carlos. 1989. "Solving the Debt Crisis: Debt Relief and

Bibliography

Adjustment." Testimony presented before the House Committee on Banking, Finance, and Urban Affairs. 6 January.

Buiter, Willem H., and Srinivasan, T. N. 1987. "Rewarding the Profligate and Punishing the Prudent and Poor: Some Recent Proposals for Debt Relief." *World Development* 15 (March): 411–17.

Bukuku, Enos S. 1988. *Income Distribution and Economic Growth in Tanzania.* Gothenberg, Sweden: Kompendietryckeriet–Källared.

Bulow, Jeremy, and Rogoff, Kenneth. 1990. "Cleaning Up Third World Debt without Getting Taken to the Cleaners." *Journal of Economic Perspectives* 4 (Winter): 31–42.

Byerlee, Derek; Eicher, Carl; and Norman, David. 1982. "Farm Systems in Developing Countries." Unpublished manuscript.

Camdessus, Michel. 1988. "The IMF: Facing New Challenges." *Finance and Development* 25 (June): 2–5.

———. 1989. "The IMF and the Global Economy: Three Addresses." Washington, DC: International Monetary Fund. September.

———. 1991. "Good News Out of Africa." *Finance and Development* 28 (December): 2.

Campbell, Bonnie K. 1985. "The Fiscal Crisis of the State: The Case of the Ivory Coast." In Henry Bernstein and Bonnie K. Campbell, eds., *Contradictions of Accumulation in Africa.* Beverly Hills, Calif.: Sage Publications, pp. 267–310.

———, and Loxley, John, eds. 1989. *Structural Adjustment in Africa.* New York: St. Martin's Press.

Campbell, Horace, and Stein, Howard, eds. 1992. *Tanzania and the IMF: The Dynamics of Liberalization.* Boulder, Colo.: Westview.

Cavanagh, John; Cheru, Fantu; Collins, Carole; Duncan, Cameron; and Ntube, Dominic. 1985. *From Debt to Development: Alternatives to the International Debt Crisis.* Washington, D.C.: Institute for Policy Studies.

Chang, P. H. Kevin, and Cumby, Robert E. 1990. "Capital Flight in Sub-Saharan African Countries." Paper presented to a World Bank Symposium on African External Finance. Washington, D.C. September.

Chelliah, Raja J.; Bass, Hessel J.; and Kelly, Margaret R. 1975. "Tax Ratios and Tax Effort in Developing Countries, 1969–71." *International Monetary Fund Staff Papers* 22 (March): 187–205.

Chenery, Hollis; Ahluwalia, Montek S.; Bell, C. L. G.; Duloy, John H.; and Jolly, Richard. 1974. *Redistribution with Growth.* London: Oxford University Press.

Chenery, Hollis B., and Strout, Alan M. 1966. "Foreign Assistance and Economic Development." *American Economic Review* 56 (September): 679–733.

Cheru, Fantu. 1989. *The Silent Revolution in Africa: Debt, Development and Democracy.* London: Zed Books.

Chow, Peter C. Y. 1987. "Causality between Export Growth and Industrial Development: Empirical Evidence from the NICs." *Journal of Development Economics* 26 (June): 155–63.

Bibliography

Cleaver, Kevin M. 1985. "The Impact of Price and Exchange Rate Policies on Agriculture in Sub-Saharan Africa." World Bank Staff Working Paper No. 728. Washington, D.C.

Cline, William R. 1984. *International Debt: Systemic Risk and Policy Response.* Cambridge, Mass.: MIT Press.

Cline, William R., and associates. 1981. *World Inflation and the Developing Countries.* Washington, D.C.: Brookings Institution.

Cobbe, James. 1991. "Economic Crisis, Structural Adjustment, and Basic Education: Ghana and Malawi Compared." Paper presented to the African Studies Association meeting. St. Louis. 23–26 November.

Cohen, Benjamin J. 1991. "What Ever Happened to the LDC Debt Crisis?" *Challenge* 34 (May–June): 47–51.

Collier, Paul, and Lal, Deepak. 1986. *Labour and Poverty in Kenya, 1900–1980.* Oxford: Clarendon Press.

Commander, Simon, ed. 1989. *Structural Adjustment and Agriculture: Theory and Practice in Africa and Latin America.* London: Overseas Development Institute.

Committee for Academic Freedom in Africa. 1991. "The World Bank and Education in Africa." *CAFA Newsletter,* no. 2 (Fall): 2–12.

Cook, Paul, and Kirkpatrick, Colin, eds. 1988. *Privatisation in Less-developed Countries.* Sussex, England: Wheatsheaf.

Cornia, Giovanni Andrea; Jolly, Richard; and Stewart, Frances, eds. 1987. *Adjustment with a Human Face: Protecting the Vulnerable and Promoting Growth.* 2 vols. Oxford: Clarendon Press.

Cuddington, John T. 1986. *Capital Flight: Estimates, Issues, and Explanations.* Princeton Studies in International Finance, no. 58. Princeton, N.J., Princeton University.

Curtin, Philip; Feierman, Steven; Thompson, Leonard; and Vansina, Jan. 1978. *African History.* Boston: Little, Brown, and Co.

Daly, Herman E. 1977. *Steady-State Economics: The Economics of Biophysical Equilibrium and Moral Growth.* San Francisco: W. H. Freeman.

Darity, William, Jr., and Horn, Bobbie L. 1988. *The Loan Pushers: The Role of Commercial Banks in the International Debt Crisis.* Cambridge, Mass.: Ballinger Publishing.

Davies, Rob, and Saunders, David. 1987. "Stabilisation Policies and the Effect on Child Health in Zimbabwe." *Review of African Political Economy,* no. 38 (April): 3–23.

Davis, J. Tait. 1991. "Institutional Impediments to Workforce Retrenchment and Restructuring in Ghana's State Enterprises." *World Development* 19 (August): 987–1005.

Delgado, Christopher L., and Jammeh, Sidi, eds. 1991. *The Political Economy of Senegal under Structural Adjustment.* New York: Praeger.

Dell, Sidney. 1991. *International Development Policies: Perspectives for Industrial Countries.* Durham, N.C.: Duke University Press.

de Larosière, Jacques. 1986. "Address before the Economic and Social Council of the United Nations." Washington, D.C.: International Monetary Fund.

de Oliveira Campos, Roberto. 1964. "Economic Development and Inflation with Special Reference to Latin America." In Organisation for Economic Cooperation and Development, *Development Plans and Programmes.* Paris: OECD Development Centre, pp. 129–37.

DeRosa, Dean. 1991. "Protection in Sub-Saharan Africa Hinders Exports." *Finance and Development* 28 (September): 42–45.

Development Assistance Committee (DAC) Aid Ministers and Heads of Aid Agencies Chairman's Report. 1989. *Development Co-operation in the 1990s.* Paris: OECD.

Devlin, Robert. 1987. "Economic Restructuring in Latin America in the Face of the Foreign Debt and the External Transfer Problem." *CEPAL Review,* no. 32 (August): 75–101.

———. 1989. *Debt and Crisis in Latin America: The Supply Side of the Story.* Princeton, N.J.: Princeton University Press.

———. 1991. "The Menu Approach." *IDS Bulletin* 21 (April): 11–16.

Diamond, Larry; Linz, Juan J.; and Lipset, Seymoure Martin, eds. 1988. *Democracy in Developing Countries.* Vol. 2. *Africa.* Boulder, Colo.: Lynne Rienner.

Diaz-Alejandro, Carlos F. 1984. "Latin American Debt: I Don't Think We Are in Kansas Anymore." *Brookings Papers,* no. 2: 335–89.

Dornbusch, Rudiger, and Fischer, Stanley. 1986. "Third World Debt." *Science* 234 (November): 836–41.

Dudley, B. J. 1972. "The Politics of Adebo." *Quarterly Journal of Administration* 6 (January): 131–70.

Economic Commission for Africa (ECA). 1983. "ECA and Africa's Development, 1983–2008: A Preliminary Perspective Study." Addis Ababa.

———. 1985. *Survey of Economic and Social Conditions in Africa, 1983–1984.* E/ECA/CM.11/16. Addis Ababa. April.

———. 1987. *The Abuja Statement.* Abuja, Nigeria. 15–19 June.

———. 1989a. *African Alternative Framework to Structural Adjustment Programmes for Socio-Economic Recovery and Transformation (AAF-SAP).* E/ECA/CM.15/6/Rev. 3. Addis Ababa. 10 April.

———. 1989b. *South African Destabilization: The Economic Cost of Frontline Resistance to Apartheid.* Addis Ababa.

Economic Commission for Africa/Organisation of African Unity (ECA/OAU). 1986. *Africa's Submission to the Special Session of the United Nations General Assembly on Africa's Economic and Social Crisis.* Addis Ababa. 31 March.

Edwards, Sebastian, and Larrain, Felipe, eds. 1989. *Debt, Adjustment and Recovery: Latin America's Prospects for Growth and Development.* Oxford: Basil Blackwell.

Eichengreen, Barry, and Portes, Richard. 1990. "The Interwar Debt Crisis and Its Aftermath." *The World Bank Research Observer* 5 (January): 69–94.

Eicher, Carl K., and Baker, Doyle C. 1982. "Research on Agricultural Develop-

Bibliography

ment in Subsaharan Africa: A Critical Survey." International Development Paper No. 1. East Lansing, Mich.: Michigan State University.

Erbe, Susanne. 1985. "The Flight of Capital from Developing Countries." *Intereconomics* 20 (November/December): 268–75.

Erzan, Refik, and Svedberg, Peter, 1991. "Protection Facing Export from Sub-Saharan Africa in the EC, Japan and the US." In Jonathan H. Frimpong-Ansah, S. M. Ravi Kanbur, and Peter Svedberg, eds., *Trade and Development in Sub–Saharan Africa*. Manchester: Manchester University Press, pp. 97–151.

Essien, Efiong, 1990. *Nigeria under Structural Adjustment.* Ibadan: Fountain Publications.

Evans, David. 1986. "Reverse Dutch Disease and Mineral-Exporting Developing Economies." *IDS Bulletin* 17 (October): 10–23.

Faini, Riccardo; de Melo, Jaime; Senhadji, Abdelhak; and Stanton, Julie. 1991. *World Development* 19 (August): 957–67.

Falola, Toyin, and Ihonrbere, Julius. 1985. *The Rise and Fall of Nigeria's Second Republic, 1979–84.* London: Zed Press.

Federal Reserve Bank of Kansas City. 1986. *Debt, Financial Stability and Public Policy.* Symposium held at Jackson Hole, Wyo., 27–29 August.

Feinberg, Richard E., and contributors. 1986. *Between Two Worlds: The World Bank's Next Decade.* New Brunswick, N.J.: Transaction Books.

Fischer, Stanley, and Husain, Ishrat. 1990. "Managing the Debt Crisis in the 1990s." *Finance and Development* 27 (June): 24–27.

Food and Agriculture Organization of the U.N. (FAO). 1991. *The State of Food and Agriculture, 1990.* Rome.

Forrest, Tom. 1986. "The Political Economy of Civil Rule and the Economic Crisis in Nigeria." *Review of African Political Economy*, no. 35 (May): 4–26.

Fransman, Martin. 1986. *Technology and Economic Development.* Boulder, Colo.: Westview.

Freund, W. M. 1981. "Class Conflict, Political Economy and the Struggle for Socialism in Tanzania." *African Affairs* 80 (October): 483–500.

Fry, Maxwell J. 1988. *Money, Interest, and Banking in Economic Development.* Baltimore: Johns Hopkins University Press.

Gaiha, R. 1989. *Structural Adjustment and Rural Poverty in Developing Countries.* Rome: FAO.

Galbraith, John Kenneth. 1975. *Money.* Boston: Houghton Mifflin.

Galtung, Johann. 1971. "A Structural Theory of Imperialism." *Journal of Peace Research*, no. 2: 81–118.

Georgescu-Roegen, Nicholas. 1971. *The Entropy Law and the Economic Process.* Cambridge, Mass.: Harvard University Press.

Ghai, Dharam, ed. 1991. *The IMF and the South: The Social Impact of Crisis and Adjustment.* London: Zed Books.

Ghai, Dharam; Godfrey, Martin; and Lisk, F. 1979. *Planning for Basic Needs in Kenya: Performance, Policies and Prospects.* Geneva: International Labour Office.

Bibliography

Ghai, Dharam, and Radwan, Samir, eds. 1983. *Agrarian Policies and Rural Poverty in Africa*. Geneva: International Labour Office.

Ghatak, Subrata, and Ingersent, Ken. 1984. *Agriculture and Economic Development*. Baltimore: Johns Hopkins University Press.

Gilbert, Christopher L. 1990. "Primary Commodity Prices and Inflation." *Oxford Review of Economic Policy* 6 (4): 77–99.

Godfrey, Martin. 1985. "Trade and Exchange Rate Policy in Sub-Saharan Africa." *IDS Bulletin* 16, no. 3: 31–38.

Goliber, Thomas J. 1989. "Africa's Expanding Population: Old Problems, New Policies. *Population Bulletin* 44 (November): 1–49.

Goode, Richard. 1962. "Personal Income Tax in Latin America." In Joint Tax Program, Organization of American States/Inter-American Development Bank/Economic Commission for Latin America. *Fiscal Policy for Economic Growth in Latin America*. Baltimore: Johns Hopkins University Press, pp. 157–71.

Goreux, L. M. 1980. "Compensatory Financing Facility." International Monetary Fund Pamphlet Series No. 34, Washington, D.C.

Grant, James P. 1989. *The State of the World's Children, 1989*. New York: Oxford University Press.

Greene, Joshua. 1991. "The African Debt Problem: What Are the Issues and Strategies for Resolution?" Paper presented to the African Studies Association meeting. St. Louis. 23–26 November.

Grosh, Barbara. 1991. *Public Enterprise in Kenya: What Works, What Doesn't, and Why*. Boulder, Colo.: Lynne Rienner.

Grubel, Herbert G. 1981. *International Economics*. Homewood, Ill.: Irwin.

Gulhati, Ravi. 1990. *The Making of Economic Policy in Africa*. Washington, D.C.: World Bank.

Guttentag, Jack, and Herring, Richard. 1985. *The Current Crisis in International Lending*. Washington, D.C.: Brookings Institution.

Gutteridge, William. 1985. "Undoing Military Coups in Africa." *Third World Quarterly* 7 (January): 78–89.

Gylfason, Thorvaldur. 1987. *Credit Policy and Economic Activity in Developing Countries with IMF Stabilization Programs*. Princeton Studies in International Finance, no. 60. Princeton, N.J.: Princeton University.

Hackett, Paul. 1990. "Economy." In *Africa South of the Sahara, 1990*. London: Europa Publications.

Hance, William A. 1967. *African Economic Development*. New York: Praeger.

Hardin, Garrett. 1974. "Living on a Lifeboat." *BioScience* 24 (October): 561–68.

Harsch, Ernest. 1989. "After Adjustment." *Africa Report* 34 (May/June): 47–50.

Hawkins, Jeffrey J., Jr. 1991. "Understanding the Failure of IMF Reform: The Zambian Case." *World Development* 19 (August): 839–49.

Heilbroner, Robert L. 1963. *The Great Ascent: The Struggle for Economic Development*. New York: Harper and Row.

Bibliography

Helleiner, Gerald. 1991. "The IMF, the World Bank, and Africa's Adjustment and External Debt Problems: An Unofficial View." Paper presented to a symposium on Structural Adjustment, External Debt, and Growth in Africa sponsored by the Association of African Central Banks. Gaborone, Botswana. February.

Heller, Peter, and Tait, Alan. 1983. "Government Employment and Pay: Some International Comparisons." *Finance and Development* 20 (September): 44–47.

Hewitt, Daniel P. 1991. "Military Expenditures in the Developing World." *Finance and Development* 28 (September): 22–25.

Hirschman, Albert O. 1963. *Journeys toward Progress: Studies of Economic Policy-making in Latin America.* New York: Twentieth Century Fund.

———. 1986. "The Political Economy of Latin American Development: Seven Exercises in Retrospect." Paper for the 13th International Congress of the Latin American Studies Association. Boston. October.

Hofmeier, Rolf. 1991. "Political Conditions Attached to Development Aid for Africa." *Intereconomics* 26 (May/June): 122–27.

Holtham, Gerald, and Hazlewood, Arthur. *Aid and Inequality in Kenya: British Development Assistance to Kenya.* London: Croom Helm, 1976.

Hoogvelt, Ankie. 1990. "Debt and Indebtedneess: The Dynamics of Third World Poverty." *Review of African Political Economy*, no. 47 (Spring): 121–122.

Huang, Yukon, and Nicholas, Peter. 1987. "The Social Costs of Adjustment." *Finance and Development* 24 (June): 22–24.

Husain, Ishrat, and Diwan, Ishac, eds. 1989. *Dealing with the Debt Crisis.* Washington, D.C.: World Bank.

Husain, Ishrat, and Underwood, John. 1992. "The Problem of Sub-Saharan Africa's Debt—and the Solutions." Unpublished paper. Washington, D.C.: World Bank.

Hyden, Göran. 1980. *Beyond Ujamaa in Tanzania: Underdevelopment and an Uncaptured Peasantry.* London: Heinemann.

Ihonvbere, Julius O. 1990. "Why I Left Nigeria." *Africa Today* 37 (3): 67–68.

Independent Commission on International Development Issues (Brandt report). 1980. *North-South: A Program for Survival.* Cambridge, Mass.: MIT Press.

International Labour Office (ILO). Jobs and Skills Programme for Africa. 1981. *First Things First: Meeting the Basic Needs of the People of Nigeria.* Addis Ababa.

———. 1982. *Rural-Urban Gap and Income Distribution: The Case of Ghana.* Addis Ababa.

International Monetary Fund (IMF). 1984. *Government Finance Statistics Yearbook,* vol. 8. Washington, D.C.

———. 1986. *World Economic Outlook.* Washington, D.C., April.

———. 1987. *World Economic Outlook.* Washington, D.C., October.

———. 1988. *World Economic Outlook.* Washington, D.C., October.

Bibliography

————. 1989a. *World Economic Outlook.* Washington, D.C., May.

————. 1989b. *World Economic Outlook.* Washington, D.C., October.

————. 1990. *World Economic Outlook.* Washington, D.C., October.

————. 1991. *World Economic Outlook.* Washington, D.C., May.

Jain, Shail. 1975. *Size Distribution of Income: A Compilation of Data.* Washington, D.C.: World Bank.

Jamal, Vali. 1988. "Getting the Crisis Right: Missing Perspectives on Africa." *International Labour Review* 127 (6): 655–78.

Jamal, Vali, and Weeks, John. 1988. "The Vanishing Rural-Urban Gap in Sub-Saharan Africa." *International Labour Review* 127 (3): 271–92.

Jeffries, Richard. 1982. "Rawlings and the Political Economy of Underdevelopment in Ghana." *African Affairs* 81 (July): 307–17.

Johnson, G. G.; Fisher, Matthew; and Harris, Elliott. 1990. *Officially Supported Export Credits: Development and Prospects.* Washington, D.C.: International Monetary Fund.

Kaldor, Nicholas. 1963. "Taxation for Economic Development." *Journal of Modern African Studies* 1 (March): 7–23.

————. 1984. "An Exchange-Rate Policy for India." *Economic and Political Weekly* 19 (14 July): 1093–95.

Kapur, Ishan; Hadjimichael, Michael T.; Hilbers, Paul; Schiff, Jerald; and Szymczak, Philippe. 1991. *Ghana: Adjustment and Growth, 1983–91.* Occasional Paper 86. Washington, D.C.: International Monetary Fund.

Kayizzi-Mugerwa, Steve. 1991. "External Shocks and Adjustment in a Mineral Dependent Economy: A Short-run Model for Zambia." *World Development* 19 (July): 851–65.

Kenen, Peter B. 1989. *The International Economy.* Englewood Cliffs, N.J.: Prentice Hall.

————. 1990. "Organizing Debt Relief: The Need for a New Institution." *Journal of Economic Perspectives* 4 (Winter): 7–18.

Khatkhate, Deena. 1987. "International Monetary System—Which Way?" *World Development* 15 (December): vii–xvi.

Khan, Haider Ali. 1990. "Economic Modeling of Structural Adjustment Programs: Impact on Human Condition." *Africa Today* 37 (4): 29–38.

Khan, Mohsin S. 1987. "Macroeconomic Adjustment in Developing Countries: A Policy Perspective." *The World Bank Research Observer* 2 (January): 23–42.

Kilby, Peter. 1969. *Industrialization in an Open Economy: Nigeria, 1945–1966.* Cambridge: Cambridge University Press.

Killick, Tony. 1978. *Development Economics in Action: A Study of Economic Policies in Ghana,* London: Heinemann.

Killick, Tony, ed. 1982. *Adjustment and Financing in the Developing World: The Role of the International Monetary Fund.* Washington, D.C.: International Monetary Fund.

————, ed. 1984. *The Quest for Economic Stabilization.* London: Overseas Development Institute.

Killick, Tony; Bird, Graham; Sharpley, Jennifer; and Sutton, Mary. 1984.

Bibliography

The IMF and Stabilisation: Developing Country Experiences. London: Overseas Development Institute.

Kindlebergor, Charles P. 1956. *The Terms of Trade: A European Case Study.* New York: Wiley.

———. 1974. "The Theory of Direct Investment." In Robert E. Baldwin and J. David Richardson, eds., *International Trade and Finance.* Boston: Little, Brown, pp. 267–85.

Kindleberger, Charles P., and Herrick, Bruce. 1977. *Economic Development.* New York: McGraw-Hill.

Kirkpatrick, Collin, and Diakosavvas, Dimitris. 1985. "Food Insecurity and Foreign-Exchange Constraints in Sub-Saharan Africa." *Journal of Modern African Studies* 23 (June): 326–42.

Klein, Martin A. 1991. "Democracy Revisited." Presidential Address to the African Studies Association meeting. St. Louis. 25 November.

Kohli, Harinder S., and Sood, Anil. 1987. "Fostering Enterprise Development." *Finance and Development* 24 (March): 34–36.

Körner, Peter, et al. 1986. *The IMF and the Debt Crisis: A Guide to the Third World's Dilemma.* Trans. Paul Knight. Atlantic Highlands, N.J.: Zed Books.

Kreinin, Mordechai E. 1987. *International Economics: A Policy Approach.* San Diego: Harcourt Brace Jovanovich.

Krueger, Ann O. 1974. "The Political Economy of the Rent-seeking Society." *American Economic Review* 64 (March): 291–301.

———. 1987. "Origins of the Developing Countries' Debt Crisis." *Journal of Development Economics* 27 (October): 165–87.

Krueger, Anne O.; Lary, Hal B.; Monson, Terry; and Akrasanee, Narongchai, eds. 1981. *Trade and Employment in Developing Countries.* Vol. 1. *Individual Studies.* Chicago: University of Chicago Press.

Krugman, Paul R., and Obstfeld, Maurice, 1990. *International Economics.* 2nd edition. Glenview, Ill.: Scott, Foresman and Co.

Kuczynski, Pedro-Pablo. 1988. *Latin American Debt.* Baltimore: Johns Hopkins University Press.

Lal, Deepak. 1983. *The Poverty of "Development Economics."* London: Institute of Economic Affairs.

Lal, Deepak, and Rajapatirana, Sarath. 1987. "Foreign Trade Regimes and Economic Growth in Developing Countries." *World Bank Research Observer* 2 (July): 189–217.

Lall, Sanjaya. 1985. *Multinationals, Technology and Exports.* New York: St. Martin's Press.

Lancaster, Carol. 1990. "Economic Reform in Africa: Is it Working?" *The Washington Quarterly* 13 (Winter): 123–24.

———. 1991. *African Economic Reform: The External Dimension.* Washington, D.C.: Institute for International Economics.

Lancaster, Carol, and Williamson, John, eds. 1986. *African Debt and Financing.* Washington, D.C.: Institute for International Economics.

Bibliography

Langdon, Steven. 1980. *Multinational Corporations in the Political Economy of Kenya*. London: Macmillan.

Larkman, Jolyon. 1990. "How a Major Creditor Views the New Proposals." *IDS Bulletin* 21 (April): 50–51.

Lawrence, Peter, ed. 1986. *World Recession and the Food Crisis in Africa*. London: James Currey.

Lecaillon, Jacques; Paukert, Felix; Morrisson, Christian; and Germidis, Dimitri. 1984. *Income Distribution and Economic Development*. Geneva: International Labour Office.

Lele, Uma. 1989. *Agricultural Growth, Domestic Policies, the External Environment and Assistance to Africa: Lessons of a Quarter Century*. Washington, D.C.: World Bank.

———. 1990. "Structural Adjustment, Agricultural Development and the Poor: Some Lessons from the Malawian Experience." *World Development* 18 (September): 1207–19.

Lemarchand, René. 1979. "The Politics of Penury in Rural Zaïre: The View from Bandundu." In Guy Gran, ed., *Zaïre: The Political Economy of Underdevelopment*. New York: Praeger, pp. 237–60.

Lessard, Donald R., and Williamson, John, eds. 1987. *Capital Flight and Third World Debt*. Washington, D.C.: Institute for International Economics.

Leys, Colin. 1974. *Underdevelopment in Kenya: The Political Economy of Neo-Colonialism*. Berkeley: University of California Press.

Lindauer, David L. 1991. "Parastatal Pay Policy in Africa." *World Development* 19 (July): 831–38.

Livingstone, Ian. 1981. "The Distribution of Income and Welfare." In International Labour Office, Jobs and Skills Programme for Africa, *Rural Development, Employment, and Incomes in Kenya*. Addis Ababa.

Lovejoy, Paul E.; Nafziger, E. Wayne; Cohen, Ronald; Goldman, Abe; Osaghae, Eghosa; Joseph, Richard; and Smaldon, Joseph P. 1992. *Nigeria: A Country Study*. Washington, D.C.: Library of Congress.

Lucas, Robert E., Jr. 1990. "Why Doesn't Capital Flow from Rich to Poor Countries?" *American Economic Review* 80 (May): 92–96.

MacEwan, Arthur, and Tabb, William K., eds. 1989. *Instability and Change in the World Economy*. New York: Monthly Review Press.

McKinnon, Ronald I. 1973. *Money and Capital in Economic Development*. Washington, D.C.: Brookings Institution.

———. 1984. "The International Capital Market and Economic Liberalization in LDCs." *Developing Economies* 22 (September): 327–55.

Mamdani, Mahmood. 1988. "Uganda in Transition: Two Years of the NRA/NRM." *Third World Quarterly*, no. 10: 1151–81.

Mapolu, H. 1984. "Imperialism, the State, and the Peasantry in Tanzania." *Mawazo* 5 (3): 3–17.

Markovitz, Irving Leonard. 1977. *Power and Class in Africa: An Introduction to Change and Conflict in African Politics*. Englewood Cliffs, N.J.: Prentice Hall.

Bibliography

Meadows, Donella H.; Meadows, Dennis L.; Randers, Jorgen; and Behrens, William W., III. 1972. *The Limits to Growth*. New York: Universe Books.

Meier, Gerald M. 1976. *Leading Issues in Economic Development*. New York: Oxford University Press.

———. 1980. *International Economics: The Theory of Policy*. New York: Oxford University Press.

Meier, Gerald M., and Steel, William F., eds. 1989. *Industrial Adjustment in Sub-Saharan Africa*. New York: Oxford University Press.

Miller, Morris. 1991. *Debt and the Environment: Converging Crises*. New York: United Nations.

Mills, Cadman Atta. 1989. "Structural Adjustment in Sub-Saharan Africa." Economic Development Institute Policy Seminar Report No. 18. Washington, D.C.: World Bank.

Mistry, Percy S. 1991. "African Debt Revisited: Procrastination or Progress?" Paper prepared for the North-South Roundtable on African Debt Relief, Recovery, and Democracy. Abidjan, Côte d'Ivoire. 8–9 July.

Moore, Will H., and Scarritt, James H. 1990. "IMF Conditionality and Polity Characteristics in Black Africa: An Exploratory Analysis." *Africa Today* 37(4): 39–60.

Morawetz, David. 1977. *Twenty-five Years of Economic Development, 1950 to 1975*. Baltimore: Johns Hopkins University Press.

Morss, Elliott R. 1984. "Institutional Destruction Resulting from Donor and Project Proliferation in Sub-Saharan African Countries." *World Development* 12 (April): 465–70.

Moseley, K. P. 1992. "West African Industry and the Debt Crisis." *Journal of International Development* (forthcoming).

Mosley, Paul; Harrigan, Jane; and Toye, John. 1991. *Aid and Power: The World Bank and Policy-based Lending*. 2 vols. London: Routledge.

Mountfield, Peter. 1990. "The Paris Club and African Debt." *IDS Bulletin* 21 (April): 42–46.

Müller, Anton P. 1991. "The Creditworthiness and International Payment Ability of Sovereign States." *Intereconomics* 26 (March/April): 74–81.

Myrdal, Gunnar. 1968. *Asian Drama: An Inquiry into the Poverty of Nations*. 3 vols. Middlesex, England: Penguin Books.

Mytelka, Lynn Krieger. 1984. "Foreign Business and Economic Development." In I. William Zartman and Christopher Delgado, eds. *The Political Economy of Ivory Coast*. New York: Praeger, pp. 149–73.

Nafziger, E. Wayne. 1977. *African Capitalism: A Case Study in Nigerian Entrepreneurship*. Stanford, Calif.: Hoover Institution Press.

———. 1983. *The Economics of Political Instability: The Nigerian-Biafran War*. Boulder, Colo.: Westview.

———. 1986. "The Japanese Development Model: Its Implications for Developing Countries." *Bulletin of the Graduate School of International Relations, International University of Japan*, no. 5 (July): 1–26.

Bibliography

————. 1988a. *Inequality in Africa: Political Elites, Proletariat, Peasants, and the Poor.* Cambridge: Cambridge University Press.

————. 1988b. "Society and the Entrepreneur." *Journal of Development Planning,* no. 18: 127–52.

————. 1990. *The Economics of Developing Countries.* Englewood Cliffs, N.J.: Prentice Hall.

Naylor, R. T. 1989. *Hot Money and the Politics of Debt.* London: McClelland & Stewart.

Nelson, Joan M., and contributors. 1989. *Fragile Coalitions: The Politics of Economic Adjustment.* New Brunswick, N.J.: Transaction Books.

Newman, Mark; Ouedraogo, Ismael; and Norman, David. 1979. "Farm-level Studies in the Semiarid Tropics of West Africa." Proceedings of the Workshop on Socioeconomic Constraints to Development of Semiarid Tropical Agriculture, International Crop Research Institute for Semiarid Tropics (ICRISAT). Hyderabad, India. 19–23 February, pp. 241–63.

Ng'ethe, Njugna. 1980. "The State and the Evolution of the Peasantry in Kenyan Agriculture: A Summary of Well-known Issues." *Mawazo* 5 (June): 191–213.

Nkrumah, Kwame. 1970. *Class Struggles in Africa.* New York: International Publishers.

————. 1973. *Revolutionary Path.* New York: International Publishers.

North-South Institute. 1988. *Structural Adjustment in Africa: External Financing for Development.* Ottawa, Canada, 25–26 February.

Nove, Alec. 1983. *The Economics of Feasible Socialism.* London: George Unwin.

Nowzad, Bahram. 1990. "Lessons of the Debt Decade: Will We Learn?" *Finance and Development* 27 (March): 9–13.

Nurkse, Ragnar. 1944. *International Currency Experience.* Princeton, N.J.: Princeton University Press.

Nurkse, Ragnar, 1953. *Problems of Capital Formation in Underdeveloped Countries.* New York: Oxford University Press.

————. 1961. *Patterns of Trade and Development.* New York: Oxford University Press.

Nyerere, Julius K. 1977. *The Arusha Declaration Ten Years After.* Dar es Salaam: Government Printer.

————. 1980. "No to IMF Meddling." *Development Dialogue,* no. 2: 7–9.

————. 1986. "An Address." *Development and Change* 17 (July): 387–97.

Nyongo, P. Anyang. 1984. "Accelerated Development and Industrialization in Africa." *Mawazo* 5 (December): 3–30.

Obasanjo, Olusegun, and d'Orville, Hans, eds. 1990. *Challenges of Leadership in African Development.* New York: Taylor & Francis.

O'Donnell, Guillermo. 1987. "Brazil's Failure: What Future for Debtors' Cartels?" *Third World Quarterly* 9 (October): 1157–66.

Ogbuagu, Chibuzo, S. A. 1983. "The Nigerian Indigenization Policy: Nationalism or Pragmatism?" *African Affairs* 82 (April): 241–66.

Bibliography

Olashore, Oladele. 1991. *Challenges of Nigeria's Economic Reform.* Ibadan: Fountain Publications.

Olukoshi, Adebayo O. 1991. *Nigerian External Debt Crisis: Its Management.* Lagos: Malthouse Press.

Onimode, Bade, ed. 1989. *The IMF, the World and the African Debt.* Vol. 1. London: Zed Books.

Organisation for Economic Cooperation and Development (OECD). 1988a. *Development Cooperation in the 1990s: Efforts and Policies of the Members of the Development Assistance Committee.* Paris.

————. 1988b. *Financing and External Debt, 1987.* Paris.

————. 1989. *Financing and External Debt of Developing Countries: 1988 Survey.* Paris.

————. 1990a. *Development Cooperation: Efforts and Policies of the Members of the Development Assistance Committee.* Paris.

————. 1990b. *Financing and External Debt of Developing Countries.* Paris.

Organisation of African Unity (OAU). First Economic Summit of the Assembly of Heads of State and Government. 1980. *Plan of Action for the Implementation of the Monrovia Strategy for the Economic Development of Africa Recommended by the ECA Conference of Ministers Responsible for Economic Development at its Sixth Meeting Held at Addis Ababa, 9–12 April 1980 (called Lagos Plan of Action).* Lagos. 28–29 April.

Overseas Development Council (ODC). 1982. *U.S. Foreign Policy and the Third World: Agenda, 1982.* New York: Praeger.

Parfitt, Trevor W. 1990. "Lies, Damned Lies and Statistics: The World Bank/ECA Structural Adjustment Controversy." *Review of African Political Economy,* no. 47 (Spring): 134–35.

Parfitt, Trevor W. and Bullock, Sandy, 1990. "The Prospects for a New Lomé Convention: Structural Adjustment or Structural Transformation." *Review of African Political Economy,* no. 47 (Spring): 104–16.

Parfitt, Trevor W., and Riley, Stephen P. 1989. *The African Debt Crisis.* London: Routledge.

Park, Young C. 1987. "Evaluating the Performance of Korea's Government-Invested Enterprise." *Finance and Development* 24 (June): 25–27.

Pastor, Manuel, Jr. 1987. "The Effects of IMF Programs in the Third World: Debate and Evidence from Latin America." *World Development* 15 (February): 249–62.

Patel, I. G. 1982. "Current Crisis in International Economic Co-operation." Association of Banks in Malaysia Annual Lecture Series, Second Tun Ismail Ali Lecture. Kuala Lumpur, Malaysia. 15 March.

Patel, Surendra J. 1964. "Economic Transition in Africa." *Journal of Modern African Studies* 2 (August): 329–49.

Paulino, Leonardo A. 1986. *Food in the Third World: Past Trends and Projections to 2000.* International Food Policy Research Institute Research Report 52. Washington, D.C. June.

Bibliography

Peace, Adrian J. 1979. *Choice, Class, and Conflict: A Study of Southern Nigerian Factory Workers*. Atlantic Highlands, N.J.: Humanities Press.

Pechman, Joseph A., and Okner, Benjamin A. 1974. *Who Bears the Tax Burden?* Washington, D.C.: Brookings Institutions.

Perry, David B. 1980. "International Tax Comparisons." *Canadian Tax Journal* 28 (January–February): 89–93.

Pickett, James, and Singer, Hans, eds. 1990. *Towards Economic Recovery in Sub-Saharan Africa: Essays in Honour of Robert Gardiner*. London: Routledge.

Polanyi, Karl. 1944. *The Great Transformation: The Politics and Economics of Our Times*. Boston: Beacon Press.

Population Reference Bureau. 1988. *1988 World Population Data Sheet*. Washington, D.C.

———. 1990. *1990 World Population Data Sheet*. Washington, D.C.

———. 1991. *1991 World Population Data Sheet*. Washington, D.C.

Portes, Richard. 1990. "Development vs. Debt: Past and Future." *IDS Bulletin* 21 (April): 7–10.

Prebisch, Raul. 1962. "The Economic Development of Latin America and its Principal Problems." *Economic Bulletin for Latin America* 7 (February): 1–22.

Preusse, Heinz Gert. 1988. "The Indirect Approach to Trade Liberalization: Dynamic Consideration on Liberalization-cum-Stabilization Policies in Latin America." *World Development* 16 (August): 883–97.

Rahimibrougerdi, Alireza. 1988. "An Empirical Investigation of the Effects of Major Exogenous Shocks on the Growth of Non-oil and Oil-exporting Developing Countries from 1965 to 1985." Ph.D. dissertation. Manhattan, Kans.: Kansas State University.

Ranis, Gustasv. 1987. "Latin American Debt and Adjustment." *Journal of Development Economics* 27 (October): 189–99.

Ray, Edward John. 1989. *U.S. Protectionism and the World Debt Crisis*. New York: Quorum Books.

Reisen, Helmut. 1991. "The Brady Plan and Adjustment Incentives." *Intereconomics* 26 (March/April): 69–73.

Reisen, Helmut, and Van Trotsenburg, Axel. 1988. *Developing Country Debt: The Budgetary and Transfer Problem*. Paris: OECD.

Remmer, Karen L. 1966. "The Politics of Economic Stabilization: IMF Standby Program in Latin America, 1954–1984." *Comparative Politics* 19 (October): 1–24.

Riddell, Roger C., ed. 1990. *Manufacturing Africa: Performance and Prospects of Seven Countries in Sub-Saharan Africa*. London: James Currey.

Ridler, Neil B. 1985. "Comparative Advantage as a Development Model: The Ivory Coast." *Journal of Modern African Studies* 23 (September): 407–17.

Rimmer, Douglas. 1984. *The Economies of West Africa*. London: Weidenfeld and Nicolson.

———. 1990. "Alternatives to Structural Adjustment and the Future of the Nigerian Economy." Paper for the Conference on Democratic Transition and Structural Adjustment in Nigeria. Stanford, Calif.: Hoover Institution. 25–29 August.

Rodney, Walter. 1972. *How Europe Underdeveloped Africa.* London: Bogle-L'Ouverture.

Roemer, Michael. 1985. "Dutch Disease in Developing Countries: Swallowing Bitter Medicine." In Mats Lundahl, ed., *The Primary Sector in Economic Development.* New York: St. Martin's, pp. 234–52.

Rogoff, Kenneth. 1990. "Symposium on New Institutions for Developing Country Debt." *Journal of Economic Perspectives* 4 (Winter): 3–6.

Rosebrock, Jens, and Sondhof, Harald. 1991. "Debt-for-Nature Swaps: A Review of the First Experiences." *Intereconomics* 26 (March/April): 82–87.

Rothchild, Donald, ed. 1991. *Ghana: The Political Economy of Recovery.* Boulder, Colo.: Lynne Rienner.

Russell, Robert. 1990. "The New Roles and Facilities of the IMF." *IDS Bulletin* 21 (April): 32–37.

Sachs, Jeffrey D. 1985. "External Debt and Macroeconomic Performance in Latin America and East Asia." *Brookings Papers on Economic Activity* 2: 523–64.

———. 1988. "The Debt Crisis at a Turning Point." *Challenge,* 31 (May/June): 17–26.

———. ed. 1989a. *Developing Country Debt and the World Economy.* Chicago: University of Chicago Press.

———. 1989b. "Making the Brady Plan Work." *Foreign Affairs* 69 (Summer): 87–104.

Sandbrook, Richard. 1985. *The Politics of Africa's Economic Stagnation.* Cambridge: Cambridge University Press.

Sandbrook, Richard, and Cohen, Robin, eds. 1975. *The Development of an African Working Class: Studies in Class Formation and Action.* London: Longman.

Sanford, Jonathan E. 1988. "Feasibility of a World Bank Interest Subsidy Account to Supplement the Existing IDA Program." *World Development* 16 (July): 787–96.

Schatz, Sayre P. 1978. *Nigerian Capitalism.* Berkeley: University of California Press.

———. 1984. "Pirate Capitalism and the Inert Economy of Nigeria." *Journal of Modern African Studies* 22 (March): 45–57.

Schatzberg, Michael G., and Zartman, I. William, eds. 1986. *The Political Economy of Cameroon.* New York: Praeger.

Schumpeter, Joseph A. 1947. *Capitalism, Socialism, and Democracy.* New York: Harper & Row.

Seidman, Ann, and Makgetla, Neva Seidman. 1980. *Outposts of Monopoly Capitalism: Southern Africa in a Changing Global Economy.* Westport, Conn.: Lawrence Hill.

Sewell, John W.; Tucker, Stuart K.; and contributors. 1988. *Growth, Exports,*

Bibliography

and Jobs in a Changing World Economy: Agenda, 1988. New Brunswick, N.J.: Transaction Books.

Shaw, Edward S. 1973. *Financial Deepening in Economic Development.* New York: Oxford University Press.

Shivji, Issa G. 1976. *Class Struggles in Tanzania.* New York: Monthly Review Press.

Shivji, Issa G. 1991. "The Democracy Debate in Africa: Tanzania." *Review of African Political Economy,* no. 50 (March): 79–91.

Short, R. P. 1983. "The Role of Public Enterprise: An International Statistical Comparison." Working Paper of the International Monetary Fund Fiscal Affairs Department. Washington, D.C. 17 May.

Silver, Maurice S. 1985. "United Republic of Tanzania: Overall Concentration, Regional Concentration, and the Growth of the Parastatal Sector in the Manufacturing Industry." In U.N. Industrial Development Organisation. *Industry and Development.* No. 15. New York.

Simonsen, Mario Henrique. 1985. "The Developing-Country Debt Problem." In Gordon W. Smith and John T. Cuddington, eds., *International Debt and the Developing Countries.* Washington, D.C.: World Bank, pp. 101–26.

Singer, Hans. 1950. "The Distribution of Gains between Investing and Borrowing Countries." *American Economic Review* 40 (May): 473–85.

Sklar, Richard. 1979. "The Nature of Class Domination in Africa." *Journal of Modern African Studies* 17 (December): 531–52.

Sonko, Karamo, N. M. 1988. "The Political Economy of IMF Presence in Africa: An Analysis of the Causes and Consequences." Paper presented to the African Studies Association. Chicago. 27–30 October.

Spraos, John. 1985. *Inequalising Trade? A Study of Traditional North/South Specialisation in the Context of Terms of Trade Concepts.* Oxford: Clarendon Press.

Squire, Lyn, 1981. *Employment Policy in Developing Countries: A Survey of Issues and Evidence.* New York: Oxford University Press.

Srinivasan, T. N. 1987. "Economic Liberalization in China and India: Issues and an Analytical Framework." *Journal of Comparative Economics* 11 (September): 427–43.

Stein, Howard. 1991. "Deindustrialization, Adjustment, and the IMF in Africa." *World Development* 19 (December).

Stein, Howard and Nafziger, E. Wayne. 1991. "Structural Adjustment, Human Needs, and the World Bank Agenda." *Journal of Modern African Studies* 29 (March): 173–89.

Stewart, Frances. 1974. "Technology and Employment in LDCs." In Edgar O. Edwards, ed., *Employment in Developing Countries.* New York: Columbia University Press, pp. 80–93.

———. 1987. "Should Conditionality Change?" Paper presented at the Seminar on the International Fund and the World Bank: Conditionality and its Impact. Uppsala, Sweden: Scandinavian Institute of African Studies. 29 January.

———. 1990. "Are Adjustment Policies in Africa Consistent with Long-run Development Needs?" Paper presented to the American Economic Association. Washington, D.C. 30 December.

Stiles, Kendall W. 1990. "IMF Conditionality: Coercion or Compromise." *World Development* 18 (July): 959–74.

Sutcliffe, Bob. 1984. "Africa and the World Economic Crisis." Paper presented to the Review of African Political Economy Conference on The World Recession and the Crisis in Africa. Keele, England: University of Keele. September.

Tait, Alan A.; Grätz, Wilfred L. M.; and Eichengreen, Barry J. 1979. "International Comparisons of Taxation for Selected Developing Countries, 1972–76." *International Monetary Fund Staff Papers* 26 (March): 123–56.

Tanzania. Ministry of Finance, Planning and Economic Affairs. 1982. *The National Economic Survival Programme*. Dar es Salaam: Government Printer. January.

Tanzi, Vito. 1966. "Personal Income Taxation in Latin America: Obstacles and Possibilities." *National Tax Journal* 19 (June): 156–62.

Tanzi, Vito. 1987. "Quantitative Characteristics of the Tax Systems of Developing Countries." In David Newbery and Nicholas Stern, eds., *The Theory of Taxation for Developing Countries*. New York: Oxford University Press, pp. 205–41.

Teal, Francis. 1986. "The Foreign Exchange Regime and Growth: A Comparison of Ghana and the Ivory Coast." *African Affairs* 85 (April): 267–82.

Toft, Anthony. 1990. "The New Roles and Facilities of the World Bank." *IDS Bulletin* 21 (April): 38–41.

Tripp, Ali. 1989. "Women and the Changing Urban Household in Tanzania." *Journal of Modern African Studies* 27 (December): 601–23.

United Nations 1987. *National Accounts Statistics: Main Aggregates and Detailed Tables, 1985*. New York.

———. 1988. *Financing Africa's Recovery: Report and Recommendations of the Advisory Group on Financial Flows for Africa*. New York.

———. 1990. *World Economic Survey, 1990*. New York.

U.N. Centre on Transnational Corporations. 1989. *International Debt Restructuring: Substantive Issues and Techniques*. New York.

U.N. Conference on Trade and Development (UNCTAD). 1991. *Trade and Development Report, 1991*. New York.

U.N. Department of Economic Affairs. 1949. *Relative Prices of Exports and Imports of Underdeveloped Countries*. New York.

U.N. Development Programme and World Bank. 1989. *African Economic and Financial Data*. Washington, D.C.

U.N. General Assembly. 1986. *Programme of Action for African Economic Recovery and Development, 1986–1990*. New York.

———. 1991. *Critical Economic Situation: Final Review and Appraisal of the Implementation of the United Nations Programme of Action for African Economic Recovery and Development, 1986–1990: Report of the Secretary-General*. A/46/324. New York: 6 August.

Bibliography

U.N. Inter-Agency Task Force. 1988. *Khartoum Conference on the Human Dimensions of Africa's Economic Recovery and Development.* Khartoum, March.

UNICEF. 1989. *The State of the World's Children, 1989.* New Delhi.

———. 1992. *The State of the World's Children, 1992.* Oxford: Oxford University Press.

U.S. Agency for International Development. 1990. *Annual Report.* Washington, D.C.

U.S. President, Council of Economic Advisors. 1973. *Economic Report of the President, 1973.* Washington, D.C.: Government Printing Office.

———. 1990. *Economic Report of the President.* Washington, D.C.: U.S. Government Printing Office.

Vengroff, Richard, and Farah, Ali. 1985. "State Intervention and Agricultural Development in Africa: A Cross-National Study." *Journal of Modern African Studies* 23 (March): 75–85.

Wagner, Adolph. 1958. "Three Extracts on Public Finance." In Richard A. Musgrave and Alan Peacock, eds., *Classics in the Theory of Public Finance.* New York: Macmillan, pp. 1–16.

Wakeman-Linn, John. 1991. "The Market for Developing Country Debt: The Nature and Importance of its Shortcomings." *World Bank Research Observer* 6 (July): 191–203.

Wangwe, S. M. 1980. "Sub-Saharan Africa: Which Economic Strategy?" *Third World Quarterly* 6 (October): 1033–59.

Weeks, John F., ed. 1989. *Debt Disaster? Banks, Governments, and Multilaterals Confront the Crisis.* New York: New York University Press.

Wheeler, David. 1984. "Sources of Stagnation in Sub-Saharan Africa." *World Development* 12 (January): 1–23.

Wheeler, Joseph C., Chairman of the Development Assistance Committee. 1990. *Development Co-operation: Efforts and Policies of the Members of the Development Assistance Committee.* Paris: OECD.

Williamson, John. 1990a. "The Debt Crisis at the Turn of the Decade." *IDS Bulletin* 21 (April): 4–6.

———, ed. 1990b. *Latin American Adjustment: How Much Has Happened?* Washington, D.C.: Institute for International Economics.

Williamson, John, and Lessard, Donald R. 1987. *Capital Flight: The Problem and Policy Responses.* Washington, D.C.: Institute for International Economics.

Wilson, Ernest T. 1991. "Making the Connection: Economic and Political Liberalization in Africa." Paper presented to the African Studies Association meeting, St. Louis, 23 November.

Winkler, Max. 1933. *Foreign Bonds.* Philadelphia: Roland Swain Co.

Wood, Gordon. 1990. "The Changing Secondary Market." *IDS Bulletin* 21 (April): 75–77.

World Bank. 1975. *Kenya: Into the Second Decade.* Washington, D.C.

———. 1978. *World Development Report, 1978.* New York: Oxford University Press.

Bibliography

————. 1980a. *World Development Report, 1980.* New York: Oxford University Press.

————. 1980b. *World Tables. 1980.* Baltimore: Johns Hopkins University Press.

————. 1981a. *Accelerated Development in Sub-Saharan Africa: An Agenda for Action.* Washington, D.C.

————. 1981b. *World Development Report, 1981.* New York: Oxford University Press.

————. 1982a. *World Debt Tables, 1982–83.* Washington, D.C.

————. 1982b. *World Development Report, 1982.* New York: Oxford University Press.

————. 1983. *World Development Report, 1983.* New York: Oxford University Press.

————. 1984. *Toward Sustained Development in Sub-Saharan Africa: A Joint Program of Action.* Washington, D.C.

————. 1985. *World Development Report, 1985.* New York: Oxford University Press.

————. 1986a. *Financing Adjustment with Growth in Sub-Saharan Africa, 1986–90,* Washington, D.C.

————. 1986b. *World Development Report, 1986.* New York: Oxford University Press.

————. 1987. *World Development Report, 1987.* New York: Oxford University Press.

————. 1988a. *Adjustment Lending: An Evaluation of Ten Years of Experience.* Washington, D.C.

————. 1988b. *World Debt Tables: External Debt of Developing Countries, 1987–88 Edition.* 2 vols. Washington, D.C.

————. 1988c. *World Development Report, 1988.* New York: Oxford University Press.

————. 1989a. *Sub-Saharan Africa: From Crisis to Sustainable Growth: A Long-Term Perspective Study.* Washington, D.C.

————. 1989b. *World Debt Tables, 1989–90: External Debt of Developing Countries.* vol. 1. *Analysis and Summary Tables.* Washington, D.C.

————. 1989c. *World Development Report, 1989.* New York: Oxford University Press.

————. 1990a. *Adjustment Lending Policies for Sustainable Growth.* Washington, D.C.

————. 1990b. *World Debt Tables, 1989–90: External Debt of Developing Countries.* Washington, D.C.

————. 1990c. *World Debt Tables, 1990–91: External Debt of Developing Countries.* 2 vols. Washington, D.C.

————. 1990d. *World Development Report, 1990.* New York: Oxford University Press.

————. 1991a. *Global Economic Prospects and the Developing Countries.* Washington, D.C.

Bibliography

————. 1991b. *World Debt Tables, 1991–92: External Debt of Developing Countries.* 2 vols. Washington, D.C.

————. 1991c. *World Development Report, 1991.* New York: Oxford University Press.

World Bank and International Monetary Fund. Joint Ministerial Committee of the Boards of Governors. 1990. *Problems and Issues in Structural Adjustment.* Washington, D.C.

World Bank and U.N. Development Programme. 1989. *Africa's Adjustment and Growth in the 1980s.* Washington, D.C.

Young, Crawford. 1982. *Ideology and Development in Africa.* New York: Yale University Press.

Periodicals

Africa

Africa Demōs (Atlanta)

African Business

African Economic Digest

Africa Report

Africa Research Bulletin (*Economic Series*)

Annual Report, Bank of International Settlements

Annual Reports and Statements of Accounts. Central Bank of Nigeria, Lagos

Country Profile for various African countries. Economist Intelligence Unit, London

Economist

Euromoney

Digest of Statistics (Quarterly), Nigeria, Office of Statistics

IMF Survey

Indicative Prices for Developing Country Debt, Salomon Brothers

International Financial Statistics, International Monetary Fund

Kansas City Star

New York Times

Quarterly Economic Review for various African countries. Economist Intelligence Unit, London

Wall Street Journal

Yearbook of International Trade Statistics, U.N., New York

Index

.

Index

Index

Index

Index

Wages *(cont'd)*
132, 157, 158, 161, 170; and adjustment, xx, 78; and debt crisis, 11
Wars, 47; and refugees, 41
Weeks, John F., 76, 84, 133
Wheeler, David, 85
White, Harry Dexter, 23–24
Wilson, Ernest T., 215
Wolpe, Howard, 93
Women, 47, 127, 145, 159; rural, 121; self-employed, 114
Workers, 82, 122, 127; effect of reducing social programs on, 24; in foreign firms, 84; and inflation, 155; lack of class consciousness by, 48; living standards for, 129; as privileged, 133; reforms and, 62; view of, on liberalization, 119
Working classes, xx, 121; weakness of, 48
World Bank, 80, 87, 108, 113–14, 122, 126, 138, 141, 163, 180, 181, 182, 183, 205, 206, 211, 217; adjustment by, xix; adjustment and reform policies of, xvii; adjustment loans by, 99, 104; adjustment policies of, 76; adjustment programs of, xxii, 47, 50, 57, 98, 100, 105, 109–10, 115, 133, 137, 152, 157, 165, 168, 173; agricultural lending from, 146; and cofinancing agreements, 15; Commodity Risk Management and Finance Unit of, 101; concessional lending by, 78; conditionality (conditions) of loans by, 25, 128, 136, 149, 150, 172, 174; criticism of Africa by, 48; on debt crisis (1983), 5; debt reduction consortium of, 192; and debt writedowns, xxiii; establishment of a "third window" by, 97; on farm prices, 110–11; front-loading of conditionality by, 138; and Fund seal of approval, xxiii; insistence of, on guarantee by state, 92; insistence of, on subsidy reduction, 132; lending by, 86, 145; liberalization sponsored by, 114; loans by, xix; on local research, 147; policy advice by, 209; policy-based lending by, 96, 123; on policy objectives, 162; on privatization, 142; program strategies of, xx, 12; recommendations by, 148, 154; refinancing of hard loans by, 139; reform by, 62,

94; reliance of, on IMF seal of approval, 102; report on African development, 39; on required reforms, 159; rescheduling model of, 204; resource transfers from, 33–34; SALs by, 106, 110; SALs and SECALs by, 135; SAP by, 127; Social Dimensions of Adjustment Projects (SDSA) of, 175; soft-loan window of, 125; strategy of, 71; structural adjustment lending by, 38, 85, 179; structural adjustment programs of, 50, 134, 166; study by, 215; as substitute for bank lending, 194; suspension of lending by, 129; on tariffs, 82; view of Africa's economic crisis, xviii, 36, 38. *See also* Multilateral institutions
Writedowns, of debt, 136
Writeoffs, 1
Wuyts, Marc, 209

Yugoslavia, 9

Zaïre, 52, 73, 78, 207; adjustment in, and minimum wage, 157–58; budget cuts in, 25; capital flight from, 33, 93–94; copper export concentration in, 66; debt and GNP in, 16; debt crisis in, in 1976, xix; debt forgiveness for, 187; debt rescheduling by, 76; debt-service ratio in, 17; dependence of, on external assistance, 86; effective exchange rate in, 85; eligibility of, for SPA, 97; international trade taxes and government revenue in, 55; MNCs in, 72; "Nigerian disease" in, 60; poor national economic management in, 20; price policy in, 110; scheduled debt service in, 15; secondary market prices of bank debt for, 3
Zambia, 9, 12, 55, 73, 78; adjustment programs by World Bank and IMF in, 122–29; as aid recipient, 131; Basic Needs Report in, 161; calories in, 159; Congress of Trade Unions (ZCTU) in, 129, 217; copper export concentration in, 66; debt rescheduling by, 76; destruction of small-scale industry in, 114; domestic currency in, 152; employment shares of parastatals in, 50; exports from, 141; foreign exchange

Designed by Laury A. Egan

Composed by World Composition Services
in Baskerville text and display

Printed by Princeton University Press on
50-lb. Glatfelter Natural, B-16,
and bound in Holliston Roxite